CONTENTS

Page

INVITED PAPERS

iii

THEATRE PAPERS

633-202
£20 Mag

Grassland Management and Nature Conservation

Occasional Symposium No. 28, British Grassland Society, 1993

Proceedings of a joint meeting between the British Grassland Society
and the British Ecological Society held at Leeds University,
27-29 September 1993

Edited by
R. J. HAGGAR AND S. I

BRITISH

GRASSLAND

SOCIETY

OCCASIONAL SYMPOSIUM NO. 28

British Grassland Society

British Library Cataloguing-in-Publication Data available

1993
ISBN 0 905944 20 8
ISSN 0572-7022

Copyright British Grassland Society

Printed by Cambrian Printers, 22 Queen Street, Aberystwyth, SY23 1PX

POSTER PRESENTATIONS

viii

THE AIM AND OBJECTIVES
OF THE BRITISH GRASSLAND SOCIETY

The aim is to provide a forum for all those with an active interest in the science and the practice of temperate grassland production and utilization by bringing together research workers, advisers, farmers and technical members of the agricultural industry.

The objectives of the society are:

(a) To encourage research and practice in all aspects of grassland and forage husbandry which will lead to improvements in the efficiency of its use.

(b) To communicate as widely as possible the results of research and practice in grassland and forage crops.

Membership

This is open to all those with a keen interest in grassland and the furtherance of the Society's objectives.

Membership is drawn from research, advisory services, agricultural education, farmers and allied interests.

There are 70 local grassland societies affiliated to the BGS.

Publications

An international journal, *Grass and Forage Science*, is published quarterly and supplied to members free of charge. Three times each year, the Society publishes *Grass Farmer*, a practically orientated publication which gives reports of farm practices, together with research and development findings in digest form. This is also available to members free of charge.

Other occasional publications include textbooks, symposia proceedings and reports of meetings and surveys.

Further information on any aspect of BGS can be obtained from:

The Secretary
British Grassland Society
No. 1 Earley Gate
University of Reading
Reading RG6 2AT

ACKNOWLEDGEMENTS AND DISCLAIMER

This conference was organized by a committee under the chairmanship of D. J. A. Milne. BGS gratefully acknowledges all those who gave time to ensure the success of the conference.

Occasional reference is made in this publication to trade names and proprietary products. No endorsement or criticism of named products is intended nor is any criticism implied of similar products which are not mentioned.

INVITED PAPERS

Current Government Policy and Existing Instruments Balance in the Countryside

G. R. WATERS
Ministry of Agriculture, Fisheries and Food
Nobel House, 17 Smith Square, London SW1P 3JR

ABSTRACT

This paper gives an overview of the impact of developments in agriculture and agricultural policy on the countryside in the post-war period, when advances in technology and the United Kingdom's system of guaranteed support prices encouraged increases in production and changes in the pattern of farming. These changes continued into the 1970s, when we joined the European Community.

Increased production from a reduced area of land gave rise to changes in the countryside which were not always welcome to the public. Pressure from those concerned with wildlife and landscape conservation in the Eighties led to a reappraisal of attitudes and a re-balancing of Government policy. The designation of the first Environmentally Sensitive Areas heralded changes in the attitudes of policy makers in the UK and the EC. These led to the adoption of the EC's Agri-Environment programme in 1992 and changes in CAP support mechanisms which enable both environmental and agricultural objectives to be served by it. An account is given of the United Kingdom's proposals for implementing these policies.

I am honoured to have been asked to address this conference on Grassland Management and Nature Conservation. I am going to talk about integrating environmental aspects with agricultural production; or, as we say in Government, promoting 'Balance in the Countryside'.

In the Sixties, I read Modern History at Oxford, which had the consequence that I was recently asked by one of my young nieces to explain the Corn Laws. Reaching for the excellent Pelican History of England in the 19th Century in order to maintain my guise as an expert, I came across this sentence: "The farmers grew corn in a big way to feed England during the wars, but they often cultivated chalk lands or moorlands that were normally uneconomic to use for corn, and after the wars when the price of corn fell they demanded protection." The wars were of course the Napoleonic Wars!

The desperate need to feed our population in the Second World War and after led to a similar disturbance of the balance in the countryside between agriculture and nature. The 1947 Agriculture Act maintained financial support for food production after the war and, indeed, it was not until 1957 that the Government set about limiting the quantities of food for which guaranteed prices would be paid.

3

In that post-war period, when I grew up in the countryside, our farmers were supported not only by taxpayers' subsidies but by advances in plant and animal breeding, by inorganic fertilisers, by newly available pesticides and by more powerful and versatile machinery. Taken together these factors enabled farmers to increase production even where the constraints of nature had previously prevented them.

By the time the United Kingdom entered the European Community in 1973 the post-war agricultural revolution was in full swing. Encouraged by higher EC support prices, the proportion of our consumption of temperate foodstuffs produced at home was set to rise to 75% by 1992 whilst the food price element of the RPI was to fall to 12% by 1992. These higher support prices and increased levels of production did of course lead to increases in the cost of the Common Agricultural Policy which eventually proved unsustainable; and to the creation of unsaleable surpluses which generated problems in world trade. These in turn contributed to the difficulty of reaching agreement in the Uruguay Round of the GATT. However, it is not with these international implications that I wish to concern myself but with the changes that the agricultural revolution wrought in the countryside at home, and on grassland in particular.

Grassland, in its many varieties, covers about 70% of farmed land in the United Kingdom. We learned to make productive use of it in the Fifties and Sixties. Figures from the Annual Survey of Fertiliser Practice, show that we increased the use of nitrogenous fertilisers to promote the growth of grass. Rates of use on permanent grass more than doubled in the Sixties, almost doubled again in the Seventies and increased still further in the Eighties. More grass meant more winter fodder, if you could cut and conserve it quickly in our unpredictable weather. So hay making gave way to silage making, to the advantage of the farmer but to the disadvantage of botanical diversity. Increased nitrogen use, silage making and earlier cutting dates meant more competition for the 'stress tolerators' (the wild flowers) and less chance for them to seed before being carted off to the farm silage clamp.

To sum up just a few of the other changes in the patterns of agriculture in the post-war period, we have seen a continuing loss of land from agriculture, a more intensive use of the land remaining in agriculture, a concentration of grazing livestock in the wetter west and upland parts of the country, a relative increase in the area used for arable production, a switch from Spring to Autumn sowing, and a significant expansion of the area sown to oilseed rape.

The outcome has been to increase the quantity of food produced in the United Kingdom. The summary figures mask the detail of more complex changes. In particular, the increases in cereals production resulted from a switch from barley into wheat and from Spring to Autumn sowing. Moreover, cereal production increased by 69% even though the area devoted to it declined by 7%.

What changes did this intensification of agriculture cause to the appearance of the countryside as a whole, as opposed to changes in agriculture? I suspect that we all think that we can recollect what our landscape and wildlife looked like in the period before we joined the European Community 20 years ago and that we can give a broad account of the main changes in the balance between agriculture and nature since then.

Probably we can. At the macro level, however, it is very hard to make accurate comparisons. Our successors will have a much fuller account of the state of our countryside in the early 1990s once the Institute of Terrestrial Ecology Countryside Survey 1990 is published. For the moment, I have to content myself with partial data, often produced by extrapolation and surmise and subject to wide margins of error. With these qualifications, let me quote from just one report, this one produced by Hunting's Technical Services Ltd, which monitored landscape change for the Department of the Environment and the Countryside Commission in the mid-Eighties.

It estimated that, between 1969 and 1980, rough grassland and neglected grassland declined from 5.8% to 5.3% of the landscape of England and Wales. Improved grassland declined from 34.5% to 31%. Cropped land increased from 30.9% to 34.6%. Upland heath remained constant at about 2.4%, having fallen from 3% in 1947, and upland grass declined from 5.2% to 4.5%. In the same period developed land increased from 8.6% to 9.7% while forest cover stayed constant at 7.9%.

All these figures are subject to very wide margins of error. By themselves, they seem to show relatively little change over that 11 year period. From them alone it would be hard to understand what led to the clashes between environmentalists and farmers over the enactment of the Wildlife and Countryside Act in 1981. (This strengthened the protection afforded to Sites of Special Scientific Interest, so that farmers had to consult the Nature Conservancy Council (NCC) before undertaking certain potentially damaging farming operations; and authorised the NCC to offer compensatory payments to farmers.) It would be hard to understand the passion that fuelled the protest over the draining of the Halvergate Marshes in the Norfolk Broads or the Levels and Moors of Somerset. But there was no mistaking the weight of the correspondence that the Minister of Agriculture received over the ploughing up of the Halvergate grazing marshes for cereal production; or that the Secretary of State for the Environment received over plans to prevent the draining of the Somerset Levels and Moors. The political balance between agriculture and nature had been upset.

The Ministry's response to that up-welling of popular dislike of the destruction of our sensitive landscapes and habitats was the first of a series of measures designed to restore the balance in the countryside by working with farmers to safeguard some of our most valued rural landscapes and habitats. In 1987, after securing the agreement of the European Community, we introduced the first of our Environmentally Sensitive Areas (ESAs) in which the Agriculture Ministry pays farmers to maintain traditional farming practices on which the preservation of the landscape or the habitat critically depends. Over the next 2 years we were to see a rapid extension of these ESAs to cover 10 particularly valuable areas of England. To these 10 original ESAs, 6 more were added earlier this year, 3 of them mainly to tackle the problems of overgrazing by sheep. 6 more ESAs are scheduled to come into operation next year. They will cover around 10% of agricultural land in England and we expect to see expenditure on them rise from zero in 1986 to £30 million this year and to £43 million in 2 years' time. There will be 6 in Wales, covering an even higher proportion of the agricultural land.

5

Each of them has its own set of objectives which has been established with the aid of our statutory advisers, the Countryside Commission, English Nature and the Department of the Environment. In every case we ask ourselves:

(i)   what is particularly valuable about the landscapes and habitats in question;

(ii)   what threat is there from agricultural practice or neglect;

(iii) is the socio-economic base (farmers and allied craftsmen) still there to counteract the threat to the landscape or habitat;

(iv) can we afford the carefully targeted financial support needed to reward them for their effort?

We in the United Kingdom have pioneered this particular form of co-operation between agriculture and the conservation of the landscape and wildlife. At the outset the simple aim was to arrest the destruction that modern agricultural technology could wreak on our landscape. We improved our chances of success by pruning right back our aid for investment in land improvement. We succeeded in our aim, as the monitoring of the first ESAs showed in 1991. Now our revised and new ESAs offer much more demanding challenges to farmers and higher rewards to those that meet them. We have succeeded in persuading enough farmers to take part in the ESAs for them to have a noticeable effect on the countryside: in terms of more wetlands for birds, more hay meadows rich in flowers and more arable land reverted to grassland. A further challenge will be to address the problem of the damage to heather in places like Dartmoor, where changes in livestock farming have occasioned great changes in the landscape and wildlife.

With the reform of the Common Agricultural Policy in 1992, our own drive for a better balance between efficiency and environmental protection in agriculture in England was taken up by the European Commission and other Member States. All Member States are now required to offer multi-annual programmes of incentives for a range of environmentally friendly farming methods. I and my colleagues negotiated intensively and successfully to get that piece of CAP reform in place and I want to say a few words about its implementation in England before I finish. However, an equally significant innovation was the introduction of direct payments for arable and livestock production to assist in the process of reducing EC support prices. That innovation enabled the EC to start greening the CAP. It is now possible to make a direct link between the subsidies that farmers receive for their produce and the protection of the environment on their farms. What is more, the systems of arable aids and livestock quotas should help to set limits to the further intensification of those types of production.

Chapter 7:20 of the Government's White Paper on the Environment 'This Common Inheritance', published in 1990, said that the Government would "seek wherever possible and worthwhile, to develop the integration of agricultural and environmental policies within the European Community, including changes to Community arrangements so that those benefiting from EC support schemes will be required in return to protect and, where possible, enhance the environment on their holdings". We said in 'Our Farming Future' in 1991, "Farmers will have to meet basic environmental requirements in order to benefit from CAP support schemes." The importance of the change in CAP mechanisms is that we can now gradually and sensibly develop the CAP so that its budgget supports environmental objectives as well as agricultural ones. Even when the EC agri-environment schemes are fully developed in 1997, they are likely to account for less than 5% of the total CAP budget of some £28 billion. By contrast 95% of CAP expenditure will continue to be devoted solely to agricultural support. If we can green some of that 95% we shall be able to integrate our environmental and agricultural policies in a cost effective and balanced manner.

Our task is to convert these principles slowly but surely into a set of sensible and balanced policies to support environmentally sensitive and efficient agricultural production in England and the rest of the United Kingdom. We have already made a start in arable policy. The environmental conditions attached to the set-aside payments require farmers to manage their set-aside land in a responsible way: by establishing a green cover, by restricting the use of fertilisers and pesticides, and by retaining important landscape and habitat features on that land. In livestock policy, we have refashioned the statutory definition of overgrazing used in our Hill Livestock Compensatory Allowances (HLCAs), so that it relates *directly* to the condition of the grass and not indirectly, as before, to the condition of the animals eating it. Throughout this year we have been drawing to the attention of hill farmers the importance of managing their stock in ways which prevent overgrazing. We count on their co-operation because the skills and knowledge of our upland farmers have created so much of the visual appeal of our hills over the centuries.

Our upland farmers are in the best position to see to it that a reasonable balance is struck between the efficient use of the uplands for grazing and the maintenance of their wider landscape and ecological value: the heather, the bird life and so on. Most of them would probably agree that we need to shift the present balance a little bit away from over-intensive agriculture. The limitation of the payment of HLCAs and other livestock subsidies to those numbers of animals that can be carried on our upland grassland without unacceptable damage to the environment has an important part to play here. We are not saying that farmers cannot farm as they wish. We are simply saying that if they want public subsidies, they will have to farm well. And *well* means farming in an environmentally sensitive way as well as in an efficient one.

Farmers, like everyone else, need encouragement to take care of the countryside. But we do not have unlimited resources and we cannot afford to get ourselves into the position of paying robbers to go away. So, as I have said, farmers can increasingly expect that basic environmental protection will be a precondition of their receipt of agricultural subsidies. From stocking densities to the protection of landscape and habitat features this idea now forms part of the reformed CAP.

Our aim will be to develop this idea in ways which reward the kind of efficient and environmentally sensitive farming on which a healthy rural economy clearly depends, not least in the less favoured areas of our country. This is not some idealistic and far-

7

fetched programme. It does not usher in an era of individual farm plans under bureaucratic control. In terms of national policy, we are contemplating a very small shift in the balance to safeguard the scenery and wildlife of our farmed countryside: a countryside in England and Wales which attracts visitors whose annual expenditure is estimated at £9 billion. That is more than the £7 billion that agriculture adds to our GDP in the United Kingdom as a whole.

We do, of course, recognise that farmers will need reward and encouragement if we want them to go further than basic agricultural and environmental standards would require. I said earlier that I would outline the measures that we propose to introduce in England to implement the Agri-Environment Regulation. Final decisions on the launch of these schemes will be made later this year but we have deposited with the European Commission plans to introduce the following schemes. Similar but not necessarily identical proposals are being put forward for Scotland, Wales and Northern Ireland.

First and foremost, we will add 6 new ESAs so that there are 22 ESAs in England; and we shall be adding 2 more in Wales so that there are 6: Cambrian Mountains, Lleyn Peninsula, Ynys Mn, Radnor, Preseli and the Clwydian Range. Besides the new ESAs, we are adding 6 other new reward schemes. We will introduce a new voluntary incentive to farmers to offer the public some access in the ESAs where it would be particularly helpful (for example to gain sight of a beautiful view, or to connect with other footpaths to make an interesting walk). Third, we will introduce a Moorland Scheme to encourage farmers to reduce the number of sheep carried on heather and particularly susceptible moorland outside the ESAs. Fourth, we will introduce a Habitat Scheme to provide incentives to farmers to take land out of production for 20 years and manage it in an environmentally beneficial way. We have in mind the grazing marshes in the inter-tidal ranges of our coastline, the waterside margins of some of our finest rivers and some of the particularly valuable habitats that have been protected under the voluntary 5-year Set-Aside Scheme. Fifth, we will provide a Countryside Access Scheme on set-aside land which will have the same purposes as the Access Scheme proposed for the ESAs, and be equally voluntary. Sixth, we will introduce an Organic Scheme to assist farmers to increase that particular form of production. Seventh, we will expand our Nitrate Sensitive Areas Scheme with the designation of 30 more areas in which farmers will be paid to farm in ways which reduce the potential leaching of nitrate into groundwater. Finally we shall include in the agri-environment programme the Countryside Stewardship Scheme now being piloted by the Countryside Commission to try out new approaches to the conservation and enhancement of valuable landscape habitats outside the ESAs.

All of this amounts to a very substantial programme which will gradually shift the balance somewhat away from the encouragement of production and towards the protection of our countryside. It is not quite a full description of our policies of encouragement because I have not mentioned the important local initiatives taken by English Nature and others to protect wildlife. But it is an impressive programme which will amount to expenditure of some £70 million in England alone in 1995/6.

The research and development R&D programme of the Ministry and the Welsh Office has itself been reorientated accordingly. Over a third of the £6 million we shall spend on grassland research in 1993/4 will be directed at maintaining species diversity and reducing pollution. On top of this, £1/2 million will be directed at improving our knowledge of heather management. This and much other R&D helps inform the advice that we make available to farmers, both directly and through Codes of Practice such as those that we issue in respect of the protection of water, soil and air.

Many of you may be asking yourselves what reason we have to believe that this change of policy, this change of balance in the countryside, this expenditure on countryside management is what people usually want. You may like to know that a contingent valuation study of our ESAs, carried out for us this year by Newcastle University, shows that people in general, whether they live in the ESAs, visit them, or just want to know that they are there, are in favour of them and are prepared to contribute substantially to their retention through taxation. In these hard times that is a reassurance that I am sure you will all welcome as much as I do. It is a genuine recognition of the valuable work our farmers can do to manage and safeguard our beautiful and varied countryside; and of the important part that Government policies have to play in helping them to do that.

UK Grasslands Now:
Agricultural Production
and Nature
Conservation

A. HOPKINS AND J. J. HOPKINS[1]

Institute of Grassland and Environmental Research,

North Wyke, Okehampton, Devon, EX20 2SB

[1]Joint Nature Conservation Committee, Monkstone House,

City Road, Peterborough PE1 1JY

ABSTRACT

Grasslands occupy over 50% of UK agricultural land, provide about 75% of the diet of ruminant livestock and are important for recreation and nature conservation. Although 50% of grassland swards are over 20 years old, most have been modified by intensive management. Fertilizer N is now applied to 85% of grassland. Reseeding, drainage and replacement of hay by silage have also contributed to reduced botanical diversity. Only a small proportion of lowland grasslands are now of conservation value; over 95% have been lost since 1930. Of the 34 grassland communities in the National Vegetation Classification, 21 are now rare enough to merit SSSI designation, and 80% of SSSI management agreements in England relate to grassland sites. Since the mid-1980s, agricultural surpluses and a 'greening' of agricultural policies have reduced the incentives for increased production; compensation schemes in Environmentally Sensitive Areas enable some integration of less intensive agriculture with conservation objectives, but elsewhere losses of habitat and species diversity continue to occur.

INTRODUCTION

Grasslands occupy a higher proportion of agricultural land in the UK than they do in most other countries. Of a total area of 12 million hectares of crops and grass, nearly 7 million hectares consist of 'permanent' or 'temporary' grasslands, the main subject of this paper. In addition, there are 6 million hectares of unenclosed 'rough grazings' (a heterogenous census category which includes heather moor, bracken and *Molinia/Nardus/Festuca* grassland, mainly in the cool, wet uplands of the north and west); some of this can also be regarded as grassland in the present context. Climate, soils and hydrology combine to give much of western Britain advantages for grass production in regions only marginally suitable for grain production. In areas such as Dyfed, Dumfries and Galloway, Northern Ireland, and in parts of north-west and south-west England, grassland accounts for over 80% of agricultural land. Grass provides most of the dietary requirements of the ruminant livestock sector, which in turn accounts for about half the farm-gate value of UK agricultural end-products.

Grassland also has an important amenity role. It dominates the landscape, particularly in the north and west where most National Parks and similar protected landscapes are situated. In some districts the income associated with the recreational and conservation value of the landscape, and its associated flora and fauna, exceeds the direct income from agricultural production, so extending employment opportunities for rural communities at a time when agricultural income is falling.

Non-agricultural roles of grassland are not new; they found their expression in the creation of parkland estates in the eighteenth century, and sporting interests have often conflicted with pressures to bring the land under the plough. Sir George Stapledon, although best remembered as a protagonist of ley farming, also argued passionately for 'a great return to nature for the nation as a whole; the urban population should have sufficient opportunity for simple enjoyment of the country' (Stapledon, 1935).

Since the second world war, food shortages, government and EC policies, and technological innovations have stimulated greatly increased production from grassland. In the 40 years to the mid-1980s, output of beef and lamb doubled, and that of milk more than trebled, while the grassland area actually fell. However, this success was achieved at the expense of a wide range of wildlife habitats and species. Grasslands of nature conservation value account for only a small proportion of the UK total, having decreased by an estimated 97% since 1930 in the lowlands (Fuller, 1987), and in some areas are virtually confined to protected sites such as Sites of Special Scientific Interest (SSSIs). Such grasslands are likely to figure prominently in the UK Biodiversity National Action Plan. They contain a higher proportion of British Red Data Book plants than does any other habitat type. A significant number of rare and threatened invertebrates, and a number of rare birds such as the corncrake *(Crex crex)* and chough *(Pyrrhocorax pyrrhocorax)*, are also dependant upon grasslands.

In this paper we review the divergent approaches to grassland taken by agriculturalists and conservationists; the development and consequences of agricultural intensification of grassland in recent decades; and the present management of grassland for agriculture and of grassland habitats for nature conservation.

GRASSLAND TYPES

The National Vegetation Classification (NVC) (Rodwell, 1991; 1992) was commissioned by the Nature Conservancy Council and aims to describe and classify the full range of British vegetation. Thirty-four grassland types found in the lowlands are described, and are further sub-divided into 107 sub-communities. This diversity reflects the complexity of regional geology, climate, hydrology and management.

The NVC divides grasslands into four main groups characterized by soils:

(a) Mesotrophic. Grasslands of circum-neutral clay and loam soils, including semi-natural grasslands (MG1 - MG5, MG8 - MG13) and highly anthropogenic grasslands created by fertilizers, liming and reseeding (MG6 - MG7) (Rodwell, 1992).

(b) Calcicolous. Grasslands on nutrient-poor soils derived from calcareous parent materials (CG1 - CG10), excluding coastal sand dunes (Rodwell, 1992).

11

(c) *Calcifugous*. Grasslands on nutrient-poor acid substrates (U1 - U6), including cover sands, but excluding coastal sand dunes (Rodwell, 1992).

(d) *Fen meadows and wet, acid grasslands*. Communities developed over acid or circum-neutral peat, or perennially wet mineral soil with a low nutrient status (M22 - M26) (Rodwell, 1991).

Many NVC grassland types have a distinctly regional pattern of distribution, reflecting the importance of climate as the second most important controlling influence upon vegetation. Regional conservation strategies are therefore required if the full range of variation is to be conserved.

The NVC is of only limited value for understanding the ecology and management of intensively managed grassland. The majority of agricultural grasslands have been affected by fertilizer use, and fall within either the MG6 *Lolium perenne - Cynosurus cristatus* grassland type (synonymous with the widespread *Lolio - Cynosuretum* found extensively in the rest of temperate Europe) or the MG7 *Lolium perenne* ley grasslands. These two vegetation types account for most agricultural and managed amenity grasslands and exhibit a complex but subtle pattern of variation.

In contrast to ecologists, agronomists have placed emphasis upon a limited number of economically important species in description and classification; mainly grasses, white clover and notable weeds such as *Rumex* spp. and *Cirsium arvense*. A simple method of botanical analysis for assessing agricultural value was used for the first grassland surveys in the 1930s, and provided the basis of grassland mapping of England and Wales (Davies, 1941). Lowland swards were classified into one of seven main pasture types, some with sub-divisions. The proportion of perennial ryegrass was the basis of classification; e.g. first-grade was defined as >30% perennial ryegrass, plus white clover and other productive grasses, and second-grade as 15-30% ryegrass and a greater abundance of *Agrostis*. These two grades accounted for less than 8% of lowland permanent pasture in the 1930s. Later grassland surveys (Forbes *et al.*, 1980; Green, 1982; Hopkins and Wainwright, 1989) continued to emphasize the percentage contribution of perennial ryegrass in relation to sward age, management and output, but by the late 1970s perennial ryegrass was so abundant that about 70% of over-20-year-old swards (and most of the younger sown grass) would have fitted the descriptions of first- or second-grade pasture. To produce a basis for classifying agriculturally improved grassland, Hopkins (1986) used cluster analysis on botanical records from 3700 fields. Eight species groups were identified: (1) *Lolium* dominant; (2-6) *Lolium* and *Agrostis* with either *Holcus lanatus*, other sown grasses, *Trifolium repens*, *Poa trivialis* or *Cirsium arvense*; (7) *Agrostis-Holcus lanatus*; and (8) *Agrostis-Festuca*. These groups were subsequently related to detailed field management records and environmental information.

The potential for grassland production varies with the length of the growing season but is modified by moisture availability, itself a function of climate and soil. Such an approach to grassland classification has been used to identify grassland yield categories, the suitability of sites for grassland being further refined by the influence of soil trafficability. Ranking land for grassland suitability seeks to express the ease with which a balance can be struck between potential production and utilization, four main classes being identified (Harrod, 1979).

Multi-site trials of both permanent swards and ryegrass leys show variation in yield due to site conditions (Morrison *et al.*, 1980; Hopkins *et al.*, 1990). However, on good grass-growing sites (which are often seasonally affected by excess soil moisture), utilization of herbage may be lower than on drier, less productive sites.

In a rational land use policy it is, of course, the land types least suited for production and utilization which are most suitable for conservation and other uses, and these approaches to classification should have considerable interest to both conservationists and agriculturalists.

RECENT HISTORICAL DEVELOPMENTS

The grassland area and its management have fluctuated with the demands of population growth and economics, but it is the period from the late 1930s (at the end of a 60-year agricultural depression) to the present that has had the greatest impact upon grassland productivity and its implications for nature conservation.

Until the early 1980s there was a degree of political consensus on countryside management. Successive governments encouraged the intensification of agriculture through guaranteed prices, capital grants and advice. Increased self-sufficiency in food production was justified on grounds of national security, and later because of its contribution to the balance of payments and rural prosperity. Although the post-war period had seen the creation of National Parks, National Nature Reserves and the Nature Conservancy, in the 1940s agriculture was not identified as a threat to the countryside (Sheail, 1976). For 40 years agricultural improvement was carried out with scant regard for conservation values.

As far as grassland was concerned, the main effect was a reduction of botanical diversity. Overall, there was an increase of ryegrass at the expense of most other species due to three developments acting together: reseeding, increased use of fertilizers, particularly nitrogen, and increased silage-making. Earlier cutting for silage favours ryegrass at the expense of late-flowering species, and has allowed the economic potential of improved ryegrass varieties and nitrogen to be realized.

Despite the impact of the wartime ploughing campaign and subsequent agricultural improvement, nearly 60% of the old grass that existed in 1939 remained unploughed 20 years later (Baker, 1960). At this time, fertilizer nitrogen use on grassland was relatively low, silage was made by only a minority of farmers, and a high proportion of the grasslands of wildlife value found in 1940 would have remained.

During the following 20 years, management changes had a major impact upon this remaining core of old grassland. The average use of nitrogen on grassland trebled. The practice of making silage increased, with a five-fold increase between 1966 and 1980; replacement of hay by silage, together with the management changes it requires or enables, probably had more effect on species diversity than any other factor. This was also a very active period for land drainage operations, encouraged and partly financed by MAFF, which affected large areas of wet lowland grasslands.

13

Reseeding of grassland also continued at a rate of about 200,000 hectares annually. The increase in arable land during this period was at the expense of grassland, including many chalk grasslands and the once highly prized fattening pastures of the East Midlands, Norfolk and Romney Marsh. Governments continued to encourage increased production from grasslands, a policy signalled very strongly in the 1975 White Paper 'Food from our own Resources'. By the end of the 1970s there was increasing disquiet at the pace of destructive change affecting the countryside. The sentiments were not confined to conservationists, and there was a rapid growth of Farming and Wildlife Advisory Groups at this time. By the mid-1980s, semi-natural grasslands were reported to cover only 4% of the lowland grassland area (Fuller, 1987), and a wide range of grassland plant and animal species had declined dramatically (Park, 1988).

The 1980s was a radical decade which saw most of the arguments for increasing agricultural production gradually fall away, and a progressive 'greening' of mainstream British politics. The 1981 Wildlife and Countryside Act heralded a change in emphasis in terms of encouraging conservation, and one of the most contentious issues of the period, the debate over the future of the Somerset Levels, focused attention upon grassland loss. The introduction of milk quotas in 1984 removed a major incentive to further increases in production, and the 1986 Agriculture Act imposed a duty for agriculture ministers to balance the needs of farming with conservation and enjoyment of the countryside, and gave ministers powers to establish Environmentally Sensitive Areas.

Despite these changes of policy and outlook, the loss of grassland continued. Fuller (1987) reports an approximate 2% per annum loss of semi-natural grasslands between 1930 and 1984, but in some areas this may have risen to 10% in the 1980s due to a combination of agricultural intensification, inappropriate management and neglect (Devon Wildlife Trust, 1990; Porley and Ulf-Hansen, 1991). Ironically, the reasons for this increased rate of loss would appear to relate to government policy. Many dairy farmers responded to milk quotas by intensifying their grassland, to reduce expenditure on bought feedstuff. Falling incomes from other livestock enterprises, and anticipation of a quota system on cattle and sheep numbers, was countered by increasing stocking rates and intensification of grassland management.

PRODUCTIVITY AND MANAGEMENT TODAY

Grass is our biggest single crop. It supplies over 75% of the dietary needs of some 12 million cattle and calves, 44 million sheep and lambs, and over 0.5 million horses. The products of grassland farms provide the livelihood for about 170,000 farming families and their staff, and for workers in associated supply, service and processing industries. The meat and milk derived from grassland on UK farms provides about 20% of the calorie intake and 30% of the protein intake of our population. Meat exports have also increased in recent years, mainly to other EC countries.

Information on grassland management, output, and sward composition is derived mainly from surveys and field trials (Forbes et al., 1980; Hopkins and Wainwright,

1989; Hopkins *et al.*, 1990). These studies, aspects of which now need updating, add substantially to data from the Survey of Fertilizer Practice (ADAS/FMA, 1992) and the annual MAFF Census.

Despite the reduction of grasslands of high conservation value, at least 50% of swards are at least 20 years old or unploughed. In a few areas, e.g. parts of the Pennines where over 60% is more than 35 years old, management changes have had little effect on old grassland (Hopkins and Wainwright, 1989). But elsewhere, modern agriculture has had a considerable impact.

Some 85% of all grassland in England and Wales now receives fertilizer N, at a mean annual rate of 160 kg N/ha; but while leys receive, on average, *c.* 200 kg N/ha, 40% of over-20-year-old grassland receives none or less than 50 kg N/ha, and the average on fields mown for hay, 100 kg N/ha, is less than half that on silage fields (ADAS/FMA, 1992). Dairy farms use, on average, more than twice the amount of fertilizer N used on beef/sheep farms. On sites with good grass-growing conditions, herbage yield responses (up to 300 kg N/ha) are *c.* 15-20 kg dry matter (DM) per kg of fertilizer N (Hopkins *et al.*, 1990). Losses in utilization prevent such responses from being fully reflected in additional livestock production, but fertilizer N is associated with higher output and profitability. Additional grass from fertilizer N is usually cheaper than purchased feeds.

Other inputs include phosphorus (P) and potassium (K), applied on *c.* 60% of grassland at average rates of 15 kg P/ha and 45 kg K/ha. Each year about 3% of grassland receives lime. Herbicide use is mainly confined to the establishment phase of leys, or for spot-treatment of perennial weeds (*Rumex* and *Cirsium* spp.) or bracken; *c.* 5-10% of the grassland area is treated each year.

Botanical composition *per se* is not a major determinant of sward productivity, but it reflects fertility and site conditions. Sown perennial ryegrass and permanent swards were compared at nine sites for 7 years under identical management: mean annual yields at 300 kg N/ha were 9.9 and 9.0 t DM/ha, respectively (Hopkins *et al.*, 1990, and in prep.). However, swards containing white clover, with no fertilizer N, can produce comparable output to grass-only swards receiving moderately high N. Research activity in this field has been very successful, and taken up enthusiastically by some farmers, but white clover-based swards have yet to be widely adopted in place of nitrogen-fertilized grass.

Output from grassland in terms of Utilized Metabolizable Energy (UME) is correlated with fertilizer N, but other factors which affect grass growth and utilization produce wide variation in output between farms using the same N rate. Average UME output on 450 farms recorded by Forbes *et al.* (1980) was 44 Gigajoules/ha for dairy farms and 40 Gj/ha for beef/sheep farms; few farms achieved over 70 Gj/ha. Present-day output (based on results from fewer farms, and allowing for general changes in livestock numbers, feed requirement, fertilizers etc.) is estimated to average at least 50 Gj/ha on beef/sheep farms, and 60 Gj/ha on dairy farms, while 80-100 Gj/ha is not uncommon for a milking herd.

15

NATURE CONSERVATION TODAY

Grasslands of nature conservation value are not extensive. Fuller (1987) estimated that in 1984 there were only 200,000 ha of unimproved lowland semi-natural grassland in England and Wales, and less can be expected in Scotland and Northern Ireland. Many of the plant communities of such grasslands are inherently species-rich, make an important contribution to the general conservation of biodiversity, and provide a reservoir of material for plant improvement programmes. However, grasslands are also very important for the conservation of the rare and threatened elements of our national biodiversity.

The British Vascular Plant Red Data Book lists seventy three grassland species - 23% of the total - giving grasslands a higher importance for rare plant conservation than any other major habitat (Perring and Farrell, 1983).

Two of the seven British Red Data Book butterflies, the chequered skipper (*Carterocephalus palaemon*) and the extinct large blue (*Maculinea arion*) are grassland species (Shirt, 1987). Studies of butterfly populations in southern England by Warren (1993) illustrate the importance of grasslands: of the twenty nine rare and local butterflies examined, twenty one species bred at grassland sites.

Ten British Red Data Book bird species are heavily dependent upon dry grassland habitat, while ten Red Data Book bird species make significant use of wet lowland grasslands as a breeding habitat, and sixteen species use wet lowland grassland for feeding and roosting (Batten *et al.*, 1990).

Of the thirty four grassland communities described in the NVC, twenty one are considered to be rare enough for examples to merit designation as SSSI. Some of these types are now very rare, such as the CG1 *Carlina vulgaris-Festuca ovina* grasslands which occur in south and west Britain on very steep, south-facing slopes with skeletal soils, and cover less than 1,000 ha; and the once relatively extensive MG3 *Alopecurus pratensis-Sanguisorba officinalis* grassland and MG4 *Geranium sylvaticum-Anthoxanthum odoratum* grassland, two meadow types which are estimated to cover less than 1500 ha.

The EC Habitats and Species Directive makes provision for the protection of three UK grassland types: the MG3 and MG4 referred to above, and all grasslands of the *Festuco-Brometea* class, which encompasses all lowland calcareous grassland types. However, there are other types found in the British Isles which are rare in Europe but not covered by the Directive, particularly the MG5 *Centaurea nigra-Cynosurus cristatus* grasslands, which are known only from the British Isles.

Grasslands account for 19% of the SSSI area in England (Smith, 1991). However, due to their high level of threat, a disproportionately large effort has been required to protect these sites from agricultural improvement. In 1992, 80% of all management agreements on SSSIs in England related to sites with grassland. This may not fully reflect the conservation problem; for instance Warren (1993) found that 33% of calcicolous grasslands of importance for butterflies were unmanaged and deteriorating as a result, 56% of these being SSSIs.

In 1987 the first Environmentally Sensitive Areas (ESAs) were declared in the United Kingdom, and by 1993 over forty such areas had been designated or proposed.

Grassland conservation is an important objective of most ESAs. However, the ESAs were also established to conserve landscapes, and not all the grasslands are of high nature conservation value. Of the five ESAs established in England in 1987, about 58% of the designated area was grassland (MAFF, 1989).

In addition, the Countryside Commission has established a Countryside Steward-ship programme, providing discretionary payments under a series of targeted schemes for environmentally sensitive land management. In 1991-92, 22% of the land subject to agreements was entered into the 'Chalk and Limestone Grassland' or 'Old Meadow and Pasture' schemes, with others such as 'Historic Landscapes' and 'Waterside Landscapes' schemes also including a significant proportion of grassland.

It will be some years before grassland sites are designated under the EC Habitats and Species Directive. Stroud *et al.* (1990) report twenty-one existing or proposed grassland sites (one calcareous and twenty seasonally flooded) for designation as Special Protection Areas (SPAs) under the EC Birds Directive.

THE FUTURE

Ruminant production is likely to remain the main use for most UK grassland, subject to no major changes in human diet or world trade. Farmers and politicians will, how-ever, face pressure to ensure that agricultural practices meet environmental and con-servation objectives. Further increases in fertilizers and other inputs are unlikely, and their use may decline. As farmers strive to achieve greater efficiency in a static or de-clining market, the total agricultural grassland area may fall: reductions of 2-4 million hectares by 2015 have been suggested (North, 1990).

In the short term, changes in support prices for cereals will reduce the cost advant-age of grass silage, relative to maize, cereals and concentrates. This will probably af-fect the amount and average quality of silage, with delayed and heavier first cuts, possibly with less fertilizer, and subsequent cuts replaced by grazing. Such changes would affect grassland production, sward structure and composition.

The lack of strategic data on how grassland has changed since the mid-1980s makes prediction about the future of grassland of conservation interest very uncertain. How-ever, evidence suggests that, despite a greening of agricultural policy in the 1980s, many semi-natural grasslands were lost as farmers tried to maintain their falling in-comes. Increased knowledge about grassland management will also have contributed to this trend.

Despite further policy mechanisms being introduced in the early 1990s to encourage nature conservation, we anticipate that, just as in the 1950s and 1960s farmers were delayed in their response to incentives to increase production, a similar delay in the uptake of conservation incentives will occur as farmers face uncertainty and attempt to make unfamiliar business judgements, resulting in further loss of semi-natural grass-lands.

This loss may, however, be of minor significance compared with the damage to sites due to neglect. Policies to reduce livestock numbers and the possibility of grazing on former arable land could well intensify this problem. Additional pressures could also

17

come from converting grassland to other uses, such as coppiced woodland for biofuel production, and from further demands for recreational use.

REFERENCES

ADAS/FMA (1992) *Fertilizer use on farm crops in England and Wales 1991.* London: MAFF.

BAKER H.K. (1960) Permanent grassland in England. In: *Proceedings of the 8th International Grassland Congress, Reading*, pp. 394-399.

BATTEN L.A., BIBBY C.J., CLEMENT P., ELLIOTT G.D. and PORTER R.F. (1990) *Red Data Birds in Britain.* London: Poyser.

DAVIES W. (1941) The grassland map of England and Wales: explanatory notes. *Journal of the Ministry of Agriculture*, **48**, 112-121.

DEVON WILDLIFE TRUST (1990) *Survey of Culm Grasslands in Torridge District.* Exeter: Devon Wildlife Trust.

FORBES T.J., DIBB C., GREEN J.O., HOPKINS A. and PEEL S. (1980) *Factors affecting the productivity of permanent grassland - a national farm study.* Hurley: GRI/ADAS Permanent Pasture Group.

FULLER R.M. (1987) The changing extent and conservation interest of lowland grasslands in England and Wales: a review of grassland surveys 1930-84. *Biological Conservation*, **40**, 281-300.

GREEN J.O. (1982) *A sample survey of grassland in England and Wales, 1970-72.* Hurley: GRI.

HARROD T.R. (1979) Soil suitability for grassland. In: Jarvis, M.G. and Mackney D. (eds.) *Soil Survey Technical Monograph* no. 13, pp. 51-70.

HOPKINS A. (1986) Botanical composition of permanent grassland in England and Wales in relation to soil, environment and management factors. *Grass and Forage Science*, **41**, 237-246.

HOPKINS A. and WAINWRIGHT J. (1989) Changes in botanical composition and agricultural management of enclosed grassland in upland areas of England and Wales, 1970-86, and some conservation implications. *Biological Conservation*, **47**, 219-235.

HOPKINS A., GILBEY J., DIBB C., BOWLING P.J. and MURRAY P.J. (1990) Response of permanent and reseeded grassland to fertilizer nitrogen. 1. Herbage production and herbage quality. *Grass and Forage Science*, **45**, 43-55.

MAFF (1989) *Environmentally Sensitive Areas.* London: HMSO.

MORRISON J., JACKSON M.V. and SPARROW P.E. (1980) The response of perennial ryegrass to fertilizer nitrogen in relation to climate and soil. *GRI Technical Report* no. 27, Hurley: GRI.

NORTH J. (1990) Future agricultural land use patterns. In: D. Britton (ed) *Agriculture in Britain: changing pressures and policies.* pp. 69-93, Wallingford: CAB.

PARK J.R.(Ed.)(1988) *Environmental Management in Agriculture.* London: Belhaven.

PERRING F.H. and FARRELL L. (1983) *British Red Data Books: 1. Vascular Plants.* Lincoln: RSNC.

PORLEY R.D. and ULF-HANSEN P.F. (1991) Unimproved neutral grassland in Dorset: survey and conservation. *Proceedings of the Dorset Natural History and Archaeological Society*, **113**, 161-165.

RODWELL J.S. (Ed.)(1991) *British Plant Communities, Vol 2, Mires and heaths*. Cambridge: CUP.

RODWELL J.S. (Ed.) (1992) *British Plant Communities, Vol 3, Grasslands and montane communities*. Cambridge: CUP.

SHEAIL J. (1976) *Nature in Trust*. London: Blackie.

SHIRT D.B. (1987) *British Red Data Books: 2. Insects*. Peterborough: NCC

SMITH I.R. (1991) *An examination of the habitat representation on SSSIs in England*. Peterborough: NCC.

STAPLEDON R.G. (1935) *The Land - Now and Tomorrow*. London: Faber and Faber.

STROUD D.A., MUDGE G.P. and PIENKOWSKI M.W. (1990) *Protecting internationally important bird sites*. Peterborough: NCC.

WARREN M.S. (1993) A review of butterfly conservation in central southern Britain: II Site management and habitat selection of key species. *Biological Conservation*, **64**, 37-49.

Objectives for Production and Conservation in Grasslands: Effects of Large Grazing Ungulates

I. J. GORDON AND P. DUNCAN[1]

Macaulay Land Use Research Institute, Craigiebuckler, Aberdeen AB9 2QJ, UK
[1]Centre d'Etudes Biologiques de Chizé, Centre National de la Recherche Scientifique (CNRS), 79 360 Beauvoir-sur-Niort, France.

ABSTRACT

Grasslands are of great importance world-wide not only for animal production, but also for the conservation of natural resources. In this paper we focus on the integration of production with the conservation of biodiversity: for some organisms such as plants, species richness in grasslands is obviously higher than in forests at large scales, it is comparable even at small scales. We describe the functioning of grassland ecosystems with particular emphasis on the impact and role of grazing animals. Factors which determine agricultural output from grasslands are reviewed, as are the criteria that are used to choose conservation objectives. The means of achieving agricultural and conservation objectives are compared and contrasted. Common elements exist, but their reconciliation will require changes in the current European agricultural policies concerning pricing and subsidies. More survey and research work is needed urgently, especially for the less well-known taxonomic groups such as invertebrates; and on the role of biodiversity in the functioning of grassland ecosystems.

INTRODUCTION

Natural grasslands, including steppes, savannas, punas and prairies in arctic, temperate and tropical regions, are second only to the oceans in the area they cover—about a quarter of the world's land surface. Man's agricultural development has been closely linked with these grassland systems, and the majority of our domestic livestock species are preferentially grazers (Thalen, 1984).

In the UK approximately 50% (12.8 Mha) of the land area comprises agricultural grasslands with rough and hill grazings, permanent grazings and silage grasslands completely dominating the landscape of much of western and northern Britain (Bunce and Barr, 1988; Alcock, 1992). Over 50% of the agricultural output of the UK comes from livestock grazing these pastures (Owen, 1987).

Production goals

As a result of the food crisis during the last war the principal goal of agricultural production policy at the national and European levels has been self-sufficiency in food.

Macroeconomic instruments, principally price interventions and subsidies, have been employed to achieve this. At the farm level, the principal goal is the maximization of profits through maximization of livestock and/or crop production. This has led to the conversion of much grassland into cropland; and subsidized livestock production systems, with subsidized inputs (fertilisers and supplementary feeds) resulting in widespread increases in grazing pressure on the fragile rough grazing and semi-natural vegetation communities in many areas within the UK. Consequently, there are currently major conflicts between the agricultural sector and conservation bodies.

Conservation issues

There are three key elements in the conservation of natural resources: the maintenance of life support systems, the sustainable utilisation of species and ecosystems, and the conservation of biodiversity (IUCN, 1990a). Grasslands play an important role in all of these. Concerning life support systems, grassland management affects the quality of water, surface and soil, as well as the regulation of atmospheric concentrations of greenhouse gases (Davidson and Herman, 1993).

The reasons for conserving biodiversity are less obvious than those for conserving life support systems; they include economic, ethical and aesthetic issues (which are dealt with in detail by the World Conservation Monitoring Centre (WCMC), 1992). In this paper we will focus on the productive use of grassland ecosystems and on the conservation of biodiversity, which used to be called "wildlife", and on their interactions. Biodiversity is an umbrella term covering the diversity of life. For conservation purposes it can be defined as the number and relative abundance of species in a given area, the genetic diversity within species and at higher levels, up to landscapes and regions (Fig. 1).

Species. Vascular plants of natural grasslands are extraordinarily diverse—at least as diverse as forests, particularly in the temperate regions. Grasslands can have up to 80 species/m^2 in Asian steppes (Knystautas, 1987) and 40 in chalk grasslands in the UK. In forests this is typically the richness of a hectare: 10-30 species in North America, 30-100 in South America (Gentry, 1988). On a different scale, in blocks of 10,000 km^2, tropical Africa's savannas are comparable with forests, with 1,000 to 2,500 species for savannas and 1,300 to 3,100 species for forests (Menaut, 1983).

Wild large herbivore communities still exist in a few grasslands, such as East Africa's Maasailand where up to 20 species of large herbivores coexist with their predators. In Europe most large mammals have become extinct in the last 100,000 years, probably because of overhunting by man (Owen-Smith, 1988).

Small mammals, reptiles, amphibians and birds have not had major radiations in this biome, and only 5% of the world's species are primarily adapted to grasslands (WCMC, 1992). However, grasslands are important for the conservation of communities of birds found nowhere else, including raptors, seed-eaters, and herbivorous ducks and geese in wetlands (cf. Goriup, 1988). Invertebrates dominate other groups in numbers of species but are so poorly surveyed that their contribution to biodiversity

21

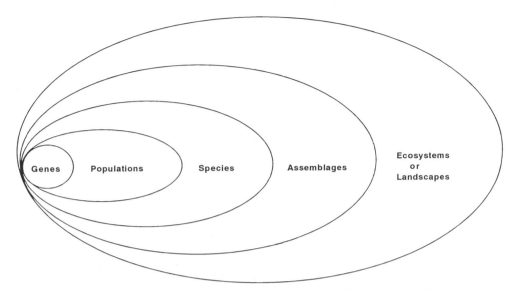

Fig. 1. The operational concept of biodiversity (from Duncan and Jarman in press).

is rarely measured: more survey work is urgently needed for all the less well-known groups, especially the invertebrates.

Populations and genotypes. Grasslands host the ancestors of many stock species, and plants of pastures and crops. Many of these occur in the Mediterranean and tropical regions, but northern European grasslands contain wild species of the genera *Lolium*, *Poa* and *Festuca* which have been used to develop some of the most productive varieties of pasture grasses. In addition these grasslands maintain some of the hardy breeds of livestock which underlie the productivity of locally adapted extensive agricultural practices. The development of genetic engineering means that these genetic resources can only be of greater importance for intensive production systems in the future.

Ecosystems, and their landscapes and processes. Some of the most valued landscapes are grasslands, like the prairies of North America, and the rolling grasslands of central Asia. Genetic material from wild plants and animals can be conserved in deep freezes, but without the conservation of whole systems the ecological processes which lead to natural selection will disappear, and with them the evolution of the species concerned. The conservation of whole systems is, therefore, of value both intrinsically, and as a means of conserving other levels of biodiversity, species and below.

Conservation goals

Though much more survey work is needed, especially for invertebrates, it is clear that the grassland biome contains exceptional biodiversity which is of great economic and aesthetic value. The primary goal of conservation in grasslands is to ensure the survival of the existing diversity of life, from the genotype to the landscape level.

Few, perhaps none of the remaining grasslands in northern Europe are natural: "The primary degradation of European grasslands has been practically total" (Beintema, 1988). As a result of agricultural selection favouring short-lived species with rapid growth rates, a few species of plants and animals have increased in abundance relative to non-agricultural species. Natural grasslands have therefore been replaced by species-poor meadows and pastures; cereal fields are the logical endpoint of this process.

In this paper we give an outline of the objectives for management of grasslands to meet agricultural and conservation goals with special emphasis to Britain. We evaluate the extent to which management to achieve production objectives is compatible with achieving conservation objectives.

The ecological functioning of natural and semi-natural grasslands

Few grasslands in northern Europe are stable, climax communities: most result from the action on climax forests of processes such as grazing by large herbivores, fire, logging or the input of nutrients by rainfall. The exact successional pathway a grassland follows, and its endpoint, varies considerably even within a given ecosystem, depending on biotic, edaphic and climatic factors. In a single chalk grassland, thirteen different possible end-points have been identified (Jones-Walters, 1990).

Succession is slowed, and diversity maintained or enhanced, by processes such as mowing and grazing which reduce the dominance of strongly competitive plants. Grazing has a greater influence on diversity than mowing as it involves defecation and urination as well as prehension; and the offtake is selective, so grazing can affect the diversity and species richness within a community (alpha-diversity) in very different ways depending on the interaction between the diet preferences of the animal species and the competitive abilities of the plants (Gordon et al., 1990). Grazing can either increase diversity (e.g. if the dominant species is preferred) or decrease diversity if the dominant species is avoided (Lubchenco, 1978). Very heavy grazing can reduce diversity. Grazing by herbivores also increases beta-diversity, the variety of communities (Bakker et al., 1983).

The abundance of invertebrates as well as many of the smaller vertebrates, is determined principally by the structure of the vegetation, so interactions of wildlife with large ungulates are also strong. In some ecosystems, short grazed swards have invertebrate communities with fewer species and lower densities than lightly grazed ones, for many invertebrates require dense cover. In others the richness of their invertebrate communities is unaffected, but their composition changes in favour of the species of open ground (Putman et al., 1989). In freshwater marshes management of the emergent vegetation (e.g. by grazing) is usually a necessary condition for their use by coot and dabbling ducks (e.g. in the Camargue, Duncan, 1992).

Large ungulates, in natural as well as pastoral systems, therefore play an essential role in the maintenance of the characteristic communities of plants and animals: they are "keystone" species in these ecosystems (Kortlandt, 1984; van Wieren, 1990). In

23

the UK, the typical vegetation of the hill and upland areas is the result of centuries of anthropogenic disturbances, primarily sheep but also fire (Miles, 1988).

PRODUCTIVE USE OF GRASSLANDS
The objectives of animal production

The strategic objective of farmers is to maximise profitability by obtaining high rates of animal production while minimising costs. Prior to the second world war the food requirements of the UK population were supplemented by imports. Agriculture was based upon a small scale matrix of extensive mixed farming enterprises, a stable, hete-rogeneous system which resulted in habitats which were ideal for wildlife. Over the past 40 years there has been a drive to reach self-sufficiency in agricultural products. This has resulted in increases in the productivity of the land through increasing inten-sification including land "improvement" by drainage and seeding to agricultural grasses, increased use of fertiliser and herbicides, increased use of preventative anthel-mintics for livestock and movement towards single commodity agricultural enterprises with high capital investments. For example, in Wales 100,000ha of marginal agricultu-ral land was improved in the 20 years to 1986 (NCC, 1990); over 1,000,000 tonnes of fertiliser nitrogen is currently added to UK grasslands every year (Owen, 1987). Many of the the costs of this intensification have been subsidised either through the British Government or the European Community.

Farmers have thus been encouraged to approach maximal rates of animal produc-tion. This depends principally on two factors: nutrient intake and animal health. Grassland structure, the quantity and quality of forage available, is the primary in-fluence on animal performance through its effect on nutrient intake. The objectives of farm management therefore focus on sward structure.

The intake of domestic ruminants responds mainly to variations in the amount and maturity of leaf material in the sward and its distribution within the sward canopy (Hodgson, 1990). Swards with abundant highly digestible material, principally leaf, tend to maximise the performance of livestock. Herbage quality only limits animal production where herbage availability is not limiting, or when quality is below some threshold. These circumstances are commonly found only in extensive livestock pro-duction systems based on semi-natural grasslands (Gordon and Illius, 1992).

In agricultural swards, the availability of plant material is usually defined in terms of herbage mass or sward surface height (Hodgson, 1990). Mean sward height has been shown to be an important determinant of intake and performance amongst both sheep and cattle (Hodgson, 1990). Increases in sward height result in higher levels of intake and higher levels of performance until an asymptote is reached above which there is little effect on intake and little improvement in individual animal perfor-mance. However, there would be a decline in the performance of the flock or herd as a whole because of the decline in the efficiency of herbage utilisation (Hodgson, 1990).

Poor health reduces animal productivity. The principal causes are food shortages (end of winter, summer droughts), disease and parasites. In domestic grazing systems the most important of these are helminths (Nansen, 1987). There are well-known interactions between food shortages and susceptibility to disease and parasitism (Holmes, 1993).

Management techniques
The quantity of herbage available to the grazing animal is the difference between the rates of growth and litter formation. Plant production on typical semi-natural and natural grasslands is highly responsive to the prevailing edaphic and climatic conditions. Rainfall, soil nutrient status and the species composition of the grassland are the primary factors influencing production. These constraints are commonly overcome through inputs in order to achieve swards on which animal production is close to maximal.

The most spectacular management intervention is the ploughing up of natural grassland and seeding with exotic plants which allow higher levels of animal production. In temperate regions sown pastures are based on only some 5 or 6 species of grass and legume; usually these are sown in cultures of at most a grass species and a legume.

The maintenance of highly productive swards, sown and native, is achieved by management based on two principal types of action: harvesting (grazing, mowing), and the use of inputs either for soil enrichment (nutrients and water) or the control of undesirable species (competing plants and herbivores, and parasites and disease).

Grazing and mowing. These necessary parts of the production process may have positive or negative effects on biodiversity. Their effects on plant structure and diversity, and the knock-on effects on animal populations have been presented in the above section on **The ecological functioning of natural and semi-natural grasslands**.

Inputs. Fertiliser input (processed or manure) is the most commonly used means of adding nutrients (nitrogen and minerals) and its use has increased sharply over the past 50 years. This liberal use of fertilisers has often resulted in decreases in the efficiency of use of the nitrogen and phosphorus by the pasture, leading to a large increase in effluents from grasslands into the groundwater, rivers and the atmosphere. This, in turn, leads to eutrophication of freshwater and the consequent detrimental effect on the environment. Legislation is now being brought in to reduce fertiliser inputs in the EC so as to ensure the levels of nutrients in the groundwater are reduced (e.g. HMSO, 1989). Fertilisation greatly reduces plant species diversity (Tilman, 1986). Irrigation has the same kind of effect because both these inputs favour the dominance of the most competitive species. If these inputs are not sufficient to maintain the desired plant species, and levels of animal production, then competing plants and herbivores are controlled by the use of herbicides and insecticides. Such inputs obviously decrease diversity, and their long term effects may be catastrophic.

To improve animal health, farmers use supplementary foods and medicines, both preventive and curative. Concentrates or supplementary feeds are commonly distributed to tide the animals over periods of food or mineral shortages. These can have environmental effects through increasing the concentration of protein or minerals in the soil or water. Medicines to prevent or to treat disease, and especially parasites, are used universally. Anthelminthics have effects on components of the grasslands other than the intestinal parasites targeted. For example, ivermectin inhibits the development of larvae from Dipteran and Coleopteran invertebrates which lay their eggs on the faeces (Madsen *et al.*, 1990).

CONSERVATION USE OF GRASSLANDS
The objectives

The planet is undergoing one of the most spectacular periods of extinction in its history (Jablonski, 1991), and we cannot save all existing biodiversity. Conservation biology is a new discipline which aims to develop the necessary scientific and technical framework for action. Research on agricultural production has been conducted intensively for over 100 years, but conservation biology is a very young discipline and in spite of considerable recent progress (cf. Soulé, 1987, 1991), there is currently no generally accepted method of measuring the costs (financial, let alone ethical) of losses of biodiversity, especially the costs outside direct human interest. There are no universally accepted methods of determining priorities for conservation action. Methods of managing populations of wild plants and animals so as to conserve their genetic diversity are in their infancy. Most professional conservationists are operating on the premise that "getting something preserved - anything at all - is acceptable regardless of the yardstick" (Erwin, 1991). The technical framework generally used for targeting conservation actions is given in Fig.2.

Inventory, priorities and monitoring. The most threatened items of biodiversity (e.g. species, genotypes etc.) are identified by surveys at different levels: global, national, local (IUCN, 1990b; ICBP, 1992). The situation in Britain is relatively good, for the

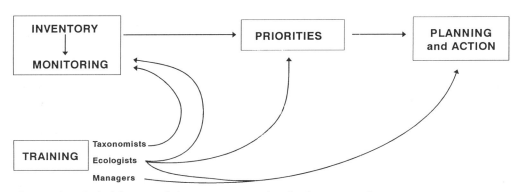

Fig. 2. A technical framework for management planning in conservation.

Biological Records Centre maintains a computerised monitoring scheme for all plant species, and the BTO (British Trust for Ornithology), in cooperation with sister organisations like the RSPB (Royal Society for the Protection of Birds) monitors the abundance of common as well as rare birds. Of the 1900 plant species in Britain less than 100 are endangered, compared with the 60 000 plant species which, it is estimated, will disappear worldwide before 2050 (IUCN, 1986).

Priorities for biodiversity conservation in grasslands. Loss of grasslands, loss of diversity due to heavy grazing pressure and intensification, and particularly the loss of the largest and most vulnerable species of vertebrates are the main issues worldwide. Britain, with its high human density, faces all these problems, in spite of its long tradition of conservation. A quarter of the semi-natural habitats were lost to intensive agriculture between 1947-80. The distribution of losses has been very uneven. There has been a 92% loss of unimproved and rough grasslands in lowland Britain, with only 0.6 Mha remaining (Fuller, 1987); 75% of chalk grasslands and 50% of wetlands have disappeared (NCC, 1984; Countryside Commission, 1986); uplands, which are relatively less diverse, have been less touched. The combined consequences have led to the loss of at least 200 species this century (Green, 1989).

At the global level, primary objectives for conservation actions are the protection of taxa and communities from extinction; at the national and local levels the priority is commonly the maintenance of diversity. The objectives are usefully divided into the categories "species" and "habitat", though they are, in most cases, closely linked. For species the objective is the maintenance of wild populations; for habitats (and ecosystems and landscapes) the maintenance of representative areas and of species diversity within them.

Conservation management in grasslands

The means of conserving and using biodiversity sustainably range from off-site, like germ-plasm banks, to on-site, like Biosphere Reserves (Soulé, 1991).

Species and genotypes. For some of the threatened vertebrate species we have adequate knowledge to identify the threats and provide solutions, usually involving protection and population management. Reintroduction and reinforcement of smaller, fast breeding species of plants, invertebrates, birds, and even some mammals, have been carried out in many grasslands. A well known example is the Large Blue butterfly, which was reintroduced into chalk grassland in the UK (Morris and Thomas, 1989). Detailed "Species Action Plans" are available for only a small minority of plants and animals. Five hundred and thirty bird species have been recorded in the UK, and 117 are threatened. Of these Action Plans exist for ten.

Habitat protection and management. Most problems of conservation of biodiversity can be solved only by broader programmes of habitat management. In the higher production farming areas, where few semi-natural grasslands remain, the most urgent action is to save the relics of the original grasslands as protected areas (PAs), state or private of adequate size (e.g. in lowland Britain, but also in the tallgrass prairies of the USA and the Ukrainian steppes).

In most grasslands management is needed to maintain their biodiversity and grazing is often an essential component. In Europe where most of the native wild large ungulates are extinct, their ecological role can be replaced only by their domestic relatives. In European PAs the diversity of grasslands is increasingly being managed by grazing with domestic stock - a practice which has many technical advantages (Gordon and Duncan, 1988; Girard *et al.*, 1990; van Wieren, 1990).

Prescriptions for biodiversity conservation in some of the more important types of grassland are available; for example, calcareous grasslands, traditional hay meadows (this volume), and heather moorland (Armstrong, 1990). It is urgent that similar prescriptions are developed for the restoration for intensively-farmed croplands and pastures.

COMMONALITIES OF OBJECTIVES IN FARMED GRASSLAND

This discussion of the factors which are important in determining the agricultural output and conservation value of grasslands shows that it is possible to harmonise agricultural and conservation uses. However, this will be difficult within an economic context where production is maximised.

The conservation value of grasslands is high where there are low levels of inputs and grazing pressure, as in extensive systems. With the current overproduction of the temperate agricultural commodities within the countries of the EC it clear that there is an opportunity to produce the food and fibre necessary for self-sufficiency from a much smaller land resource (North, 1991). With the social requirement to maintain populations in rural areas, much farming on marginal lands will change towards extensification. Greater financial constraints on inputs and financial investment in agricultural practices which are beneficial to the conservation of wildlife (e.g the ESA scheme in the UK; Potter *et al.*, 1991) will be a necessary condition to favour extensification. However much more will be needed - in particular new technical frameworks for farmers which are adapted to present economic conditions. The social and psychological dimensions of changes which appear retrogressive are aspects which will need to be addressed if these new technical frameworks are to be accepted by rural communities.

The harmonisation of production and conservation goals will also be promoted by the diversification of economic activities on farms: naturalists, like ornithologists are attracted to farms with diverse plant and animal communities. This will allow farmers to base their farm incomes less on subsidies provided by government to produce a commodity which is in surplus, and more on services for which the urban population desire and are willing to pay.

Finally the functional role of biodiversity in ecological production is poorly understood: further research on this important question may promote commonalities of objectives.

CONCLUSIONS

1. The goal of an agricultural enterprise is to maximise profitability. Currently macroeconomic instruments reduce the costs of inputs and therefore favour enterprises which tend towards maximal rates of production.

2. Conservation goals aim to maintain or enhance biodiversity. In grasslands, this involves maintaining:
   - threatened animal populations. These objectives are achieved through reintroduction, reinforcement, predator control, and species-oriented habitat management.

 - grasslands as diverse systems, by the creation of reserves to maintain them as a component of the landscape, and by appropriate management of grasslands as habitats for wild plants and animals, both in reserves and in the wider countryside. Such management includes:
   : disturbance of the grasslands to slow succession, and to maintain a variety of niches, and thus plant species diversity;
   : maintaining heterogeneous, relatively tall swards as habitats for invertebrate and vertebrate communities;
   : reducing or eliminating biocides.

3. Conservation and production goals are therefore completely different, and in grasslands high rates of production are associated with lower biodiversity. As a consequence the strategic, management objectives to achieve production and conservation goals overlap only by coincidence, and only exceptionally.

4. The development of common objectives must be based on more extensive production, aimed at reducing costs and improving conservation (water quality as well as biodiversity), and reducing inputs of nutrients, water, biocides and grazing pressures, especially in sheep-grazed areas. In protected areas this is already occurring; in the wider countryside progress requires changes in macroeconomic policy, through freer trade and through reduced subsidies for inputs to favour extensification rather than intensification, and profitability rather than productivity.

REFERENCES

ALCOCK M.M. (1992) Role in landscape and wildlife conservation. In: Phillips, C. and Piggins, D. (eds.) *Farm Animals and the Environment*, pp. 383-410. Wallingford: CAB International.

ARMSTRONG H. (1990) Modelling the effects of vertebrate herbivore populations on heather moorland vegetation. In: Whitby, M. and Grant, S. (eds.) *Modelling Heather Management - a Workshop Report*, pp. 56-67. Department of Agricultural Economics: University of Newcastle upon Tyne.

BAKKER J.P., DE BIE S., DALLINGA J.H., TJADEN P. and DE VRIES Y. (1983) Sheep grazing as a management tool for heathland conservation and regeneration in the Netherlands. *Journal of Applied Ecology*, **20**, 541-560.

BEINTEMA A.J. (1988) Conservation of grassland bird communities in the Netherlands. In: Goriup, P.D. (ed) *Ecology and Conservation of Grassland Birds. International Council for Bird Preservation Technical Publication* No. 7. Cambridge, U.K.

BUNCE R.G.H., TRANTER R.B., THOMPSON A.M.N., MITCHELL C.P and BARR C.J. (1984) Models for predicting change in rural land use in Great Britain. In: Jenkins, D. (ed.) *Agriculture and the Environment*, pp. 37-44. Cambridge: Institute of Terrestial Ecology.

COUNTRYSIDE COMMISSION, (1986) *Monitoring Landscape Change*. Cheltenham: Countryside Commission.

COUNTRYSIDE COMMISSION, (1991) *The seven pound trip. Countryside Commission News* No. 50, Manchester, U.K.

DAVIDSON E.A., HERMAN D.J., SCHUSTER A. and FIRESTONE M.K. (1993) Cattle grazing and oak trees as factors affecting soil emissions of nitric oxide from an annual grassland. *American Society of Agronomy Special Publication* No. 55, pp.109-119. Madison, U.S.A.

DUNCAN P. (1992) The nutritional ecology of equids and their impact on the Camargue. *Horses and Grasses*. New York: Springer.

DUNCAN P. and JARMAN P.J. (in press) The conservation of biodiversity in managed rangelands, with special emphasis on the ecological effects of large grazing ungulates, domestic and wild. *Proceedings of the XVII International Grasslands Congress*.

ERWIN, T.L. (1991) An evolutionary basis for conservation strategies. *Science*, **253**, 750-752.

FULLER R.M. (1987) The changing extent and conservation interest of lowland grasslands in England and Wales; a review of grassland surveys 1939-84. *Biological Conservation*, **40**, 281-300.

GENTRY A.H. (1988) Tree species richness of upper Amazonian forests. *Proceedings of the National Academy of Science*, **85**, 156-159.

GIRARD N., DUNCAN P., ROSSIER E., DOLIGEZ E. GLEIZE J.C., BOULOT S. and TESSON J.L. (1992) *L'élevage extensif de chevaux pour la protection des espaces naturels. Paris:* CEREOPA.

GORDON I.J. and DUNCAN P. (1988) Pastures new for conservation. *New Scientist*, **117** (1604), 54-59.

GORDON I.J. and ILLIUS A.W. (1992) Foraging strategy: from monoculture to mosaic. In: Speedy, A.W. (ed.) *Progress in Sheep and Goat Research*, pp. 153-177. Wallingford: CAB International.

GORDON I.J., DUNCAN P., GRILLAS P. and LECOMTE T. (1990) The use of domestic herbivores in the conservation of the biological diversity of European wetlands. *Bulletin d'Ecologie*, **21**, 49-60.

GORIUP P.D. (1988) *Ecology and conservation of grassland birds. International Council for Bird Preservation Technical Publication* No. 7. Cambridge, U.K.

GREEN B. (1989) The impact of agricultural management practices on the ecology of grasslands. In: *Environmentally Responsible Grassland Management. British Grassland Society Winter Meeting*, pp. 1.1-1.13. London.

HMSO (1989) Water, England and Wales. *The Water Quality (Water Supply) Regulations 1989. Statutory Instruments 1989*, No. 1147.

HODGSON J. (1990) *Grazing Management. Science into Practice. Hong Kong: Longman.*

HOLMES P.H. (1993) Interactions between parasites and animal nutrition: the veterinary consequences. *Proceedings of the Nutrition Society*, **52**, 113-120.

ICBP (1992) *Putting Biodiversity on the Map*. Cambridge: International Council for Bird Preservation.

IUCN (1990a) *Caring for the World: A Strategy for Sustainability*. Gland: IUCN/UNEP/WWF.

IUCN (1990b) *Red List of Threatened Species*. Gland: IUCN.

JABLONSKI D. (1991). Extinctions: a palaeontological perspective. *Science*, **253**, 754-757.

KORTLANDT A. (1984) Vegetation research and the bulldozer herbivores of tropical Africa. In: Chadwick, A.C. and Sutton, C.L. (eds.) *Tropical Rainforest. Special Publications of Leeds Philosophical and Literary Society*, pp. 205-226.

KNYSTAUTAS A. (1987) *The Natural History of the USSR*. London: Century.

LUBCHENCO J. (1978) Plant species diversity in a marine intertidal community: importance of herbivore food preference and an algal competitive ability. *American Naturalist*, **112**, 23-29.

MADSEN M., OVERGAARD NIELSEN B., HOLTER P., PEDERSEN O.C., BROCHNER JESPERSEN J., VAN JENSEN K.M., NANSEN P. and GRONVOLD J. (1990) Treating cattle with Ivermectin: effects on the fauna and decomposition of dung pats. *Journal of Applied Ecology*, **27**, 1-15.

MENAULT J.C. (1983) The vegetation of African savannas. In: Bourliere, F. (ed.), *Tropical Savannas. Ecosystems of the World*, 13. pp. 109-149. Amsterdam: Elsevier.

MILES J. (1988) Vegetation and soil changes in the uplands. In: Usher, M.B. and Thompson, D.B.A. (eds.) *Ecological Change in the Uplands. Special Publication of the British Ecological Society*, pp. 57-70. Oxford: Blackwell Scientific Publications.

MORRIS M.J. and THOMAS J.A. (1989) Re-establishment of insect populations, with special reference to butterflies. In: Heath, J. and Emmet, A.M. (eds.) *The Moths and Butterflies of Great Britain and Ireland*, pp. 22-36. Colchester: Harley Books.

NANSEN P. (1987) Production losses and control of helminths in ruminants of temperate regions. *International Journal of Parasitology*, **17**, 425-433.

NATIONAL RIVERS AUTHORITY (1990) *Toxic Blue-green Algae. Water Quality Series* No. 2. Northants: Stanley L. Hunt (printers) Limited.

NCC (1984) *Nature Conservation in Great Britain*. Peterborough: Nature Conservancy Council.

NCC (1990) *Nature Conservation and Agricultural Change. Focus on Nature Conservation* No. 25. Peterborough: Nature Conservancy Council.

NORTH J. (1991) Technology and future land use patterns. In: Britton D. (ed.) *Agriculture in Britain: Changing Pressures and Policies*, pp. 45-93. Wallingford: CAB International.

OWEN D. (1987) *Report to the Priorites Board, Grassland and Forage Research Committee*. MAFF, DAFS, AFRC.

OWEN-SMITH R.N. (1988) *Megaherbivores: The Influence of Very Large Body Size on Ecology*. Cambridge: Cambridge University Press.

POTTER C., BURNHAM P., EDWARDS A., GASSON R. AND GREEN B. (1991) *The Diversion of Land - Conservation in a Period of Farming Contraction*. London: Routledge.

PUTMAN R.J., EDWARDS P.J., MANN J.C.E., HOW R.C. and HILL S.D. (1989) Vegetational and faunal changes in an area of heavily grazed woodland following relief of grazing. *Biological Conservation*, **47**, 13-32.

SOULE M. (1987) *Viable Populations for Conservation*. Cambridge: Cambridge University Press.

SOULE M. (1991) Conservation: Tactics for a constant crisis. *Science*, **253**, 744-750.

THALEN D.C.P. (1984) Large mammals as tools in the conservation of diverse habitats. *Acta Zoologica Fennica*, **172**, 159-163.

TILMAN D. (1986) Resources, competition and the dynamics of plant communities. In: Crawley, M.J. (ed.) *Plant Ecology*, pp.51-75. Oxford: Blackwell Scientific Publications.

VAN WIEREN S. (1990) Management of populations of large mammals. In: Spellerberg, I.F., Goldsmith, F.B. and Morris, M.G. (eds.) *The Scientific Management of Temperate Communities for Conservation. 31st Symposium of the British Ecological Society*, pp. 103-127. Oxford: Blackwell Scientific Publishers.

WCMC (World Conservation Monitoring Centre) (1992) *Global Biodiversity: Status of the Earth's Living Resources*. Chapman & Hall, London.

Sward Structure With Regard to Production

J.A. MILNE AND G.E.J. FISHER[1]

The Macaulay Land Use Research Institute, Craigiebuckler, Aberdeen AB9 2QJ

[1]The Scottish Agriculture College, Auchincruive, Ayr KA6 5HW

ABSTRACT

The relationships between the structure of grass swards and net herbage growth, herbage intake and animal production from dairy cows, beef cattle and sheep are described. There are curvilinear relationships between sward height and net herbage growth and herbage intake with a decreasing response at higher sward heights. Individual animal performance increases with increasing sward height to an asymptote with the asymptote varying with animal species and sward density as affected by previous management of the sward. Because of economic and welfare constraints on individual animal performance, animal production per hectare in the UK relates to sward height in a similar manner to that of individual animal performance. Similar relationships to those for grass swards exist for grass/clover swards. At greater sward heights than those used in most current grazing systems, the structure of swards change and patchiness increases. A simple model was developed to demonstrate that patchiness will lead to a considerable reduction in animal production per hectare.

INTRODUCTION

Sward structure has a major influence on animal production per unit area from sown and permanent grassland. It influences the quality and quantity of the diet ingested and hence determines the intake of metabolisable energy (ME) and the performance of individual animals. Sward structure also affects animal production per unit area by influencing dry matter (DM) biomass production.

Sward structure can be usefully described in terms of its vertical and horizontal dimensions. In a mono-specific sward, such as that typified by perennial ryegrass (*Lolium perenne*), sward height has an overriding influence on DM biomass production, particularly when continuously grazed. Within the sward canopy live leaf, dead leaf and stem are distributed such that live leaf is mainly at the top of sward with dead material, stems and leaf bases, which contribute most of the total biomass, at the bottom of the sward. Since most ruminants graze from the top of the sward, this ensures that in many circumstances a diet of high digestibility and hence ME concentration can be ingested from live leaf material. Except when hay or silage harvests are included as part of the grazing management, density of grass tillers, as a measure of the horizon dimension of structure, is high and hence there is insufficient variation in most grazed swards to cause the horizontal dimension to have large effects on animal production.

In this paper the major emphasis will be placed on the effects of sward height on animal production from sheep and cattle grazing perennial ryegrass and perennial ryegrass/ white clover swards. As sward heights increase, the manner in which they are grazed by those species leads to some areas being unselected, often associated with defaecation and urination on such areas. During the grazing season these patches will decline in ME content, mainly associated with seed-head formation, and create a sward which is visually patchy and which represents an important element of the horizontal dimension of structure. Animal productivity from these swards is likely to be lower than from uniform leafy swards and the extent to which a reduction may occur is considered.

EFFECT OF SWARD STRUCTURE ON ANIMAL PERFORMANCE FROM CONTINUOUSLY GRAZED GRASS SWARDS

Bircham and Hodgson (1983) described the effect of sward height on the productivity of a N-fertilised, dense and predominantly ryegrass sward continuously grazed by ewes and lambs from May to July. Growth increased with sward height at a diminishing rate. Senescence increased linearly with sward height resulting in net production reaching a maximum at around 4 cm and then declining slightly. Net production describes the amount available to the animal for ingestion. In the autumn over the same height range both growth and senescence were found to increase linearly with sward height, such that net growth also increased linearly (Hepp, 1989). The differences in net growth between summer and autumn are likely to be due to a lower quantity of light and lower temperatures in the autumn. The results of these studies indicate that higher sward heights are required in the autumn than in the summer for maximum net growth but that the range in height to achieve this objective is relatively small.

Hepp (1989) also considered the effect of sward density on herbage production from grazed predominantly perennial ryegrass swards. Swards were manipulated between May and July by either grazing continuously with sheep or by cutting for silage to create dense and open swards in August. These swards were then grazed by ewes or weaned lambs from August until October. Table 1 shows the effect of tiller density on herbage growth, senescence and net growth. With the sward with the lower tiller density, mean growth, senescence and net growth over the period from August to October were all reduced compared to those on the sward with the higher tiller density. These results demonstrate the penalty in DM biomass production in the autumn that occurs when a silage or hay cut is taken.

Under continuous grazing herbage intake increases to a maximum as sward height rises (see Hodgson (1990)). The relationships differ for different classes of livestock so that a maximum intake is reached at approximately 5-6 cm for sheep and 8-10 cm for dairy cows. A similar value of 8-10 cm has been obtained for suckler beef cows by Wright et al., (1989). It is likely that at greater sward heights than these herbage intake will decline. This is because at greater sward heights, sward density will be less, resulting in lower intake (see Table 1). This is due to reduced bite mass, which is an important determinant of herbage intake.

In general terms intake and digestibility of the diet are positively correlated. The digestibility of the diet is high and constant at sward heights up to the maximum height for intake but tends to decline at greater sward heights because of the greater quantity

Table 1. Effect of sward structure created by previous management on the mean tiller density and biomass productivity of swards continuously grazed by ewes and weaned lambs from August to October, and on the herbage intake and digestibility of the diet ingested by weaned lambs (from Hepp, 1989).

	Previous Management	
	Continuously Grazed	Aftermath following 2 silage cuts
Tiller density (tillers m^{-2})	15,000	12,000
Growth	47	28
Senescence	21	12
Net growth (kg DMha^{-1}day^{-1})	26	16
Herbage intake (g OM kgLW^{-1}day^{-1})	30.0	26.7
Digestibility of OM	0.783	0.764

Table 2. The effect of sward height in spring on herbage mass, tiller density, ME content of herbage, herbage intake and milk yield of dairy cows in late summer.

Spring sward height (cm)	Herbage mass (t DM ha^{-1})	Tiller density (live tillers m^{-2})	ME content of herbage (MJ kg DM^{-1})	Herbage intake (kg DM day^{-1})	Milk yield (kg day^{-1})
6-7	0.8	25.0	10.4	9.6	24.3
3-4	1.0	29.9	11.1	10.9	26.2
2-3	1.2	31.1	11.3	16.0	29.0
SED				2.22	2.20

(Roberts D.J., Fisher, G.E.J. and Hameleers A.J.L., unpublished data)

of flowering stem and dead material in taller swards. The lower herbage intakes at greater sward heights are also related to the lower digestibility of the diet ingested on these swards.

Swards with a lower tiller density result in a lower herbage intake, associated with a lower bite mass and a slightly lower digestibility in the diet selected (see Table 1).

Relationships between individual animal performance and sward height under continuous grazing conditions (see Figure 1) reflect those described for intake since digestibility of the diet remains relatively constant.

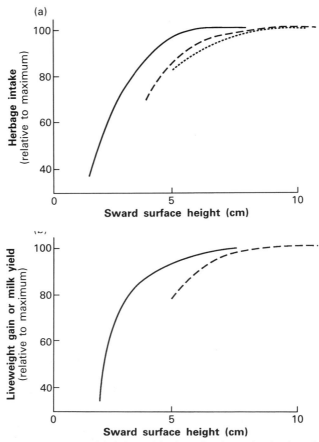

Fig. 1. Relationship between sward height and herbage intake and animal performance (expressed relative to maximum) for sheep and cattle: (a) herbage intake (———— sheep, ▬▬▬▬▬ dairy cows, •••••••• suckler beef cows) and (b) animal performance (———— liveweight gain of of lambs, ▬▬▬▬▬milk yield of cows (after Hodgson, 1990).

Since tiller density can be manipulated by varying the height of the sward in the early part of the grazing season, it is possible to develop management systems which allow higher levels of animal performance later in the season at a fixed sward height as a result of manipulation of sward height early in the season. An example of the effect of such manipulations is given in Table 2. Sward heights were maintained at three different levels in the spring by cows in late lactation or by sheep and then grazed in late summer at a sward height of 8 cm by cows in early lactation. In the late summer, tiller density and DM biomass were greater, ME content was higher and herbage intake and milk yield elevated on the swards that had been managed to maintain the lowest sward heights in the spring.

Animal production systems in the UK tend to operate at moderately high levels of individual animal performance for economic, welfare and management reasons. This means that the theoretical optimum for animal production per hectare, which would be at lower sward heights than for individual animal performance and near the optimum for net herbage growth, is seldom sought and the economic maximum for animal production per hectare is often near that for individual animal performance.

It is worth pointing out that management strategies are associated with the seasonality of herbage production in the UK. This requires that a proportion of the area of herbage which could potentially be grazed is conserved as hay or silage for use as fodder in the winter and that the finished product, for example a lamb at an appropriate liveweight, needs to be achieved before herbage growth ceases in the autumn. Such considerations have an effect of creating some diversity of herbage structure in most grazing systems.

EFFECT OF SWARD STRUCTURE ON ANIMAL PERFORMANCE FROM GRASS/CLOVER SWARDS

There is no direct experimental evidence which describes the relationship between the DM biomass productivity of continuously grazed swards with a moderate to high proportion of clover (20 to 40% of DM) in the sward and sward height. Cutting studies have generally shown that grass DM biomass production is higher on N-fertilised grass swards when 150 kg ha^{-1} or above is applied than on unfertilised grass/clover swards under similar cutting management.

The relationships between sward height of continuously grazed swards and herbage intake have been established to be similar for grass/clover swards as compared to grass swards (Orr *et al.*, 1990). There are slight differences in the nutritive value of white clover relative to grass such that, although their ME contents are similar, the balance of absorbed amino acids to ME intake appears to be greater for ruminants on grass/clover swards so that liveweight gains are higher with a higher proportion of white clover in the diet (Thomson, 1984). This is particularly so for lambs. Structure, in terms of height or density, does not affect *per se* the nutritive value of the diet selected when a grass/clover sward is grazed. It is the case, however, that managements that create low sward densities and which allow the clover to be present in the grazed horizon of the sward will increase the proportion of clover in the diet (Milne *et al.*, 1982) and hence may improve the nutritive value of the total diet.

Empirical evidence on responses in animal performance supports the statements made above. In a study which investigated the use of grass/clover swards by autumn-born Hereford × Fresian steers from 1984 to 1989, grazing days per hectare were 19% less and the liveweight gain per hectare was 24% less on average for a grass/clover system compared to a grass/nitrogen system (see Table 3). The steers weighed 200kg LW at the start of grazing and both sward types were grazed to the same height (7 cm in early and 8 cm in late season). The grass/clover swards received 40 kg N/ha/year until 1986, after which no fertiliser N was used, and the grass/nitrogen swards received 270 kg N/ha/year. The differences in grazing days and production per ha reflected differences in herbage production from the two sward types. There did not appear to be a nutritional advantage to grazing mixed swards in this experiment; indeed, steers on

Table 3. Total grazing days and liveweight gain by beef steers on grass/clover or grass/nitrogen swards grazed from May-September, between 1984 and 1989.

	Grass/Clover	System Grass/Nitrogen	SE Mean
Total grazing days ha^{-1}	1228	1509	48
Individual liveweight gain (kg day^{-1})	0.92	0.99	0.011
Liveweight gain (kg ha$^{-1)}$	1120	1481	44

Younie, D. and Heath, S.B. (1990)

the grass/nitrogen system had a significantly higher average daily liveweight gain over the six years (Table 3), even though the mixed sward contained an average of 33% clover in the herbage DM, compared with 7% in the grass/nitrogen sward.

A study by Vipond *et al.*, (1993) of the use of perennial ryegrass/white clover swards for lamb production demonstrated in a 3-year experiment that the daily liveweight gains of lambs from birth to weaning were 35 g/day higher on the grass/clover sward (250g day^{-1}) than on the grass sward receiving 160 kg Nha^{-1} annually (215g day^{-1}). Liveweight gain per hectare in the summer, however, was greater on the N-fertilised grass sward (1143 v 1014 kg), presumably reflecting the greater productivity of the N-fertilised grass sward. These results relate to sward heights maintained continuously at 4-5 cm from May to August. In the same study sward heights were also allowed to rise slightly in July and August. This resulted in greater liveweight gains of lambs, particularly on the grass/clover sward such that total output per hectare was similar in these grass and grass/clover systems.

This latter result indicates that simple management strategies which result in changes in sward structure can be used to increase animal performance. The use of sequential grazing of cattle followed by sheep to alter sward structure has also been found to improve animal performance. By grazing grass/clover swards in the period from May to July with cattle or sheep at sward heights maintained at 4 or 8 cm and following this with grazing by weaned lambs at 4 or 8 cm, the liveweight gain of the lambs was significantly higher on those swards grazed previously by cattle at both of the sward heights studied (I. A. Wright, personal communication). This was at least partially due to the higher clover content of the swards following cattle grazing, compared to following sheep grazing.

EFFECT OF PATCHINESS OF SWARDS ON ANIMAL PERFORMANCE

In swards continuously grazed at greater than 8 cm, the uniformity of the sward is reduced. Wright and Whyte (1989) shows that, when a sward is continuously grazed by suckler cows and their calves at 12 cm, approximately 20% of the grazing area is not grazed, i.e. rejected, by August. This rejected area will be tall, having developed seed heads, and its ME content will be approximately 8.0 MJ ME kgDM^{-1}, which is 30% lower than that of a continuously grazed short sward. Thus with taller swards, particularly under cattle grazing, patchiness will develop. This increase in structural diversity in a sward may lead to an increase in nature conservation value (see Mitchley 1993) but is likely to lead also to a reduction in animal production per hectare associated with reduced diet quality and lower total DM biomass production. Quantification of this reduction cannot be made from empirical observations as no studies have, as yet, been conducted.

In an attempt to provide this quantification, data from a number of studies have been drawn together. In the studies of Baker and Leaver (1986) and Fisher *et al.*, (1990) the interval between defoliation of grass tillers was measured when dairy cows grazed swards of a range of heights in the spring. The defoliation interval was between 5 and 30 days with the interval being greater at greater sward heights and lower stocking densities, as would be expected. A positive and linear relationship between defoliation interval, covering the range described above, and the proportion of tall grass in the sward was then derived. The data of Fitzgerald and Crosse (1989) were then used to derive a relationship between the proportion of tall grass in the sward and that in the diet (see Figure 2). The relationship described shows a typical response to the grazing of a preferred and a less preferred component in the diet. As the proportion of the less preferred component of the increases, there is an increasing proportion of that component in the diet.

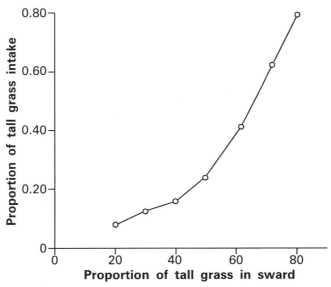

Fig. 2. Relationship between the proportion of tall grass in the sward and proportion of tall grass in the diet (after Fitzgerald and Crosse, 1989).

Assuming that the short grass has an ME concentration of 11.0 MJ kgDM^{-1} and that of the long grass is 8.0 MJ kgDM^{-1}, and extrapolating the relationship shown in Figure 2 to the whole grazing season, the impact of the proportion of tall grass in the sward, on reduction in ME intake and hence liveweight gain relative to a uniform sward can be established for a sward grazed at a low grazing pressure throughout the season. It can be seen from Figure 3 that there will be reductions of 3, 10 and 20% when the proportion of tall grass is 0.20, 0.40 or 0.60 of the total grazing area respectively. There will be a further reduction in animal production per hectare if the DM biomass production of the tall patches is less than that of the short patches. If the proportion reduction in DM biomass production was 0.30, then it can be calculated that the reduction in animal production per hectare would be 10, 25 and 35% when the proportion of tall grass is 0.20, 0.40 and 0.60 of the total grazing area respectively.

This latter conclusion only applies to the latter part of the grazing season when tall grass has had the opportunity to develop following the imposition of a lax grazing pressure. It may be that a necessary condition to meet nature conservation objectives is that the sward is patchy throughout the season. This would require that there was no grazing on the sward in the winter and in such a case the reductions in animal production per hectare for the grazing season would be of the order described above. Experimental quantification of these possible reductions in animal production is required and one of the aims of several experiments currently being conducted on the extensification of sheep production in the UK is to provide such information.

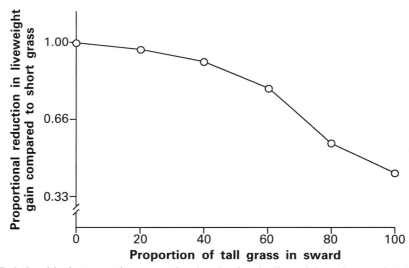

Fig. 3. Relationship between the proportional reduction in liveweight gain associated with tall grass in the sward compared to a uniform sward of short grass, and proportion of tall grass in the sward.

CONCLUSIONS

In terms of structure it has been shown that sward height has an important effect on animal production from grass and grass/clover swards continuously grazed by sheep and cattle. Sward density has a lesser effect but lower densities, produced by the introduction of hay or silage cuts into a management system, reduce subsequent individual animal performance and animal production per hectare. Management systems can be created which manipulate sward structure or its composition of grass and clover. These may create a greater diversity of structure during the season without reducing animal production per hectare compared to uniform swards. At greater sward heights patchiness will develop and this will lead to substantial reductions in animal production per hectare. It is concluded that any major alteration in the structure of swards, currently managed for agricultural production, to improve the nature conservation value of grasslands will lead to a substantial reduction in animal production.

REFERENCES

BAKER A-M.C. and LEAVER J.D. (1986) Effect of stocking rate in early season on dairy cow performance and sward characteristics. *Grass and Forage Science*, **41**, 333-340.

BIRCHAM J.S. and HODGSON J. (1983) The influence of sward condition on rates of herbage growth and senescence in mixed swards under continuous stocking management. *Grass and Forage Science*, **38**, 323-331.

FISHER G.E.J., ROBERTS D.J. and LAWSON A. (1990) The manipulation of grass swards for summer calving dairy cows. *British Grassland Society Research Meeting*, No. 2, Session VI, Paper 2.

FITZGERALD S. and CROSSE S. (1989) Production and utilisation of short grass and tall grass growing around dung pats in a perennial ryegrass sward grazed by dairy cows. *XVI International Grassland Congress, Nice*, pp. 1147-1148.

HEPP C. (1989) *Interactions between sward conditions and the intake and grazing behaviour of sheep in the autumn.* M.Phil. thesis, University of Edinburgh.

HODGSON J. (1990) *Grazing management - science into practice.* London, Longman Group, p. 81.

MILNE J.A., HODGSON, J., THOMPSON, R., SOUTER, W.G. and BARTHRAM G.T. (1982) The diet ingested by sheep grazing swards differing in white clover and perennial ryegrass content. *Grass and Forage Science*, **37**, 209-218.

MITCHLEY J. (1993) Sward structure with regard to conservation. In: Haggar R.J. and Peel S. (eds.) *Grassland Management and Nature Conservation.* Occasional Symposium of the British Grassland Society No. 28.

ORR R.J., PARSONS A.J., PENNING P.D. and TREACHER T.T. (1990) Sward composition, animal performance and the potential production of grass/white clover swards continuously stocked with sheep. *Grass and Forage Science*, **45**, 325-336.

THOMSON D.J. (1984) The nutritive value of white clover. In: Thomson D.J. (ed.) *Forage Legumes. Occasional Symposium of the British Grassland Society* No. 16, pp. 78-92.

41

VIPOND J.E., SWIFT G., MCCLELLAND T.H., FITZSIMONS J.A., MILNE J.A. and HUNTER E.A. (1993) A comparison of diploid and tetraploid perennial ryegrass and tetraploid ryegrass/white clover swards under continuous sheep stocking at controlled sward heights. 2. Animal Production. *Grass and Forage Science*, **48**, 290-300.

WRIGHT I.A. and WHYTE T.K. (1989) Effects of sward surface height on the performance of continuously stocked spring-calving cows and their calves. *Grass and Forage Science*, **44**, 423-432.

YOUNIE D. and HEATH S. B. (1990) Beef cattle output from clover-based and nitrogen-fertilised swards over six grazing seasons. *Animal Production*, **50**, 546 (Abstract)

Sward Structure with Regard to Conservation

J. MITCHLEY
Wye College, Ashford, Kent TN25 5AH

ABSTRACT

Sward structure is the vertical and horizontal arrangement of sward components through space and time and has a profound influence on biotic diversity at all scales. As a general rule the greater the variety of plant parts in the vegetation the greater the diversity of associated animals and plants. In temperate grasslands management treatments have a crucial influence on vegetation structure and therefore on the associated plant and animals populations. Integrated management strategies are therefore required for conservation of existing grasslands as well as for improving opportunities for the construction of new ones. More widespread cooperation is required between plant and animal ecologists in autecological and experimental studies of grassland structure with regard to wildlife conservation and in the communication of the results to the agriculturalists and conservationists responsible for their management.

INTRODUCTION

Sward structure is the arrangement of sward components in three-dimensional space and through time (Brown, 1991); plants and animals influence vegetation structure and, in turn, are influenced by it. The classic study of the relationship between the physical structure of plants and species richness of animals was that of MacArthur and MacArthur (1961) and this has been followed by a great deal of research (see for example Bell *et al.*, 1991 for a review). In general I restrict my comments to limestone grasslands where most research has been done and to higher plants, invertebrates and large vertebrate herbivorous since these are the dominant groups of organisms which influence and are influenced by grassland sward structure.

ELEMENTS OF SWARD STRUCTURE WHICH PROMOTE BIOTIC DIVERSITY

Horizontal sward structure and plant species diversity

At large spatial scales beta-diversity in grasslands is determined through the responses of plants and animals to variation in soil properties, hydrology, topography or management treatments within or between habitats (Rodwell, 1992). Smaller-scale pattern is influenced by biotic influences such as the growth-form of plants, the impact of grazing animals and features such as ant hills (King, 1977), rabbit scrapes (Grubb, 1976) and dung and urine patches (Putnam *et al.*, 1991). Vertebrate herbivores profoundly influence horizontal sward structure and all show some degree of diet selectivity and preferred vegetation types (Hodgson *et al.*, 1991; Putnam *et al.*, 1991). When herbivores feed preferentially on what would otherwise be the dominant plant species, botanical richness is normally increased and grazing (or suitable alternative treatments) is thus essential for the maintenance of plant species richness in grassland vegetation (Grime, 1979; Crawley, 1983).

Horizonal sward structure and invertebrate species diversity
In terms of invertebrate diversity spatial scale is again important and larger patches of host plants house more species due to increased habitat heterogeneity, increased encounter frequency and reduced probability of extinction (Lawton, 1983). However, plant spatial pattern influences the exploitation by herbivores due to differences in mobility, diet selectivity and search characteristics, and invertebrate herbivore feeding is generally patchy, even in uniform plant populations and may lead to food wastage and reduced equilibrium population densities (Crawley, 1983). However, more significantly, it may also lead to population stability since the wasted plants act as a powerful stabilizing force (Crawley, 1983). More diverse communities of plants tend to hold richer assemblages of insects (but often lower equilibrium population densities) than, for example, monocultures due to the effects of a multi-species vegetation on invertebrate movement, search efficiency and dispersal and because the non-host plants hide the host or masks the hosts plant's chemical attractants (Crawley, 1983; Andow, 1991; Denno and Roderick, 1991). Temporal heterogeneity (due to combinations of fluctuating weather conditions, plant phenology, plant successional change or soil disturbance) is the key factor affecting population change in most herbivores. Species with high intrinsic rates of increase tend to track temporal changes, while species with low rates of increase tend to show reduced equilibrium densities in highly variable environments.

Vertical sward structure and plant species diversity
Most information in the literature comes from studies of above-ground shoots and very much less on litter and on roots (but see Marshall, 1979). The effect of vertical structure on plant diversity may be direct through plant-plant competition, or indirect, through the impact of microclimate on the regeneration niche of species (Grubb, 1977; Fliervoet, 1984; Barkman, 1989). Competition can occur above-ground for light, or below-ground for nutrients and water. The precise impacts of competition in structuring grassland vegetation are difficult to unravel (Grace, 1993) but there is no doubt that changes in, for example, fertilizer management affect the competitive relations between plant species and result in corresponding changes in sward structure and in species diversity (Grime, 1979; Bobbink, 1991; Bakker, 1989; Willems *et al.*, 1993). Plants regenerate by seed or by vegetative expansion in gaps in the sward, and gap shape, size and timing together with the associated influences of weather, other plants, pests and diseases all affect the chances of successful regeneration (Grubb, 1977). Many grasslands are composed of perennial matrix-forming species with short-lived annual, biennial and pauciennial species in the interstices (Grubb *et al*, 1983; Grubb, 1986). Control of population size in the short-lived species depends on the combined effects of several factors including drought, nutrient supply, herbivory, predation, disease and life history features (van Tooren, 1990). Small fluctuations in, for

example, sward height strongly affect the total number of flowering individuals implying that a well defined microhabitat is required for completion of life cycles (Verkaar et al., 1983; During et al., 1985; Grubb, 1986; Kelly, 1989; van Tooren, 1990). Nutrient limitation in the surrounding matrix limits growth of the matrix perennials and the short-lived species have enough time to complete their life-cycle before the gap closes. Where atmospheric pollution elevates nitrogen availability in the soil closure of gaps accelerates and populations of short-lived species decline (Bobbink, 1991).

Grime's (1979) "hump-back model" indicates that the potential for species richness in temperate grassland vegetation falls within a narrow window of productivity measured as peak standing crop of above-ground biomass plus litter (Grime, 1979; though see also van der Maarel and Titlyanova, 1989). The model predicts the decline in plant species richness which is often observed when biomass is elevated by increased fertility or decreased grazing pressure. However, biomass must be viewed as a surrogate measure of vegetation structure and different stands of vegetation with similar small-plot biomass may have quite different plant species diversity. Variation in species richness has been observed often to be much greater at lower levels of biomass than at higher levels (Grime, 1979; Wheeler and Shaw, 1991) and some of this variation is undoubtedly due to structural differences of the swards (Willems et al., 1993). These observations indicate that simple above-ground biomass measures are not wholly adequate for analysing the more subtle impacts of sward structure on plant diversity.

Vertical sward structure and invertebrate species diversity

Larger, more complex plants with greater variety and persistence of above-ground parts, or more complex plant communities will present a greater range of plant structures for specialization by feeding guilds of herbivorous invertebrates (Strong et al, 1984). It will also provide more non-trophic resources such as nesting, resting, basking, mating, overwintering and oviposition sites and enemy free space (Denno and Roderick, 1991). Similarly, a more complex plant community provides greater heterogeneity in microclimate (Barkman, 1979; Fliervoet, 1984) and in spatial and temporal plant patterns (Stinson and Brown, 1983; Brown, 1991).

Sward height is a further surrogate measure of sward structure and for many groups of invertebrates it is possible to demonstrate a good correlation between species richness and sward height (e.g. Morris, 1990a). In general, moderately tall grassland supports more species of invertebrates than very short grassland. However, this result should not be used as evidence to encourage taller grassland universally because there is a risk of losing a valuable fauna only to be replaced by a more ordinary one and in any case after a period of time the richness of the tall grassland community would decline as litter builds up and the composition of the vegetation changes (Kirby, 1992). Clearly in this case "quality" of diversity is more significant than "quantity" of diversity.

Some invertebrate groups show a distinct requirement for short swards. For example climate and microclimate are of great significance for the population dynamics of thermophilous butterflies at the northerly limit of their range in the UK, such as the adonis blue (*Lysandra bellargus*) (Thomas, 1991). The larval stages are monophagous on a fairly common grassland plant, horse-shoe vetch, (*Hippocrepis comosa*), but the presence of the food plant is not sufficient in itself to ensure survival of the population. Instead, host plants growing in hot microclimatic conditions are selected for egg laying, for example sunny south-facing slopes, sheltered hollows and bare ground (and in addition the presence of mutualistic ants) is required.

Some invertebrates require different micro-habitats for feeding, sheltering and breeding sites. For example, the wart-biter bush cricket (*Decticus verrucivorus*) requires a mosaic of vegetation structure for different stages of the life cycle: bare ground, short and taller turf (Cherrill and Brown, 1990). Such habitat mosaics may be important in promoting diversity both by allowing species which need several habitat components to persist, and by increasing the range of components, each of which supports its own suite of species (Brown *et al.*, 1990). The implication is that for a good representation of the calcareous grassland invertebrate fauna overall it is important that the management treatment results in a range of sward heights. The effects of myxomatosis in the UK combined with post-war reduction in sheep and cattle grazing of chalk downland have resulted in a decline in those invertebrate dependent on short sward compared with longer grass species, thus the conservation priority must be to maintain areas of short sward (McLean, 1990; Thomas, 1991). Insect populations respond quickly to changes in habitat structure and, while their foodplant populations may also be affected, changes are more gradual. A well documented example is that of the large blue butterfly (*Maculinea arion*) which became extinct from all of its sites in southern Britain despite the continued presence of the larval food plant, wild thyme (*Thymus praecox*), at all of them (Thomas, 1991).

SWARD STRUCTURE AND CONSERVATION MANAGEMENT TREATMENTS

Effective management is the key to grassland management whether it is for production or for wildlife conservation or indeed for both. The most common treatments, grazing, mowing, burning and nutrient applications, have major impacts on vegetation 3structure and hence diversity of plants and animals in grasslands.

Fire

In some cases burning may restore botanical diversity in derelict limestone grasslands (Lloyd, 1968). However, this must be balanced against the usually deleterious impact on invertebrate populations (Kirby, 1992). Burning can provide a last resort treatment for restoration of botanical diversity in derelict grasslands, but its effectiveness depends on the timing and extent of the burn. The influence of management by fire on vegetation structure and biotic diversity is discussed further by Mushinsky and Gibson (1991).

Nutrient applications

Applications of different major plant nutrients affects sward structure in different ways. Applications of nitrogen increase the grass component and tend to produce a tall dense sward structure (Bobbink, 1991), while applications of phosphorus increase the legume component and may lead to clumped sward structure (Willems *et al.*, 1993). The increased productivity and herbage quality of the sward under fertilizer applications may result in increased populations of certain phytophagous invertebrates but the general effect is to reduce species diversity of both plants and invertebrates (Morris, 1990b). Treatments which result in reduced soil nutrient levels can be expected to result in increased biotic diversity, a principal which is significant in grassland restoration/creation (Gibson *et al.*, 1987; Bakker, 1989; Marrs and Gough, 1989).

Grazing

The influence of grazing management by large herbivores on plant species richness has long been appreciated and the magnitude of this impact is indicated by the dramatic changes in vegetation structure and composition which followed the outbreak of myxomatosis in the 1950's (e.g. Sumption and Flowerdew, 1985).

Grazing management for conservation aims to achieve a habitat mosaic of short and tall sward and bare ground. The intensity and timing of grazing is crucial and should be heavy enough to create a patchy short sward, yet light enough to enable survival of grazing sensitive species and to allow more tussocky grassland in some areas Kirby (1992). Timing of grazing is even more vital for invertebrates than for plants since individual species may be easily excluded by single events in key phases of their life cycle (Brown *et al.*, 1990). The impact of grazing on invertebrates is variable and seasonal grazing is generally better than both rotational and continuous grazing and spring and summer grazing may be deleterious to more species than autumn/winter grazing (Brown *et al.*, 1990; Morris, 1990a; Kirby, 1992).

The type of stock grazed has a profound impact on sward structure and in general grazing by sheep or by horses produces the most even sward while cattle and rabbits produce the most uneven sward. Thus, Kirby (1992) suggests that grazing by cattle or by rabbits provide the most suitable management treatments for invertebrate conservation, while sheep or rabbits are generally considered most suitable for botanical conservation. However, there are no hard and fast rules and much depends on the management objectives and the topography of the site as well as the resources available. For example while horses are generally poorly regarded as grazers for nature conservation one of the best chalk grassland sites in south-east Kent is maintained in excellent condition both botanically and entomologically through year-round grazing by horses! The success in this case rests principally on the low intensity of grazing and the large and varied topography and the coastal nature of the site.

Mowing or cutting

Management by mowing can lead to high plant species richness by removing most tissue from the most abundant and potentially dominant species (Crawley, 1983; Bakker, 1989). A good example of this is the traditionally mown Estonian meadow described by Kalevi and Martin (1991) in which 25 species of higher plant were recorded in a sample of vegetation measuring just 10 cm square! Timing of defoliation is crucial and ideally should be related to the phenology of species, to ensure adequate regeneration of species from seeds (Smith and Jones, 1991). In contrast, cutting reduces invertebrate diversity (Morris, 1990a; Kirby, 1992). Both grazing and cutting involve defoliation, but the most significant difference between cutting and grazing is the catastrophic nature of the cut. Very often the even traditional hay-cuts occur at a time when invertebrate populations are developing, especially those dependent on flower, fruit or seed resources (Volkl *et al.*, 1993). While cutting can be an ideal management for maintaining botanical diversity of hay meadows (Smith and Jones, 1991) and very effective at increasing plant species richness to derelict chalk grassland swards dominated by coarse grasses (Bobbink, 1991) invertebrate diversity may suffer under such management. This is not to say that such treatments are to be universally discouraged, but that they will be most appropriate only when botanical diversity is the overriding objective at a site.

Conflicts in management strategies for conservation of plant and animal diversity

There has been the temptation in grassland conservation to say 'if we manage for the plants the animals will look after themselves'. However, this will only be appropriate if the invertebrate guilds are perfectly correlated with the plant communities. Most evidence suggests that herbivore feeding is patchy and that, rather than being perfectly correlated, insect guilds tend to track spatially distinct parts of the vegetation community; in general phytophagous invertebrates tend to track their food plants (e.g. leaf miners (Sterling *et al.*, 1992)) while predatory invertebrates track certain plant structures (e.g. spiders (Gibson *et al.*, 1992)). However, the generalization is not perfect and leaf hoppers appear to be intermediate (Brown *et al.*, 1992). Other groups may track temporally distinct parts of the vegetation community, e.g. one (or more) phenological or successional stage (Southwood *et al*, 1979; Stinson and Brown, 1983). Thus the occurrence of most insect guilds may be only indirectly correlated with vegetation communities and management for a particular vegetation type will not ensure the survival of viable populations of invertebrates. Thus, management should be for the particular structure/architectural complex in space and time which satisfies the life-history requirements of the species concerned.

Relatively few invertebrate species are confined to calcareous grasslands in Britain and the ones that are tend to feed exclusively on plants confined to these habitats (McLean, 1990). A much higher (and variable) proportion regularly occur in calcareous grasslands as well as other habitats, e.g. dry dunes, heaths and neutral grasslands (and fens). Some of these require more than one habitat, either at different life stages, or within different generations. The majority of invertebrates have annual life cycles and their life history needs must be satisfied each year of they are to persist at a site. Many insects have different requirements for the various life stages (egg, pupa and adult) and this adds to the complexity of their life history needs. Some species are highly mobile, but most are relatively sedentary which restricts their ability to recolonize sites following local extinctions or to colonize new sites without assistance. Some plants support a rich assemblage of phytophagous insects, each of which in turn may be the target of specialist or generalist predators and parasitoids. Compared with this degree of complexity, the requirements of plants seem quite straight forward. We might just as well state that if we manage for the animals the plants will look after themselves!

The message then is that management for spatial and temporal heterogeneity will maximise both plant and invertebrate diversity. Maintenance of large scale habitat variation will take care of beta-diversity, and alpha-diversity can be tackled through the use of periodic rather than continuous grazing, in seasonal or rotational bouts and with a range of stock types and breed. Where grazing is not possible creation of artificial disturbances may be desirable (Grubb, 1976). Such treatments should provide a satisfactory strategy for conserving all the common and many of the rare species of plats and animals at a site, as well as creating opportunities for establishment of populations of new ones. However in reality animals and plants display an almost endless spectrum of life-histories and some species will not respond to general management strategies outlined above, indeed some will be adversely affected. Fine tuning of the management strategy requires detailed understanding of the species at a site and their life history characteristics.

Management of sward structure for habitat creation

Creative conservation has received growing attention in recent years in the UK but attempts at grassland habitat creation are doomed to failure without effective management (Wells, 1983; Gibson et al., 1987; Morris, 1990b; Gibson and Brown, 1991; Ash et al., 1992). There are three main methods of grassland habitat creation. Firstly, colonization is allowed to proceed naturally, e.g. secondary succession after arable abandonment, grazing (or cutting) management is essential even on skeletal soils otherwise succession proceeds towards species-poor coarse grassland or scrub (Gibson et al., 1987). Secondly, sowing a non-aggressive grass mix and allowing natural regeneration thereafter. Here, the ability of the grass sward to diversify depends on the invadability of the grass sward established and so the species mix sown as well as the soil conditions are important (Morris, 1990b). Thirdly, sowing a complete seed mixture of native (or, less desirably, exotic) grasses and herbs. This is the belt and braces approach but in fertile sites a dense sward of grasses will hinder the establishment of the herb species due to high levels of competitive exclusion (F M Burch pers. comm.) and techniques for reducing soil fertility may need to be used (Marrs and Gough, 1989). The last two methods are the least likely to result in development of good invertebrate communities (Kirby, 1992) especially where sources of colonists are distant. However, where use of seed mixtures cannot be avoided, introduction of invertebrates by vacuum net is a possible option (Morris, 1990b).

CONCLUSIONS

There is a large literature on the effects of management treatments on plant and animal diversity and population dynamics in grasslands. Less information exists on the influence of sward structure on plant and animal diversity - though this research is more extensive for invertebrate animals than it is for plants. A general conclusion is that management for habitat heterogeneity at all scales will conserve most of the biotic diversity at a site. Ideally there should be a complete succession from bare ground to patchy scrub; topographic variation especially south-facing slopes, structural variation maintained by grazing, a large proportion of plants able to flower and set seed; additional habitats at their margins and within the grassland providing shelter, hibernation and structural variation. The needs of individual groups or of rare species which conflict with the above must be dealt with by fine-tuning based on their specific needs. Such data can only be obtained from autecological and population studies and experimental perturbations of species and their habitats to elucidate suitable management strategies. Integrated studies by plant and animal specialists are not common, however, because management treatments have such diverse and not infrequently conflicting effects on the plants and animals of grasslands, progress really demands ecological collaboration across taxonomic boundaries. Further, only recently have management prescriptions been devised which integrate the needs of plants and animals at a site. More widespread cooperation is needed between plant and animal ecologists in the study of grassland structure with regard to wildlife conservation and in the communication of the results to the conservationists and agriculturalists responsible for their management (Hillier *et al.*, 1990).

REFERENCES

ANDOW D.A. (1991) Vegetational diversity and Arthropod population response. *Annual Review of Entomology*, **36**, 561-586.

ASH H.J., BENNETT R. and SCOTT R. (1992) *Flowers in the Grass: Creating and Managing Grasslands with Wild Flowers*. Peterborough: English Nature.

BAKKER J.P. (1989) *Nature Management by Grazing and Cutting*. Dordrecht: Kluwer Academic.

BARKMAN J.J. (1989) The investigation of vegetation texture and structure. In: Werger, M.J.A. (ed.) *The Study of Vegetation*. pp. 125-160. The Hague: W. Junk.

BELL S.S., McCOY E.D. and MUSHINSKY H.R. (1991) *Habitat Structure: The Physical Arrangement of Objects in Space*. London: Chapman and Hall.

BOBBINK R. (1991) Effects of nutrient enrichment in Dutch chalk grassland. *Journal of Applied Ecology*, **28**, 28-41.

BROWN V.K. (1991) The effects of changes in habitat structure during succession in terrestrial communities. In: Bell, S.S, McCoy, E.D. and Mushinsky, H.R. (eds.) *Habitat structure: The Physical Arrangement of Objects in Space*. pp. 141-168. London: Chapman and Hall.

BROWN V.K., GIBSON C.W.D. and STERLING P.M. (1990) The mechanisms controlling insect diversity in calcareous grassland. In: Hillier, S.H., Walton, D.W.H. & Wells, D.A. (eds.) *Calcareous Grasslands - Ecology and Management*. pp. 79-87. Huntingdon: Bluntisham.

CHERRILL A.J. and BROWN V.K. (1990) The habitat requirements of the wart biter *Decticus verrucivorus* (L.) (Orthoptera: Tettigoniidae) in southern England. *Biological Conservation*, **53**, 145-157.

CRAWLEY M.J. (1983) *Herbivory: The Dynamics of Animal-Plant Interactions*. Oxford: Blackwell.

DENNO R.F. and RODERICK G.K. (1991) Influence of patch size, vegetation texture, and host plant architecture on the diversity, abundance and life history styles of sap-feeding herbivores. In: Bell, S.S, McCoy, E.D. and Mushinsky, H.R. (eds.) *Habitat structure: The Physical Arrangement of Objects in Space*. pp. 169-196. London: Chapman and Hall.

DURING J.J., SCHENKEVELD A.J., VERKAAR H.J. and WILLEMS J.H. (1985) Demography of short-lived forbs in chalk grasslands in relation to vegetation structure. In: White, J. (ed.). *The Population Structure of Vegetation*. pp. 341-370. Dordrecht: Junk.

FLIERVOET L.M. (1984) *Canopy structures of Dutch Grasslands*. University of Nijmegan, Unpublished Thesis.

GIBSON C.W.D., WATT T.A. and BROWN V.K. (1987) The use of sheep grazing to recreate species-rich grassland from abandoned arable land. *Biological Conservation*, **42**, 165-183.

GIBSON C.W.D., HAMBLER C. and BROWN V.K. (1992) Changes in spider (Araneae) assemblages in relation to succession and grazing management. *Journal of Applied Ecology*, **29**, 132-142.

GIBSON C.W.D. and BROWN V.K. (1991) The nature and rate of development of calcareous grassland in southern BritaIn. *Biological Conservation*, **58**, 297-316.

GRACE J.B. (1993) The effects of habitat productivity on competition intensity. *Trends in Ecology and Evolution*, **8**, 229-230.

GRIME J.P. (1979) *Plant strategies and Vegetation Processes*. Chichester: Wiley.

GRUBB P.J. (1976) A theoretical background to the conservation of ecologically distinct groups of annuals and biennials in the chalk grassland ecosystem. *Biological Conservation*, **10**, 53-76.

GRUBB P.J. (1977) The maintenance of species richness in plant communities: the importance of the regeneration niche. *Biological Reviews*, **52**, 107-145.

GRUBB P.J. (1986) Problems posed by sparse and patchily distributed species in species-rich plant communities. In: Diamond, J. and Case T.J. (eds.) *Community Ecology*. pp. 207-225. New York: Harper and Row.

GRUBB P.J., KELLY D. and MITCHLEY J. (1982) The control of relative abundance in communities of herbaceous plants. In: Newman, E.I. (ed.). *The Plant Community as a Working Mechanism*. pp. 79-97. Oxford: Blackwell.

HILLIER S.H., WALTON D.W.H. and WELLS D.A. (eds.) (1990) *Calcareous Grasslands - Ecology and Management*. Huntingdon: Bluntisham.

HODGSON J., FORBES T.D.A., ARMSTRONG R.H., BEATTIE M.M. and HUNTER E.A. (1991) Comparative studies of the ingestive behaviour and herbage intake of sheep and cattle grazing indigenous hill plant communities. *Journal of Applied Ecology*, **28**, 205-227.

KALEVI K. and MARTIN Z. (1991) High species richness in an Estonian wooded meadow. *Journal of Vegetation Science*, **2**, 711-714.

KELLY D. (1989) Demography of short-lived plants in chalk grassland. II. Control of mortality and fecundity. *Journal of Ecology*, **77**, 770-784.

KING T.J. (1977) The plant ecology of ant-hills in calcareous grasslands. I. Pattern of species in relation to ant hills in southern England. *Journal of Ecology*, **65**, 235-256.

KIRBY P. (1992) *Habitat Management for Invertebrates: A Practical Handbook*. Royal Society for the Protection of Birds, Joint Nature Conservation Committee, National Power.

LAWTON J.H. (1983) Plant architecture and the diversity of phytophagous insects. *Annual Review of Entomology*, **28**, 23-39.

LLOYD P.S. (1968) The ecological significance of fire in limestone grassland communities of the Derbyshire Dales. *Journal of Ecology*, **56**, 811-826.

VAN DER MAAREL E. and TITLYANOVA A. (1989) Above-ground and below-ground biomass relations in steppes under different grazing conditions. *Oikos*, **56**, 364-370.

MacARTHUR R.H. and MacARTHUR J.W. (1961) On bird species diversity. *Ecology*, **42**, 594-598.

MARRS R.H. and GOUGH M.W. (1989) Soil fertility - a potential problem for habitat restoration. In: Buckley G.P. (ed.). *Biological Habitat Reconstruction*. London: Belhaven.

MARSHALL J.K. (1977) *The below-Ground Ecosystem*. Fort Collins: Colorado State University.

MCLEAN I.F.G. (1990) The fauna of calcareous grasslands. In: Hillier, S.H., Walton, D.W.H. & Wells, D.A. (eds.) *Calcareous Grasslands - Ecology and Management*. pp. 41-46. Huntingdon: Bluntisham.

MORRIS M.G. (1990a) The effects of management on the invertebrate community of calcareous grassland. In: Hillier, S.H., Walton, D.W.H. & Wells, D.A. (eds) *Calcareous Grasslands - Ecology and Management*. pp. 128-133. Huntingdon, Bluntisham.

MORRIS M.G. (1990b) The Hemiptera of two sown calcareous grasslands. III. Comparisons with the Auchenorhyncha faunas of other grasslands. *Journal of Applied Ecology*, **27**, 394-409.

MUSHINSKY H.R. and GIBSON D.J. (1991) The influence of fire periodicity on habitat structure. In: Bell, S.S., McCoy, E.D. and Mushinsky, H.R. (eds.) *Habitat structure: The Physical Arrangement of Objects in Space*. pp. 237-259. London: Chapman and Hall.

PUTNAM R.J., FOWLER A.D. and TOUT S. (1991) Patterns of use of ancient grassland by cattle and horses and effects on vegetational composition and structure. *Biological Conservation*, **56**, 329-347.

RODWELL J.S. (1992) British Plant Communities. Volume 3: Grasslands and Montane Communities. Cambridge, Cambridge University Press.

SMITH R.S. and JONES L. (1991) The phenology of mesotrophic grassland in the Pennine Dales, Northern England: historic hay cutting dates, vegetation variation and plant species phenologies. *Journal of Applied Ecology*, **28**, 42-59.

SOUTHWOOD T.R.E., BROWN V.K. and READER P.M. (1979) The relationship of plant and insect diversities in succession. *Biological Journal of the Linnean Society*, **12**, 327-348.

STINSON C.S.A. and BROWN V.K. (1983) Seasonal changes in the architecture of natural plant communities and its relevance to insect herbivores. *Oecologia (Berlin)*, **56**, 67-69.

STERLING P.H., GIBSON C.W.D. and BROWN V.K. (1992) Leaf miner assemblies: effects of plant succession and grazing management. *Ecological Entomology*, **17**, 167-178.

STRONG D.W., LAWTON J.H. and SOUTHWOOD T.R.E. (1984) Insects on Plants. Oxford: Blackwell.

SUMPTION K.J. and FLOWERDEW J.R. (1985) The ecological effects of the decline in Rabbits (*Oryctolagus cuniculus* (L.) due to myxomatosis. *Mammal Review*, **15**, 151-186.

THOMAS. (1991) Rare species conservation: case studies of European butterflies. In: Spellerberg, I.F., Goldsmith, F.B. and Morris, M.G. (eds.) *Scientific Management of Temperate Communities for Conservation*. pp. 149-197. Oxford: Blackwell.

VAN TOOREN B.F. (1990) Recruitment and establishment of short-lived flowering plant species in Dutch chalk grassland. In: Hillier, S.H., Walton, D.W.H. & Wells, D.A. (eds.) *Calcareous Grasslands - Ecology and Management*. pp. 100-105. Huntingdon: Bluntisham.

VERKAAR H.J., SCHENKEVELD A.J. and BRAND J.M. (1983) On the ecology of short-lived forbs in chalk grasslands: micro-site tolerances in relation to vegetation structure. *Vegetatio*, **52**, 91-102.

VOLKL W., ZWOLFER H., ROMSTOCK-VOLKL M. and SCHMELZER C. (1993) Habitat management in calcareous grasslands: effects on the insect community developing in flower heads of Cynarea. *Journal of Applied Ecology*, **30**, 307-315.

WELLS T.C.E. (1983) The creation of species-rich grasslands. In: Warren, A. and Goldsmith, F.B. (eds.) *Conservation in Perspective* pp. 215-232. London: Wiley.

WHEELER B.D. and SHAW S.C. (1991) Above-ground crop mass and species richness of the principal types of herbaceous rich-fen vegetation of lowland England and Wales. *Journal of Ecology*, **79**, 285-301.

WILLEMS J.H., PEET R.K. and BIK L. (1993) Changes in chalk-grassland structure and species richness resulting from selective nutrient additions. *Journal of Vegetation Science*, **4**, 203-212.

Minerals, Water and Pesticides with Regard to Production

S. C. JARVIS

AFRC Institute of Grassland and Environmental Research

North Wyke, Okehampton, Devon EX20 2SB

ABSTRACT

Opportunities exist to increase DM yield closer to the potential for a given soil and site with inputs of nutrients/minerals, water and pesticides. The general responses of swards to nutrients and water are well established. Although irrigation and drainage can improve sward growth, both have had only limited economic attraction. There are also substantial effects of pests and diseases but despite this, only small areas of grassland receive chemical treatment. Appropriate supplies of all nutrients are essential to sustain high sward yields and N supply has been the key to production and profitability. Responses to N fertilizer are substantial even at large application rates. There are opportunities to make better use of the N cycling within farming systems, and to make better use of existing data bases for climate and soil type and characteristics to enable more environmentally benign managements.

INTRODUCTION

Although in many senses it is more appropriate to consider the final outputs from grassland production systems i.e. meat, milk or wool, they are in the first instance dependent upon primary, herbage dry matter production. It is this, the accumulation of organic materials by the process of photosynthesis, which interacts with and reacts to the factors discussed in the present paper. Under most circumstances for intensively managed grassland, water availability and nitrogen (N) supply are the key constraints to achieving yield potentials under a particular management and environment. The attainment of desired responses to either of these or any other factor is dependent upon all others being at appropriate levels. Thus, whilst under UK conditions the impact of other 'minerals' (nutrients) may be less dramatic and have less influence as determinants of final yield than N, adequate supplies of P, K, etc are essential. It has also been increasingly clear that yield is reduced by pests and diseases. All of these factors, either individually, or collectively, have the potential to influence the realization of potential yield and productivity. Because of this the main objective of grassland researchers, advisors and farmers has been to manipulate and/or manage these factors with economic optimum as the major if not only aim. This will remain an important criterion, but increasingly other constraints - environmental, legislative -will be imposed and will have to be considered as part of a management decision package.

PRODUCTION RESPONSES TO MINERALS

Nitrogen. Our perceptions and understanding of the general nature of the response to fertilizer N (and of other nutrients) have not changed markedly over many years and the general principles are well understood. Various comprehensive reviews describe the reactions of grass swards under different management and cutting regimes to inputs of N (Archer, 1985; Van Burg *et al.*, 1981). Although the detail of recommendations has been improved recently, the general concepts underlying N recommendations have not changed substantially.

In brief, grass swards respond to added N in a characteristic way with an average linear response of 15-20/30 kg dry matter (DM)/ha per kg of added N up to an overall annual N addition of 250-350 kg/ha. The extent of this response will be determined by local conditions, soil type/moisture, past management, patterns of application, frequency of defoliation, etc. The law of diminishing returns then operates and DM decreases to 5-15 kg DM per kg N applied; usually this is at rates of 350 - 450 kg N/ha. Thereafter, the response rate declines until a maximum yield is reached which may be anywhere between 500-800 kg N/ha. Morrison *et al.* (1980) found that, under a 4 week cutting regime, the quantity of N required to give maximum yield varied from 540 - 678 kg N/ha over a wide range of sites in England and Wales. With less frequent cutting, the average amount of N required for maximum yield was lower, but ranged between 396 - 754 kg N/ha. The rate at which the DM response falls to 7.5 kg N/ha is usually taken to define the target yield and the target N rate (N optimum) (see Thomas *et al.*, 1991), although others define optimum rates where response falls to 10 kg DXM/kg N (Holmes, 1989). At the former rate it can be assumed that 90% of the maximum yield can be achieved with less than 60% of the N required for the maximum. A response of this size may be economic for some production systems, but not for others (especially beef or sheep) where the economic output per kg DM utilized is lower. Economic returns may be achieved with smaller responses in some circumstances, but there are penalties in terms of inefficiency in utilization and resultant losses. Analysis of data from 133 replicated field trials of the response of cut grass to fertilizer N has established a strong positive relationship between optimum levels of addition, as defined above, and yield response (P. Dampney, pers. comm.). This relationship, i.e. increased response over that with no added N with increasing N optimum rates, demonstrates the very wide range of variability in background N supplies

Table 1. Maximum N application rates for UK grassland. (MAFF in press)

Management	Soil N supply		
	Low	Medium	High
Silage	420	380	340
Dairy cow grazing	380	340	300
Beef/sheep grazing	330	290	250

Table 2. Criteria for determining grassland soil N status (from MAFF, in press, and Thomas *et al.*, 1991).

Category	Previous management
Low	• Cereal or sugar beet cropping • Short term ley, <100 kg N/ha, no clover • Continuous grass, reseeded, <100 kg N/ha, no clover • Long term established grass, < 100 kg N/ha, no clover
Moderate/medium	• Potatoes, rape, peas, beans • Short term ley, 100-250 kg N/ha, or good clover content • Long term established grass, 100-250 kg N/ha, or good clover content
High	• Short term ley >250 kg N/ha • Continuous grass, reseeded, >100 kg N/ha or large clover content • Long term, established grass, > 250 kg N/ha • Long term, established grass with large amounts of slurry

from soil organic matter and its effects on fertilizer needs. The range for N optimum was from 131 to over 600 (mean 407) kg N/ha.

Field trials indicate very clearly that opportunity exists at high rates of fertilizer to increase substantially dry matter production, and current recommendations (Table 1) reflect this. In practice, although a significant proportion (11%) of intensively managed UK grasslands receive more than 300 kg N/ha, average applications are much lower than either experimentation or recommendations would indicate.

Decisions on appropriate levels of application depend upon the site/soil characteristics, soil N and whether, for example, the sward is cut or grazed. Thomas *et al.*, (1991) defined a site class on the basis of a combination of soil texture and depth and summer rainfall. Using this scheme, application rates for a medium N status soil range from 255 kg/ha for a site class 5 (shallow and sandy soils, < 350 mm summer rain) to 450 kg/ha for site class 1 (other soil types, > 500 mm summer rain). As far as soil N is concerned, differentials are based on only three basic categories reflecting past history (Table 2) to give low, medium/moderate or high N availability. A system under development in the Netherlands, based on 36 long-term field experiments over a 30 year period, pays particular attention to organic matter contents and the total apparent N supply from the soil (Oxenema *et al.*, 1992) (Table 3).

Although taking some account of the importance of soil N, current recommendations are therefore still relatively crude. Release of N from soil organic matter can be large and will influence the losses which may occur. As well as the differences indicated by the wide range in N optimum values, cut swards grown in the absence of added N provide similar information. Cut swards at different sites in the UK have yielded, in the absence of added N, between 1.45 and 8.85 t DM/ha containing 11-136

Table 3. Effects of soil organic matter and moisture supplying capacities on N responses by cut grass (Oenema *et al.*, 1992).

Organic matter class	Soil N (tonnes/ ha)	Apparent N supply kg/ha/ yr)	Apparent recovery	Optimum N application rate (kg/ha/yr) Moisture supplying capacity		
				Low	Medium	High
Poor	<5	75	80	315	-	-
Medium	5-10	100	80	285	-	-
Poor	<5	125	80	-	385	455
Medium	5-10	150	80	-	355	420
Humus	10-15	200	80	-	295	360
Mesotrophic peat	15-20	250	60	-	205	280
Eutrophic peat	>20	350	60	-	0	120

kg N/ha in the harvested forage (Hopkins *et al.*, 1990; Morrison *et al.*, 1980). If it is assumed that off-take represented 60% of total uptake and that efficiency of uptake was 80%, then net annual mineralization under a cutting management ranged between 23-283 kg N/ha. Field incubation methods have been used recently to provide *in situ* measurements of net mineralization. On an inherently poorly-drained soil in SW England, 63, 144, 141 and 279 kg N/ha were mineralized in undrained and drained soils with 400 kg fertilizer N/ha, respectively (Scholefield and Blantern, 1989). Other measurements on well-drained soil in SE England have found net mineralization rates over a grazing season of 310 - 415 kg N/ha (Hatch *et al.*, 1991). Clearly the supply of N from this source can be substantial but highly variable and merits greater definition in order to influence fertilizer practice and recommendations.

For nutrients generally, and N particularly, to be at their most effective, availability should be synchronized with plant growth. There are recognised patterns of dry matter accumulation under different managements (Holmes, 1989), and the general nature of seasonal variation is well established although the absolute response will vary according to management and location. Temperature is an important determinant, its most significant effect being to influence the length of the growing season. The most important time for N fertilizer is at the start of the growing season, and timing of first applications can vary from early February in the SW to mid April in the North. One approach to determine the optimum timing for first applications has been the T sum 200 which was designed to indicate when grass growth starts. There has been much effort in assessing T sum 200 (i.e. when the sum of daily temperatures $> 0°C$ since January 1st reaches $200°C$), but the results from England and Wales (Archer, 1985) and the Netherlands (Van Burg *et al.*, 1981) have shown that the system is not reliable and only provides a broad indication of when to apply N.

Generally, application patterns have a reducing rate to avoid high N contents at the end of the season as growth slows. There have been numerous response trials with variation in timing and patterns of application (Frame, 1992). Sample recommendations derived from this type of information are given by Thomas *et al.* (1991). As well as the herbage responses there are environmental considerations, with potential for direct losses from the applied fertilizer by leaching/runoff or denitrification to be avoided. At any one time, the availability of N for uptake is dependent on the interactions and balance of supply (from fertilizer, soil or excreta) and removal (by uptake, denitrification and leaching). The further interaction of these with management and current weather conditions may mean that there may be a substantial excess of N over immediate sward demands and the opportunity for loss becomes much larger. Current recommendations make only crude allowance for this, i.e. to reduce inputs if drought develops and to omit applications if the drought is severe or prolonged.

For other nutrients, soil tests can provide information which is of relevance through a growing season. With N, which is much more mobile, this is not so feasible. However, an interest has been re-stimulated in the use of soil testing as a tool for more rational N use. Recent studies (Titchen and Scholefield, 1992) examined the possibility of avoiding accumulations of soil mineral N by tactically altering the rate and timing of applications. The basis for this is a rapid and accurate field estimate of soil mineral N which, with simple models for predicting rates of mineralization, denitrification and plant uptake, provides information to allow adjustment of fertilizer requirements at frequent intervals to avoid excesses in the soil (Titchen and Scholefield, 1992). The net result is to maintain dry matter production at lower N fertilizer rates and reduced losses. There is scope to better match supplies of N to sward demands: much information already exists to help define the envelope of potential growth response on the site concerned, e.g. by overlaying data bases for average rainfall and evapotranspiration with information about the available water storage capacity of the soil. Adding in current weather information and soil mineral N status would allow further fine tuning.

An important complicating factor in assessing the N requirements of a sward is the grazing animal. Large quantities of N are recycled in excreta much of which, especially in urine, is available for uptake with effects on N requirements. There is, however, little information for grazed swards because of (a) the logistics involved in conducting large scale animal experiments and (b) the approaches required to obtain relevant DM yield data in the presence of animals (Holmes, 1989). However, studies have shown an enhanced response under grazing compared to cutting (Holmes, 1974), and Baker (1986) describes 8 cattle grazing experiments in which continuously grazed swards yielded more than cut swards especially at lower fertilizer rates (Table 4).

Current recommendations take some account of excreta (Table 1), but perhaps not to the extent that could be expected from a knowledge of the quantities involved. There are a number of reasons for this; firstly, only recently has a general appreciation of the amounts recycled become widespread. Secondly, reservations must be expressed about some of the techniques that have been used to estimate herbage responses under grazing. Further, and most importantly, the discrete and random nature of excretal returns also prevents an efficient utilization of the N, especially from urine. Local soil contents under a urine patch will substantially outweigh plant demands even though

58

Table 4. Yield responses under cutting or grazing at 8 UK trials (Baker, 1986).

Fertilizer N applied kg/ha	Dry matter (t/ha)	
	Cutting	Grazing
100	4.14	5.38 (+30%)
250	6.51	7.46 (+15%)
450	7.70	8.40 (+9%)
750	8.46	8.56 (+1%)

(Numbers in parenthesis indicate percentage increase with grazing)

neighbouring areas may be deficient in N and the opportunities for losses may be greater than from cut counterparts. Over the longer term the effects of residual, less immediately mobile, N from excreta will contribute to an enhanced fertility which is not adequately accounted for in current recommendations.

Another effect of the animal may be to reduce the importance of seasonal patterns of fertilizer application, because recycled N removes the effect of a particular application being restricted solely to the next harvest. This has been shown in simulated grazing trials (Morrison *et al.*, 1980) and in a grazing trial in SW England, where three different patterns of N application had no statistically significant impact on herbage and animal production (Table 5).

Table 5. Effects of patterns of N fertilizer applications to grazed swards. Values are averages for 3 years (from Titchen *et al.*, 1989).

Treatment (kg/ha)	Total N applied (kg/ha)	DM yield (t/ha)	Liveweight gain (kg/ha)
6 × 50	300	12.2 (± 1.18)	1207 (± 74)
4 × 75	300	12.3 (± 0.30)	1520 (± 95)
4 × 75 + additional N	425	13.6 (± 0.48)	1713 (± 116)

Other Nutrients. In order to achieve the potential yields defined by N inputs, it is necessary that all other aspects of soil fertility are non-limiting. In the main this will involve P, K and lime status, although S supplies may become more limiting as a result of reduced emissions into, and deposition from, the atmosphere. Dampney and Unwin (1992) noted that yield responses to added S of over 20% have been found and suggested that all areas receiving less than 30 kg/ha/year are potentially deficient, especially second and later silage cuts on medium and light textured soils. Responses under grazing are less likely although this has not been examined critically.

Soil tests have been used as key components of cost-effective fertilizer management for P, K and lime status. It is generally accepted that lime should be applied as soon as pH values fall significantly below 6.0. Lower values are acceptable on peat soils but clover-based swards are more demanding. Inputs of lime to grassland soils have declined and there is a need to quantify overall effects and to ascertain the importance of maintaining this aspect of soil quality. This may become more and more important as cropping regimes change or there is a return to either legume-based or mixed farming. The patterns of responses to P and K fertilizer addition are well documented. The current practice is to maintain a Soil Index of 2 (16 - 25 mg extractable P/l soil) for P and Index 2 (121-240 mg K/l soil) for cutting and Index 1 (61-121 mg K/l soil) for grazing (MAFF, in press). This is usually achieved by considering the offtake in herbage. A typical silage cut of 5 tonnes DM/ha will remove only 13-18 kg P/ha but over 100 kg K. The recommended rates (Table 6) indicate the inputs required for soils of different nutrient status; off-takes under grazing are small and inputs therefore lower. Dampney and Unwin (1992) have indicated that there is a substantial deviation from an optimum soil Index 2 with over 40% of UK soils being below this and 30% above for P, and 48% below and 10% above for K. Although P and K recommendations are not related to the rates of N applied, the greater amounts of P and K needed with increasing rate of N are achieved by making applications for each succeeding cut.

Table 6. Recommendations for P and K fertilizer rates (kg/ha) for grassland soil of different nutrient status (MAFF, in press).

Management	Soil index							
	0		1		2		>2	
	P	K	P	K	P	K	P	K
Grazing	26	52	18	26	9	0	0	0
Grass clover	26	52	18	26	9	0	0	0
Cut grass 1st	44	120	26	86	13	52	13	26
2nd	22	103	13	86	13	69	0	35
3rd	0	69	0	52	0	35	0	17

PRODUCTION RESPONSES TO WATER

Water shortage. Water is a major determinant of yield: DM accumulation is reduced with either excess or deficiency. Although swards can extract water down to 0.7 - 1.0 m, growth is generally restricted when the soil moisture deficit in the top 30 cm exceeds 40 - 50 mm and, on average, some response to irrigation would be found in most of lowland Britain. Fluctuations in growth brought about by water shortage, although not unexpected, are often unpredictable and caused by variation in rainfall pattern. Drought is most likely to limit production during mid to late summer with annual production averaging 25% less than the potential yields in SE England and 5% less in much of the W and N of Britain (Garwood, 1979). There is considerable interaction between N requirement and the quantity of available water and summer rainfall, Morrison *et al.* (1980). The influence of soil physical characteristics and water supply is also shown by the Dutch method of assessment for N supply (Table 3). The general effects of supplying water to increase yield substantially are generally well appreciated but there has been only limited economic attraction in doing this.

Water excess. Much grassland is on poorly drained soil. Of 500 permanent grassland farms in the UK, only 21% were freely drained, 45% imperfectly drained and 30% poorly or badly drained (Forbes *et al.*, 1980). Recent results from drained and undrained treatments on an impermeable clay loam in SW England indicated that overall benefits were slight (Tyson *et al.*, 1992). The increase in production associated with drainage would not have paid for costs, certainly over the short term. Much of any improvement in DM yield was apparently associated with a greater availability of N rather than a reduction in anaerobic conditions, damaged plant roots or poaching of the sward. A further consequence of the improved N availability is that leaching losses may be enhanced.

PRODUCTION RESPONSES TO PESTICIDES

Grassland swards are hosts to a wide range of invertebrate pests, fungal, bacterial and viral diseases and weed infestations. Whilst damage on an epidemic scale is unusual, there can be substantial effects in both newly sown and established crops which, although often difficult to assess, are well recognised. Johnson (1991) suggested that weeds, pests and diseases together could reduce dry matter production by approximately 20%. Clements *et al.* (1990) have related damage assessments to livestock production and valued the losses at £500 - 750 M. Effects are usually insidious with the major pests being frit fly in short term swards and leatherjackets in longer term pastures. The most important disease is likely to be ryegrass mosaic virus, but rusts, mildew and other fungi have significant effects. White clover has a particular suite of problems but with slugs and Sitona weevils causing widespread damage. There is much recent evidence to show that effects of pesticide application can be substantial. Clements and Bentley (1985) have shown for example that there are a number of ways in which grass seedling pests can be controlled and damage minimized and that integrated strategies are a feasible, effective means of managing swards. Integration with management and prevailing environmental conditions is important. There is greater risk of insect damage when grass follows grass or when direct drilling rather than full cultivation methods are used (Clements and Bentley, 1985).

Despite the mounting evidence for a widespread and substantial suite of effects, there is generally a low use of pesticides. Over 80% of managed grassland receives no pesticide application (Johnson, 1991): of that the majority is as herbicides which account for 98% of the products applied. Current economic and environmental pressures are unlikely to promote a greater use. A particular concern is that pesticides are non-specific and may have detrimental effects on neutral and beneficial species. However, there are certain situations which may offer opportunities for greater use where the application precision and specificity can be better targeted, for example in short term intensive managed pastures (Clifford, 1991).

61

CONCLUSIONS

Opportunities for increased production are considerable. Wilkins (1987) argued that a full adoption of existing technologies, principally by the use of N fertilizer, could enable a two to three fold increase in production. Technology has advanced and production potential further increased. However, the perceptions of the needs of, and controls over, production and demands placed by environmental constraints are creating a need to produce better integrated managements. For example, whilst N fertilizers have been and are likely to remain a key management tool, there are considerable opportunities for more efficient utilization of the considerable quantities of N that are cycled within production systems. Adoption of these and integration with the other components of management and greater use of existing data bases for climate, soil moisture characteristics will allow more environmentally benign agricultural systems to be developed whilst meeting economically acceptable targets.

REFERENCES

ARCHER J. (1985) *Crop Nutrition and Fertilizer Use*. Ipswich: Farming Press.

BAKER R.D. (1986) Efficient use of nitrogen fertilizers. In: Cooper, J.P and Raymond, W.F. (eds.) *Grassland Manuring, Occasional Symposium of the British Grassland Society*, No. 20, pp.15-27.

CLEMENTS R.O.and BENTLEY B.R. (1985) Incidence, impact and control of insect pests in newly-sown grassland in the UK. In: Brockman, J.S. (ed.) *Weeds, Pests and Diseases of Grassland and Herbage Legumes. Occasional Symposium of the British Grassland Society*, No. 18, pp. 165-172.

CLEMENTS R.O., MURRAY P.J., BENTLEY B.R., LEWIS G.C. and FRENCH N. (1990) The impact of pests an diseases on the herbage yield of permanent grassland at eight sites in England and Wales. *Annals of Applied Biology*, **117**, 349-357.

CLIFFORD B.C. (1991) Future options for pest and disease control in UK grassland. In: *Strategies for Weed, Disease and Pest Control in Grassland. Proceedings British Grassland Society Conference*, 1991, pp. 9.1-9.11.

DAMPNEY P.M.R. and UNWIN R.J. (1992) More efficient and effective use of NPK in today's conditions. In: Hopkins, A. and Younie, D. (eds.) *Forward with Grass into Europe. Occasional Symposium of the British Grassland Society*, No. 27, 62-72.

FORBES T.J., DIBB C., GREEN J.O., HOPKINS A and PEEL S. (1980) Factors affecting the productivity of permanent grassland: a national farm study. GRI/ADAS Report, Hurley.

FRAME J. (1992) *Improved Grassland Management*. Ipswich: Farming Press.

GARWOOD E.A. (1979) The effect of irrigation in grassland productivity. In: *Water Control and Grassland Productivity, Proceedings Winter Meeting of the British Grassland Society*, pp. 2.1-2.8.

HATCH D.J., JARVIS S.C. and REYNOLDS S.E. (1991) An assessment of the contribution of net mineralisation to N-cycling in grass swards using a field incubation method. *Plant and Soil*, **138**, 23-32.

HOLMES W. (1974) The role of nitrogen fertilizer in the production of beef from grass. In: *The Role of Nitrogen in Grassland Productivity. Proceedings of the Fertilizer Society*, **142**, 57-69.

HOLMES W. (1989)*Grass, its Production and Utilization.* Oxford: Blackwell Scientific Publications.

HOPKINS A., GILBEY J., DIBB C., BOWLING P.J. and MURRAY P.J. (1990) Response of permanent and reseeded grassland to fertilizer nitrogen. I. Herbage production and herbage quality.*Grass and Forage Science*, **45**, 43-55.

JOHNSON J. (1991) Importance of the problem, practical solutions. In: *Strategies for Weed, Disease and Pest Control in Grassland. Proceedings British Grassland Society Conference, 1991*, pp. 1.1-1.13.

MAFF (in press). *Fertilizer Recommendations* (Consultation Document) Reference Book 209, 6th Edition, London: MAFF.

MORRISON J., JACKSON M.V. and SPARROW P.E. (1980) The response of perennial ryegrass to fertilizer nitrogen in relation to climate and soil. *Grassland Research Institute, Technical Report 27*, Hurley: GRI.

OENEMA O., WOPEREIS F.A. and RUITENBERG G.H. (1992) Developing new recommendations for nitrogen fertilization of intensively managed grassland in the Netherlands. In: *Nitrate and Farming Systems. Aspects of Applied Biology*, **30**, 249-253.

SCHOLEFIELD D. and BLANTERN P.J. (1989) Continuous long-term measurement of net mineralization of N in grazed pasture soils. *Proceedings of 2nd AFRC Meeting on Plant and Soil Nitrogen Metabolism*, AFRC: Swindon.

THOMAS C., REEVE A. and FISHER G.E.J. (1991) *Milk from Grass.* ICI/SAC/IGER.

TITCHEN N.M. and SCHOLEFIELD D. (1992) The potential of a rapid test for soil mineral nitrogen to determine tactical applications of fertilizer nitrogen to grassland. In: *Nitrate and Farming Systems. Aspects of Applied Biology*, **30**, 223-229.

TITCHEN N.M., WILKINS R.J., PHILIPPS L. and SCHOLEFIELD D. (1989) Strategies of fertilizer nitrogen applications to grassland for beef: effects on production and soil mineral N. *Proceedings XVI International Grassland Congress, Nice*, pp.183-184.

TYSON K.C., GARWOOD E.A., ARMSTRONG A.C. and SCHOLEFIELD D. (1992) Effects of field drainage on the growth of herbage and the liveweight gain of grazing beef cattle. *Grass and Forage Science*, **47**, 290-301.

VAN BURG P.F.J., PRINS W.H., DEN BOER D.J. and SLUIMAN W.J. (1981) Nitrogen and intensification of livestock farming in EEC countries. *Proceedings of the Fertilizer Society*, **199**, 78 pp.

WILKINS R.J. (1987) Grassland into the Twenty-first Century. In: *Farming into the Twenty-first Century* pp95-115. Ipswich: Norsk Hydro.

Effects of Fertilisers on Plant Species Composition and Conservation Interest of UK Grassland

R.S.SMITH
The University of Newcastle upon Tyne,
Newcastle upon Tyne NE1 7RU.

ABSTRACT

Fertiliser effects are reviewed in the context of the range of UK grasslands described by the National Vegetation Classification and the controlling management and environmental factors. The influence of fertiliser on the yield, species richness and species composition of plagioclimax grasslands is reviewed; together with fertiliser interactions with grazing and cutting. Usually the effect of fertiliser use is detrimental to the nature conservation interest. Prediction of the effect of fertiliser on species richness is difficult with existing models. These particularly need to incorporate the interacting effects of management and environmental factors.

INTRODUCTION

Forty two of the 134 grassland communities described by Rodwell (1992) are not dependent upon management for the maintenance of their species composition, being maintained solely by extreme climatic and/or edaphic factors (Table 1). Most of these 'natural' types are calcifugous grasslands of high montane environments, such as those associated with snow beds and high plateaus. Eight are calcicolous grasslands, including those that are the end points of successional changes initiated by the cessation of grazing. Four are mesotrophic grasslands found under very particular upland (MG2) and coastal (MG12) environments.

The commoner plagioclimax grasslands have a species composition dependent upon particular grazing, fertilizing and cutting regimes as well as edaphic and climatic factors. Fertiliser is particularly used on mesotrophic grasslands and has been blamed for considerable reductions in unimproved permanent pasture (Fuller, 1987; Hopkins and Wainwright, 1989). Although the cessation of livestock grazing also has implications for plant species composition and diversity (Fig. 1).

THE EFFECT OF FERTILIZER ON YIELD AND SPECIES RICHNESS

Soil nitrogen supply primarily limits grass yield, the relationship between nitrogen fertiliser rates and yield being linear up to about 250-530 kg N/ha. Yield increase reaches a maximum (5.2-14.3 t/ha) and then progressively declines at very high fertiliser applications (Morrison, 1987). However, the low availability of phosphorus and potassium

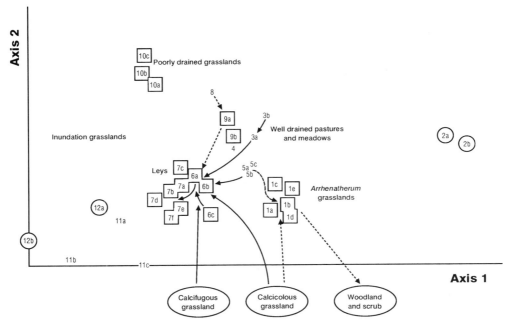

Fig. 1. Wildlife interest, 'naturalness' and vegetation transitions initiated by fertiliser use and the cessation of grazing in mesotrophic grassland (after Rodwell 1992).
———→ addition of fertilizer; — — — → cessation of grazing; □, communities of limited wildlife interest (from Nature Conservancy Council (1989)); ○, 'natural' mesotrophic grassland.

may also limit yields (Kirkham and Wilkins in press A and B). Empirical regression models that relate hay yield to nitrogen fertiliser use allow dry-matter yields to be predicted for a proposed fertiliser regime. Over the full range of fertiliser dose rates these are polynomial regressions, eg. on the Somerset Levels (Kirkham and Wilkins 1993):
Yield = 5140 + 9.1N - 0.05N^2 (r^2=0.90 p<0.001).........(1),
yield and nitrogen supply (N) being in kg per ha.

At the lower dose rates r$_{b02}$elevent to wildlife conservation they are linear regressions, eg. in the Pennine Dales (Smith, 1985):
Yield = 2842 + 39.8N (r^2=0.76 p<0.001)................(2).

Species richness per unit area is a community characteristic with some montane tall herb communities having an average of 54 species per 4m^2 (Rodwell, 1992). At the other extreme 5-14 species per 4m^2 are often found in fertilized mesotrophic swards. Calcicolous grasslands usually contain more species (often between 20-34 species per 4m^2) than mesotrophic and calcifugous grassland (generally 10-24 species per 4m^2).

The fertiliser effect on species richness could be predicted if hay yield could be related to species richness. Grime's (1979) 'hump-back' model associates high species richness with calcareous soils and a maximum above-ground standing crop of 3.5-7.5 t/ha; environmental stress and high productivity respectively limiting species richness at the lower and upper ends of this range. There is support for this model when it is

65

Table 1. British plant communities* (after Rodwell (1992)).

Mesotrophic grasslands.
Arrhenatherum elatius grasslands. MG1(5), **MG2(2)**.
Well drained pastures and meadows. MG3(2), MG4, MG5(3), MG6(3).
Long term leys and related grasslands. MG7(6).
Ill drained pastures. MG8, MG9(2), MG10(3).
Grass-dominated inundation communities. MG11(3), **MG12(2)**, MG13.

Calcicolous grasslands.
South-east lowlands. **CG1(6)**, CG2(4), CG3(4), **CG4(3)**, CG5(2), **CG6(2)**, **CG7(5)**.
Sesleria albicans grassland. CG8(3), **CG9(5)**.
North-west uplands. CG10(3), CG11(2), CG12, **CG13(2)**, **CG14**.

Calcifugous grasslands and montane communities.
Submontane. U1(6), U2(2), U3, U4(5), U5(5), U6(4).
Low- and middle-alpine snowfields. **U7(3)**, **U8(2)**, **U11(2)**, **U12(3)**.
Moss- and rush-heaths of low- to middle-alpine plateaus. **U9(2)**, **U10(3)**.
Mesotrophic montane swards and herb-rich banks and ledges. **U13(2)**, **U14**, **U15**, **U16(3)**, **U17(4)**.
Calcifuge fern communites. **U18**, **U19**, **U20(3)**, **U21**.

* These are listed using the standard codes from Rodwell (1992); the number of subcommunities

applied to a range of habitats (Marrs, 1993; Van Meer and Berendse, 1983). However, it's usefulness in predicting species richness within a limited range of habitat types has been questioned (Marrs, 1993; Wheeler and Shaw, 1991; Moore *et.al.* 1989). Management experiments in various mesotrophic grasslands show that after four years there is large variation in species richness over a wide range of hay yields (Fig. 2). Species richness appears to be influenced by autumn grazing with cattle rather than low rates of fertiliser use (<50 kg N/ha).

Therefore, whilst reasonably accurate predictions of yield can be obtained for a given fertiliser application, predicting the species richness from these yield estimates is prone to error. This may be due to: (1) the young age of many grasslands (Berendse *et al.*, 1992; Oomes, 1990); (2) the role of grazing and mowing in maintaining species richness; (3) the incompatability of the data sets used to construct Fig. 2, with data collected at different times in the growing season. In Upper Teesdale meadows, the yield increases linearly throughout the early part of the growing season, flattening off in late July and August, but the species richness is greatest in May and June (Fig. 3). Consequently these grasslands are classified as 'northern' meadow (MG3) in May/June, and as *Lolium perenne - Cynosurus cristatus* grassland (MG6) in July/August.

THE EFFECT OF FERTILIZER ON PLANT SPECIES COMPOSITION
The experimental addition of fertiliser to dune grassland (Willis, 1963), calcareous grassland (Bobbink, 1991; Bobbink and Willems, 1987; Davy and Bishop, 1984;

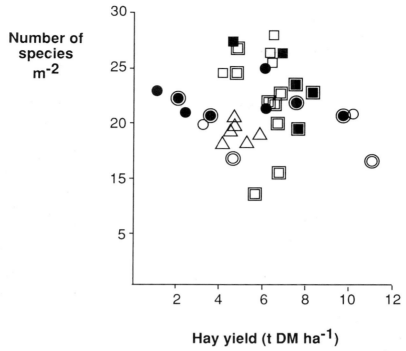

Fig. 2. Species richness and hay yield after four years of experimental treatments in mesotrophic grassland.

□ Somerset Levels; ○ Upper Teesdale;Acklington, Northumberland; infilled symbols were aftermath grazed with cattle; outlined symbols were fertilized (N50kg per ha). Data provided by Mike Bullard (MAFF), Francis Kirkham (IGER) and Ross Chapman (University of Newcastle upon Tyne).

————→addition of fertiliser;————→cessation of grazing;

□ communities of limited wildlife interest (from Nature Conservancy Council (1989));○'natural' mesotrophic grassland.

Grime and Curtis, 1976; Jeffrey and Pigott, 1973; Lloyd and Pigott, 1967; Smith, *et al.*, 1971), upland *Festuca-Agrostis* grassland and calcifugous *Molinia* grasslands (Jones, 1967) has emphasised the importance of low-moderate fertility for the maintenance of the original species composition. Fertiliser addition encourages the growth of competitive species, usually resulting in the loss of many species. Similar changes occur when fertiliser is used in moderately productive mesotrophic pastures and meadows (Mountford *et al.*, 1993; Smith, 1985, Van Hecke *et al.*, 1981). Some experiments have been of very long duration, eg. the Park Grass Experiment at Rothamsted Experimental Station (Brenchley and Warrington, 1958; Silvertown, 1980; Thurston, 1969; Thurston *et al.*, 1976) and the Palace Leas hay meadow trial at Cockle Park, Northumberland (Smith, 1987). These demonstrate a number of features about the response of grassland communities to fertilisers.

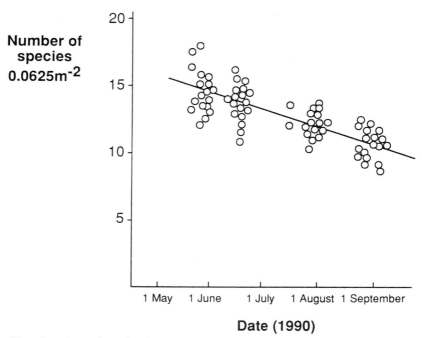

Date (1990)

Fig. 3. The phenology of species richness in mesotrophic grassland in Upper Teesdale (from data provided by H.Buckingham).

(1) There is a major effect with nitrogen fertilisers. Nitrogen encourages the growth of competitive species. Species lost can include *Carex nigra*, *Juncus inflexus*, *Lotus pedunculatus*, *Lysimachia nummularia*, *Prunella vulgaris*, *Ranunculus acris*, *Ranunculus repens* and *Trifolium repens* (Mountford *et al.*, 1993). Without nitrogen a greater mix of species is possible, with many legumes in communities created by the use of phosphorus fertilisers.

(2) When soil phosphorus and potassium deficiencies are rectified with fertiliser there is often an interaction with nitrogen. This results in even greater growth of competitive species and a further loss in wildlife interest. When the nitrogen is supplied as ammonium sulphate soil acidification occurs and this produces a distinctive, species-poor community that can only be rectified by reducing the soil acidity with lime, to a pH greater than 4.5.

(3) The quantity of applied fertiliser dictates the rate at which change occurs in the species composition. Applications in excess of 50 kg nitrogen per ha per annum rapidly change the species composition within four years. The magnitude of the change can be considerable in a short time, especially when pH, phosphorus and potassium deficiencies are made good. With nitrogen fertiliser applied at 25 kg/ha significant species change is slower but inevitable, with decreases in *Plantago lanceolata*, *Brachythecium rutabulum* and *Eurhynchium praelongum* (Mountford *et al.*, 1993).

(4)   There is a difference between organic sources of nutrients such as farmyard manure (FYM) and sources such as mineral fertiliser. FYM applied at 12.5 tonnes per ha is acceptable in management regimes aimed at enhancing the wildlife interest of meadows in the Lake District and the Pennine Dales Environmentally Sensitive Areas (ESAs) (MAFF, 1992a,b). This is half the quantity used in the recent past (Davies, 1970) and is equivalent to adding 19 kg nitrogen, 11 kg phosphorus and 42 kg potassium (Cooke, 1975). The nutrients are only slowly made available by organic matter mineralisation throughout the growing season, particularly, in the uplands, in May and June as temperatures rise. However, excessive use of FYM can have an adverse effect on species composition. This can be seen locally in the vegetation of latrine areas created by the distinctive grazing patterns of cattle and horses in mesotrophic meadows (Putman *et al.*, 1991; Van Den Bos and Bakker, 1990).

(5)   Fertiliser use often masks the influence of edaphic and climatic factors, converting different grassland communities to one or other of the improved communities recognised by Rodwell (1992) as *Lolium perenne-Cynosurus cristatus* grassland (MG6) and *Lolium perenne* leys (MG7). Diverse communities characterised by species associated with the wetland origin of the grassland on the Somerset Levels and with the woodland origin of meadows in Upper Teesdale, are replaced by similar mixtures of *Alopecurus pratensis*, *Holcus lanatus*, *Lolium perenne*, *Poa trivialis* and *Phleum pratense*.

THE INTERACTING EFFECTS OF FERTILISER, GRAZING AND CUTTING

With the exception of high input-high output management regimes, grazing and cutting can be important in maintaining the species density and composition of various grasslands (Bobbink and Willems, 1991; Bakker, 1989; Gibson and Brown, 1991; Parr and Way, 1988; Smith and Rushton *in press*). It has been suggested that the adverse effects of moderate fertiliser applications on the wildlife interest of grassland can be reduced when the grass crop is harvested by appropriate grazing and cutting regimes (Marrs, 1993); the creation of bare patches by the treading action of livestock being particularly important for the maintenance of regeneration niches for the shorter lived species (Grubb, 1977; Hillier, 1990). Consequently, defoliation by mowing is not a substitute for grazing. The response of plant species to such grazing and cutting can be estimated from their biology (Grime, *et al*, 1988); for example, the cessation of spring or autumn grazing in meadows has been shown to result in the subsequent loss of species that regenerate from seed at these times (Smith and Rushton *in press*).

The effects of fertiliser on grasslands must, therefore, be seen alongside the effects of grazing and haycutting. On its own the cessation of grazing reduced the species richness in upland meadows within three years (Table 2) and in the longer term can result in the development of species-poor *Arrhenatherum elatius* grassland (MG1) from a range of plant communities (Rodwell 1992). This rapid loss of species was greater than that produced by the application of 80 kg nitrogen per hectare. Earlier or later than normal hay cutting also reduced the species richness and this was further reduced when fertiliser was also applied. In the long term, when management regimes are

Table 2. Plant species richness and diversity (in parentheses) in a mesotrophic meadow (MG3) in Upper Teesdale, after three years of various fertiliser, cutting date and grazing regimes[*].

		Grazing treatment		
		Autumn-cattle and spring-sheep.	Autumn-cattle only	No grazing
UNFERTILISED PLOTS				
Cut date:	14 June	15.0 (7.6)	13.3 (8.0)	11.9 (8.0)
	21 July	16.6 (9.5)	15.4 (8.9)	13.9 (7.4)
	1 Sept.	15.7 (8.1)	15.4 (8.2)	13.7 (6.8)
FERTILISED PLOTS[**]				
Cut date:	14 June	12.4 (8.1)	13.1 (8.1)	10.6 (4.5)
	21 July	16.2 (8.6)	16.1 (8.8)	12.3 (6.0)
	1 Sept.	13.8 (7.1)	12.9 (6.5)	9.9 (4.5)

There were significant differences in diversity and species density at all main treatment levels (fertiliser, grazing and cut date); with significantly lower species richness on fertilised and early or late cut plots.

[*] species richness is the number of species per 0.0625 m^2; the diversity index is the inverse of Simpsons Index.
[**] application rate was 400 kg ha 20:10:10 NPK fertiliser.

stable the interactions between management and edaphic factors produces a range of grassland types within a farm (Smith and Jones 1991).

Wildlife management prescriptions must address these complexities if practical grassland management for conservation is to be successfully implemented; see, for example, the prescriptions for grassland management in ESAs (Ministry of Agriculture, Fisheries and Food, 1992A and 1992B) (Smith, 1988).

REFERENCES
BAKKER J.P. (1989) *Nature Management by Grazing and Cutting.* Dordrecht: Kluwer Academic.

BERENDSE F., OOMES M.J.M., ALTENA H.J. and ELBERSE W.TH. (1992) Experiments on the restoration of species-rich meadows in The Netherlands. *Biological Conservation*, **62**, 59-65.

BOBBINK R. (1991) Effects of nutrient enrichment in Dutch chalk grassland. *Journal of Applied Ecology*, **28**, 28-41.

BOBBINK R. and WILLEMS J.H. (1987) Increasing dominance of *Brachypodium pinnatum* (L.) Beauv. in chalk grasslands: a threat to a species-rich ecosystem. *Biological Conservation*, **40**, 301-314.

BOBBINK R. and WILLEMS J.H. (1991) Impact of different cutting regimes on the performance of *Brachypodium pinnatum* in Dutch chalk grassland. *Biological Conservation*, **56**, 1-21.

BRENCHLEY W.E. and WARRINGTON K. (1958) *The Park Grass plots at Rothamsted 1856-1949*. Rothamstead: Rothamsted Experimental Station.

COOKE G.W. (1975) *Fertilizing for maximum yield*. London: Granada.

DAVIES H.T. (1970) Manuring of meadows in the Pennines. *Experimental Husbandry*, **18**, 8-24.

DAVY A.J. and BISHOP G.F. (1984) The response of *Hieracium pilosella* in Breckland grassheath to inorganic nutrients. *Journal of Ecology*, **72**, 319-330.

FULLER R.M. (1987) The changing extent and conservation interest of lowland grasslands in England and Wales: a review ofgrassland surveys 1930-84. *Biological Conservation*, **40**, 281-300.

GIBSON C.W.D. and BROWN V.K. (1991) The nature and rate of development of calcareous grassland in southern Britain. *Biological Conservation*, **58**, 297-316.

GRIME J.P. (1979) *Plant strategies and vegetation processes*. London: Wiley.

GRIME J.P. and CURTIS A.V. (1976) The interaction of drought and mineral nutrient stress in calcareous grassland. *Journal of Ecology*, **64**, 976-998.

GRIME J.P., HODGESON J.G. and HUNT R. (1988) *Comparative Plant Ecology*. London: Unwin Hyman.

GRUBB P.J. (1977) The maintenance of species-richness in plant communities: the importance of the regeneration niche. *Biological Reviews*, **52**, 107-145.

HILLIER S. (1990) Gaps, seed banks and plant species diversity in calcareous grasslands. In: Hillier, S.H., Walton, D.W.H. and Wells, D.A. (eds.) *Calcareous Grasslands Ecology and Management*, pp. 57-66. Bluntisham: Bluntisham Books.

HOPKINS A. and WAINWRIGHT J. (1989) Changes in botanical composition and agricultural management of enclosed grassland in upland areas of England and Wales, 1970-86, and some conservation implications. *Biological Conservation*, **47**, 219-235.

JEFFREY D.W. and PIGOTT C.D. (1973) The response of grasslands on sugar-limestone in Teesdale to application of phosphorus and nitrogen. *Journal of Ecology*, **61**, 85-92.

JONES L.I. (1967) Studies on Hill Land in Wales. *TechnicalBulletin of the Welsh Plant Breeding Station*, No.2.

KIRKHAM F.W. and WILKINS R.J. (in press A) The productivity and response to inorganic fertilisers of species-rich wetland haymeadows on the Somerset Moors: nitrogen response under haycutting and aftermath grazing. *Grass and Forage Science*.

KIRKHAM F.W. and WILKINS R.J. (in press B) The productivity and response to inorganic fertilisers of species-rich wetland haymeadows on the Somerset Moors: the effect of nitrogen, phosphorus and potassium on herbage production. *Grass and Forage Science*.

LLOYD P. and PIGOTT C.D. (1967) The influence of soil conditions on the course of succession on the chalk of southern England. *Journal of Ecology*, **55**, 137-146.

MARRS R.H. (1993) Soil fertility and nature conservation in Europe: theoretical considerations and practical management solutions. *Advances in Ecological Research*, **24**, 241-300.

MINISTRY OF AGRICULTURE, FISHERIES AND FOOD (1992a) *Environmentally Sensitive Areas: The Lake District*. London: Ministry of Agriculture, Fisheries and Food.

MINISTRY OF AGRICULTURE, FISHERIES AND FOOD (1992b) *Environmentally Sensitive Areas: The Pennine Dales*. London: Ministry of Agriculture, Fisheries and Food.

MOORE D.R.J., KEDDY P.A., GAUDET C.L. and WISHEU I.C. (1989) Conservation of wetlands: do infertile wetlands deserve a higher priority. *Biological Conservation*, **47**, 203-217.

MORRISON J. (1987) Effects of nitrogen fertiliser. In: Snaydon, R.W. (ed.) *Ecosystems of the World 17B. Managed Grasslands: Analytical Studies*, pp.61-70. Amsterdam: Elsevier.

MOUNTFORD J.O., LAKHANI K.H. and KIRKHAM F.W. (1993) Experimental assessment of the effects of nitrogen addition under haycutting and aftermath grazing on the vegetation of meadows on a Somerset peat moor. *Journal of Applied Ecology*, **30**, 321-332.

NATURE CONSERVANCY COUNCIL (1989) *Guidelines for selection of biological SSSIs*. Peterborough: Nature Conservancy Council.

OOMES M.J.M. (1990) Changes in dry matter and nutrient yields during the restoration of species-rich grasslands. *Journal of Vegetation Science*, **1**, 333-338.

PARR T.W. and WAY J.M. (1988) Management of roadside vegetation: the long term effects of cutting. *Journal of Applied Ecology*, **25**, 1073-1087.

PUTMAN R.J., FOWLER A.D. and TOUT S. (1991) Patterns of use of ancient grassland by cattle and horses and effects on vegetational composition and structure. *Biological Conservation*, **56**, 329-347.

RODWELL J.S. (1992) *British Plant Communities Volume 3 Grasslands and Montane Communities*. Cambridge: Cambridge University Press.

SILVERTOWN J. (1980) The dynamics of a grassland ecosystem: botanical equilibrium in the Park Grass Experiment. *Journal of Applied Ecology*, **17**, 491-504.

SMITH C.T., ELSTON J. and BUNTING A.H. (1971) The effects of cutting and fertiliser treatment on the yield and botanical composition of chalk turfs. *Journal of the British Grassland Society*, **26**, 213-219.

SMITH R.S. (1985) *Conservation of northern upland meadows*.Bainbridge: Yorkshire Dales National Park.

SMITH R.S. (1987) The effect of fertilisers on the conservation interest of traditionally managed upland meadows. In: Bell, M. and Bunce, R.G.H. (eds.) *Agriculture and Conservation in the Hills and Uplands*, pp.38-43, ITE symposium no. 23, Grange-over-Sands: Institute of Terrestrial Ecology.

SMITH R.S. (1988) Farming and the conservation of traditional meadowland in the Pennine Dales Environmentally Sensitive Area. In: Usher M.B. and Thompson

D.B.A. (eds.) *Ecological change in the uplands*, pp. 183-199. British Ecological Society, Special Publication No. 7. Oxford: Blackwell Scientific Publications.

SMITH R.S. and JONES L. (1991) The phenology of mesotrophic grassland in the Pennine Dales, Northern England: historic hay cutting dates, vegetation variation and plant species phenologies. *Journal of Applied Ecology*, **28**, 42-59.

SMITH R.S. and RUSHTON S.P. (in press) The effects of grazing management on the vegetation of mesotrophic (meadow) grassland in Northern England. *Journal of Applied Ecology*.

THURSTON J.M. (1969) The effect of liming and fertilisers on the botanical composition of permanent grassland, and on the yield of hay. In: Rorison, I.H. (ed.) *Ecological aspects of the mineral nutrition of plants*, pp. 1-10, Symposium of the British Ecological Society, No. 9, Oxford: Blackwell Scientific.

THURSTON J.M., WILLIAMS E.D. and JOHNSTON A.E. (1976) Modern developments in an experiment on permanent grassland started in 1856: effects of fertilisers and lime onbotanical composition and crop and soil analyses. *Annals of agronomy*, **27**, 1043-1082.

VAN DEN BOS J. and BAKKER J.P. (1990) The development of vegetation patterns by cattle grazing at low stocking density in The Netherlands. *Biological Conservation*, **51**, 263-272.

VAN HECKE P., IMPENS I. and BEHEAGHE T.J. (1981) Temporal variation of species composition and species diversity in permanent grassland plots with different fertiliser treatments. *Vegetatio*, **47**, 221-232.

VER MEER J.G. and BERENDSE F. (1983) The relationship between nutrient availability, shoot biomass and species richness in grassland and wetland communities. *Vegetatio*, **53**, 121-126.

WHEELER B.D. and SHAW S.C. (1991) Above-ground crop mass and species richness of the principal types of herbaceous rich-fen vegetation of lowland England and Wales. *Journal of Ecology*, **79**, 285-301.

WILLIS A.J. (1963) Braunton Burrows: the effects on the vegetation of the addition of mineral nutrients to the dune soils. *Journal of Ecology*, **51**, 353-374.

Effects of Inorganic Fertilisers in Flower-rich Hay Meadows on the Somerset Levels

J. O. MOUNTFORD, J. R. B. TALLOWIN[1], F. W. KIRKHAM[1] AND K. H. LAKHANI

NERC Institute of Terrestrial Ecology,
Monks Wood, Abbots Ripton, Cambs PE17 2LS
[1]AFRC Institute of Grassland and Environmental Research
North Wyke Research Station, Okehampton, Devon EX20 2SB

ABSTRACT

The objectives were: to establish whether a 'safe' amount of fertiliser nitrogen existed which could be applied to species-rich meadows on the Somerset Levels without reducing their floristic diversity; to measure the agricultural output achievable within any such limit; and to establish the speed and nature of reversion in botanical composition following the cessation of fertiliser inputs.

No such 'safe' amount of fertiliser nitrogen input was identified. Rates as low as 25 kg N/ha increased the dominance of grasses such as Lolium perenne *and* Holcus lanatus, *significantly reducing species diversity within 6 years. Botanical change was much more severe when high inputs of phosphorus were used in addition to nitrogen fertiliser. Agricultural output was consistent with fertiliser N response models developed for agricultural grasslands in the UK. Three years after fertiliser inputs ceased, species richness was still reduced in formerly fertilised plots and it appears that species impoverishment will persist for several years, particularly where high inputs of N and P have been used. Disturbance of the species impoverished vegetation showed limited value in accelerating reversion, and re-introducing seed of lost species gave no improvement.*

INTRODUCTION

It is well known that the application of fertiliser increases the abundance of sown grasses at the expense of indigenous species, and reduces floristic diversity of species-rich grassland (Brenchley and Warington, 1958; Tilman, 1982; Wells, 1989). Data on specific and/or community effects of fertiliser use on semi-natural grasslands are mainly limited to those from a few long-term experiments in dry mesotrophic plant communities, such as the classic "Park Grass" at Rothamsted (Digby and Kempton, 1987). It is not certain how far this data can be used to predict the response to fertilisers of other species-rich grassland types. It became clear in the early 1980s that a prediction was needed of the degree of damage likely to be caused by agricultural intensification in species-rich meadows on the Somerset Levels and Moors. In 1986 the

Ministry of Agriculture, Fisheries and Food, English Nature and the Department of the Environment commissioned the Institutes of Grassland and Environmental Research and Terrestrial Ecology to establish whether there was a 'safe' amount of fertiliser nitrogen that could be applied to these meadows without reducing floristic diversity, also to establish the agricultural output achievable within any such safe fertiliser limit and the output foregone by adhering to it. The objectives were extended in 1990 to investigate the speed and nature of botanical change when fertiliser inputs ceased and to test techniques for rehabilitating species-rich grassland.

This paper discusses botanical and agronomic data from two experiments involving continued use of fertilisers over 7 years (1986 to 1993) and the cessation of inputs after 4 years of use. More details are available elsewhere (Mountford *et al.*,1993; Kirkham and Wilkins, 1993a and b).

METHODS

Two experiments were established in 1986 within 20 hectares of the Tadham and Tealham Moors SSSI. The soil was of Altcar 1 series peat (Soil Survey of England & Wales, 1983) to a depth of 125-160cm, pH 5.7. Two major grassland communities (Rodwell, 1992) were present: *Centaureo-Cynosuretum cristati* (MG5) and *Senecioni-Brometum racemosi* (MG8). Previous management had involved late hay cutting followed by aftermath grazing with no artificial fertiliser inputs.

Main Experiment

Five nitrogen (N) treatments were applied within a randomised block design with three replicates : 0 (control), 25, 50, 100 and 200kg N/ha per year 1986-89 in split amounts, half in the spring the other half after a hay crop in mid-summer. The amounts of phosphorus (P) and potassium (K) removed in the hay were replaced by fertiliser inputs in mid-summer on all plots except controls. Plots ranged from 1.1 to 0.6 ha depending upon fertiliser treatment, designed to support a minimum of two steers grazing the aftermath continuously. Plots were cut for hay after the 1 July each year. A compressed sward height (rising plate) of 5.5-6.5cm was maintained during aftermath grazing by continuous, variable stocking (Tallowin *et al.*, 1990). Production was measured in terms of hay yield, animal liveweight production and utilized metabolisable energy (UME).

In 1990 plots were split, with one half continuing to receive fertiliser inputs as previously until April 1993 (N+), whilst fertiliser treatments ceased on the other half (N-). Production was measured between 1990 and 1993 on the N+ and N- halves of each plot separately.

Between 1986 and 1990, vegetation was recorded on 24 randomly placed m² quadrats per plot in May each year, with 16 quadrats per half-plot from 1991-93. All vascular plant species and bryophytes were scored individually for percent ground cover within each quadrat and the following values were derived for each plot: mean number of plant species (species richness) per m², and per 24 m² (1986-1990) or per 16 m² (1990-1993); number of species in flower at the time of observation; and Simpson's index (**I**) of diversity (Simpson, 1949). A detailed account of the methodology is given in Mountford *et al.* (1993).

Small-scale Experiment

A wider range of P and K inputs than those used in the Main Experiment were applied from 1986 to 1989 to 7.5m^2 plots in a randomised block experiment with three replicates. Additional fertiliser treatments included 0N with P and K replaced, 100 or 200kg N/ha with 0P and K replaced, 0 or 100 or 200kg N/ha with 75kg P/ha and K replaced and 200kg N/ha, 75kg P/ha with 200kg K/ha. The plots were cut at the same time as the hay in the Main Experiment followed by two aftermath cuts. All fertiliser inputs to these plots ceased in 1990. The yields of herbage and of N,P and K were measured at each cut between 1986 and 1993, with botanical composition assessed in May each year in two 0.4 × 1.27m quadrats per plot.

Reversion Experiments

The impact of disturbance on the recovery of species richness, and the effects of re-introducing seed of 'lost' species by sowing their seed, were investigated in a randomized small plot (8.0 m^2) experiment set up on a N200- main plot in 1990. Treatments, replicated three times, were: autumn rotavation; spring rotavation; spring gap creation using herbicide; and an undisturbed control, all with + or — seed introduction. Botanical assessments were made in May on four 25 × 25cm quadrats per plot.

Statistical Analysis

In Phase I (1986 to 1990), analyses of variance (ANOVA) and tests for linear response to N rate were performed on data for each botanical variable for each year. In Phase II (1990 to 1993), data from the N+ and N− treatments were analysed separately. Contrasts (Z = N− — N+) were used to compare discontinued with continued treatments for each variable. The agronomic and small plot data were examined for treatment effects within years by ANOVA and regression.

RESULTS AND DISCUSSION

Botanical Changes in Main Experiment

All linear trends in species richness and diversity against N were negative (Tables 1A and 1B). The N50 (except 1991), N100 and N200 plots became poorer in species (per m^2) than control plots from 1989 onwards. Species diversity (**I**) showed a similar pattern to the number of species per m^2, except in 1991 when there was no significant linear effect of N. Changes in **I** were associated with increases in the abundance of *Holcus lanatus*. The number of species per plot showed a significant negative linear trend, with N100 and N200 poorer in species than control from 1987 onward, N50 plots from 1989 onwards and N25 plots in 1992. The number of species in flower per plot showed a similar trend in time to the other variables, but only became significantly lower than the control in the N100+ and N200+ plots in 1992.

Table 1. Summary of the ANOVA results for **M** (= mean number of species per quadrat), **S** (=total number of species per 'plot'), **S'** (= total number of flowering species per 'plot') and **I** (= Simpson's index of diversity per 'plot'). Showing: **(a)** the significance of the F-test and **(b)** treatments significantly different from control, M_1. The sign of all the slopes was negative.

A) Phase I (1986-90)

		M	S	S'	I
1986	(a)	N/S	$\star$	N/S	N/S
	(b)	none	none	none	none
1987	(a)	$\star$	$\star\star$	N/S	$\star$
	(b)	none	M_4,M_5	none	none
1988	(a)	$\star\star\star$	$\star\star\star$	$\star\star$	$\star\star\star$
	(b)	none	M_4,M_5	none	M_5
1989	(a)	$\star\star\star$	$\star\star$	$\star\star$	$\star\star\star$
	(b)	M_3,M_4,M_5	M_3,M_4,M_5	none	M_4,M_5
1990	(a)	$\star\star\star$	$\star\star\star$	$\square$	$\star\star$
	(b)	M_3,M_4,M_5	M_3,M_4,M_5	none	M_4,M_5

Phase II (1991-93)
B) N+ plots receiving the same fertiliser inputs as in 1986-90.

		M	S	S'	I
1991	(a)	$\star\star$	$\star\star$	N/S	N/S
	(b)	M_4,M_5	M_3,M_4,M_5	none	none
1992	(a)	$\star\star\star$	$\star\star\star$	$\star\star\star$	$\star$
	(b)	M_3,M_4,M_5	M_2,M_3,M_4,M_5	M_4,M_5	none

C) N- plots receiving no fertiliser application after 1989.

		M	S	S'	I
1991	(a)	$\star\star$	$\star\star\star$	$\star$	$\square$
	(b)	M_4,M_5	M_3,M_4,M_5	M_2	none
1992	(a)	$\star\star\star$	$\star\star\star$	$\star\star$	$\star$
	(b)	M_3,M_4,M_5	M_3,M_4,M_5	M_5	M_5

Note: Significance
NS: not significant $\square$: $p<10\%$ $\star$: $p=<5\%$
$\star\star$: $p<1\%$ $\star\star\star$: $p=<0.1\%$

Changes in individual species

Agrostis stolonifera, *Bromus hordeaceus*, *Phleum pratense*, *Poa trivialis* and particularly *H. lanatus* and *Lolium perenne* were all increased by N. The mean cover of *H.lanatus* and *L.perenne* increased from c. 3.5% in 1986 to 15.7% and 16.9% respectively by 1992 when averaged over the N50+, N100+ and N200+. In 1992, the swards in the hiigher N+ treatments were dominated by a mix of *Anthoxanthum odoratum*, *B. hordeaceus*, *H. lanatus*, *L. perenne* and *Rumex acetosa*. *Deschampsia cespitosa*, *Agrostis capillaris*, *Cynosurus cristatus* and *Festuca rubra* responded negatively to N. In 1986 the latter three species together accounted for >15% of the sward but they had declined by 1992 in all fertilised plots; in the N50+ plots their combined cover was 3%.

Few forbs increased with N. Those that did included docks (*Rumex acetosa* and *R.crispus*), chickweeds (*Cerastium fontanum* and *Stellaria media*) and *Taraxacum* agg.. These may have benefited from the application of replacement P and K in the N plots since *R.acetosa* and *Taraxacum* compete poorly where nitrate is applied alone (Brenchley and Warington, 1958; Gupta and Rorison, 1975).

Most sedge, rush, forb and moss species showed a negative linear trend with N. The number of species showing this trend increased from 1987 to 1992, most of these trends increasing in significance in later years. The pleurocarpous mosses *Brachythecium rutabulum*, *Calliergon cuspidatum*, *Climacium dendroides*, *Eurhynchium praelongum* and *Rhynchostegium confertum* reacted similarly, apparently unable to compete for light or space with increased shading by grasses in fertilised plots. Mosses were almost eliminated by N200+ and were significantly reduced in the N25 and N50 plots. The fertilisers may also have had some herbicidal effect on the mosses (Rabotnov, 1977).

Many low-growing forbs such as, *Leontodon autumnalis*, *Prunella vulgaris* and *Stellaria graminea* declined between 1986 and 1992 where high N rates were applied, whilst *Lysimachia nummularia*, *Plantago lanceolata*, *Potentilla reptans* and *Ranunculus repens* were also reduced by N25 and N50 compared with controls. *Cirsium palustre*, *Myosotis discolor* and *Trifolium dubium* also declined. These species depend upon light for germination and seedling establishment, and their decline may be related to increases in spring grass growth caused by fertilisers. *Centaurea nigra*, *Filipendula ulmaria* and *Ranunculus acris* also showed a significant negative linear trend against N. The phenology of these species may be relevant since both *C.nigra* and *F.ulmaria* grow and flower late in the year, and thus may be suppressed by early-growing grasses.

Most legumes showed similar trends to other forbs and declined with high N. By the end of Phase I, the largest cover of legumes was in the N25 plots, probably due more to the replacement of P and K than to the small amount of N applied (Tilman, 1982).

Small-scale Experiment

The botanical changes caused by fertilisers in this experiment up to 1990 were broadly similar to those in the Main Experiment, with grasses increasing at the expense of forbs, sedges, rushes and mosses, particularly with high inputs of N, P and K. *Holcus lanatus* in particular was enhanced in the plots receiving the combination of high N

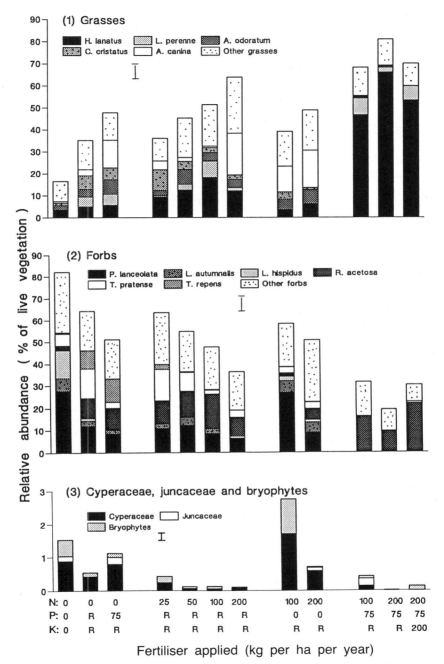

Fig. 1. Species abundance in May 1990 in the Small-scale Experiment. Vertical bars are effective standard errors of the means for the major species groupings, i.e. whole columns.

with high P (Fig. 1). *Leontodon autumnalis* and *L. hispidus*, both common in the control plots, were amongst species to be almost eliminated from the high N high P plots. *Rumex acetosa* was the only non grass species able to sustain a high abundance in fertilized plots, increasing significantly in plots receiving high N, P and K.

Phosphorus was more important than N in determining botanical change; in the plots receiving N and K but no P, changes in botanical composition were relatively small compared with the control, whereas inclusion of high P severely reduced species diversity (Table 2).

Table 2. Species richness (number of species per 7.5 m^2 plot) on the Small-scale Experiment.

Treatment	1986	1987	1988	1989	1990	1991	1992
					\multicolumn{3}{c}{Treatments discontinued}		
N0, P0, K0	33.3	37.3	35.3	33.0	31.7	31.3	26.7
N0, P & K replaced	32.0	36.7	34.7	32.7	30.3	31.3	29.7
N25, P & K replaced	29.7	37.0	34.0	29.7	29.7	25.3	27.7
N50, P & K replaced	30.7	37.0	32.0	29.7	30.7	27.3	27.0
N100, P & K replaced	29.3	33.7	28.3	27.3	27.3	26.7	26.7
N200, P & K replaced	30.0	36.0	29.7	28.7	28.3	22.7	25.7
N100, PO, K replaced	28.3	36.0	33.7	32.3	27.0	28.3	28.7
N200, P0, K replaced	31.3	35.0	30.0	31.3	26.3	28.3	27.0
N0, P75, K replaced	31.3	37.0	34.7	32.0	32.7	27.7	26.3
N100, P75, K replaced	28.7	34.3	27.0	23.3	26.0	23.7	19.7
N200, P75, K replaced	29.0	31.0	27.0	19.0	18.3	19.0	16.3
N200, P75, K200	29.7	30.0	26.3	22.0	19.7	19.7	24.3
			★★	★★★	★★★		★★

Significance as in Table 1

Table 3. UME production from hay and aftermath grazing averaged over 1986-89 in the Main Experiment (GJ/ha).

	Hay	**Grazing**	**Hay & Grazing**
N0	28.8	11.9	40.7
N25	29.9	14.5	44.4
N50	37.6	20.1	57.7
N100	36.4	19.3	55.7
N200	39.8	22.1	61.9
	★★★	★★★	★★★

Significance of effects as in Table 1

AGRICULTURAL OUTPUT

Hay yield and total annual production were significantly increased by fertilisers (Table 3). The total UME outputs obtained (40.7-61.9 GJ /ha per year) compare favourably with those recorded for non-suckler beef farms in a National Farm Study of permanent grassland (Forbes *et al.*, 1980). Overall, hay production contributed about two-thirds of the total UME output, equating with the seasonal distribution of production from grazed permanent pastures elsewhere (Tallowin *et al.*, 1990).

There was an attenuation of the response at rates above 50kg N / ha (Table 3) which contrasts with the general response of permanent pastures in the UK, where herbage production normally increases with inputs of up to 300kg N /ha (Hopkins *et al.*, 1990). This attenuated response was attributable to deficiencies in P and K supply (Kirkham and Wilkins, 1993a). When P and K were provided in non-limiting amounts in the Small-scale Experiment (Table 4), output was similar to that obtained from a wide range of permanent pastures in the UK (Hopkins *et al.*, 1990; Kirkham and Wilkins, 1993b).

Table 4. DM yield (t/ha) from the Small-scale Experiment 1986-92 and the difference in P yield (kg/ha) between treatments and control 1991-92.

Treatment	DM t/ha	Treatments discontinued			Difference in P yield (kg/ha)	Treatments discontinued	
	1986-89	1990	1991	1992	1990	1991	1992
N0, P0, K0	4.69	2.93	3.72	4.91	-	-	-
N0, P & K replaced	6.69	5.27	4.80	5.55	2.0	1.3	1.4
N25, P & K replaced	6.99	4.84	4.84	5.92	1.8	1.2	2.2
N50, P & K replaced	7.17	4.30	4.94	6.00	0.5	1.1	1.2
N100, P & K replaced	7.39	4.94	4.79	5.16	1.4	1.2	1.0
N200, P & K replaced	7.96	5.28	5.02	6.13	1.3	1.0	1.0
N100, P0, K replaced	5.81	4.21	4.45	5.13	0.7	0.4	0.1
N200, P0, K replaced	5.71	4.38	4.33	4.88	1.0	0.5	0.2
N0, P75, K replaced	6.85	5.07	5.51	6.83	10.0	12.8	10.9
N100, P75, K replaced	8.76	5.60	6.09	5.67	11.9	15.9	6.6
N200, P75, K replaced	8.84	6.13	5.19	5.70	13.0	12.3	8.3
N200, P75, K200	10.46	6.30	6.27	6.46	12.0	12.0	8.6
	***	***	***	*	Significance not tested		

Significance as in Table 1.

THE EFFECT OF CESSATION OF FERTILISER APPLICATION
Changes in community diversity and individual species — Main Experiment

Species diversity in N- plots had not recovered by 1992, two years after fertiliser application ceased (Table 1C). In addition to the species shown in Table 5, fifteen other species of sedge, forb and bryophyte showed significant negative linear trends with

Table 5. Summary of ANOVA results for the contrasts $(N^- — N^+)$. Results for individual plant species for 1991 and 1992.

Species name	Trends against N		Significance	
	1991	1992	1991	1992
Agrostis canina	-	-	NS	★★
Agrostis capillaris	-	-	NS	★★★
Alopecurus pratensis	+	+	★	★
Anthoxanthum odoratum	-	-	□	□
Bromus hordeaceus	+	+	★	★
Bromus racemosus	+	+	NS	□
Centaurea nigra	-	-	□	NS
Cerastium fontanum	+	+	□	NS
Cynosurus cristatus	-	-	★	★★
Elytrigia repens	+	+	NS	★
Holcus lanatus	+	+	NS	★
Lysimachia nummularia	-	-	NS	★
Plantago lanceolata	-	-	NS	□
Potentilla reptans	-	-	NS	★★★
Rumex acetosa	+	+	★	NS
Stellaria graminea	-	-	NS	★★★
Stellaria media	+	+	NS	★
Taraxacum spp.	-	-	NS	★★
Trifolium repens	-	-	NS	★

Significance as in Table 1

previous N input in the N- plots in 1991 and/or 1992. Most of these showed no sign of recovery, whilst *B. perennis* and *P. vulgaris* continued to decline despite discontinued fertiliser use.

Agrostis canina, *A.capillaris*, *Anthoxanthum odoratum* and *Cynosurus cristatus* were significantly more abundant in the N- than in the N+ plots in 1992 (Table 5). *Agrostis capillaris* and *A. odoratum* had partially replaced *L. perenne* in the N- plots by 1992, but there was still more *L.perenne* in the N100- and N200- than in the controls. *Alopecurus pratensis*, *Bromus hordeaceus*, *B.racemosus*, *Elytrigia repens* and *H. lanatus* were more common constituents of the N+ than the N- plots. The cover of *F.rubra* had increased by 1992 in the control plots, but remained low in previously treated plots. *Rumex acetosa* and *Taraxacum* agg. remained more abundant in N- plots than in controls.

Carex flacca, *Lysimachia nummularia*, *Plantago lanceolata*, *Potentilla reptans*, *Stellaria graminea*, *Taraxacum* spp., *Trifolium repens* and *Ceratodon purpureus* were significantly more common by 1992 in N- than in N+ plots. Most of these had continued to decline since 1990 in the N+ plots, but had increased in the N- plots.

82

Residual effects of previous P inputs on vegetation — Small-scale Experiment

The former high P plots have shown the least tendency to revert of all former treatments. Species diversity was still lower in the former high N high P plots compared with the control two years after treatments ceased, with no increase in diversity (Table 2). *Anthoxanthum odoratum, Centaurea nigra, Leontodon hispidus, Leontodon autumnalis* and *Trifolium pratense*, all common constituents of control plots, were still significantly lower in former high N high P plots two years after fertiliser inputs ceased, whereas *Holcus lanatus, Ranunculus repens* and *Rumex acetosa* remained significantly higher.

Residual effects on agricultural output and nutrient yield in herbage

There were no residual effects of previous fertiliser input on either hay yield, N yield, beef production or annual UME output in any year in the Main Experiment. In the Small-scale Experiment, herbage yields remained enhanced by all former treatments in 1990 and in 1991 particularly by those which had included high P (Table 4), but by 1992 the residual effects of previously high P inputs on herbage yield were only evident in the autumn. Phosphorus yield was enhanced by all former high P treatments throughout phase ll.

A total of 23 kg P/ha was harvested from unfertilized control plots between 1986-89. Assuming that this amount was available from the soil on all plots in addition to the amounts applied, then the same figure represents an excess of input over off-take where the latter was 'replaced' on fertilized plots. Extrapolating the mean amounts removed from these plots per year 1990-92 suggests that it would take 13-25 years under current cutting management to deplete the excess P, even assuming continued linearity of P removal.

Accelerating reversion

All treatments that disturbed the established vegetation enhanced species richness relative to control in the year after treatment (Table 6a). Total grass cover was reduced by autumn rotavation and/or spring herbicide treatment (Table 6b), although *H. lanatus* abundance was enhanced by all disturbance treatments. Total cover of forbs, particularly of *R. repens*, was enhanced by disturbance, particularly by autumn rotavation, but sowing seed did not increase the abundance of any of the sown species significantly compared with control.

SYNTHESIS

There was no 'safe' amount of fertiliser N input that did not reduce floristic diversity. Even 25kg N/ha per year reduced overall diversity and the abundance of most of the distinctive hay meadow species within 6 years. Using TABLEFIT (Hill, 1991) showed that, under high rates of N, rich grasslands (MG5 and MG8 of the National Vegetation Classification — Rodwell, 1992) were replaced by more species-poor types e.g. MG6. Despite the initially species-rich vegetation, the production response to fertilisers of the meadows was consistent with that of a wide range of permanent pastures in the UK and was predictable from existing N response models.

Table 6. The effect of either autumn rotavation (RA), spring rotavation (RS) or spring herbicide (H) treatment on species number and cover.

	RA	RS	H	C	Significance
a) number of species per 25 × 25 quadrat in June 1992					
Total diversity	18.2	16.6	16.9	15.6	★ (2)
Grasses	7.4	7.3	7.9	8.1	NS
Forbs	10.3	8.8	8.8	7.8	★★ (2)
b) % cover					
Grasses	47.9	61.0	53.5	61.1	★★★ (1), ★ (2)
Forbs	50.6	40.4	45.0	36.9	★★ (1), ★ (2)
Agrostis capillaris	5.9	8.4	4.0	12.6	★★ (1), ★★★ (2)
Anthoxanthum odoratum	13.2	17.9	10.6	13.0	★ (1), ★ (2)
Holcus lanatus	12.1	12.9	15.6	9.3	★ (2)
Cerastium fontanum	4.2	5.6	4.2	1.4	★★★ (1), ★★★ (2)
Ranunculus repens	10.5	3.8	4.0	2.8	★ (1), ★★ (2)
Rumex acetosa	2.9	4.5	0.8	4.2	★★ (1), ★★★ (2)

Significance of effects on angular transformed data. 1 = treatment, 2 = disturbance versus no disturbance

The sensitivity to fertilisers of these meadows suggests little room for compromise with agricultural practice for this vegetation in the Somerset Levels ESA and elsewhere. The considerable "inertia" in vegetation composition after fertiliser application ceased was almost certainly due to enhanced residues of available nutrients, particularly P. It is estimated that it would take a minimum of 13 years before the P status in formerly fertilized plots declined to former levels. Attempts to accelerate reversion involving disturbance of the soil and vegetation and sowing of lost species showed little success and it seems that future attempts should be linked to techniques of reducing soil fertility.

REFERENCES

BRENCHLEY W.E. and WARINGTON K. (1958) *The Park Grass Plots at Rothamsted 1856-1949. Rothamsted Experimental Station, Harpenden.*

DIGBY P.G.N. and KEMPTON R.A. (1987) *Multivariate Analysis of Ecological Communities.* London: Chapman & Hall.

FORBES T.J., DIBB C., GREEN J.O., HOPKINS A. and PEEL S. (1980) *Factors affecting the productivity of permanent grassland.* A National Farm Study. Hurley: Joint GRI/ADAS Permanent Pasture Group.

GUPTA P.L. and RORISON I.H. (1975) Seasonal differences in the availability of nutrients down a podzolic profile. *Journal of Ecology*, **63**, 521-534.

HILL M.O. (1991) *TABLEFIT. Program manual (Version 1).* Institute of Terrestrial Ecology, Huntingdon.

HOPKINS A., GILBEY J., DIBB C., BOWLING P.J. and MURRAY P.J. (1990) Response of permanent and reseeded grassland to fertiliser nitrogen. 1. Herbage production and herbage quality. *Grass and Forage Science*, **45**, 43-55.

KIRKHAM F.W. and WILKINS R.J. (1993a) The productivity and response to inorganic fertilisers of species-rich wetland hay meadows on the Somerset Moors: nitrogen response under hay cutting and aftermath grazing. *Grass and Forage Science*. (in press).

KIRKHAM F.W. and WILKINS R.J. (1993b) The productivity and response to inorganic fertilisers of species-rich wetland hay meadows on the Somerset Moors: the effect of nitrogen, phosphorus and potassium on herbage production. *Grass and Forage Science*. (in press).

MOUNTFORD J.O., LAKHANI K.H. and KIRKHAM F.W. (1993) Experimental assessment of the effects of nitrogen addition under hay-cutting and aftermath grazing on the vegetation of meadows on a Somerset peat moor. *Journal of Applied Ecology*, **30**, 321-332.

RABOTNOV T.A. (1977) The influence of fertilisers on the plant communities of mesophytic grassland. In: Kraus W. (ed.) *Applications of Vegetation Science to Grassland Husbandry*. pp. 461-497. The Hague: Junk.

RODWELL J.S. (1992) *British Plant Communities. Volume 3. Grasslands and montane communities*. Cambridge.

SIMPSON E.H. (1949) Measurement of diversity. *Nature*, **163**, 688.

SOIL SURVEY OF ENGLAND and WALES (1983) *1:250,000 Map of England and Wales: six sheets and legend*. Soil Survey of England & Wales, Harpenden.

TALLOWIN J.R.B., KIRKHAM F.W., BROOKMAN S.K.E. and PATEFIELD M. (1990) Response of an old pasture to applied nitrogen under steady-state continuous grazing. *Journal of Agricultural Science, Cambridge*, **115**, 179-194.

TILMAN D. (1982) *Resource Competition and Community Structure*. Princeton: Princeton University Press.

WELLS T.C.E. (1989) Responsible management for botanical diversity. In: *Environmentally Responsible Grassland Management*. pp 4.1-4.16. British Grassland Society.

Management Options to Achieve Agricultural and Nature Conservation Objectives

R. J. WILKINS AND H. J. HARVEY[1]

AFRC Institute of Grassland and Environmental Research,
North Wyke, Okehampton, Devon EX20 2SB

[1]National Trust, 33 Sheep Street, Cirencester, Gloucestershire GL7 1QW

ABSTRACT

The compatibility between managements imposed for agricultural purposes and specific aspects of wildlife is reviewed. Generally actions to increase fertility and efficiency of grassland utilisation, whilst increasing productivity and profitability will reduce the diversity of higher plants with consequent reductions in populations of insects, particularly butterflies, and birds. High levels of utilisation also reduce numbers of ground-nesting birds and small mammals. Variations in cutting date, reseeding, the use of herbicides and pesticides and drainage often have little effect on productivity, but may have major effects on wildlife. It is argued that a general marginal lowering in intensity of management will often result in little wildlife benefit, but considerable loss in productivity and profitability. In most circumstances the best combination of agricultural and conservation objectives will be achieved by applying contrasting managements to particular fields within a farm.

INTRODUCTION

This paper takes an integrated approach to optimizing management from the dual viewpoints of agriculture and nature conservation. Objectives are considered in the first section, followed by discussion on the compatibility between the contrasting objectives and the impacts of specific management strategies on productivity, flora and fauna. A final section analyses different approaches for producing optimal solutions. The main context of the paper is neutral and acid-neutral grassland in the lowlands, although the principles developed are often of widespread application.

MANAGEMENT OBJECTIVES
Agricultural objectives
The principal objective of farmers in managing grassland is to contribute to farm profitability, generally through conversion of the herbage grown to milk and meat. The quest for maximum profitability is tempered by concern to avoid risks, and often factors relating to the availability of capital and labour, incentive and 'quality of life' (see Johnson and Bastiman, 1981).

There is a close positive relationship on grassland farms between output from grassland measured as utilized metabolizable energy (UME) and gross margin and margin over feed and fertilizer cost, as found by Forbes *et al.* (1980) for both dairy and beef farms.

Conservation objectives

These objectives may be very diverse, relating variously to maintaining a varied flora and fauna through the landscape, preservation of particular habitats and preventing the disappearance of plant and animal species from particular areas.

Green (1989a) drew attention to pressures from agriculture which have led to extinctions of several species, with serious declines or endangered populations for 149 species of plants, 13 of butterflies, 36 of birds and several of mammals; many of these being species of grassland. The Nature Conservancy Council (1984) concluded that only 5% of lowland neutral grasslands had significant wildlife interest.

On farmed land, an important vehicle providing financial incentives to maintain or enhance species richness is the Environmentally Sensitive Area (ESA) scheme, whilst protection of particular examples of habitats and species is often achieved through designation of areas as Sites of Specific Scientific Interest (SSSI) with management restrictions. Considerable areas have also been acquired by voluntary Conservation Bodies, with some 185,000 ha of land managed principally for nature conservation in non-statutory protected areas (Department of the Environment, 1993).

IMPACT OF MANAGEMENT VARIABLES ON PRODUCTIVITY AND ON WILDLIFE

Table 1 is an attempt to summarise the impact of key management options on utilized output and on different classes of wildlife, using information of varying quality from a wide range of sources.

Agricultural productivity

The key features under management control that determine utilized output from grassland are fertility (particularly the supply of N to the sward) and the efficiency with which herbage is utilized by grazing or as conserved forage. The positive relationship between fertilizer N and UME found by Forbes *et al.* (1980) is well recognised but the driving force for production is the total supply of N to the sward, with fertilizers, soil organic matter, returns of excreta and slurry and biological N fixation all of importance. Substantial production may be sustained in old permanent grassland receiving no inorganic fertilizer, with Hopkins *et al.* (1990) reporting average yields on 16 sites of 4.3 t DM/ha. Farm studies carried out by Peel *et al.* (1988) highlighted the large variation in efficiency of utilization both at grazing (with the percentage of the herbage grown which was utilized varying between farms from 51 to 83%) and with silage-making (55 to 73%).

Other management variables may have only small effects on utilized output. Hopkins *et al.* (1990) showed that reseeding with perennial ryegrass, although increasing production markedly in the first year, had little effect on yields in the longer term. The increase in beef production from reseeding over a 5 year period was only 7%

87

Table 1. Generalised effects of agricultural management options on utilised output and on wildlife.

	Utilized output	No. higher plants	Insects	Birds	Small mammals
Increase fertility	+	-	-	-	0
Increase level of utilisation*	+	(-)	-	-	-
Increase proportion reseeded	(+)	-	-	-	(-)
Improve drainage	(+)	-	-	-	?
Use herbicides	(+)	-	-	V	?
Use pesticides	(+)	0	-	V	(-)
Increase proportion early-cut	(+)	-	-	-	(-)
Increase proportion late-cut	(-)	+	+	+	+
Graze with cattle rather than sheep	(-)	(+)	+	+	+
Graze intermittently rather than continuously	0	V	+	+	V

The direction of change, either positive or negative is indicated with symbols. Those not in parentheses indicate major effects. V signifies that direction of effect varies in different situations.
* Particularly increased severity of grazing.

(Tyson *et al.*, 1993). In the same experiment over a 10 year period, drainage only increased beef production/ha by 7%. Pesticides and fungicides are not widely used in grassland. Clements *et al.* (1990b) found that insecticide plus molluscicide treatment increased yield of permanent swards by 11% on average over 8 sites for 2 years. In the long-term, however, repeated pesticide use may not increase production because of adverse effects on soil biological activity and soil structure (Clements *et al.*, 1990a). The use of herbicides on grassland is decreasing and Johnson (1991) estimated an overall adverse effect of weeds on grassland output of only 2%.

Wildlife

There are linkages between different classes of wildlife in their responses to variation in agricultural management. Actions that result in increased number and diversity of higher plant species will generally also support higher populations of phytophagous insects, including butterflies, and in turn higher populations of insectivorous birds.

The hump-back model of Grime (1979) in which botanical diversity is at a maximum at intermediate levels of biomass (or productivity) is widely accepted (Fig. 1). However, the baseline productivity of old grassland without fertilizer use in Britain is relatively high, so that options in managing grassland are normally concerned only with the right-hand side of the graph in Fig. 1, as recognised by Grime (1979). Silvertown (1980) demonstrated close negative relationships between biomass productivity (hay yield) and species numbers in the Park Grass experiment at Rothamsted. In re-

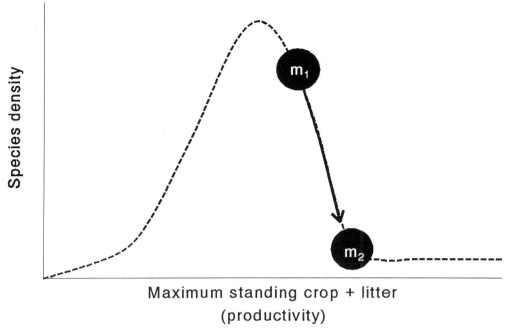

Fig. 1. The alteration in species density resulting from the application of a heavy dressing of fertilizer to a species rich meadow ($m_1 \rightarrow m_2$) (from Grime, 1979).

cent experiments in the Somerset Levels, UME output was negatively correlated with species numbers. Even the lowest rate of fertilizer applied (25 kg N/ha) had significant adverse effects on species numbers (Mountford *et al.*, 1993). Silvertown (1980), however, noted that botanical diversity, at any level of productivity, may be reduced in conditions of low soil pH.

A further major conflict between agricultural management and wildlife results from variation in the intensity of utilization of the herbage grown. Severity of defoliation rather than method of grazing (e.g. rotational vs. continuous grazing) has the predominant effect on utilized output (Robson *et al.*, 1989). Wildlife values, in contrast, are generally higher with lax grazing as this will give a mosaic of short and tall patches, providing a wide range of micro-environments for wildlife with benefits for ground-nesting birds (Lack, 1992) and small mammals (Harris and Woollard, 1990). Wildlife may be much affected also by the time of grazing and species of animal used (Bacon, 1990). For some classes of biota there are advantages from grazing in winter. Grazing with cattle rather than sheep is often recommended by conservationists, because of the greater variability in sward structure that results and the greater exposure of bare soil through hoof damage.

Silage is now the predominant method of grass conservation, with many fields cut in May and at frequent intervals thereafter. Whilst ensiling is a reasonably efficient and weather-proof method of conservation for the farmer, it has a devastating effect on ground-nesting birds and contributes to reducing floral diversity in grasslands.

The matrix within Table 1 does, however, indicate that some agricultural management have relatively little impact on output, but substantial effects on wildlife. The effect of reseeding on output is modest, but it results in massive disturbance to the ecosystem with adverse effects on wildlife. Woiwod and Stewart (1990), for instance, noted that ploughing and reseeding with modern cultivars eliminates all known larval food plants of UK butterflies. Thomas (1984) stated that unimproved patchy pasture supported 23 butterfly species per site, compared with only one species for grass-clover leys. Likewise, drainage may have little impact on utilized output, but poor drainage status is often associated with high levels of diversity of both flora and fauna. Withholding pesticides and herbicides results in little economic sacrifice in grassland but potentially large wildlife benefits.

Thus, though some steps to combining agricultural and wildlife objectives can be made through using permanent grassland, avoiding pesticides and herbicides and by not draining land, major conflicts remain in relation to fertility and method and level of utilization.

APPROACHES TO MEETING AGRICULTURAL AND WILDLIFE OBJECTIVES

The direction of government policies towards reduction of agricultural output gives increased opportunity for seeking wildlife benefits from grassland, but individual farmers still need to maintain their levels of income. We discuss whether these requirements are best achieved by a reduction in intensity of production over the total area or by targeting particular areas.

It seems reasonable to suppose that nature conservation value remains at a low or negligible value until a certain attribute reaches a threshold level and then may increase rapidly. Considering higher plant species, nature conservation value will be negligible whether there is, say, 1 or 5 species/m^2. Thresholds would vary with sward type, but swards are unlikely to attract substantial nature conservation value until there are more than, say, 15 to 20 plant species/m^2. A negative linear relationship in a particular situation between utilized output and number of species present and a positive linear relationship between utilized output and agricultural profitability may be assumed, as discussed earlier. These conceptual relationships between nature conservation value (in relation to higher plant species), agricultural value and utilized production for a particular site are illustrated in Fig. 2. This illustrates that a reduction of intensity of production from X to Y will give considerable sacrifice in agricultural returns, without compensatory increase in conservation value. Intensity needs to be reduced below Y to give a conservation value which may compensate for reduced agricultural returns.

Whilst this relationship can at present only be schematic, it suggests that a general marginal reduction in intensity of agricultural management may give negligible conservation benefits. If, on the other hand, all grassland were managed to give high species numbers, the reduction in agricultural output would be large and probably unacceptable. It is our view that a better solution is to target management for wildlife.

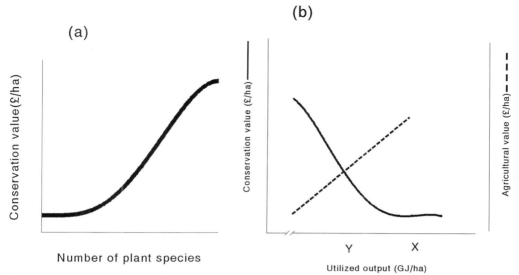

Fig. 2. Schematic relationships between number of plant species and nature conservation value (a) and between utilized output, agricultural value and nature conservation value (b).

Thus a proportion of grassland could be managed specifically for agricultural productivity with due regard to profitability, sustainability and prevention of pollution, whilst other areas could be managed within an agricultural context, but for specific conservation objectives.

Such targeting of land management could be achieved either within a field, through imposing different managements at the margins compared with the main part of the field, or within a farm, by designating different fields to different purposes, or at a district or regional level.

Whilst the hedge and associated banks may provide valuable refuges for insects, small mammals and birds and provide links between areas of diversity on the farm, there are both biological and practical problems in exploiting a wider field margin to increase nature conservation value. Even without the use of fertilizer N in the field margins, fertility in that area may remain high in grazing conditions, because of transfer of N in excreta from the main field area. There may also be problems with selectivity of grazing between contrasting areas and in grass conservation, because of differences in composition and maturity between different areas of the sward. Whilst recognising the possible value of hedges and field boundaries for many nature conservation purposes, we do not think that wider field margins with discrete management have a major part to play in grassland.

There is attraction in targeting different managements to different areas within a particular farm. This, of course, is not a new concept and has been widely advocated by advisors of the Farming and Wildlife Advisory Group. Particular characteristics of soil and terrain, current and potential wildlife status and agricultural manageability help identify blocks of land for particular purposes. If the wildlife objective is to increase botanical diversity (with associated benefits for butterflies) then key management factors will probably be the absence of fertilizers and the use of low intensity grazing (to give a mosaic of grazed and ungrazed areas) or late cutting for hay or silage. If ground-nesting birds are also a target, then late cutting together with aftermath grazing will be appropriate.

Defoliation is important to prevent shrub regeneration and maintain high wildlife values in grassland, but many areas moving out of agricultural use remain ungrazed and rapidly decline in wildlife value. Appropriate grazing (and cutting) management is more readily achieved in grassland that is managed in a farm context than when management is totally separated from farming. Grazing animals and farm machinery and the appropriate stockmanship and expertise are available. It should be possible to plan hay or silage-making and appropriate grazing in the target areas to satisfy wildlife objectives without prejudicing the success of the animal enterprises.

There are, however, problems. The quality of herbage is likely to be lower than that in the main agricultural area, but utilization by stock with (at the particular time) low nutrient requirements (e.g. dry cows) is likely to be quite feasible. The difficulties of utilizing herbage from areas devoted principally to wildlife increase the greater the proportion of such land becomes on the farm, largely because of the low quality of hay or silage taken from the mature crops. Also, farmers may be reluctant to use stock from their main enterprises for grazing swards perceived to be of low quality. In order to achieve acceptable rates of animal production, substantial levels of supplementation may be required at times of the year. Unfortunately though, this would lead to importation of nutrients onto the farm and thus an increased load of nutrients to be returned to the land, with possible adverse effects on wildlife. It is contended by Green (1989b) that modern lowland breeds rarely make much impact on coarse grasses which usually dominate amenity grassland. Although there is considerable anecdotal evidence on this point (e.g. Bacon, 1990), there has been little rigorous experimentation. It would be a significant disadvantage to the approach we are suggesting if farmers had to have different breeds to utilize different grassland areas on their farms.

Whilst the concept of devoting particular fields on a farm to particular purposes is attractive, there are circumstances in which larger areas may need to be managed specifically for wildlife. Minimum breeding areas required for viable colonies of particular species need to be considered. Thomas (1984) pointed out that for many butterfly species, areas of 0.5 ha are sufficient, but for some species, e.g. *Apatura iris*, the required area is above 50 ha. Considerably larger areas under a defined management may be required for maintenance of adequate populations of some predator species and meta populations of other wildlife species. Drainage and water control systems required for the maintenance of some wetland habitats may need major capital investments with the result that substantial areas, rather than fields within farms, would need to be devoted to nature conservation. Benefits from tourism are also more likely to be captured through management of a high proportion of the land in a particular area for wildlife benefits.

Financial incentives must be provided to farmers in order to combine grassland and wildlife objectives within the framework of the farm. ESA-type schemes should be more widely available. It is particularly important that support is given for measures to protect or enhance nature conservation for parts of farms rather than support being available only at the whole farm level. Also in view of the adverse effects on wildlife of even small applications of fertilizer, we consider that, in terms of nature conservation, better value for money is likely to be given by the more restrictive higher tiers included in many ESA's than the lower tiers, which allow application of considerable quantities of fertilizers (see MAFF, 1992).

CONCLUSIONS

The major conflicts between agricultural and wildlife objectives relate to soil fertility and the efficiency and timing of utilization. The use of permanent swards, the withholding of pesticides and herbicides and the acceptance of poor drainage status may, however, increase wildlife value with little sacrifice in agricultural output. The best combination of agricultural productivity and wildlife conservation is likely to be achieved by targeting different areas of the farm specifically for agricultural or wildlife management rather than endeavouring to satisfy both agricultural and wildlife criteria from the same area of land.

REFERENCES

BACON J.C. (1990) The use of livestock in calcareous grassland management. In: Hillier, S.H., Walton, D.W.H. and Wells, D.A. (eds). *Calcareous Grasslands - Ecology and Management*, pp. 121-127, Huntingdon: Bluntisham Books.

CLEMENTS R.O., MURRAY P.J., BENTLEY B.R. and HENDERSON I.F. (1990a) Herbage yield and botanical composition over 20 years of a predominantly ryegrass sward treated frequently with phorate pesticide and three rates of nitrogen fertilizer. *Journal of Agricultural Science*, **115**, 23-27.

CLEMENTS R.O., MURRAY P.J., BENTLEY B.R., LEWIS G.C. and FRENCH N. (1990b) The impact of pests and diseases on the herbage yield of permanent grassland at eight sites in England and Wales. *Annals of Applied Biology*, **117**, 349-357.

DEPARTMENT OF THE ENVIRONMENT (1993). *Digest of Environmental Protection and Water Statistics*. HMSO.

FORBES T.J., DIBB C., GREEN J.O., HOPKINS A. and PEEL S. (1980) *Factors Affecting the Productivity of Permanent Grassland*. Hurley: Grassland Research Institute and Agricultural Development Advisory Service.

GREEN B.H. (1989a) The impact of agricultural management practices on the ecology of grasslands. In: *Environmentally Responsible Grassland Management*, British Grassland Society Winter Meeting, December 1989, pp. 1.1-1.19.

GREEN B.H. (1989b) Grassland management for wildlife conservation and amenity. In: Holmes, W. (ed.). *Grass: Its Production and Utilization*, pp. 240-257, Oxford: Blackwell Scientific Publications.

GRIME J.P. (1979) *Plant Strategies and Vegetation Processes*. Chichester: John Wiley and Sons.

HARRIS S. and WOOLLARD T. (1990) The dispersal of mammals in agricultural habitats in Britain. In: Bunce, R.G.H. and Howard, D.C. (eds.) *Species Dispersal in Agricultural Habitats*, pp. 159-188, London: Belhaven Press.

HOPKINS A. GILBEY J., DIBB C., BOWLING P.J. and MURRAY P.J. (1990) Response of perennial and reseeded grassland to fertilizer nitrogen. 1. Herbage production and herbage quality. *Grass and Forage Science*, **45**, 43-55.

JOHNSON J. (1991) Importance of the problem - practical solutions. In: *Strategies for Weed, Disease and Pest Control in Grassland*, pp. 1.1-1.13. Proceedings British Grassland Society Conference, Feb. 1991.

JOHNSON J. and BASTIMAN B. (1981) Social and human factors in grassland farming. In: Jollans, J.L. (ed.). *Grassland in the British Economy*, pp. 268-288, CAS Paper 10, Reading: Centre for Agricultural Strategy.

LACK P. (1992) *Birds on Lowland Farms*. London: HMSO.

MINISTRY OF AGRICULTURE, FISHERIES AND FOOD (1992) *The Somerset Levels and Moors ESA - Guidelines for Farmers*. Ministry of Agriculture, Fisheries and Food, PB 0756, SLM/ESA/2.

MOUNTFORD J.O., TALLOWIN J.R.B. and KIRKHAM F.W. (1993) Case study on Somerset Levels. *Occasional Symposium No. 28*, British Grassland Society (in press).

NATURE CONSERVANCY COUNCIL (1984) *Nature Conservation in Britain*. Nature Conservancy Council.

PEEL S., MATKIN E.A. and HUCKLE C.A. (1988) Herbage growth and utilized output from grassland on dairy farms in southwest England: case studies of five farms 1982 and 1983. II. Herbage utilization. *Grass and Forage Science*, **43**, 71-78.

ROBSON M.J., PARSONS A.J. and WILLIAMS T.E. (1989) Herbage production: grasses and legumes. In: Holmes, W (ed.). *Grass: Its Production and Utilization*, pp. 7-88, Oxford: Blackwell Scientific Publications.

SILVERTOWN J. (1980) The dynamics of a grassland ecosystem: botanical equilibrium in the Park Grass experiment. *Journal of Applied Ecology*, **17**, 491-504.

THOMAS J.A. (1984) The conservation of butterflies in temperate countries: past efforts and lessons for the future. In: *The Biology of Butterflies*, pp. 334-353, London: Academic Press.

TYSON K.C., HAWKINS J.M.B. and STONE A.C. (1993) *Final Report on the AFRC-ADAS drainage experiment 1982-1993*. Okehampton: North Wyke Research Station.

WOIWOD I.P. and STEWART A.J.A. (1990) Butterflies and moths - migration in the agricultural environment. In: Bunce, R.G.H. and Howard, D.C. (eds). *Species Dispersal in Agricultural Habitats*, pp. 189-202, London: Belhaven Press.

The Swiss Grassland System

J. NÖSBERGER

Swiss Federal Institute of Technology, ETH 8092 Zurich

ABSTRACT

Switzerland is a small country with a wide range of climatic and edaphic conditions. The average farm size is 11.4 ha, small and medium farms predominate. More than 70% of the agricultural land is covered by grass. Dairy cows produce 75% of their milk from the grass grown on the farm. During the last 10 years public opinion has become increasingly concerned about maintaining the quality of the countryside, landscape and environment. Swiss grassland practices are based on the following principles: management must be site-specific and support long-term, floristic stability pastures. A floristic composition in which grasses contribute 50-60%, legumes 20-30% and the other species 10-20% to the yield is considered appropriate. The plant nutrient cycles should be balanced. For fertilization, farm manure should primarily be used. The seed mixtures for leys should include grasses and legumes. Herbicides should only exceptionally be used. Management aims are not directed towards profit maximization, but take into consideration the concerns of the majority of the population regarding the quality of the landscape and the environment. Such an integrative approach attempts to balance the objectives of agriculture and nature conservation. Very intensive management should be restricted to sites where it is ecologically acceptable. Extensive management is a prerequisite for maintaining species-rich pastures, but results in low yield and poor quality. Farmers can only integrate both objectives if they receive a financial compensation. The majority of the population expects grassland systems to provide more than just food.

INTRODUCTION

Switzerland is a small country with a wide range of climatic and soil conditions, where small and medium size farms predominate. The average farm size is 11.4 ha. Farmers own about 60% of the agricultural area. The economic importance of dairy production is reflected by its 40-45% contribution to the gross receipts of the farms.

In many regions the climate and topography are not suitable for arable cultivation. Switzerland is a grassland country; more than 70% of the agricultural land is covered by grass. Permanent grassland in the lowlands and uplands exceeds the area utilized for temporary grass by a factor of seven. Pastures in the alpine region are generally situated at more than 1000 m above sea level.

Only 4.2% of the working population earn their living on farms. The great majority of our society still regard the countryside as part of their heritage. Many of the most valued landscapes of Switzerland are the product of farming systems based on varying sorts of grassland management. Many of our rare habitats are grassland. During the last 10 years public opinion has become increasingly concerned about maintaining the quality of the countryside, landscape and environment. Intensive cultivation and an excessive number of animals per unit of farm area are regarded as threats to the environment. The government has tried to satisfy the three major aims of Swiss agricultural policy: national security, the maintenance of a healthy rural and family farm population and the preservation of the environment. This policy and the prosperity of the country have largely influenced the development of diverse grassland systems.

AGRICULTURAL OBJECTIVES OF THE GRASSLAND SYSTEMS

We can distinguish 4 different categories of roughage producing areas:

i) *Alpine pastures* cover 25% of Swiss territory. About two thirds of this area can be used as pasture. During the summer the animals stay only in this region; many farms have to rely on this important additional forage source. Alpine pastures also have a great recreational value during summer and winter.

ii) *Permanent pastures and meadows* in the lowlands and uplands constitute more than 60% of our agricultural area. Only 12% is used exclusively for grazing; the other areas are used for cutting as well as grazing. (The term "permanent pasture" will be used in this review for permanent grassland independent of the modes of utilization: grazing and/or cutting.)

iii) *Leys* that are mostly a mixture of grasses and legumes are a traditional factor in crop rotation. They produce the forage for mixed farms that cultivate diverse arable crops. Leys are usually sown for a duration of two or more years; they cover about 12% of the agricultural area and are also considered an important element in the landscape.

iv) *Maize for silage and other fodder plants* like fodder beet account for the smallest proportion of forage producing land.

In making decisions regarding the management of grassland, the Swiss system takes into consideration the following principles:

1) Management must be site-specific and support a long-term stable floristic composition of the pastures. Experience has shown that too intensive a management, especially in the uplands, leads to degenerated pastures in which the percentage of undesired species is increasing and the sward density is decreasing. In the lowlands and uplands, we are aiming at a floristic composition of 50 - 60% grass, 20 -30% legumes and 10 -20% other species. At higher altitudes the proportion of other species increases at the expense of the other components.

2) A high proportion of the ruminant production should be derived from grazing and conserved grass. On average in Switzerland, dairy cows produce upto 77% of their milk from the grass produced on the farm. This production (national average 5000 kg milk /cow/year) can be achieved by pastures with a relatively high number of species, but it requires energy-rich young grass.

3) The nutrient cycles should be balanced for each pasture. A nutrient supply that exceeds the plant nutrient exports generates ecological problems. These can lead to pasture degeneration, especially if the growing conditions for perennial ryegrass (*Lolium perenne*), Italian ryegrass (*Lolium multiflorum*) or meadow fox-tail (*Alopecurus*

pratensis) are unfavourable. This emphasizes the crucial importance of the number of animals per unit farm land, the input of mineral fertilisers and the amount of concentrates used for the plant nutrient balance.

4) For fertilization, farm manure should primarily be used. This helps to solve the disposal problem in a cost-effective and ecologically meaningful way. Herbicides should only be used if stubborn weeds have to be controlled. A recent survey has shown that less than 5% of the grassland is treated with herbicides. Other pesticides are not used.

5) The recommended seed mixtures for leys should include legumes as well as grasses in order to enhance the quality of the forage, and to reduce the need for mineral nitrogen as well as contributing to biological diversity.

OPERATION OF AN INTEGRATED GRASSLAND SYSTEM

To economists, the above-summarized grassland system of Switzerland is probably difficult to understand because it is not directed towards profit maximization. Farmers, however, derive their satisfaction from a number of activities which count for more than a balance-sheet profit. As they constitute only a small percentage of the total population, farmers have to rely on the attitudes of the great majority in determining the quality of the landscape and the environment. There has been a noticeable shift in public attitudes (which are often emotional) as in other densely populated and industrialized countries. Current perceptions do not favour the techniques that modern grassland management has produced. The Swiss Grassland Society has pondered these changes, in intensive discussions with nature conservationists, with the aim of developing mutual understanding and achieving a far-reaching cooperation. One result of such discussions was an extensive research project on the management of species-rich pastures and the nutritive value of their component vegetation. This project, based on cooperation between the Grassland Society, several research stations and the nature conservation authorities, had a positive influence on policy adjustments. It generated a more rational discussion about agricultural, social and environmental objectives and created a positive climate for the work done at the research and extension level. The demands of the public population were routinely built into the research and extension programmes, so that advances in grassland management could simultaneously contribute to environmental improvement. The following examples should briefly characterize the various types of grassland, indicate how they are managed and suggest which questions should be addressed by research for integrated grassland systems.

Botanical composition and management of leys

The present list of standard seed mixtures includes 27 different recipes (Lehmann *et al.*, 1992). It always includes grasses and legumes and takes into account the expected duration, mode of utilization and climatic conditions (suitable for perennial ryegrass). For most mixtures, expected yields range from 10 — 15 t DM/ha. This production should need less than 150 kg N/ha/year. The number of defoliations per growing season may vary from 2 to 6 (Lehmann and Meister, 1985). Two cuts would be typical for a traditional, extensive hay meadow. One mixture is offered with two different sets of wild flowers: one set with 15 species is more adapted to drier regions; the other with 13 species was developed for wetter sites. For deteriorated pastures 4 special mixtures are available.

Variation in the management of permanent pastures

Edaphic, climatic and technical factors, plus floristic composition are the main sources of variation in grass production and of the varied responses of pastures to management decisions. It is necessary to take these many factors into account when models of management are elaborated.

Very intensive management. In the mild and humid valley regions of central and northern Switzerland a type of permanent meadow developed in which Italian ryegrass (*Lolium multiflorum*) dominates. It can account for more than 80% of the forage yield. This type of vegetation developed from an *Arrhenatherion* community containing about 30 species. Two or three decades ago this grassland was managed with moderate intensity. The changes introduced were frequent defoliation (6 — 7 cuts per year), a very early first cut and a high nutrient supply with liquid manure. This intensification strongly favored the competitive ability of Italian ryegrass (which is able to produce up to 19 t DM /ha). This type of grassland is adapted to a very intensive management. However, the few species in this association and the short life of the main grass are responsible for the unstable floristic composition of this sward. It was necessary to study the regeneration of Italian ryegrass to get some indication as to how the floristic composition could be made more stable. The results suggested that, in addition to the vegetative regeneration, a periodic renewal of the sward from seed shedding is necessary if Italian ryegrass is to persist (Bassetti and Nösberger, 1989). As a consequence, a combination of long cutting intervals to enable seed-dispersal and short intervals that promote tillering and seedling establishment is considered to be important for a dense and stable Italian ryegrass stand (Bassetti 1989; Wilda 1992). With a comparable management intensity, swards that were only grazed, or grazed only in spring, also developed pastures with a high proportion of perennial ryegrass or smooth meadow grass (*Poa pratensis*) and white clover. Management systems were developed to control the proportion of grasses and legumes (Thöni and Schüpbach, 1988). The quality of the grass obtained from these pastures is excellent and accounts for the high levels of milk produced from them (Table 1). This type of grassland is a prerequisite in grassland systems with a moderate output/low N input strategy. It helps to reduce the purchase of concentrates and does not damage nutrient cycling.

Intermediate intensity of management. When growing conditions are unfavourable for ryegrasses and the management of the grassland is characterized by high fertilization and frequent cutting (but the first cut is not before inflorescence emergence), then the number of species increases up to 30. The proportion of grasses (mainly cocksfoot (*Dactylis glomerata*), yellow oat grass (*Trisetum flavescens*), and meadow foxtail (*Alopecurus pratensis*)) varies from 30 to more than 70%. Characteristic of the group of 'other

Table 1. Milk production record of a Swiss farm with intensively managed grass-legume pastures (yield proportions : 70 % grasses, 18 % other species, 12 % white clover) BRÜLI-SAUER (1993) written communication.

	1985	1986	1987	1988	1989	1990	1991	1992
Milk (kg/cow/year)	5725	5915	6024	6175	6300	6469	6456	6226
kg accounted for by forage*	5200	5450	5500	5500	5650	5800	5800	5650
% accounted for by forage*	91	92	91	89	90	90	90	91

* during winter the ration included 3 kg/cow/day maize silage

species 'are cow parsley (*Anthriscus sylvestris*), cow parsnip (*Heracleum sphondylium*) and meadow buttercup (*Ranunculus friesianus*). Legumes may be rare in such associations (*Arrhenatherion*). The floristic composition varies greatly with the intensity of management. Liquid manure is applied to the most frequently cut meadows after each utilization. They are mostly located near farms or on very accessible land. The limit of intensification for this type of vegetation is reached when the sward starts to deteriorate. This can be a slow or a fast, quantitative or qualitative, response of the floristic composition to management decisions introduced recently or one, or even two, decades ago. This observation suggests that the time factor plays a crucial role in the evolution of the vegetation. The deterioration is obvious when species other than grasses or legumes start to become too competitive.

Extensive management. When the amount of organic manure and PK supplied to nutrient-poor soils is moderate, and the first cut (used for conservation) is taken after inflorescence emergence of the grasses, then an *Arrhenatherion* will probably develop in the lowlands and a *Trisetion* in the uplands and mountainous regions. The number of species in this type of vegetation ranges from 30 to 45, with a great diversity in floristic composition, depending on site influences. In comparison to the intensively managed associations, where a high cutting frequency and a high rate of fertilization are the dominating factors, here soil and climate have a greater effect on botanical composition. Species with specific requirements can develop; these vegetation types offer many niches for colourful wild flowers.

The highest number of species, including rare ones, is found in unfertilised dry sites where a haycut follows after flowering of the grasses. These *Mesobromions* (Thomet, 1980) are very colourful associations and have always attracted the attention of conservationists. A cooperative research programme was developed to determine the nutritive value of this grass (Table 2). The hays had similar, low nutrient concentrations, in spite of their very different botanical composition. They were characterized by high fibre levels and low crude protein and phosphorus contents. The *in vivo* digestibility

Table 2. Digestibility of the main nutrients of different permanent pasture associations (Daccord, 1990).

			Associations			
	Mesobro-	Arrhena-	Festucion	Agrostido	Nardion	Se
Organic matter	60.2	59.1	63.1	54.8	64.8	1.2
Crude protein	49.3	51.4	55.8	52.3	53.1	1.6
Crude fibre	60.1	54.8	58.9	51.1	63.8	1.7
NDF*	61.2	55.8	60.9	51.9	65.6	1.6
ADF**	56.0	52.3	56.1	48.3	58.4	1.4

*: Neutral Detergent Fibre; **: Acid Detergent Fibre. (Data are based on 41 hays collected from species-rich meadows and pastures located at altitudes between 300 and 2000m above sea level. The samples were cut from mid-June to mid-August at dates considered appropriate in practical farming).

of the main nutrients was generally low and was little affected by cutting date and botanical composition. This very low nutritive value of the hay strongly restricts its use in ruminant rations. These results from the Swiss Federal Research Station for Animal Production in Posieux were not only important for agriculture, they were referred to in discussions with policy makers and nature conservationists. Subsequently, animal nutritionists began to investigate the possibilities of using such herbage in the ration of different productivity categories of ruminants and horses, and came to the conclusion that on an average farm, 10 -15% of the roughage does not need to have quality higher than this hay (Daccord and Jans, personal communication).

SUCCESS AND LIMITATIONS IN INTEGRATING AGRICULTURAL AND NATURE CONSERVATION OBJECTIVES

Experience has shown that it is possible to integrate the objectives of agriculture and nature conservation to a high degree. The objectives can be achieved with different types of grassland. In Table 3, yields and some important characteristics for permanent pastures are summarized. Agricultural value is maximized by intensively managing ryegrass-pastures ; for nature conservation, the diversity of the flora and fauna of the *Mesobromion* and other associations must be accorded a high priority. At most sites the *Mesobromion* are easily intensified; yield can increase from 30 up to 50%, and a higher nutritive value can be achieved in a short time.

The farmer maintaining this type of pasture must consequently forego any possible improvement of his grassland and gives voluntarily higher priority to nature conservation. In extreme cases, the harvested grass can become a side product of the environmental goods produced. This is a change of paradigm in grassland management. However, it will only be viable if the majority of the population is willing to offer farmers an acceptable financial compensation for the loss of revenue resulting form low yields, poor quality and activity in favour of nature conservation. Experience in our country has shown that the cantonal parliaments strongly supported farmers who

100

Table 3. Yield, number of species, and energy content of the hay of different permanent pasture associations (Jeangros and Schmid, 1991).

	Ryegrass pastures	Arrhenatherion (1)	Arrhenatherion (2)	Mesobromion (2)(3)
Intensity of management	very high	intermediate	low	very low
Number of species	≃20	≃30	≃40	≃60
Yield (t DM/ha)	10-13	9-11	5-8	1-3.5
Energy lactation (MJ/kg DM)	6.0	5.2	4.9	4.6

(1)   main species: perennial ryegrass, rough meadow-grass, dandelion, white clover; hay cut at begining of inflorescence emergence of the grass.

(2)   mainly used for hay production; cutting at inflorescence emergence (intermediate intensity) or just after inflorescence emergence (low intensity)

(3)   on dry and infertile soils, no or very moderate fertilization; late hay cut.

contracted to integrate the objectives of nature conservation into their grassland systems. Models from the cantons were then taken over by the federal government. The farmer decides voluntarily. If he is interested in the programme, he has to sign a contract. Such strong public support would not have been achieved without the positive popular response to the cooperation between agriculture and nature conservation. For agriculture it was a new public "good". An integrated grassland system could be developed which strongly influenced the differentiation between very intensive and extensive management of the grassland at the farm level. Management principles were elaborated to help the farmer to continue, where appropriate, an environmentally responsible, very intensive management, or an extensive one, where objectives other than productivity are given higher priority. The Grassland Society worked out guiding principles for the future development of the grassland system with the Federal Research Stations, the agricultural schools and the extension service. The main objective reads as follows:

The Swiss grassland system is aiming at a site specific and environmentally responsible grassland management, which allows a high proportion of the animal production to be produced profitably from the forage grown on the farm.

The recommendations for management have to take into account both edaphic and climatic conditions, floristic make-up, topography and the intended mode of utilization (Dietl, 1987; Thöni et al., 1991). In the uplands and mountainous regions, maps that summarise vegetation types, as well as soil and climatic factors, can be used as tools for diagnosing agricultural grassland and predicting the most probable quantitative and qualitative responses of floristic composition to management decisions. However, these empirical approaches urgently need a scientific background knowledge about the processes leading to such changes. Objectives other than enhancing productivity measured in terms of additional forage, have to be addressed. The range of products that are relevant has increased because the opportunity exists for grassland systems to create a rural environment that does much more than just produce food. Developing an integrated, multipurpose approach, is therefore a tremendous challenge for research at different levels of complexity and development.

CONCLUSIONS

This case-study tried to show that grassland systems can be developed that take agricultural and nature conservation objectives into consideration. This system requires more site-specific variation in the management of permanent grassland. The farmer who voluntarily supports this multipurpose approach must consequently forego any possible improvement of his grassland and give higher priority to nature conservation. He needs a finacial compensation for the environmental goods produced. This proposed integrated approach offers challenges at the scientific, technical and political level and it requires strong cooperation between farmers and nature conservationists.

REFERENCES

BASSETTI P. (1989) *Einfluss der Bewirtschaftung auf die Regeneration von Italienisch Raygrass (Lolium multiflorum Lam.).* [Influence of management on the regeneration of Italian ryegrass]. Ph. D. thesis No 8976, Eidgenössische Technische Hochschule Zürich [Swiss Federal Institute of Technology].

BASSETTI P. and NÖSBERGER J. (1990) Einfluss der Schnittfrequenz und der Stickstoffdüngung auf die reproduktive Selbstverjüngung von *Lolium multiflorum* Lam. [Influence of cutting frequency and nitrogen fertilization on the reproductive regeneration of Italian ryegrass]. *Das wirtschaftseigene Futter*, **35**, 265-277.

DACCORD R. (1990) Nährwert von Heu aus artenreichen Wiesen. [Nutritive value of hay from species-rich pastures]. *Landwirtschaft Schweiz*, **3**, 620-624.

DIETL W. (1987) Standortsgemässe Nutzung von Mähwiesen und Weiden im Berggebiet. [Site-specific management of meadows and pastures in mountainous regions]. *Zeitschrift für Kulturtechnik und Flurbereinigung*, **28**, 329-336.

JEANGROS B. and SCHMID W. (1991) Production et valeur nutritive des prairies permanentes riches en espèces. [Production and nutritive value of species-rich permanent pastures]. *Fourrages*, **126**, 131-136.

LEHMANN J. and MEISTER E. (1985) Advantages and management of grass-legume associations in forage production. *Proceedings of the 15th International Grassland Congress*, pp 582-584.

LEHMANN J., ROSENBERG E., BASSETTI P., and MOSIMANN E. (1992) Standardmischungen für den Futterbau. [Standard seed mixtures for leys]. *Landwirtschaft Schweiz*, **5**, 389-400.

SCHMID W. and JEANGROS B. (1990) Artenreiche Wiesen der Schweiz und ihr Ertrag. [Yield of species-rich permanent pastures in Switzerland]. *Landwirtschaft Schweiz*, **3**, 610-619.

THOMET P. (1980) *Die Pflanzengesellschaften der Schweizer Juraweiden und ihre Beziehung zur Bewirtschaftungsintensität.* [Plant associations of the Swiss Jura and their relationship to the management intensity]. Ph. D. thesis No 6629, Eidgenössische Technische Hochschule Zürich.

THÖNI E., JEANGROS B. et AMAUDRUZ M. (1991) Recommandations pour la fumure des prairies et des pâturages. [Recommendations for the fertilization of meadows and permanent pastures]. *Revue suisse d'Agriculture*, **23**, 91-98.

THÖNI E. and SCHÜPBACH H. (1988) *Futterbau und Futterkonservierung.* [Forage production and forage conservation]. Landwirtschaftliche Lehrmittelzentrale Zollikofen.

WILDA CH. (1992) *Die Entwicklung von Jungpflanzen von Italienisch-Raigras (Lolium multiflorum Lam.) in intensiv bewirtschafteten Grasbeständen.* [The development of seedlings from Italian ryegrass in intensively managed swards]. Ph. D. thesis No 9726, Eidgenössische Technische Hochschule Zürich.

Wildflowers in Grassland Systems

J. FRAME, G.E.J. FISHER[1] AND G.E.D. TILEY[1]

13 St Vincent Crescent, Alloway AYR KA7 4QW

[1]Scottish Agricultural College, Auchincruive AYR KA6 5HW

ABSTRACT

Herbage production from commercial wildflower mixtures differed markedly with both hay and silage cutting regimes; mixtures containing white and/or red clover were most productive and had highest mineral concentrations. Several wildflower species did not establish or were of poor persistence, indicating the need for less complex, locally adapted mixtures. In experimental mixtures, wildflower herbage production was best with the non-competitive grasses such as crested dogstail, sweet vernal, meadow fescue and timothy. Nitrogen and mineral concentrations were usually higher in wildflowers than grasses but organic matter digestibilities were lower. Overall, the most persistent and productive wildflowers were chicory, ox-eye daisy, ribwort, yarrow, kidney vetch and knapweed. In a field-scale low-input system, wildflower contents were maintained under one-cut and two-cut regimes but were reduced by winter applications of cattle slurry. Supplementation with a high protein/high energy concentrate was necessary to ensure adequate liveweight gains by dairy youngstock fed on hay or silage. It is concluded that viable animal production systems are attainable from extensively managed wildflower swards; however, further research, including whole ecosystem studies, is required to ascertain the effects of selective grazing on species persistence and the value of such swards as wildlife habitats.

INTRODUCTION

The sowing of wildflowers to increase species diversity in grassland is a recent development aimed at counterbalancing the devastating loss of semi-natural species-rich grassland which has occurred during the last 50 years in Britain due to the intensification of agriculture (Wells *et al.*, 1989). Estimates of the loss of wildflower-rich grassland habitat vary from 50 to 99% (Nature Conservancy Council, 1984; Wells *et al.*, 1989). The most serious losses have occurred in the lowland "neutral" grasslands. These have been most susceptible to agricultural intensification by drainage, reseeding, use of fertilisers and herbicides, change from hay to silage, and much increased stocking densities which have replaced the practices of annual hay cropping and little manuring.

Recent changes in agricultural policy have moved away from a production-orientated direction towards encouraging countryside amenity and wildlife conservation. Measures include the creation of Environmentally Sensitive Areas (ESAs), with financial help for specific conservation work, Extensification Schemes, with compensation for loss of income due to destocking, and new agro-environmental initiatives.

The creation of local and National Nature Reserves (Nature Conservancy Council, 1984) has ensured the protection of the most important examples of old semi-natural grassland. The notification of additional areas of high conservation interest as sites of special scientific interest (SSSIs) increased the area of protected grassland. However, the total area of protected grassland habitat is only a tiny fraction of the total grassland area in Britain.

An opportunity to promote the re-introduction of broad-leaved wildflowers exists in some areas of agricultural grassland to increase plant diversity which in turn will support a wider range of insects and other wildlife. This is being encouraged by recent trends in Government policy. Species-rich grasslands require lower fertility and are inherently less productive and some form of commercially acceptable support is necessary to encourage their establishment (Green, 1990).

From 1987 at The Scottish Agricultural College (SAC), a series of experiments on wildflower swards explored the concept of combining floral diversity and agricultural management at nil to moderate inputs of plant nutrients, whether inorganic or organic. As well as using a range of cutting regimes to simulate practical methods of utilization, wildflower productivity and persistence were also assessed on a field-scale, low-input system of grazing and conservation for dairy youngstock. Progress reports on aspects of the work, which was undertaken on agriculturally productive soils at SAC Auchincruive and Crichton Royal Farms, have been reported, for example, see Frame and Tiley (1990), Tiley and Frame (1990) and Fisher and Roberts (1992).

In the work described below the term *wildflower* embraces broad-leaved species other than red and white clover which can be added to grassland to increase species diversity, though excluding competitive weed species such as docks (*Rumex* spp.) or chickweed (*Stellaria media*). Some authors use the American term *forb* to include any non-grass species. Within the group of wildflower species are forage herbs such as ribwort (*Plantago lanceolata*) or yarrow (*Achillea millefolium*) which have often been added to grass seed mixtures to provide leafy, mineral-rich herbage (Foster, 1988).

GENERAL MATERIALS AND METHODS

The agronomic experiments, normally lasting three harvest years, were established at Auchincruive on a sandy loam soil classed as freely to imperfectly-drained and with pH maintained at *circa* 6.0. Soil analyses taken regularly are used to maintain soil P, K and Mg status at adequate levels for productive agriculture. Experimental plots, 5 × 1.5 m, were established by sowing seed without a cover crop using an Øyjord drill. Normally a replicated randomized-block statistical design was used. Whole plots were harvested with a Haldrup plot harvester leaving a stubble height of *circa* 30mm. Grazing, silage or hay managements were simulated by varying the number of cuts during the growing season; for example, a silage system comprised cuts in early June, mid July, late August and mid October. Botanical estimates of complex mixtures were made by visual scoring and point quadrat analyses, but components of simple mixtures were determined by hand separation. Total herbage and in some cases, constituent components, were analysed for dry matter (DM) content and for one or more of the following parameters: *in vitro* organic matter digestibility (OMD), N and mineral concentrations (P, K, Ca, Mg, Na).

The low-input system work was undertaken at Crichton Royal Farm, Dumfries on a soil classed as a medium loam overlying clay, and with soil fertility previously maintained at adequate levels for intensive dairy farming. The seeds were sown with a farm seed drill and subsequent hay or silage harvesting and handling operations carried out with typical farm-scale equipment. No inorganic fertiliser was applied. British Holstein/Friesian dairy replacement heifers were used for grazing and feeding investigations.

COMMERCIAL WILDFLOWER MIXTURES

With the objective of measuring the performance and persistency of individual constituents, 10 mixtures, listed A-J, from two commercial seed firms (British Seed Houses Ltd and W.W. Johnson and Son Ltd) were monitored under both hay and silage cutting regimes. Except for A and B, all mixtures contained secondary or amenity grasses, e.g. red fescue (*Festuca rubra* ssp. *rubra*), golden oat-grass (*Trisetum flavescens*). The content of wildflowers ranged from 8 to 20, forage legumes 1 to 7 and grasses 0 to 9 species. Inorganic fertiliser providing 25, 50 and 50 kg/ha N, P_2O_5 and K_2O, respectively, were applied each year in March and again after the July cuts.

Under hay management, annual DM production differed significantly (P<0.001) among mixtures each year. Table 1 illustrates second harvest year data. Mean 3-year DM production varied between 7.6 and 11.0 t/ha with 60% of production at the main

Table 1. Annual and main hay cut DM production and OMD values for harvest year 2 from commercial wildflower mixtures.

Mixture	DM (t/ha)		OMD	
	Annual	Hay cut	Annual	Hay cut
A	11.4	7.7	61.2	58.1
B	9.3	7.1	58.5	55.9
C	11.1	7.4	61.8	57.9
D	8.2	5.6	59.6	55.4
E	7.3	5.4	57.8	54.9
F	6.4	4.2	61.5	57.3
G	10.2	6.1	63.3	57.9
H	7.0	5.5	56.5	53.6
I	7.0	5.2	58.9	56.0
J	6.9	5.2	58.4	55.0
Mean	8.5	5.9	59.7	56.2
SED±	0.49	0.39	0.008	0.010
Signif.	***	***	***	***

Table 2. Total silage DM production, N and mineral concentrations for harvest year 3 from commercial wildflower mixtures.

Mixture	DM (t/ha)	N and minerals (g/kg DM)					
		N	P	K	Ca	Mg	Na
A	9.2	28	3.9	25	15	3.3	3.7
B	8.7	30	3.9	29	13	3.8	2.7
C	9.3	29	3.8	25	12	2.8	4.3
D	8.7	28	3.5	22	11	2.9	2.8
E	8.6	28	3.6	24	12	2.7	2.4
F	8.7	30	3.7	22	12	2.7	3.0
G	9.9	27	3.3	25	11	2.8	3.1
H	8.9	27	3.8	26	13	2.6	3.1
I	9.6	26	3.6	23	12	2.5	3.3
J	9.0	26	3.6	26	13	2.7	3.3
Mean	9.1	28	3.7	25	12	2.7	3.3
SED±	0.85	1.2	0.10	1.2	0.7	0.16	0.44
Signif.	NS	*	***	***	***	***	*

hay cut in mid July. Annual OMD values also differed significantly ($P<0.001$) each year with 3-year values ranging from 62.4 to 66.9, and main hay cut values, 58.3 to 61.8; the highest values were associated with the most productive mixtures, which contained white clover (*Trifolium repens*) and/or red clover (*Trifolium pratense*).

When cut under a silage regime, DM production from the mixtures differed significantly ($P<0.001$) in harvest years 1 and 2 but not 3. Table 2 illustrates third year data. Mean 3-year DM production ranged from 7.5 to 10.8 t/ha with 55% of production at the main silage cut in early June. In years 1 and 3 when N and mineral concentrations were determined in the herbage, the highest annual concentrations, excepting K and Na, were associated with the most productive mixtures; differences were significant mainly at the $P<0.001$ level except for N and Na in year 3 (see Table 2).

Many wildflower constituents failed to establish while others lacked persistence. Ribwort, yarrow, ox-eye daisy (*Leucanthemum vulgare*), autumn hawkbit (*Leontodon autumnalis*) cat's ear (*Hypochoeris radicata*) and sorrel (*Rumex acetosa*) were the most abundant wildflowers. White clover thrived throughout the course of the experiment while red clover was prominent in harvest years 1 and 2. The most persistent grasses were bents (*Agrostis* spp.) and fescues (*Festuca* spp.).

BINARY WILDFLOWER/GRASS MIXTURES

To evaluate their performance and persistency with different companion grasses of differing competitive ability, 9 wildflowers, with red clover for comparison, were sown in binary mixtures with each of three grass species: crested dogstail (*Cynosurus cristatus*), meadow fescue (*Festuca pratensis*) and perennial ryegrass (*Lolium perenne*). Fertiliser applications totalled 150, 45 and 90 kg/ha N, P2O5 and K2O, respectively, in harvest year 1 (6-cut system) and half these rates in year 2 (3-cut system) applied as aliquot dressings per cut, and nil fertilization in year 3 (3-cut system).

The most persistent and productive wildflowers were chicory (*Cichorium intybus*), ribwort, ox-eye daisy and to a lesser extent burnet (*Poterium sanguisorba*) and yarrow. Wild carrot (*Daucus carota*), sheep's parsley (*Petroselinum crispum*), caraway (*Carum carvi*) and self-heal (*Prunella vulgaris*) all persisted poorly. Wildflower performance was best with non-competitive crested dogstail and meadow fescue companions. Nitrogen and mineral concentrations were usually higher in the wildflowers than in the grasses but OMD values were usually lower. Table 3 illustrates data from the first harvest year.

Table 3. Mean annual DM production, OMD, N and mineral concentrations of wildflower and grass fractions of sown binary mixtures in harvest year 1.

Species	DM (t/ha)	OMD	N and minerals (g/kg DM)				
			N	P	K	Ca	Mg
Red clover	6.8	70.5	35	3.0	26	15	3.8
Ribwort	6.0	71.3	20	3.5	23	26	1.9
Chicory	4.6	73.0	23	4.2	51	16	2.7
Ox-eye daisy	2.7	69.8	22	4.3	44	13	2.4
Wild carrot	1.7	78.0	20	3.6	41	19	3.0
Burnet	0.9	60.5	20	3.2	18	18	4.7
Yarrow	0.7	68.3	27	4.3	43	12	2.2
Caraway	0.6	79.6	23	5.8	50	14	3.2
Sheep's parsley	0.1	75.0	21	5.4	35	19	3.8
Self-heal	0.1	75.0	19	5.4	40	12	5.4
Perennial ryegrass	8.1	83.7	15	2.9	25	4	1.4
Meadow fescue	6.5	81.1	16	2.9	25	4	1.3
Crested dogstail	5.1	76.1	17	2.9	25	3	1.5

SIMPLE WILDFLOWER/GRASS MIXTURES

Seventeen species, including red and white clovers for comparison, were each sown in mixture with a common blend of meadow fescue and red fescue to assess productivity and nutritive value. A hay cutting regime was imposed and no fertiliser was applied to the plots.

The wildflowers made a substantial contribution to herbage production and for example, in the second harvest year, comprised between 26% and 70% of the annual DM output; the ranking order was birdsfoot trefoil (*Lotus corniculatus*), ribwort, ox-eye daisy, knapweed (*Centaurea nigra*), dandelion (*Taraxacum officinale*), thyme (*Thymus serpyllum*), tufted vetch (*Vicia cracca*), field scabious (*Knautia arvensis*), kidney vetch (*Anthyllis vulneraria*), chicory, yarrow, burnet, autumn hawkbit, ragged robin (*Lychnis flos-cuculi*), red campion (*Lychnis dioica*). Nutritive value data were similar to those in the previous experiment.

WILDFLOWER BLEND/COMPANION GRASS MIXTURES

With the objective of evaluating the suitability of grass species for sowing in mixture with wildflowers, 10 seed mixtures, each with a single grass species and a common blend of wildflowers (the same 15 species as used in the previous experiment) were monitored under an annual cutting regime simulating early bite, late hay and aftermath grazing. No fertilization was applied.

Differences among mixtures in the parameters of annual total herbage, grass or wildflower DM were not significant in either harvest year 1 or 2. Figure 1 illustrates the grass and wildflower DM production data and second year results point to sweet vernal, crested dogstail, meadow fescue, timothy and rough-stalked meadow grass as providing a balance between total production and wildflower content. The OMD of

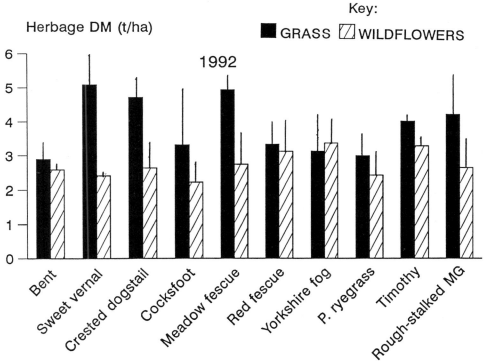

Fig. 1. Annual DM production from components of the wildflower blend/companion grass mixtures in harvest year 2 (bars indicate SEs).

the mixtures in year 2 ranged from 56.0 (with perennial ryegrass) to 61.9 (with York-shire fog). These relatively low values reflect the late cut (20 July).

DEFOLIATION MANAGEMENT REGIMES

This experiment examined the effect on a wildflower/grass mixture of 16 differing de-foliation regimes. The mixture comprised 12 wildflower species and 5 grass species. No fertiliser was applied. The basic defoliation regime of 6 cuts to simulate grazing (G) was compared with regimes within which silage (S) or hay (H) cuts were inter-posed at different times during the season by extending the growth period to encom-pass the equivalent of two 'grazing' defoliations for silage and three for hay (see Table 4). The imposition of conservation cuts, particularly when there was a silage and a hay cut increased total herbage and wildflower production but not always grass produc-tion. A late hay cut following an early defoliation markedly improved wildflower pro-duction compared with the regime where early defoliation was omitted (G--HGG vs --HGGG). Differences between defoliation regimes were significant for wildflower and total herbage in both harvest years but not for the grass fraction. Table 4 shows the production performance from a selection of the defoliation regimes in harvest year 2.

Table 4. Herbage DM production from differing defoliation in harvest year 2.

Defoliation system§	DM (t/ha)			
	Wildflowers	Grasses	Others	Total
G G G G G G	2.3	1.5	0.0	3.8
G G − S G G	2.9	1.5	0.1	4.5
− S G G G G	3.0	1.5	0.5	4.9
G − S − S G	3.5	1.2	0.1	4.8
− S − S G G	4.4	1.6	0.0	6.0
G G − S − S	3.9	1.3	0.0	5.2
− S − S − S	4.1	2.0	0.1	6.2
− S − − H G	6.0	1.5	0.0	7.5
G − − H G G	4.8	1.1	0.1	6.0
− − H G G G	2.4	2.0	0.0	4.4
Mean	3.7	1.5	0.1	5.3
SED±	1.55	0.31	-	1.32
Signif.	**	NS	-	**

§ G= simulated grazing; S = silage cut; H = hay cut

FIELD-SCALE SYSTEMS DEVELOPMENT

The objective was to evaluate the performance of wildflower swards under commercial conditions including grazing and conservation without inorganic fertiliser. Swards were established by ploughing and reseeding, or existing swards were direct drilled

WITHOUT SLURRY

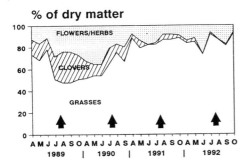

WITH SLURRY

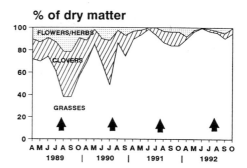

ONE-CUT SYSTEM

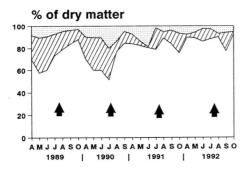

TWO-CUT SYSTEM

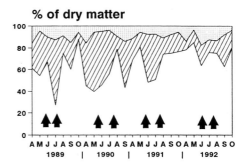

C,G

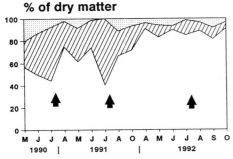

G,C,G

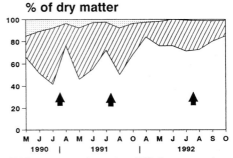

Fig. 2. Gross botanical composition of herbage from wildflower swards under differing extensive management systems. (Arrows indicate timing of cuts for conservation).

with a wildflower mixture. The basic mixture used was based on 12 wildflowers, 2 clovers and 5 grasses. Conservation was partly by big bale silage and partly by hay. Experiments investigated the effects of (a) cattle slurry application in late winter, providing 100 kg/ha available N, (b) a one-cut versus two-cut system of conservation and (c) early grazing at a high stocking rate (6.4 L.U./ha) as a precursor to conservation.

Figure 2 illustrates botanical composition data from samples taken by cutting to ground level monthly over a 4-year period. Slurry application reduced wildflower content although total herbage production was increased; clover content, and consequently N concentration, were enhanced. Cutting system did not affect herbage production and both systems maintained wildflower content; however, content of clovers was improved by the two-cut system, mainly white clover in the later years rather than red clover. Early grazing reduced the grass fraction but the main beneficiaries were the clovers rather than wildflower components (Figure 2). Detailed botanical data are given by Fisher *et al.* (1993).

At Crichton Royal Farm, the daily liveweight gain target for dairy heifers is 0.6 to 0.7 kg/head in order to achieve first calving at 24-30 months. This was achieved (0.82 to 1.15 kg/head) at grazing without supplementation but a high energy/high protein concentrate was required to supplement the silage or hay fed during winter, this being a reflection of the low feed quality associated with late cutting (Fisher and Roberts, 1993; Isselstein, 1993).

CONCLUSIONS

The small-plot agronomic experiments demonstrated that many species of wildflower had considerable agricultural potential although current commercial mixtures are too complex and lack seed purity and germination guarantees. The use of simpler mixtures with species adapted to local conditions would be a better option. Vigorous development of clovers featured in some mixtures, probably to the detriment of wildflower content, but wildflowers made an important contribution to production and species diversity. This was in accord with New Zealand work in which mixtures were maintained under sheep grazing (Ruz-Jerez *et al.*, 1991); nevertheless, the role of clovers requires further appraisal. Results of small-plot work also indicated the superior N and mineral contents of many of the wildflowers, compared with grass. With non-competitive grasses, mixtures also provided a favourable balance of herbage production and persistence of wildflowers. As judged by performance, the wildflower swards showed resilience to a wide range of defoliation regimes, although production from and persistence of wildflowers was highest with infrequent cutting. This was in agreement with the findings of other small-plot work (Frame and Tiley, 1993).

Field-scale work confirmed that extensively managed wildflower swards were suitable for animal production systems - in this case dairy heifer rearing - but their potential for other enterprises requires assessment. The use of slurry applications to increase herbage production was detrimental to the persistence and abundance of wildflowers in sown pastures, although a two-cut regime did not reduce the diversity and abundance of wildflowers compared with a one-cut system. Applying a high stocking rate in spring to reduce the competitive ability of grasses on a fertile soil allowed increased development of clovers, but not wildflowers.

Further research is needed to ascertain the effect of selective grazing by differing animal species on wildflower persistence and the value of the swards as wildlife habitats, including, for example, the diversity of resident invertebrate species. Study of the whole ecosystem is necessary if the value of habitat creation and wildlife conservation is to be properly evaluated.

Also, acceptability and intake characteristics of wildflowers require measurement. For example, Derrick *et al.* (1993) found that the voluntary intake of ribwort plantain and dandelion (and some weed species) by sheep, was higher than might have been predicted from their digestibility.

REFERENCES
DERRICK R.W., MOSELEY G. and WILMAN D. (1993) Intake, by sheep, and digestibility of chickweed, dandelion, dock, ribwort and spurrey, compared with perennial ryegrass. *Journal of Agricultural Science, Cambridge*, **120**, 51-61.

FISHER G.E.J., BAKER L.J. and ROBERTSON D.A. (1993) Effects of seeds mixtures, cutting/grazing management and slurry application on herbage yield and the occurrence of species in sown extensive pastures. In: Haggar, R.J. and Peel, S. (eds) *Occasional Symposium of The British Grassland Society*, No. 28, pp. (in press).

FISHER G.E.J. and ROBERTS D.J. (1992) Management of extensive grasslands containing wildflowers and herbs. *Proceedings of the 14th General Meeting of the European Grassland Federation*, Lahti, Finland, pp. 307-311.

FISHER G.E.J. and ROBERTS D.J. (1993) The management of extensive pastures for dairy youngstock. *Proceedings of the XVII International Grassland Congress, Palmerston North*, New Zealand/Rockhampton, Australia (in press).

FOSTER L. (1988) Herbs in pastures. Development and research in Britain, 1850-1984. *Biological Agriculture and Horticulture*, 5, 97-133.

FRAME J. and TILEY G.E.D. (1990) Herbage productivity of a range of wildflower mixtures under two management systems. *Proceedings of the 13th General Meeting of the European Grassland Federation*, Banská Bystrica, Czechoslovakia, Volume II, pp. 359-363.

FRAME J. and TILEY G.E.D. (1993) The performance of wildflower mixtures with grass under hay and silage cutting managements. *Proceedings of the XVII International Grassland Congress*, Palmerston North, New Zealand/Rockhampton, Australia (in press).

GREEN B.H. (1990) Agricultural extensification and amenity in British grasslands: a review of historical change and assessment of future prospects. *Grass and Forage Science*, **45**, 365-372.

ISSELSTEIN J. (1993) Forage nutritive value and ensilability of some common grassland herbs. *Proceedings of the XVII International Grassland Congress*, Palmerston North, New Zealand/Rockhampton, Australia (in press).

113

NATURE CONSERVANCY COUNCIL (1984) *Nature Conservation in Great Britain.* Edinburgh: Nature Conservancy Council.

RUZ-JEREZ B.E., BALL P.R., WHITE R.E. and GREGG P.E.H. (1991) Comparison of a herbal ley with a ryegrass-white clover pasture and pure ryegrass sward receiving fertiliser nitrogen. *Proceedings of the New Zealand Grassland Association*, **54**, 23-26.

TILEY G.E.D. and FRAME J. (1990) An agronomic evaluation of forage herbs in grassland. *Proceedings of the 13th General Meeting of the European Grassland Federation*, Banská Bystrica, Czechoslovakia, Volume II, pp. 163-166.

WELLS T.C.E., COX R. and FROST A. (1989) The establishment and management of wildflower meadows. *Focus on Nature Conservation*, No. 21. Shrewsbury: Nature Conservancy Council.

Nature Management in Dutch grasslands

J.P.BAKKER

Laboratory of Plant Ecology, University of Groningen
PO Box 14, 9750 AA Haren, The Netherlands

ABSTRACT

As long as nutrient inputs in agriculture are relatively low, the best nature management is to continue former agricultural practices once such grassland has become a nature reserve (i.e. maintenance management). The recent high input of nutrients in agriculture has forced authorities in charge of nature management to introduce grazing or hay-making without the application of fertilisers (i.e. restoration management). This type of management directly affects canopy structure in the short-term and, indirectly, nutrient availability in the long-term, with varying effects on plants and meadow birds. It is, however, the only nature management practice compatible with agricultural practices involved with milk production. Management aiming at affecting the substrate by direct reduction of nutrient availability though the removal of the topsoil is becoming increasingly popular. The most effective and sustainable management in the long-term involves regulation of hydrological processes, since these indirectly govern nutrient availability. Changing hydrological processes involves perspectives from nature management of converting semi-natural replacement communities towards the development of natural communities.

INTRODUCTION

The general aim of nature management can be formulated as the maintenance or creation of conditions for the occurrence of as many kinds of organism as possible. Many endangered grassland plant species grow under mesotrophic or oligotrophic conditions. Hence nature management objectives of grassland systems often aim at such conditions. Mesotrophic and oligotrophic conditions have been the result of agricultural practices until the introduction of artificial fertilisers. As long as the nutrient input in agriculture was relatively low, the best nature management was to continue former agricultural practices once such grassland had become a nature reserve. We refer to that as maintenance management.

Maintenance management is not sufficient once grasslands have had fertilisers applied. Such grasslands need management practices which aim at the reduction of nutrient availability. Such nature management is referred to as restoration management. It is obvious that the first action is the cessation of fertiliser application. Some results of subsequent restoration management on wet and dry soils will be presented. The successes and limitations, and the changes in thinking about the scale of restoration management, will feature as major topics.

115

RESTORATION MANAGEMENT BY AFFECTING THE VEGETATION

Hay-making on dry sandy soils, with hydrological conditions featuring infiltration, results in a decrease of above-ground standing crop. Species replacement involves a decrease of species indicating eutrophic soil conditions, namely *Lolium perenne*, *Rumex obtusifolius* and *Anthriscus sylvestris*, and an increase of species indicating mesotrophic soil conditions, namely *Agrostis capillaris* and *Festuca rubra* (Table 1). On moist peaty

Table 1. Dynamics of species replacement on dry sandy soil cut for hay in July and receiving no fertiliser application after 1972. Percentage cover of characteristic species.

	1972	1974	1976	1978	1980	1982	1984	1986	1988	1990	1992
Bromus hordeaceus	40	4	1	1	-	-	4	-	1	-	-
Glechoma hederacea	10	4	2	4	4	4	1	1	1	1	-
Poa pratensis	10	4	1	1	1	2	1	1	2	1	-
Rumex obtusifolius	-	10	4	20	20	12	4	4	1	-	-
Dactylis glomerata	-	4	1	4	12	30	20	10	2	1	-
Anthriscus sylvestris	-	1	-	-	2	2	4	2	1	1	1
Festuca rubra	-	4	2	4	1	12	40	20	50	30	40
Agrostis capillaris	-	-	-	1	1	1	4	20	20	12	10
Anthoxanthum odoratum	-	-	-	1	-	-	1	1	1	1	2

Table 2. Dynamics of species replacement on moist peaty soil with calcium-poor seepage cut for hay in July and receiving no fertiliser application after 1972. Percentage cover of characteristic species.

	1972	1974	1976	1978	1980	1982	1984	1986	1988	1990	1992
Alopecurus geniculatus	10	4	1	10	1	1	1	-	-	-	
Festuca pratensis	40	4	4	2	2	1	1	1	2	2	2
Anthoxanthum odoratum	-	2	1	1	8	2	8	10	1	12	4
Festuca rubra	-	-	-	1	1	1	1	1	8	12	1
Juncus effusus	-	-	-	1	1	-	1	1	4	8	10
Rhinanthus angustifolius	-	-	1	-	20	20	2	1	1	-	1
Juncus acutiflorus	-	-	-	-	-	-	1	1	1	1	1
Leontodon autumnalis	-	-	-	-	-	-	1	1	1	1	2
Caltha palustris	-	-	-	-	-	-	-	1	1	1	2
Lotus uliginosus	-	-	-	-	-	-	-	1	-	1	1

soils, with hydrological conditions featuring superficially seepage water, the above-ground standing crop also decreases, but not as a result of the appearance of *Juncus acutiflorus* (Bakker,1991). Species replacement involves a decrease of species indicating eutrophic soil conditions, namely *Alopecurus geniculatus*, and an increase of species indicating mesotrophic soil conditions, namely *Rhinanthus angustifolius* and *Anthoxanthum odoratum* (Table 2). On wet peaty soils with hydrological conditions featuring deep seepage water, species replacement again involves a decrease of species indicating eutrophic soil conditions, namely *Glyceria maxima* and *Poa trivialis*, and an increase of species indicating mesotrophic soil conditions, namely *Caltha palustris* and *Crepis paludosa* (Table 3).

Table 3. Wet peaty soil with calcium-rich seepage: Dynamics of species replacement on a sward cut for hay in July and receiving no fertiliser after 1972. Percentage cover of characteristic species.

	1972	1974	1976	1978	1980	1982	1984	1986	1988	1990	1992
Glyceria maxima	40	10	-	1	-	-	-	-	-	-	-
Poa trivialis	10	4	1	10	2	2	2	1	1	2	1
Carex acutiformis	10	10	20	20	20	20	30	30	20	20	20
Crepis paludosa	1	4	10	10	12	12	30	12	30	12	40
Caltha palustris	1	-	-	-	-	4	4	12	8	10	10
Ajuga reptans	-	2	1	1	2	2	2	1	-	-	1
Cirsium palustre	-	-	1	-	1	-	-	1	-	1	1
Rhinanthus angustifolius	-	-	-	8	2	2	1	1	-	1	1
Lotus uliginosus	-	-	-	-	8	12	4	1	2	2	2

In these three examples, hay-making proves successful. This can be attributed to the removal of nutrients in the hay. The timing of hay-making can be important. Cutting in late autumn results in a dominance of *Brachypodium pinnatum* in chalk grasslands and a subsequent decrease of characteristic species. The problem is solved by cutting in late summer, at the time when *Brachypodium* has not yet started to re-allocate nutrients to below-ground storage organs. By this re-allocation the nutrient input from atmospheric deposition is monopolized by *Brachypodium* (Bobbink and Willems, 1987). So hay-making is only effective if the removal of nutrients is higher than the amount of nutrients resulting from atmospheric deposition. It may, therefore, be impossible to reach oligotrophic conditions with low production by just hay-making. Affecting the substrate is more appropriate then, as will be outlined below.

Hay-making has, however, more limitations especially in moist and wet sites. Some examples are: (i) the shift of a community with *Caltha palustris* towards a stand dominated by *Holcus lanatus* and *Rumex acetosa*, and a large increase in above-ground standing crop, (ii) despite a low standing crop a curtailment of the species replacement at a stage with *Festuca rubra* and *Agrostis capillaris*, and (iii) the shift of a community with *Caltha palustris* towards a community with *Juncus acutiflorus*. The apparent limitations of hay-making will be discussed in connection with resoration management affecting hydrological processes.

Cattle and sheep-grazing on dry sandy soils with infiltration results in a species replacement similar to that of hay-making. Some differences are, however, found. Grazing creates patterns of lightly grazed patches with a tall canopy alternating with heavily grazed patches with a short canopy. In the latter patches rosette plants like *Hypochaeris radicata* and *Leontodon autumnalis* increase quicker than under hay-making. Although nutrient cycling is faster under heavy grazing than under hay-making, the rosette plant species indicating mesotrophic soil conditions may spread as a result of lack of competition for light on the heavily grazed sites. Wet peaty soils with deep seepage are rarely grazed since the herbivores prefer drier sites within the fenced area. Species replacement involves a decrease of characteristic species, namely *Caltha palustris* and *Crepis paludosa*, and an increase of tall plants, namely *Carex acutiformis* and *Glyceria maxima* (Table 4). Here, grazing seems successful in dry sites until mesotrophic conditions prevail,and certainly not in wet sites. These limitations will be discussed in connection with restoration management affecting hydrological processes.

Table 4. Wet peaty soul, calcium-rich: Dynamics of species replacement of a grazed sward receiving no fertiliser after 1971. Percentage cover of characteristic species.

	1978	1980	1982	1984	1986	1988	1990	1992
Bromus racemosus	1	1	-	-	-	-	-	-
Crepis paludosa	1	1	-	-	-	-	-	-
Ajuga reptans	2	2	-	-	-	-	-	-
Myosotis palustris	1	2	1	-	1	-	1	-
Caltha palustris	1	2	1	4	1	-	-	-
Lychnis flos-cuculi	1	1	1	-	1	-	-	-
Carex acutiformis	2	8	30	30	30	40	20	10
Filipendula ulmaria	-	1	1	1	1	8	2	-
Glyceria maxima	-	-	-	4	10	30	50	50
Mentha aquatica	-	-	-	1	1	2	4	8

RESTORATION MANAGEMENT BY AFFECTING THE SUBSTRATE

In dry sandy areas, on heathland which has been deep ploughed and supplied with fertilisers for the last century, restoration management, by hay-making and grazing do not prove successful achieving oligotrophic soil conditions. The removal of the topsoil (5-10cm) results in species replacement involving a decrease of species indicating eutrophic soil conditions and an increase of species indicating mesotrophic and oligotrophic soil conditions, namely *Erica tetralix*, *Calluna vulgaris* and *Juncus squarrosus* (Table 5). Although nutrients are removed with the topsoil, the appearance of species indicating oligotrophic soil conditions largely depends on their presence in the seed bank. The longer ago the reclamation from heathland took place, the poorer the soil seed bank reflects the former plant community (Stieperaere and Timmerman, 1983). In that case the species indicating oligotrophic soil conditions have to spread from

118

Table 5. Dynamics of species replacement on dry sandy soil after sod removal cut for hay in July and receiving no fertiliser application after 1971. Percentage cover of characteristic species.

	1974	1976	1978	1980	1982	1984	1986	1988
Bellis perennis	4	10	1	-	-	-	-	-
Trifolium repens	10	10	1	-	-	-	-	-
Sagina procumbens	2	4	1	-	-	-	-	-
Agrostis capillaris	10	4	20	20	4	4	8	12
Hypochaeris radicata	4	2	8	12	8	12	4	2
Calluna vulgaris	2	2	4	12	10	20	20	20
Erica tetralix	2	2	2	8	4	4	2	2
Juncus squarrosus	-	1	1	1	1	2	1	1
Juncus conglomeratus	-	-	1	1	-	1	-	-
Luzula campestris	-	-	-	1	1	1	1	-

elsewhere and seed dispersal might be a limiting factor for their establishment. The removal of the topsoil leaves the major part of the nutrient pool of the former agricultural layer untouched. Moreover, there is an input of nutrients from atmospheric deposition. One might fear, therefore, that it is still difficult to reach oligotrophic soil conditions. Restoration management is going on now in which the complete former agricultural layer including all organic material, often 50cm thick, was removed. It implies that not only all nutrients are removed but also the complete soil seed bank. When the seed bank still contains species indicating oligotrophic soil conditions an optimum may be searched for between the removal of nutrients and the maintenance of the soil seed bank. If there is no opportunity to dispose of the removed former agricultural layer the soil might be re-ploughed deeply. Oligotrophic soil is thereby brought to the surface and species indicating oligotrophic soil conditions present in the seed bank will appear in the developing plant community (Table 6).

In summary, affecting the substrate by removal of nutrients is successful on sandy soils in creating oligotrophic soil conditions, but may also remove the soil seed bank. Removal of the topsoil in peaty soils has not yet been practiced. It has been discussed recently in connection with restoration management affecting hydrological processes.

RESTORATION MANAGEMENT BY AFFECTING HYDROLOGICAL PROCESSES

Continuous flow of seepage water has resulted in high groundwater tables and hence caused the development of marsh vegetation on peat soil in brookvalley systems. Depending on the composition of the groundwater, different plant communities have established under hay-making regimes in the past. Sites fed by deep calcium-rich seepage water feature communities with Caltha palustris, whereas Juncus acutiflorus is a characteristic species in sites fed by superficial calcium-poor seepage water (Grootjans, 1980).

Table 6. Dry sandy soil after deep-ploughing to 60 cm: Dynamics of species replacement of a sward cut for hay in July and receiving no fertiliser after 1971. Percentage cover of characteristic species.

	1979	1981	1983	1985	1987	1989
Bellis perennis	-	1	1	-	-	-
Plantago major	-	1	1	-	-	-
Agrostis capillaris	4	1	30	40	40	30
Hypochaeris radicata	1	4	4	4	4	4
Calluna vulgaris	1	2	8	8	12	8
Erica tetralix	1	2	2	2	2	8
Juncus squarrosus	-	1	1	1	1	1
Juncus conglomeratus	-	1	1	1	1	4
Luzula campestris	-	-	-	-	-	1

In the aforementioned examples, restoration management by grazing or hay-making was not successful because of limitations in the framework of groundwater table and groundwater composition. Deep drainage ditches are a common feature of conventional agriculture. These ditches are maintained after an area has become a nature reserve, to aid drainage of the agricultural hinterland outside the reserve. This practice is enforced by the authorities in charge of the water management. It now appears that the continued development of marsh vegetation has therefore been interrupted, depending on the particular local situation in such a brookvalley system.

The development of a community dominated by *Glyceria maxima* and *Carex Acutiformis* cannot only be attributed to a lack of grazing. The establishment of a tall forb community is greatly stimulated by the drainage ditches which are still functioning. The drainage leads to superficial decomposition of the peat which in turn results in an increase in available nitrogen. During the growing season the mineralization can rise to levels higher than 100 kg N/ha.

The increase of the above-ground standing crop from 3 to 6 t DM/ha, and the development of a stand dominated by *Holcus lanatus* and *Rumex acetosa*, occurred on a site where the groundwater table dropped ca. 100cm. The mineralization of the topsoil amounted to 400 kg N/ha/yr. Even nitrophilous plant species like *Cirsium arvense*, *Urtica dioica*, *Anthriscus sylvestris* and *Stellaria media* apppeared. These changes took place in the first years after the drainage had started (Grootjans *et al.*,1985)

On sites where no further species replacement can be observed other than to *Festuca rubra* and *Agrostis capillaris*, the reason might be the irreversible loss of soil texture. The disturbed peat soil cannot maintain capillary rise of the groundwater and the vegetation suffers from drought.

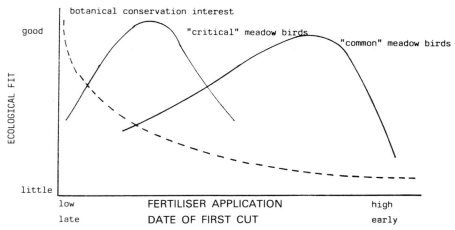

Fig. 1. Simplified relationships between the intensity of agricultural practices and the ecological fit for botanical and meadow bird conservation interest (after Dijkstra, 1991).

The previous examples have in common a drop in groundwater table as an explanation of the occurrence of the particular plant communities. There is, however, another example in which the groundwater table remained high but, nevertheless, the vegetation changed. In this case a plant community with *Caltha palustris* shifted towards a community with *Juncus acutiflorus*. The deep drainage ditches resulted in a fast discharge of deep calcium-rich seepage water. This type of groundwater is replaced by superficial calcium-poor seepage water and rainwater (Bakker and Grootjans, 1991). Here, the change in groundwater composition can also be the explanation for species replacement.

The point in common in these four examples is the lowering of the groundwater table or the replacement of deep calcium-rich seepage water by calcium-poor rainwater. Hay-making or grazing are then insufficient practices for restoration management. The management should, therefore, focus on affecting hydrological processes by changing the hydrological conditions. The groundwater table can be raised by preventing the discharge of water or by lowering the soil level through removal of the soil. The proportion of calcium-rich deep seepage water can be increased by just filling the deep drainage ditches with the adjacent dried peat layer in sites with strong deep seepage. In sites with a weaker deep seepage there is the danger of stagnant rainwater, although this can be prevented by using shallow ditches for the discharge of rainwater. Further experiments investigating hydrological processes now seem timely.

IMPLEMENTATION OF NATURE MANAGEMENT
Since the costs of restoration management are high the question arises as to what extent it can feasibly be carried out by organizations for nature management. Only hay-making and/or grazing may be appropriate for agricultural purposes. In a series of plant communities moving from a dominance of *Lolium perenne* (> 200 kg N/ha/yr) to-

wards a dominance of *Agrostis canina* (no fertiliser) the forage production dropped from 12 t/ha/yr to 3-5 t/ha/yr, whereas the forage quality decreased from 970 VEM/kgdm (VEM=unit of net energy necessary for milk production) and 180 g crude protein/kgdm towards 750 VEM/kgdm and 75 g crude protein/kgdm (Table 7) (Altenburg and Wymenga, 1991; Dijkstra, 1991). For the standard milk production of 6000 kg milk/yr the net energy value should be 900 VEM kgdm. This implies that in plant communities with a dominance of *Holcus lanatus* the forage quality is too low to sustain agricultural production and only heifers or beef cattle can be fed.

Table 7. Plant species composition, fertiliser application, herbage production, and forage quality of various plant communities cut after mid-June (after Altenburg and Wymenga, 1991; Dijkstra, 1991).

Plant community	A dry	A wet	B dry	B wet	C dry	C wet	D dry	D wet	E dry	E wet
Lolium perenne	D[*]	-	D	-	F	-	-	-	-	-
Alopecurus geniculatus	R	D	R	D	R	D	-	R	-	-
Agrostis stolonifera	R	D	R	D	R	D	-	R	-	-
Poa pratensis	F	-	F	-	F	-	F	-	-	-
Poa trivialis	F	F	R	F	F	F	R	F	-	-
Holcus lanatus	R	-	D	-	D	-	D	-	R	-
Rumex acetosa	R	R	F	R	F	F	F	R	R	R
Cardamine pratensis	R	R	-	F	R	R	R	R	-	-
Anthoxanthum odoratum	-	-	R	R	R	R	F	F	R	F
Agrostis capillaris	-	-	R	-	D	-	D	-	D	-
Caltha palustris	-	-	-	R	-	R	-	R	-	R
Agrostis canina	-	-	-	-	R	R	F	D	R	D
Myosotis palustris	-	-	-	R	-	R	-	R	-	R
Carex nigra	-	-	-	-	-	F	-	F	-	F
Plantago lanceolata	-	-	-	-	-	-	F	-	R	-
Luzula campestris	-	-	-	-	-	-	-	-	F	-
Rhinanthus angustifolius	-	-	-	-	-	-	-	-	R	F
Fertiliser application kg N/ha/yr	>200		50-200		50-200		0-50		0	
Production Herbage DM/ha/yr	12		8-11		8-11		6-7		3-5	
Forage quality VEM/kgdw[**]	970		900		825		800		750	
crude protein g/kgdw	180		160		140		125		75	

[*] D = dominant, F = frequent, R = rare
[**] Vem = unit of energy necessary for milk production

Reduction of fertiliser application to about 200 kg N/ha/yr and a first cut in the second half of June favours "common" meadow birds like Lapwing, Oystercatcher and Blacktailed godwit. Reduction of fertiliser application to 50 kg N/ha/yr and a first cut in the second half of June encourages "critical" meadow birds like Red shank, Snipe and Ruff. No fertiliser application at all causes a reduction in meadow birds because of impoverishment of the soil. Such management is, however, connected to plant communities adapted to mesotrophic soil conditions. Their variance depends on the local hydrological conditions (Fig. 1) (Dijkstra, 1991).

Reduction in fertiliser application in agricultural practices may be welcomed in terms of preventing environmental problems and increasing meadow birds. It can, however, play no part in restoration management for plant communities on mesotrophic soils, since these require cessation of fertiliser application. This might be achieved in narrow strips along the fields, but when it has to be carried out throughout whole fields, this can only be by organizations for nature management.

PERSPECTIVES ON NATURE MANAGEMENT

Restoration management aiming at mesotrophic or ologotrophic soil conditions on dry sites can be carried out by grazing and/or hay-making, but removal of the topsoil should be considered. On moist and wet sites it can only be carried out by hay-making under proper hydrological conditions, i.e. high groundwater table and a proportion of deep calcium-rich seepage water, fitting into the regional landscape and ecological setting. Since this is how restoration management started it can be referred to as "classic" nature management. It is also "classic" with respect to the continuation of former agricultural practices with low fertiliser input.

In areas still receiving low fertiliser inputs (50 kg N/ha/yr) agricultural exploitation and maintenance management actually meet. Once fertiliser input has increased restoration management is necessary. Reduction of fertiliser inputs to very low levels is encouraging meadow birds, but not plant communities on mesotrophic soils. This is particularly the case if an increase of fertiliser input was attended by changes in hydrological conditions, which is nearly always true. This implies that agricultural exploitation and restoration management exclude each other. This being said it should be considered whether the restoration of the semi-natural replacement communities of natural communities should be strived at. These developed as a by-product of agricultural exploitation by grazing and hay-making. As agricultural exploitation is no longer possible, the expensive annual management can only be carried out by organizations for nature management.

REFERENCES

ALTENBURG W. and WYMENGA E. (1991) Beheerovereenkomsten in veenweidegebieden, mogelijk effecten op vegetatie en weidevogels [The effects of adjusted farming on vegetation and meadow bird densities]. *Landschap*, **8**, 33-45.
BAKKER J.P. (1989) *Nature management by grazing and cutting*. Kluwer Academic Publishers: Dordrecht.

BAKKER J.P. and GROOTJANS A.P. (1991) Potential for regeneration in the middle course of the Drentsche A brook valley (The Netherlands). *Verhandlungen Gesellschaft für Ökologie*, **20**, 249-263.

BOBBINK R and WILLEMS J.H. (1987) Increasing dominance of *Brachypodium pinnatum* in chalk grasslands: a threat to a species-rich ecosystem. *Biological Conservation*, **40**, 301-314.

DIJKSTRA H. (1991) Natuur- en landschapsbeheer door landbouwbedrijven [Nature and landscape management by agricultural enterprises]. *COAL-publikatie* No. 60.

GROOTJANS A.P. (1980) Distribution of plant communities along rivulets in relation to hydrology and management. In: Wilmanns, O and Tüxen, R (eds.) *Epharmonie* pp.143-170. Cramer: Vaduz.

GROOTJANS A.P., SCHIPPER P.C. and VAN DER WINDT H.J. (1985) Influence of drainage on N-mineralization and vegetation response in wet meadows. I. *Calthion palustris* stands. *Oecologia Plantarum*, **7**, 403-417.

STIEPERAERE H. and TIMMERMAN C. (1983). Viable seeds in the soils of some parcels of reclaimed and unreclaimed heath in the Flemish District (Northern Belgium). *Bulletin de la Societé Royale de Botanique Belgique*, **116**, 62-73.

Re-creation of Species-rich Calcicolous Grassland Communities

V.K. BROWN AND C.W.D. GIBSON[1]

Imperial College, Silwood Park, Ascot, Berkshire SL5 7PY

[1]Bioscan (UK) Ltd., Bagley Croft, Hinksey Hill, Oxford OX1 5BD

ABSTRACT

A long-term, ongoing study at Wytham, Oxfordshire is assessing the potential for re-creating calcicolous grassland on ex-arable land. The vegetation of a field, abandoned from agriculture some 10 years ago, has been monitored regularly and quantified in terms of community structure and characteristics of the individual species. Three invertebrate taxa, the spiders, leaf miners and leaf hoppers, have been selected to represent groups which show different relations to the species composition and structure of the vegetation. After 10 years, a large number of typical calcicolous grassland plant and invertebrate species have colonized the field. However, comparison with nearby ancient calcicolous grassland shows that both plant and invertebrate communities are vastly different. Management, by different regimes of sheep (ewe) grazing, modifies the succession of both plants and animals and can be used to steer it in the right direction, but it cannot mimic the effects of time. However, the study has shown that an attractive and valuable (for nature conservation) vegetation and associated invertebrate fauna can be established on ex-arable land, within a relatively short time span, providing appropriate management is applied.

INTRODUCTION

Ancient calcicolous grasslands in southern Britain derive their high conservation value from the richness of both their flora and fauna. In addition to their diversity, they often contain rare or highly specialized species (Ratcliffe, 1977; McClean, 1990). Consequently, it is hardly surprising that the massive fragmentation and destruction of these grasslands in recent times is a cause of great concern. Attempts to re-create or transplant them are therefore attractive (see for example, Hopkins, 1989; Newbold, 1989) and deserve careful consideration. Furthermore, changes in agricultural policy, involving land coming out of intensive agricultural production, are providing a wealth of sites where re-creation programmes can be initiated.

The extensive literature on grassland succession (Bard, 1952) provides a useful general background for such re-creation programmes. From this, we know the likely pattern of plant species diversity (Tramer, 1975), plant structure (Brown and Southwood, 1987), the need for management to restrict scrub invasion (Ward, 1990) and the variable timescale of different successions (van der Maarel, 1988), although we know far less about the associated fauna (but see Brown and Southwood, 1987; Brown,

1990). Clearly, detailed information on attempts to re-create specific habitats is now needed. However, this is only pertinent where there is adjacent natural habitat for comparison. In this way, the "success" of such programmes can be assessed and the underpinning processes highlighted. It is an attempt to fulfil these aims, in respect of the re-creation of calcicolous grassland, that an ongoing, long-term experiment at Wytham, Oxfordshire was begun in 1984. This experiment has involved the regular monitoring of the developing vegetation and invertebrate fauna of an area of ex-arable land, and its comparison with nearby unimproved ancient grassland. The study has addressed three questions: (i) What are the characteristics of the successional stages between ex-arable land and ancient calcicolous grassland? (ii) How long does each of these stages take? (iii) What effect does management have on the duration and nature of these stages? The answer to the latter question lies in a comparison of the effects of different sheep (ewe) grazing regimes on the establishing grassland.

THE EXPERIMENTAL SYSTEM

The main study area (Upper Seeds) is a 10 ha field within Wytham Woods, Oxfordshire, together with a series of small patches of ancient grassland. Three of these patches are adjacent to the field, with the remaining 10 within 1.5 km. All are on shallow soil overlying Jurassic corallian limestone. The patches vary in age from 40 to well over 100 years, since the last major disturbance and provide the potential source for calcicolous grassland plants. The field was under arable cultivation from 1960 to 1982, when it was abandoned after a crop of winter wheat was sown but not harvested. In early 1985, the field was fenced to provide areas for 5 different sheep grazing treatments. Three of these (ungrazed controls, short-period spring and short-period autumn grazing) have been applied in two square 90 x 90 m grids, each comprising 9 paddocks of 30 x 30 m. There were thus 6 replicates of each treatment, with the grazing treatments occurring for 2 weeks, when three Blue Leicester x Swaledale "mule ewes" were admitted to the relevant paddocks. Outside the paddocks, the field is divided into areas grazed by sheep (approximately 6 animals ha^{-1}) from April to November, with the grazing pressure halved from June to August (referred to as 'long-period spring and autumn grazing') or grazed from late August to November (referred to as 'long-period autumn grazing').

Long-period spring and autumn grazing was also applied from 1988 to 2 ancient grassland patches, one approximately 50 years old at the time (Bowling Alley) and the other (Sundays Hill) over 100 years old. Prior to this, these grasslands had only been lightly grazed by wild animals since myxomatosis killed most of the rabbits in the mid fifties. As a result, there was considerable invasion of tor grass (*Brachypodium pinnatum*) and scrub.

In 1987, quadrats were also recorded in a number of different grassland patches of known ages within Wytham Woods to determine the local ancient grassland vegetation. In addition to the Bowling Alley, data are presented from Upper Seeds Reserve (40 years old) and the Quarry and Rough Common (both over 100 years old).

VEGETATION AND INVERTEBRATE SAMPLING

Permanent quadrats, 1 m^2, were used throughout the study to sample plant species composition. This size was considered appropriate for the scale of spatial patterning to be detected. Since 1984, 4 of these were sampled from each of the 18 paddocks. In 1986, 12 further quadrats were set up in each of the long-period grazed areas, and in 1988, a further 12 were set up in each of the 2 ancient grassland patches. Vegetation was assessed in each quadrat by species counts in each of 25 cells. In most cases, counts were undertaken 4 times during the growing season (late April, early July, August and late September). In addition, regular species censuses of the experimental grids and the entire field enabled species colonisation (and extinction) to be monitored at different spatial scales (Gibson and Brown, 1991a).

The invertebrates are represented by three groups, selected for their different relationships with the vegetation. The leaf miners are used to represent a solely phytophagous group, which contains many specialist feeders and relatively few generalist species. Thus, they may be expected to depend more strictly on plant species composition than many other groups. As larvae, they are confined within the tissues of the host plant, where their mines are conspicuous. They can thus be sampled more comprehensively and accurately than more mobile groups. In addition, the mines often persist after the completion of larval feeding, thereby providing more permanent evidence of their presence. In this study, they were sampled in the same 1 m^2 quadrats as the plants (see Sterling et al., 1992). The spiders represent a strictly predatory group, known to rely on the structure of the vegetation for web spinning and prey capture. The leafhoppers are another phytophagous group but contain few taxonomic specialist feeders, being mainly species oligophagous on grasses. They are also known to be dependent on the structure of their host plants. The latter 2 groups were sampled by D Vac suction (see Gibson et al., 1992; Brown et al., 1992) from within two specially defined 3 x 3 m quadrats within each replicate of each treatment.

SUCCESSIONAL COMMUNITIES OF PLANTS AND INVERTEBRATES

Plants. After abandonment in 1982, until the start of the study in 1984, Upper Seeds was characterized by a typical ruderal plant community, with many arable weed species as well as volunteer wheat from the previous crop. However, this changed rapidly, as grasses established and other herb species colonized. By 1993, over 250 plant species had colonized Upper Seeds and some of the treatments bore a superficial resemblance to the older nearby grasslands. To compare the nature of the different aged communities, multivariate analyses, based on species occurrence, are appropriate. These were carried out using CANOCO (ter Braak, 1987); the details of the method and its application to these data are given in Gibson and Brown (1992).

Fig. 1 illustrates the relative positions of the samples (quadrats), from the different aged grasslands, by plotting their scores on the first 2 axes of the ordination of the data. It is immediately clear that all the quadrats from Upper Seeds had very low scores on Axis 1 (describing successional age), while they had a range of scores on Axis 2, which reflected a contrast between stress-tolerators and ruderal plant strategies (*sensu* Grime *et al*, 1988) with high scores and competitor species with low scores. By contrast, the older sites had scores well spread along the first axis, with the 100 year old site having highest values on this and Axis 2. The intermediate aged grasslands have intermediate scores on both axes. Thus, from a community standpoint, there is a vast difference between Upper Seeds and the older grasslands.

The impact of the various grazing treatments on succession can be seen by examining the polygons at the left side of Fig. 1. Each polygon encloses the smallest area which includes all the scores for one particular treatment from 1984-1989. It is clear that the heavier grazing treatments retained higher scores on Axis 2. The temporal progression of scores was generally dominated by a rise in Axis 1 scores, coupled by a decrease in those for Axis 2. However, continuous spring and autumn grazing slowed

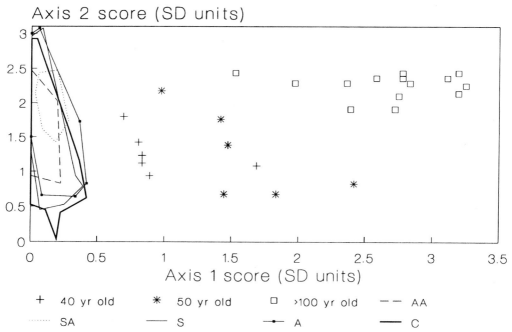

Fig. 1. (a) Relative positions of samples (species composition in 1 m^2 quadrats over a 5 year period) from grasslands of different successional age on the first 2 axes of a DCA ordination. Shaded rectangle includes all data from the experimental field. "40 yr old", "50 yr old" and ">100 yr old" respectively denote the time in years since the last major disturbance (e.g. ploughing or quarrying) on a grassland patch. The positions of samples from the experimental field under different management regimes on the same DCA axes are also shown, with all time points from all quadrats enclosed by a polygon for each treatment. The treatments are; AA long-period autumn grazed, SA long-period spring and autumn grazed, S short-period spring grazed, A short-period autumn grazed, and C ungrazed control. (From Gibson and Brown, 1992)

the increase on Axis 1, while maintaining high values on Axis 2. It would therefore seem that the vegetation in this treatment was moving, albeit very slowly, towards that of the herb rich, older grasslands, seen in Fig. 1.

Invertebrates. The substantial difference between the plant species assemblages of the early successional and older grasslands is suggestive of differences, at least as marked, in the invertebrates. Intuitively, the spiders, being a strictly predatory group, should be less sensitive to plant species composition, except when this covaries with architecture. In community analyses of the spider fauna, plant structure was indeed found to be of major importance. The ungrazed controls on Upper Seeds consistently had the highest species richness and abundance (e.g. in May 1989, 207 individuals/m^2 cf. 50.7 in the continuous spring and autumn grazed treatment). However, the impoverished fauna of the heavily grazed grassland patches was distinctive, as we shall see later. Interestingly, the leaf hoppers showed similar trends. Although there were subtle successional changes in the ex-arable field, it was the intensity of grazing which had the greatest influence on their community structure, with the older grazed grasslands again supporting a distinctive fauna. Both leafhoppers and spiders therefore represent fauna mainly determined by their response to vegetation structure, with only a few relationships with particular plant species. In addition, older grasslands have distinctive leafhopper and spider faunas, perhaps because of some species' poor dispersal ability.

Some 60 leaf miner species were recorded, of which only 4 were restricted to the older grasslands. In this group, community ordination analyses were restricted to the early successional grassland. In directly comparable analyses of the vegetation, 70.7% of the variation in plant ordination axes was explained by grazing, local position (grid) and year, while only 49.9% was explained in the case of leaf miners. This suggests a substantial contribution from other factors to leafminer composition. Sterling *et al.* (1992) showed that plant species composition, grazing treatment and year were likely to be important as well as a greater natural year-to-year variability in this insect group than in the plants. Their analysis was based on CANOCO version 2.0 (ter Braak, 1987), but re-analysis using the more sophisticated modelling and significance tests available in CANOCO version 3.12 (ter Braak 1991) has since confirmed their results. Fig. 2 shows the positions of miner taxa in respect of Axis I and II of a DCCA ordination analysis and in relation to 4 vegetation axes (V1 - V4) and autumn and spring grazing treatments. These are similar to those described for the vegetation in that the first axis is related to successional age. The second miner axis is largely related to local variation in the plant community. Modelling of the DCCA relationship by forward selection of environmental variables and Monte Carlo testing of each variable and model showed that each vegetation axis, each grazing treatment and successional age explained significant (p<0.01) and independent components of the leaf miner community. Of these variables, successional age was the most important, followed by the vegetation axes indicating plant species composition (reflected in the lengths of the biplot arrows in Fig. 2). The effects of grazing treatments were the smallest of these categories of variables. This shows that, although plant species composition and grazing

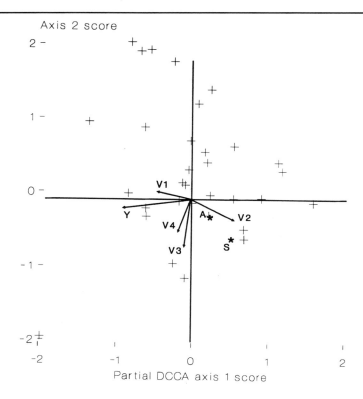

Fig. 2. Positions of individual leaf miner species on the first and second canonical axes (scores in units standard deviation) of a DCCA ordination in relation to four vegetation axes (V1 - V4), successional age (Y) and grazing treatment - A (autumn grazing) and S spring grazing). (Based on re-analysis of data in Sterling *et al.*, 1992).

have significant independent effects, the strongest determinant of the leaf miner assemblage appears to be a directional change through time (i.e. succession) which is independent of the successional trends in their foodplants. Possible causes of this trend include natural enemy effects and/or colonisation events.

SPECIES TRENDS AND STRATEGIES

Plant species. The colonisation and establishment of species in the sward is influenced by the seed bank and/or seed rain, the nature of the gaps in the sward and the competitive interactions between established species (e.g. Hillier, 1990). The seed bank of Upper Seeds has been thoroughly researched by Woodell and Steel (1990), while Watt and Gibson (1987) investigated the gap dynamics under the experimental treatments. In addition, the species composition of the adjacent ancient grassland patches provides information on potential colonists to the field.

Ten years after abandonment, Upper Seeds had accumulated a total of more than 250 species, though a few of these were already extinct from the sward by this time.

a)

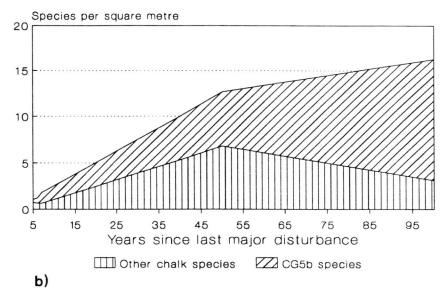

Species per square metre

Years since last major disturbance

☐☐☐ Other chalk species   ▨ CG5b species

b)

Species per square metre

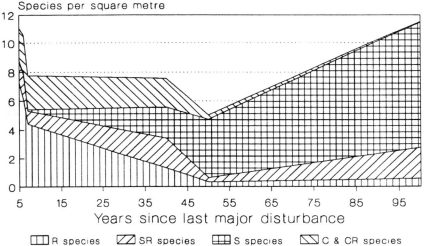

Years since last major disturbance

☐☐☐ R species   ▨ SR species   ⊞ S species   ⟍⟍ C & CR species

Fig. 3. Number of plant species belonging to different categories in grasslands of different age. Species categories are plotted cumulatively on the axes, and species falling into categories other than those indicated are not shown. (a) Species reported at 20% constancy or more in community CG5b in the NVC (CG5b species) or in other calcicolous grassland communities in the NVC (Other chalk species). (b) Species classified according to Grime *et al.* (1988) as ruderal species (R species), stress tolerant ruderals (SR species), stress-tolerators (S species), and competitive ruderals with competitors (C & CR species).

131

A large proportion of these species (over 43%) were recorded in the seed bank by Woodell and Steel. Of the remainder, all occurred in the surrounding vegetation within the Wytham estate. Based on the NVC (Rodwell, 1992), no less than 77 species establishing were calcicolous grassland species. Thus, even after such a relatively short period of time, over one third of the species were those typical of the habitat type.

Those species absent from the initial seed bank were considered to have dispersed into the field. An analysis of the life-history strategies of these species, according to some of Grime *et al.* (1988) categories, revealed no consistent trends. Surprisingly, for example, method of seed dispersal had no influence on colonisation rate or did the species germination requirements or propagule weight (Gibson and Brown, 1991a). The intensity and timing of grazing affected the number and type of species colonising. Ungrazed controls and short-period autumn grazed treatments acquired species more rapidly, though the heavier grazed treatments favoured the colonisation of perennial species.

The species composition in the grasslands of different age varied according to different categories (Fig. 3, using data from Gibson and Brown, 1992). Species representative of the CG5 Community in the NVC increased monotonically with grassland age while other calcicolous species (representative of communities other than CG5b) were more abundant in grasslands 40-50 years old than in the 100 year old grassland (Fig. 3a). Using the categories of Grime *et al.* (1988) (Fig. 3b), species designated as stress-tolerators showed a monotonic increase, reflecting the wide representation of these species in CG5b. Ruderal species declined steeply after initial abundance, while competitive ruderals showed a more gradual decline. Stress-tolerant ruderals showed no clear relation to grassland age.

Ten years' continuous monitoring of the vegetation has begun to reveal additional features of vegetation change which are not so easy to explain. Such patterns are especially marked in short-lived species which most frequently re-establish from seed. For example, cut-leaved cranesbill (*Geranium dissectum*) is an annual which follows no particular successional trends, and only the heaviest grazing treatment stands out as promoting the species. It also appears to do better in drier summers when more gaps are available in the turf for seedling establishment, having been especially abundant in drier summers during the experimental period as well as when the monitoring was started in 1984, also a dry summer. It remains to be seen whether or not the pattern is a regular cycle. The pauciennial black medick (*Medicago lupulina*) showed similar patterns but was more clearly affected by grazing intensity. Such patterns suggest a combination of weather or climate effects interacting with grazing and possibly with other factors to generate fluctuations. It is important that a study of the typical length of 3 to 5 years would have missed these patterns completely: only a long term study can even detect them, let alone hope to design the appropriate experiments to find out the underlying causes.

Invertebrate species. The life-history traits of the species predispose them to particular habitats (Brown, 1986, 1990). Thus, in addition to differences in community characteristics, such as species richness and abundance, the nature of the assemblages at different stages of grassland succession and under different grazing regimes is likely to change (Brown *et al.*, 1990; Sterling *et al.*, 1992). This was seen in the 3 groups investigated. Spiders can be divided into different foraging types: e.g. raptorial, sheet web, orb web, tangle web and scaffold species. Although they are all dependent on vegetation structure, they have different requirements. Thus, the larger web-spinning species are restricted to the ungrazed controls, where tall, structurally complex plant species persist. In the heavily grazed treatments, the impoverished spider fauna consisted mainly of the small, sheet web-producing Linyphiidae, while other web-forming species were noticeably absent. Interestingly, many Linyphiids are typical of recently disturbed ex-arable land since their habit of aerial ballooning as immatures and their multivoltine life-cycle makes them good colonists. The older grasslands, though less species rich than the ungrazed controls on the ex-arable field, had a distinctive fauna with species restricted to these areas. Despite the mobility of spiders, 7 years after abandonment, many species had failed to colonize the ex-arable field.

Unlike the spiders, where there was a general accumulation of species with the increasing age of the ex-arable field (particularly in the ungrazed controls), the leafhoppers showed considerable turnover of species. This lability was seen both in early succession and in the older grasslands. For this group, detailed records exist from the mid sixties for the older sites (Whittaker, 1969) which reveal considerable differences to the present day fauna. Even so, the older grasslands had a richer and distinctive fauna, with almost 20% of the species only found in these patches. Some of this difference can be related directly to host plant occurrence, though other factors, such as dispersal constraints of the species themselves, must also be involved. Most leafhopper species feed on grasses and respond mainly to differences in grass structure, brought about in the current study by the different grazing regimes. However, individual species show different responses and this brings about certain anomalies. For example, sparse grass cover with bare ground is characteristic of recently disturbed habitats and of heavily grazed areas. Leafhopper species favouring this type of grassland can therefore be found in very young or ancient grasslands.

The leafminer fauna presents a complex picture which cannot be fully understood from the short run of data so far but which is likely to prove a powerful tool for the understanding of succession in the long run. So far, it is clear that this group of relatively specialised species responds strongly to foodplant species composition and also to grazing (probably via both structure and incidental predation). These responses are less important than an independent directional trend through time. Unpublished data from a continuation from this study and associated work suggest that there is a time-lag in colonisation of many species associated with calcareous grassland plants by their miners, over and above the colonisation rate of the plants themselves. Such old-grassland leaf-miner species include both univoltine and multivoltine species, taxonomic specialists and generalists. Colonisation problems are unlikely to be the whole story; a full understanding needing data on the way in which further trophic levels (i.e. natural enemies of leaf miners) accumulate through the succession.

CONCLUSIONS AND FUTURE DIRECTIONS

The results of the current study have clearly demonstrated that an attractive and valuable (for nature conservation) vegetation and associated invertebrate fauna can be established on ex-arable land within a relatively short time span. This is indeed important at the current time, when agricultural policy is forcing much land out of intensive production. The process of vegetation change is initially rapid, and within 10 years the grassland can superficially resemble the goal, namely ancient calcicolous grassland. This is especially true under appropriate management, the present study showing that grazing by sheep is particularly apt. One of the main attributes of multivariate community analyses, such as those employed here, is that the structure of communities of different successional age can be compared quantitatively. In so doing, we can see the extent of the difference between Upper Seeds and nearby ancient grassland. Obviously, Upper Seeds will take decades (at least) to develop into calcicolous grassland. What we have achieved is to initiate the process and to steer it in the right direction by appropriate management.

However, we should not be discouraged by what we have achieved. Already, over 250 plant species have colonized Upper Seeds of which a third are typical calcicolous grassland species (defined according to the NVC: Rodwell, 1992). Putting it another way, nearly three-quarters of the calcicolous grassland species recorded from the ancient grassland patches at Wytham have already become established on Upper Seeds. This suggests that succession is not limited by dispersal, but by processes operating subsequently. Such processes include not only those traditionally associated with succession, but external forces such as annual changes in climatic variables (these are now the subject of experimental manipulation on Upper Seeds). The invertebrate fauna is partly driven in a deterministic manner by the vegetation changes (via species composition and structure), but is also more labile and shows successional trends independent of those in the plant community. This shows that an understanding of the plant community alone is insufficient to judge the success of grassland restoration or recreation projects.

Our future objectives are to determine whether the processes we have initiated will continue and to put our results into context by comparison with other sites. A programme for the latter has already been initiated (Gibson and Brown, 1991b).

ACKNOWLEDGEMENTS

We are grateful to the Nuffield Foundation for support from 1985-87, the Nature Conservancy Council for support from 1988-1990 and Bioscan (UK) Ltd. for support from 1988 onwards. Oxford University's Wytham Management Committee gave permission for the work to be undertaken and the grazing management was undertaken by the staff of Oxford University's Experimental Farm.

REFERENCES

BARD G.E. (1952) Secondary succession on the Piedmont of New Jersey. *Ecological Monographs*, **22**, 195-215.

BROWN V.K. (1986) Life cycle strategies and plant succession. In Taylor, F. and Karban, R. (eds.) *The Evolution of Insect Life Cycles*; pp. 105-124. New York: Springer-Verlag.

BROWN V.K. (1990) Insect herbivores, herbivory and plant succession. In: Gilbert, F. (ed.) *Genetics, Evolution and Co-ordination of Insect Life-cycles*; pp. 183-196. New York: Springer-Verlag.

BROWN V.K., GIBSON C.W.D. and KATHIRITHAMBY J. (1992) Community organisation in leaf hoppers. *Oikos*, **65**, 97-106.

BROWN V.K. and SOUTHWOOD T.R.E. (1987) Secondary succession: patterns and strategies. In: Gray, A.J., Crawley, M.J. and Edwards, P.J. (eds.) *Colonization, Succession and Stability*; pp. 315-337. Oxford: Blackwell Scientific Publications.

BROWN V.K., STERLING P.H. & GIBSON C.W.D. (1990) The mechanisms controlling insect diversity in calcareous grasslands. In: Hillier, S.H., Walton, D.W.H. and Wells, D.A. (eds.) *Calcareous Grasslands - Ecology and Management*; pp. 79-87. Huntingdon: Bluntisham Books.

GIBSON C.W.D. and BROWN V.K. (1991a) The effects of grazing on local colonisation and extinction during early succession. *Journal of Vegetation Science*, **2**, 291-300.

GIBSON C.W.D. and BROWN V.K. (1991b) The nature and rate of development of calcareous grassland in southern Britain. *Biological Conservation*, **58**, 297-316.

GIBSON C.W.D. and BROWN V.K. (1992) Grazing and vegetation change: deflected or modified succession? *Journal of Applied Ecology*, **29**, 120-131.

GIBSON C.W.D., HAMBLER C. and BROWN V.K. (1992) Changes in spider (Araneae) assemblages in relation to succession and grazing management. *Journal of Applied Ecology*, **29**, 132-142.

GRIME J.P., HODGSON J.G. and HUNT R. (1988) *Comparative Plant Ecology: a Functional Approach to Common British Species*. London: Unwin Hyman.

HILLIER S.H. (1990) Gaps, seed banks and plant species diversity in calcareous grasslands. In: Hillier, S.H., Walton, D.W.H. and Wells, D.A. (eds.) *Calcareous Grasslands - Ecology and Management*; pp. 57-66. Huntingdon: Bluntisham Books.

HOPKINS J.J. (1989) Prospects for habitat creation. *Landscape Design*, **179**, 19-23.

McCLEAN I.F.G. (1990) The fauna of calcareous grasslands. In: Hillier, S.H., Walton, D.W.H. and Wells, D.A. (eds.) *Calcareous Grasslands - Ecology and Management*; pp. 41-46. Huntingdon: Bluntisham Books.

NEWBOLD C. (1989) Semi-natural habitats or habitat re-creation: conflict or partnership? In: Buckley, G.F. (ed.) *Biological Habitat Reconstruction*; pp. 9-17. London: Belhaven Press.

RATCLIFFE D.A. (ed.) (1977) *A Nature Conservation Review*. Cambridge: Cambridge University Press.

RODWELL J. (1992) *British Plant Communities. Vol. 3*. Cambridge: Cambridge University Press.

STERLING P.H., GIBSON C.W.D. and BROWN V.K. (1992) Leaf miner assemblies: effects of plant succession and grazing management. *Ecological Entomology*, **17**, 167-178.

ter BRAAK C.J.F. (1987) *CANOCO: a FORTRAN program for canonical community ordination by (partial) (detrended) (canonical) correspondence analysis (version 2.1).* Wageningen, Netherlands, TNO Institute of Applied Computer Science, Statistics Department.

ter BRAAK C.J.F. (1991) *CANOCO: a FORTRAN program for canonical community ordination by (partial) (detrended) (canonical) correspondence analysis (version 3.12).* Wageningen, Netherlands, TNO Institute of Applied Computer Science, Statistics Department. Distributed by Cornell University, Ithaca, New York.

TRAMER E.J. (1975) The regulation of plant species diversity on an early successional old field. *Ecology*, **56**, 905-914.

van der MAAREL E. (1988) Vegetation dynamics: patterns in time and space. *Vegetatio*, **77**, 7-19.

WARD L.K. (1990) Management of grass-scrub mosaics. In: Hillier, S.H., Walton, D.W.H. and Wells, D.A. (eds.) *Calcareous Grasslands - Ecology and Management*; pp. 134-139. Huntingdon: Bluntisham Books.

WATT T.A. and GIBSON C.W.D. (1987) The effects of sheep grazing on seedling establishment and survival in grassland. *Vegetatio*, **78**, 91-98.

WHITTAKER J.B. (1969) Quantitative and habitat studies of the froghoppers and leafhoppers (Homoptera, Auchenorrhyncha) of Wytham Woods, Berkshire. *Entomologist's Monthly Magazine*, **105**, 27-37.

WOODELL S.R.J. and STEEL J. (1990) *Changes in the seed bank and vegetation of an abandoned arable field at Wytham, Oxfordshire, between 1982 and 1989.* Haslemere, Report to the Nature Conservancy Council. Bioscan (UK).

Hay Meadow Management In The Pennine Dales, Northern England

A. YOUNGER AND R. S. SMITH

Department of Agriculture, and Department of Agricultural and Environmental Science,
The University of Newcastle upon Tyne NE1 7RU

ABSTRACT

In the Pennine Dales, traditional farming practices have helped to produce a landscape which is valued for its walls, buildings and its grasslands. In particular, the hay meadows contain a large number of species and are of conservation interest. In order to discourage the more intensive farming practices which tend to threaten this habitat, the Pennine Dales ESA was established. Farmers are financially compensated for continuing to use the traditional management techniques which maintain species diversity. The scheme has been well received and seems to offer a practical solution to the possible conflict between agriculture and conservation. The management guidelines can be further refined from research evidence.

INTRODUCTION

Farming in the Pennine Dales as a whole is varied, ranging from arable crop production and intensive forms of animal production in the lower Dales where soil and environmental conditions permit, to less intensive forms of livestock rearing in the upper Dales. In the upper Dales, the combination of altitude, topography and climate determines that crop production and intensive forms of livestock production are not possible, so less intensive forms of livestock rearing predominate. In these areas, traditional practices have been used for many years to rear beef cattle and sheep, making use of the rough grazings on the hill sides and tops during the summer months, and utilizing the better land nearer to the farm buildings to provide conserved forage for use during the winter, and to provide better quality grazing at certain important stages in the production cycle of the livestock. To protect these better areas from uncontrolled grazing, stone walls were built around the pastures and meadows, and to provide shelter for both livestock and stored forage over the winter, stone barns were constructed in the meadows. The resulting landscape, characterized by stone walls, field barns, woodland, pastures and meadows is widely recognised for its beauty.

Whilst the walls and buildings certainly contribute to the overall attractiveness of the area, the conservation interest centres around the characteristic hay meadows which are an integral and vital part of the whole system.

137

TRADITIONAL HAY MEADOW MANAGEMENT

In these upland environments, the topography and ground conditions dictate that relatively few fields are suitable for cutting on most farms, therefore those which are suitable, have been cut every year. Indeed, Smith and Jones(1991) stated that within an individual farm, fields are usually cut in the same sequence each year. Superimposed on this very consistent pattern is a sequence of defoliation practice which has also been followed very regularly.

Firstly, meadows are grazed in spring, when they provide good quality grazing for sheep after lambing, and before they are turned onto the rougher hill grazings for the summer.

Secondly, the meadows are closed up during May for a period of uninterrupted growth which terminates with the cutting of the hay crop in July or August.

Thirdly, the regrowth of herbage after the hay crop is used to provide grazing in the autumn/winter period.

In their study of historic hay cutting dates, Smith and Jones (1991) found that the date of starting hay cutting tended to be around 1 July on the farms investigated, and that this date had not changed significantly between the 1950's and the 1980's except where the change to silage making involved an earlier start on one particular farm. In contrast, the date of finishing hay cutting had varied with time and was 12-27 days earlier in the 1970's than in the 1950's. September finish dates, which were once relatively common, are now much less so.

In addition to this defoliation regime, the other standard feature of the management has concerned the use of nutrients. Little or no inorganic fertiliser has been used on the meadows, whereas the manure from the barns has been used, especially on the meadows closer to the farmstead (Smith and Jones,1991).

CONSERVATION VALUE OF THE MEADOWS

The main conservation interest in the meadows derives from the high diversity of plant species in the vegetation. The species present in a sward are influenced by the gradient, soil pH, drainage status and fertility as well as by the management which has been employed. Thus the communities do vary both between and within fields (Smith,1988). J. Rodwell (National Vegetation Classification) recognises a distinctive 'northern' meadow, characterized particularly by the presence of *Geranium sylvaticum* and *Anthoxanthum odoratum* as well as an 'old grassland' type characterized by *Cynosurus cristatus* and *Centaurea nigra*. Local variants are also recognised (Alcock, 1982; Smith, 1985).

The species richness of the 'old grasslands' ranges from 17 to 41 species/m^2 with a mean of 27 whereas the 'northern' meadow has 14-34 species/m^2 and a mean of 23 (Smith, 1988). Some less common grassland types, for example on limestone, have a mean species-richness of greater than 30 species/m^2.

The main conservation objective is therefore to maintain the species richness of these traditional plant communities and in some instances to increase the species richness of communities in which the numbers of species have declined as a result of recent management practices.

THE POTENTIAL CONFLICT BETWEEN AGRICULTURE AND CONSERVATION

Within grassland farming in the UK there have been a number of important trends in response to political/financial pressures and to technological developments. Firstly, there has been a significant move towards silage as the main form of conserved feed (Murdoch, 1989) as the understanding of the silage fermentation process has increased and technological developments in terms of mechanisation and additives have enabled good quality silage to be made on farms quite regularly. Secondly, research has consistently demonstrated the increases in DM yield that can be achieved by the use of additional nutrients, especially nitrogen (Morrison et al., 1980; Hopkins et al.,1990). In attempting to increase animal production from grassland, and to increase profitability, farmers have been gradually increasing the amount of fertiliser N that they apply to swards (Church and Kershaw, 1987).

Whilst farmers in the upper parts of the Pennine dales may not have been very interested in changing to conventional silage making, because of the high capital cost of silos and equipment and because silage had to be made and used in bulk, the advent of big bale silage has provided a much more attractive alternative. Silage making is less weather dependent than haymaking, and the nutritional value of the product is less variable than that of hay. In order to conserve a crop of high organic matter digestibility, earlier cutting is practiced and the crop is removed from the field after a shorter wilting period.Within the bag or wrapper, a restricted fermentation takes place. Big bale silage making has become quite popular with UK farmers (Haigh, 1990), especially in the uplands where it replaces, at least in part, the traditional hay crop. Linked to this development, fertiliser N can be used on the crop without adversely affecting it's storage capacity, whereas adding N to a crop for hay simply made the drying time longer and therefore increased the risk of spoilage.

If farmers in the Pennine dales were to follow the national trends towards earlier cutting and rapid removal of the crop which are associated with silage making, and increased fertiliser use, then conservation interests would be threatened. Some species would be defoliated before setting seed, and the rapid harvesting process may further inhibit seed dispersal. One example of this effect was observed in an experiment in upper Teesdale when the rather conspicuous annual species, hay rattle (*Rhinanthus minor*) decreased in ground cover (estimated in June1991) from 7.6% to 1.8% as a result of cutting hay in mid June rather than mid July 1990. The increased use of fertiliser N would be likely to encourage the more competitive species eg *Lolium perenne* and would tend to be detrimental to species diversity (Jones, 1967).

THE CURRENT SOLUTION

The potential conflict between agricultural and conservation interests has been recognised by MAFF, and in1987 the Pennine dales Environmentally Sensitive Area (ESA) was designated. It has since been expanded.

Within the ESA, farmers are financially rewarded for farming in accordance with management guidelines designed to protect or to enhance the environment. Currently, farmers who decide to enter the first tier of this voluntary scheme receive £140/ha for meadow land and £70/ha for other grassland in return for following the guidelines issued by the Ministry of Agriculture, Fisheries and Food (MAFF, 1992). A higher level of payment is available to those who opt for tier 2, which is aimed at increasing the area and conservation quality of hay meadows. The guidelines, which were initially introduced in 1987, are based on a combination of best available evidence and on the application of basic principles, and have been updated in the light of experience and further evidence. Basically, they seek to define the standard management which has been responsible for creating the swards. The main components of direct relevance to the meadows are as follows:

Maintain grassland and do not plough, level or reseed the land. Cultivate meadows only with a chain harrow or roller as early as possible in spring as soon as stock are removed.

Land to be managed as meadow must be identified on the contract map and must continue to be managed as such for the length of the agreement.

Exclude stock from meadows at least 7 weeks before the first cut for hay or silage and by 1 June at the latest.

Do not cut hay or silage in any year before 8 July. All meadows must have their first cut in August at least once every 5 years. The aftermath must be grazed.

If grass is cut for silage, it must be wilted and turned before removal and the aftermath must be grazed.

Do not exceed the existing level of inorganic fertiliser and in any case do not exceed 25 kg N, 12.5 kg P_2O_5 and 12.5 kg K_2O/ha/yr or the equivalent in artificial organic fertiliser. This must be applied in one application.

Do not apply slurry or poultry manure.

Apply only manure produced on the farm, and do not exceed the existing level of application on any fields. In any case, do not use more than 12.5 t/ha/yr and apply it in a single dressing.

Do not use fungicides and insecticides.

Do not apply herbicides except to control bracken, nettles, spear thistle, creeping or field thistle, curled dock, broad-leaved dock or ragwort. When applying herbicides always use a weed wiper or spot treatment. Where bracken cannot be controlled by mechanical means, asulam may be used.

Do not spray existing areas of rushes in pastures

Do not apply lime, slag or any other substance to reduce soil acidity.

Do not graze land so as to cause poaching, overgrazing or under-grazing.

Do not install any new drainage system or substantially modify any existing drainage system.

Whilst many of these guidelines place restrictions on farmers, the scheme still seems to be acceptable to a large proportion of them. A recent estimate (MAFF, personal communication) suggests that some 65% of farmers eligible to enter into the newly enlarged scheme have already chosen to do so. Those who are more reluctant to join, tend to be farming further down the dales and are more attracted by the possibility of intensification

THE FUTURE

It is clear that the employment of traditional management practices has enabled botanically diverse swards to persist, and the management guidelines have sought to ensure that the traditional practices are continued. Whilst many of the guidelines are readily accepted, others are more controversial. A good example is the guideline about cutting date which, when rigidly applied can lead to a delay in the start of hay cutting during a period of dry weather. The loss of opportunity to preserve a crop of good quality in conditions which would otherwise be ideal for haymaking can be very frustrating, and the lack of flexibility has been criticised.

In future, it is important to refine the guidelines to minimize the practical problems without compromising the conservation objectives. It is necessary to continue with experimental work to identify the relative importance of the different components of the traditional management system in terms of maintaining species diversity. This should enable the correct emphasis to be placed on each component within the management guidelines in future, and perhaps enable some flexibility to be incorporated without detriment to conservation interests. Equally there is a role for experimental work aimed at increasing species diversity in swards where the number of species has declined. In this context, work in progress in upper Teesdale is investigating the importance of hay cutting date, fertiliser use and grazing management on the vegetation dynamics and agricultural productivity of a traditional hay meadow. At Ingleborough, a similar experiment has some additional treatments involving the introduction of seeds to increase the number of species present.

In Teesdale, treatments involving hay cutting in mid July have consistently produced high yielding crops of hay whilst maintaining species richness and diversity (Table 1). Cutting earlier, in mid June, significantly reduced hay yield and had a negative effect on botanical composition.

Table 1. The species richness (No. of species in 25 × 25 cm quadrat) and diversity (inverse Simpsons index) of vegetation within each treatment in the Teesdale meadow in June 1992, and the DM yield (t/ha) at the time of cutting (mean of 3 years 1990-92).

Hay cutting dates	Species richness	Diversity	DM yield
14 June	12.8	7.1	3.8
21 July	15.3	7.9	5.4
3 September	13.6	6.9	5.7
Grazing treatments			
No grazing	12.1	6.0	5.7
Autumn grazing	14.7	8.0	4.9
Autumn and spring grazing	15.0	8.0	4.3
Fertiliser treatments			
No fertiliser	14.8	7.9	4.2
$80N:40P_2O_5:40K_2O$	13.0	6.7	5.7

Although grazing in autumn and/or spring had a predictable negative effect on the DM yield of hay, the results show that some form of grazing is needed to maintain species numbers and diversity.

The effect of fertiliser, applied at a rate considerably in excess of that allowed in the guidelines (80 kgN, 40 kg P_2O_5, 40 kg K_2O/ha) was to increase DM yield at the time of hay cutting from 4.2 to 5.7 t/ha, a response of 19kg DM/kg N applied. Species richness and diversity were decreased by the use of fertiliser but perhaps by a smaller amount than might have been predicted.

The data indicate that the conservation objectives were more seriously affected both by early cutting and by failure to graze than by the use of fertiliser. More work is needed to establish the mechanisms behind these effects.

CONCLUSIONS

The need to encourage farmers to continue farming in sympathy with this sensitive environment has been recognised.

The Environmentally Sensitive Area scheme is a practical, and reasonably successful way of balancing the potentially conflicting interests of agriculture and conservation.

In future, it should be possible to further refine the management guidelines in the light of research evidence, perhaps to achieve a greater degree of flexibility without compromising the conservation objectives of maintaining, or increasing species diversity.

ACKNOWLEDGMENTS

The authors wish to acknowledge the major role played by Helen Buckingham and Mike Bullard in the collection and calculation of data from the Teesdale experiment.

REFERENCES

ALCOCK M.R. (1982) *Yorkshire grasslands: a botanical survey of hay meadows within the Yorkshire Dales National Park*. Project Report Number 10, England Field Unit, Nature Conservancy Council, Banbury.

CHURCH B.M. and KERSHAW C.D. (1987) Survey work in the statistics department. *Rothamsted Experimental Station, Report for 1986*, 227-235

HAIGH P.M. (1990) The effect of dry matter content on the preservation of big bale grass silages made during the autumn on commercial farms in South Wales 1983-7, *Grass and Forage Science*, **45**, 29-34.

HOPKINS A., GILBEY J., DIBB C., BOWLING P.J. and MURRAY P.J. (1990) Response of permanent and reseeded grassland to fertiliser nitrogen. 1. Herbage production and herbage quality. *Grass and Forage Science*, **45**, 43-55.

JONES L.I. (1967) Studies on Hill Land in Wales. *Technical Bulletin of the Welsh Plant Breeding Station*, No. 2.

MINISTRY OF AGRICULTURE, FISHERIES AND FOOD (1992) *Environmentally Sensitive Areas: The Pennine Dales*. London: Ministry of Agriculture, Fisheries and Food.

MORRISON J., JACKSON M.V. and SPARROW P.E. (1980) The response of perennial ryegrass to fertiliser nitrogen in relation to climate and soil. *Technical Report No. 27*. Grassland Research Institute, Hurley.

MURDOCH J.C. (1989) The conservation of grass. In: Holmes W. (ed.) *Grass, its production and utilization*, pp 173-213, Oxford: Blackwell Scientific Publications.

SMITH R.S. (1985) *Conservation of northern upland meadows*. Bainbridge: Yorkshire Dales National Park.

SMITH R.S. (1988) Farming and the conservation of traditional meadowland in the Pennine Dales Environmentally Sensitive Area. In: Usher M.B. and Thompson D.B.A. (eds.) *Ecological change in the uplands*, pp 183-199. British Ecological Society, Special Publication No. 7 Oxford: Blackwell Scientific Publications.

SMITH R.S. and JONES L. (1991) The phenology of mesotrophic grassland in the Pennine Dales, Northern England: historic hay cutting dates, vegetation variation and plant species phenologies. *Journal of Applied Ecology*, **28**, 42-59.

Grassland Management and Nature Conservation at Kingston Hill Farm

P. CHRISTENSEN

Kingston Hill Farm, Kingston Bagpuize, Abingdon, Oxfordshire

ABSTRACT

A 17 year case study is presented based on Kingston Hill Farm in Oxfordshire, aimed at combining profitable farming and conservation interests. Defining conservation objectives proved difficult. Bird populations were used as the main yardstick for monitoring conservation changes. Barn owls have just appeared.

INTRODUCTION

The Demonstration Farm Project

Following publication in 1974 of a study entitled 'New Agricultural Landscapes', the Countryside Commission decided to establish a series of 10 demonstration farms throughout England and Wales to answer:-

a) whether it is possible to combine profitable farming and conservation interests; and

b) what are the most cost effective ways of managing both existing and new landscape features?

The results were to be demonstrated to farmers, students, land managers and advisers.

METHODS AND MATERIALS

Kingston Hill Farm

Kingston Hill Farm, a 750 acre farm in Oxfordshire, was the first farm established, and continues to demonstrate the lessons learned, now through the auspices of the Farming and Wildlife Advisory Group (FWAG). The farm is owned by St. John's College, Oxford and is rented by the Christensen family. The farm runs south from the river Thames and consists of a narrow strip of gravel adjacent to the river (65 acres of grade 5), a north facing slope of Oxford clay (350 acres of grade 3 and 4) and a south facing slope of light sandy loam (335 acres of grade 2).

1993 cropping consists of 92 acres of maize, 18 acres of set-aside (grass cover) and 575 acres of grass (mostly long-term). Ten acres are non-cropped (buildings, ponds, ditches, roads, tracks etc) and 55 acres are in woodland and scrub. The stocking consists of 350 milking cows, 55 single sucklers and 395 followers and suckled calves (800 in total).

Project development

In 1976, 'single purpose plans' were formulated for the development of Kingston Hill Farm by specialist interest groups (eg. County Council, Royal Society for the Protection of Birds (RSPB), Butterfly group, Landscape Architect, Archaeology, Small Mammal Group, Conchologists, Landlord and Tenant, etc). A compromise composite plan was agreed by all of the interest groups at a memorable meeting in Oxford in July 1976. This evolved into an agreed development plan for Kingston Hill Farm, phased over 10 years.

A major difficulty to emerge at the planning stage was defining a conservation objective which was as focussed as the farming objective. Most of the serious argument occurred between the conservation interests.

The guiding principles agreed were that any conservation measures adopted were to be as low cost as possible, commensurate with being effective, and that no commitment be undertaken which required a high level of habitat management, particularly if it meant a clash with peak work loads on the farm. The emphasis was to be on maintaining and improving existing habitats, with limited habitat creation. Where planting was to be undertaken, only locally occurring and indigenous species were to be used.

It was decided to monitor the breeding bird populations as an indicator of the effectiveness of the conservation measures.

It was accepted by all groups involved that the profitability of the farming activities should not be seriously compromised by conservation activities. Without a profitable farming enterprise, conservation considerations would be seriously jeopardised.

Practical actions

The major landscape features were identified (tree lines, woodland, parish boundary, buildings, ruins including world war two bunkers, ponds, the river, ditches etc). Limited tree and shrub plantings were carried out to enhance or soften these features.

A parish boundary was widened to 10m to preserve a very ancient boundary. Part of a fir wood was reclaimed to farm use, leaving sufficient fir trees to provide habitat for goldcrests. Woodland was to be managed on a coppicing regime. All hedges were to be trimmed in late winter/early spring to preserve foodstocks for overwintering birds. Wherever possible, tree species within hedges were to be tagged and allowed to grow. Double fencing of hedges was to be undertaken to widen and strengthen them. Some areas were to be fenced off and allowed to develop naturally.

Water courses were to be dredged as necessary to keep water flowing, but only from one side and on a rotational basis. Ponds were to be kept open to the sunlight on the south side and dredged as necessary to keep open water.

Farming activities were to be carefully controlled in respect of keeping spray drift, fertilizer and manures out of non cropped areas. The objective was to reduce as much as possible the level of fertility in the non-cropped areas.

Costs

Capital costs, at 1979 prices, for tree planting, woodland planting, fencing to encourage natural regeneration, building and reclamation work amounted to £1995 spread over 5 years. Annual management costs extra to normal farming operations were calculated in 1979 to be about £135 per year.

RESULTS AND DISCUSSION

It is now 17 years since the inception of the Demonstration Farm Project and it is worth remembering that the general climate with regard to conservation and the environment was very different to now. It pre-dates milestones such as Marion Shoard's book 'Theft of the Countryside', and the establishment of grant structures for Environmentally Sensitive Areas and Stewardship Schemes. The dutch elm disease epidemic had only just started and farmers were still very defensive about their land and their rights to do with it as they wished.

Personal experience remembers that early visits by farmer groups to Kingston Hill Farm were very much on the basis of coming to look at the idiots getting involved with the 'green and hairies'!

What lessons have been learned? At a general level, the definition of a conservation objective has proved to be the most difficult. At Kingston Hill Farm we have set ourselves the target of leaving at least as many species on the farm at the end of our tenure, as at the beginning. I recognise this to be imperfect but we do need targets (we have them in every other aspect of our farming activity) and they do need to be measureable.

I have difficulty with the word 'conservation', as it means different things to different people and can in fact let the uncommitted off the hook. (I have planted two trees this year and am therefore a 'conservationist'!)

The approach at Kingston Hill Farm has not addressed the fundamental problems of farming large habitats whose value depends on their size and low levels of stocking. It is refreshing that grant and subsidy policies have recognised this basic problem and are making funds available for the extensification of grassland systems. Kingston Hill Farm falls within the Upper Thames ESA and we look forward to being able to return the water meadows to a traditional meadow management regime.

However, the increase in species diversity is likely to be a slow business if we just reduce fertility and stocking rates. Seven years ago we decided to stop any fertilizer or spray applications to a 7 acre water meadow, because we had identified quaking grass (*Briza media*) and several vetches in the field margin. There has been no marked change in sward composition during that 7 years, other than a dramatic increase in the population of creeping thistles (*Cirsium arvense*).

It has become very evident that all of the habitats are very inter-dependant; altering one may have a major effect on others. The whole farm is an eco-system, with very imprecise understanding of the effect of management changes. Measuring the effect of management change is also very difficult. Although at Kingston Hill Farm we have used bird populations as a yardstick, it is difficult to separate out climatic and other effects.

The attached Appendix is an estimate of breeding pairs of birds over the last 16 years. It represents a staggering committment by members of the Didcot RSPB group, and I pay great tribute to their efforts over this time. A total of 73 species are recorded as having nested since 1977, with a peak of 63 in any one year (1977) plunging to a low of 50 (1979). It is difficult to draw firm conclusions but certainly some loss of species is due to our farming activities.

The loss of the redshank was directly due to draining a large wet area in the centre of the farm. Leaving some conifers after reclaiming the wood was insufficient to retain the goldcrest. The lesser spotted woodpecker faded away as the dead elms were cleared.

A notable success was the establishment of a breeding pair of barn owls. A decision was made in 1990 not to cut a 3 m strip around the headlands when making silage, the intention being to encourage seed-eating birds by allowing these strips to run to head. We do not know if this was successful, but the barn owls are seen hunting these strips for food and it is assumed that enough was created for them to breed successfully.

CONCLUSIONS

For effective conservation, it is important that conservation objectives be identified (for instance, that there will be more species of wildlife at the end of my tenure than at the beginning). Conservation measures should be encompassed as part of the farm management plan, not something you do if you have time when you have finished the farming operations.

Conservation is not a cissy activity for the seriously cranky, but a vital activity for anyone who manages land. The loss of any single species due to the uncaring or thoughtless activity of man is a loss to us all and a threat to our future prosperity.

Profitable farming and species conservation are not incompatible, but require a partnership approach of the land manager and government research and development agencies, along with their consultancy services.

APPENDIX
COMMON BIRD CENSUS, 1977-1992: ANNUAL ESTIMATES OF BREEDING PAIRS FROM TERRITORY MAPS.

	77	78	79	80	81	82	83	84	85	86	87	88	89	90	91	92
Mallard	15	12	14	8	7	15	12	7	10	12	10	12	10	13	14	7
Mute swan	1	1	1	1	2	2	1	1	1	2	2	2	1	2	1	1
Canada goose	—	—	—	2	—	—	2	1	1	2	4	6	6	6	2	—
Moorhen	11	10	15	15	20	9	8	7	6	7	4	9	5	5	4	3
Coot	11	14	12	10	6	4	3	—	2	1	3	1	2	5	5	1
Kingfisher	1	—	—	—	1	1	1	1	1	—	1	—	—	—	—	—
Sparrow hawk	1	2	—	—	1	—	1	—	—	—	1	—	1	1	1	1
Kestrel	2	2	1	1	2	2	1	2	2	2	2	2	2	2	2	2

COMMON BIRD CENSUS, 1977-1992: ANNUAL ESTIMATES OF BREEDING PAIRS FROM TERRITORY MAPS—(Continued)

	77	78	79	80	81	82	83	84	85	86	87	88	89	90	91	92
Hobby	—	—	—	—	—	—	—	—	—	—	1	—	—	—	—	—
Tawny owl	2	2	2	2	3	2	2	1	1	—	1	—	1	—	1	—
Little owl	3	3	4	2	2	4	2	6	4	5	5	4	6	2	3	3
Barn owl	—	—	—	—	—	—	—	—	—	—	—	—	—	—	—	1
Red leg partridge	5	4	—	1	1	5	6	10	7	5	7	4	4	5	8	6
Grey partridge	8	7	6	8	9	6	12	13	7	7	8	3	6	5	6	3
Pheasant	9	10	6	5	11	6	12	8	7	5	6	9	9	5	9	7
Lapwing	7	5	5	5	8	19	6	10	15	16	7	5	4	5	16	14
Redshank	1	—	—	—	1	—	1	—	—	—	—	—	—	—	—	—
Curlew	—	—	—	—	—	—	—	—	1	—	—	—	—	1	—	—
Skylark	27	27	1	1	26	12	23	23	19	21	1	24	17	18	17	17
Meadow pipit	—	—	—	—	1	1	—	—	—	—	1	—	—	—	—	—
Stock dove	4	2	1	1	—	2	4	3	2	5	3	4	5	9	10	8
Turtle dove	1	2	2	2	1	—	3	2	—	1	—	—	2	1	1	—
Collared dove	2	1	3	1	1	2	—	—	—	1	1	—	—	—	1	1
Feral pigeon	—	—	—	—	—	—	—	—	—	—	—	—	—	—	1	—
Wood pigeon	63	27	nc	nc	nc	12	26	22	12	7	9	15	34	18	17	27
Swift	5	2	—	—	—	—	—	1	—	—	—	1	2	3	2	—
Swallow	11	3	—	—	nc	1	5	8	6	9	11	12	12	13	6	9
House martin	3	—	—	—	—	—	—	—	—	1	3	nc	1	1	—	1
Green woodpecker	—	—	—	—	—	1	1	—	1	—	—	1	—	1	1	—
Lesser spotted WP	1	2	1	—	—	1	—	—	—	—	—	—	—	—	—	—
Greater spotted WP	3	4	4	3	2	2	2	2	3	3	2	1	2	2	1	2
Carion crow	8	5	3	5	4	5	5	2	3	6	6	3	3	6	5	5
Jay	1	1	1	—	—	1	—	2	—	—	2	—	1	1	1	2
Magpie	5	3	3	1	3	4	4	4	4	6	7	8	8	5	7	10
Jackdaw	4	11	5	6	6	12	13	11	9	9	7	9	9	10	14	13
Rook	48	53	33	nc	159	70	245	179	184	178	167	154	191	294	259	256
Great tit	20	24	13	13	21	17	29	29	26	24	27	27	22	25	21	19
Blue tit	44	56	35	29	34	26	37	43	42	36	42	41	44	39	22	38
Coal tit	4	5	2	3	—	—	2	1	—	—	—	1	1	—	1	—
Marsh tit	3	3	2	4	3	2	3	23	2	1	2	1	—	2	2	2
Willow tit	1	1	—	—	—	—	2	—	1	—	—	—	—	—	—	—
Long tailed tit	7	7	3	1	5	—	4	9	5	2	2	4	8	5	6	7
Treecreeper	6	6	4	3	2	1	3	2	3	—	2	—	1	—	2	2
Nuthatch	—	—	—	—	—	—	—	—	—	—	—	1	—	—	2	1
Wren	42	60	19	29	41	11	36	41	27	43	42	40	75	61	32	61
Dunnock	26	24	17	16	32	18	24	26	23	31	26	31	42	42	23	29
Pied flycatcher	1	—	—	—	—	—	—	—	—	—	—	—	—	—	—	—
Spotted flycatcher	5	2	2	3	1	1	2	—	1	2	—	—	—	—	—	—
Blackbird	65	59	37	29	48	33	50	62	38	46	46	47	54	64	54	50
Mistle thrush	3	5	3	1	4	3	1	3	3	4	3	3	1	1	1	2

COMMON BIRD CENSUS, 1977-1992: ANNUAL ESTIMATES OF BREEDING PAIRS FROM TERRITORY MAPS—(Continued)

	77	78	79	80	81	82	83	84	85	86	87	88	89	90	91	92
Song thrush	10	5	4	3	5	3	5	2	2	3	3	6	2	2	1	3
Robin	38	30	23	26	26	12	18	37	17	31	23	34	38	39	20	41
Whitethroat	6	3	2	3	4	7	7	9	8	11	14	17	13	22	10	10
Lesser whitethroat	5	1	1	1	3	3	3	4	5	1	3	3	2	2	3	—
Blackcap	1	8	5	5	5	8	9	9	8	11	10	13	12	12	12	10
Willow warbler	9	4	4	3	7	7	14	10	16	17	17	20	14	14	13	5
Sedge warbler	—	—	—	1	—	—	—	—	—	—	1	—	—	—	—	2
Chiffchaff	8	7	7	6	8	5	8	4	8	7	12	16	22	36	14	19
Goldcrest	5	7	2	3	3	1	2	2	2	—	1	1	1	—	—	—
Pied wagtail	4	—	1	1	4	2	3	1	1	1	1	1	2	3	3	2
Yellow wagtail	—	—	—	1	2	2	1	1	2	2	2	1	2	3	1	—
Starling	19	15	3	9	nc	25	13	18	11	22	23	23	35	17	17	12
Greenfinch	4	4	—	3	1	2	1	1	1	3	1	1	1	4	3	4
Goldfinch	4	4	2	3	4	2	4	8	3	3	6	7	4	6	8	8
Bullfinch	4	5	—	4	4	1	2	1	2	3	1	5	2	2	—	2
Chaffinch	77	66	55	60	60	58	79	96	73	92	103	119	120	100	93	97
Yellowhammer	23	15	10	8	21	27	32	47	40	38	46	43	37	26	29	33
Corn bunting	6	11	—	—	1	1	2	1	1	—	—	1	—	—	—	1
Reed bunting	6	4	1	2	5	—	5	3	2	4	5	5	5	3	5	5
Tree sparrow	5	2	1	4	5	5	4	6	6	3	5	4	1	—	2	2
House sparrow	9	12	6	2	25	25	50	14	12	29	11	18	22	13	15	15
Cuckoo	5	2	2	5	4	2	3	2	2	2	2	2	2	5	1	4
Linnet	2	2	—	—	1	—	1	1	—	1	1	1	2	4	9	9
Total species	63	58	50	54	57	55	60	56	56	52	58	55	57	54	58	54

(Mean for 1977—1992, 56 species)

Martin Down National Nature Reserve: a Case Study

P. TOYNTON

English Nature, The Limes, Damerham, Hants SP6 3EU

ABSTRACT

At the time of purchase in 1978 Martin Down had been ungrazed for many years and as a result there had been a huge increase in rank grassland and invasion of scrub. This had led to a severe decline in the herb-rich areas and to a reduction in many species of butterflies.Active management with the reintroduction of grazing and clearance of scrub from herb-rich grassland has led to a spectacular recovery, with once rank grassland now full of flowers and butterfly species such as adonis blue and Duke of Burgundy much increased.

INTRODUCTION

Martin Down NNR is an area of 336 ha at the extreme eastern end of the Dorset Downs. It lies mainly on gently undulating land ranging from 30m to 100m OD but there is a ridge rising to 160m OD, at the southern end. The reserve is mainly of northerly aspect but some warm sheltered slopes are provided by a small valley at the southern end and the Bokerley Dyke along the south-western edge. The reserve lies wholly on the Upper Chalk but this is covered by various drift deposits, with residues of Eocene deposits at the southern end. Lower slopes are covered with loessic material of periglacial origin.

Archaeological interest is high with a Stone Age long barrow, numerous Bronze Age earthworks, Celtic fields, a Romano-British dyke and areas of broad-rig ploughing. The Down has a well recorded history and there is information about its stocking from the 15th century. The parish was enclosed very early, probably before 1600, and this may have saved the Down from later enclosures. There are still common rights and the areas is grazed by sheep belonging to local farmers.

There are rights for nearly 1200 sheep but these are not all exercised. Indeed if they were the Down would be overgrazed from the point of view of conservation. These rights were associated with sheep flocks which grazed on the Down by day and were folded on arable fields at night. Even then the area was apparently kept in short turf and the same number of sheep for 24 hours a day would certainly not allow the development of the mosaic of long and short grass and scrub which is so valuable for the wildlife today. Disputes between the owners and the commoners in the 1960s led to a court case to establish the rights, and even though the commoners won the action it proved difficult to graze the area without the cooperation of the owners. Consequently, the area was neglected until it was purchased for conservation by the Nature Conservancy Council (NCC) and Hampshire County Council in 1978.

The southern part of the reserve has been under grassland cover for perhaps 600 years whilst most of the the northern part was ploughed from 1943 to 1957 when it was turned back to grass.

The lack of grazing on the Down after the cessation of rabbit grazing in the 1950s to the time of purchase in 1978 had led to the deterioration of the chalk grassland with an increase in upright brome (*Bromus erectus*) which had become rank over much of the site and to the invasion of scrub from the already established small blocks. Torgrass (*Brachypodium pinnatum*) had also invaded some areas with large patches of up to 10 metres across. The less vigorous chalk grassland species were being lost from the grassland and many species of butterflies were becoming rare, particularly the adonis blue (*Lysandra bellargus*) and silver-spotted skipper (*Hesperia comma*).

It was agreed that NCC would manage the whole site on behalf of the owners, sheep grazing was introduced and scrub cleared from some of the areas of herb-rich grassland. The commoners were encouraged to put sheep back on the Down and NCC purchased its own sheep flock in April 1979. The Down is not fenced and stock are contained by electric fences which has enabled us to use a paddock system with a wide variety of grazing regimes.

The grassland supports several rare or local species of plants and there are areas of chalk heath. The site is very rich in butterflies with 40 species recorded in many years including adonis blue, silver-spotted skipper and Duke of Burgundy (*Hamearis lucina*). Dark-green fritillaries (*Argynnis aglaja*) are abundant through much of the longer grassland as are marbled whites (*Melanargia galathea*) and meadow browns (*Maniola jurtina*).

There are large areas of mixed scrub which support a wide range of invertebrates as well as providing breeding areas for many birds, particularly nightingales (*Luscinia megarhynchos*), willow warblers (*Phylloscopus trochilus*), blackcaps (*Sylvia atricapilla*) and lesser whitethroats (*Sylvia curruca*). Some woodland has developed at the northern and southern ends of the reserve, with oak (*Quercus robur*) dominant in most places and a small area of ash (*Fraxinus excelsior*).

There are several types of grassland on the reserve and these can be categorized botanically using the National Vegetation Community (NVC) types and also by structure. *Bromus erectus* grassland (CG3) is by far the most abundant, covering much of the older grassland and a good deal of the land reverting from arable. There are some smaller areas amounting to some 10 ha of *Festuca/Avenula grassland* (CG2) and very small areas of CG7 *Hieracium/Thymus* grassland which has developed on bare chalk since 1940. *Arrhenatherum* (MG1) grassland was dominant over much of the old arable but has declined with the increased grazing.

The upright Brome (*Bromus erectus*) areas are subdivided for management purposes into short herb-rich, medium length and long grasslands and it is the management of these which has proved the most interesting and rewarding over the past 15 years as the shorter and already herb-rich grassland was less in need of active management. There are also many areas where there is a mosaic of scrub and grassland and these are important for many species, in particular Duke of Burgundy butterflies.

MANAGEMENT

The management of the reserve is aimed at maintaining this mosaic of habitats and a grazing system has been adopted to achieve this. Scrub is an important part of the reserve and much active management takes place with rotational cutting and clearance from the better grassland.

The very short herb-rich grassland is managed by hard winter grazing, either each year on the more fertile areas where upright brome (*Bromus erectus*) is the dominant species or in alternate years on the less fertile ones.

The medium length grassland is perhaps the most important on the Down. Short herb-rich turf is represented in the region on several sites, but the taller upright brome grass (*Bromus erectus*) is poorly covered by the National Nature Reserves series. These areas were grazed in 1979 with large flocks of sheep belonging to the commoners both during the summer and winter. After this initial grazing they were grazed on a more precise pattern with about 2 to 3 weeks in the autumn at 40 ewes/ha and then again in spring to remove the first flush of the upright brome (*Bromus erectus*). The aim is to have a short sward by the beginning of May. The area is then left until the resumption of grazing in the autumn and this leads to an open but quite long grassland during the summer.

This has resulted in a tremendous increase in flowers and butterflies. Quadrats were established in 1979 and an average of 18 species per metre square was recorded. In recent years this has risen to about 30 species with many of the strict calcicoles such as horseshoe vetch (*Hippocrepis comosa*) and orchids greatly increased. Dark-green fritillaries and marbled whites are abundant.

The areas of longer grassland are managed in two ways: Either by annual grazing in early winter which applies to the larger part or, on a rotation of one year in three. The longer rotation is designed to keep the long grassland cover throughout the year for invertebrates. The annual grazing maintains a reasonably rich grassland which supports large populations of meadow browns and marbled whites as well as high densities of skylarks (*Alauda arvensis*).

Scrub/grassland mosaics and the transition zone between the two habitats are extremely important and are one of the main features of the reserve. They are much harder to manage than any of the other communities as it is difficult to maintain a balance between the two. There are two main approaches. Firstly, scrub is cut on a regular basis to prevent the canopy closing. This usually means removing about a third of the scrub at each cutting. As there is so much invading scrub it is best to treat cut stumps with a herbicide rather than be faced with coppiced regrowth in a few years. Secondly, the areas are grazed to maintain the grassland interest and to maintain the transition between grass and scrub. Fences are placed at different distances from blocks of scrub at each grazing to prevent a sudden transition area and to maintain the long grass/scrub edge.

Several of these areas support colonies of Duke of Burgundy butterflies and these are generally grazed on a three year rotation to maintain the shaded cowslips (*Primula veris*) necessary for the larvae.

One of the most interesting developments on the reserve has been the reclamation of the old arable land. This was in arable from 1943 to 1957 and was then returned to grassland. The area had sporadic grazing and was occasionally cut for hay until the Down was purchased in 1978. At this time it was dominated by *Arrhenatherum elatius* with smaller areas of *Bromus erectus* and was very rank. Since then the areas have been grazed on and off throughout the year, mainly by sheep belonging to the commoners, and this has led to a spectacular increase in flowers with pyramid orchids (*Anacamptis pyramidalis*) now found in thousands and burnt-tip orchids (*Orchis ustulata*) well established in some parts. Horshoe vetch and kidney vetch (*Anthyllis vulneraria*) are gradually invading from nearby grassland and many other species are now recorded. Quadrats established in 1979 averaged 18 species per square metre but now average 26. It is not however the number of species as much as the increase in calcicoles which is so interesting.

There are areas of chalk heath scattered through the reserve and 3 types have been recognised: the plateau heath which has developed on remnants of the Reading Beds which are found at the southern end on the highest ground, loessic heath on the middle slopes and Combe Deposit heath in the valley bottoms. In these areas there has developed a mixed flora of calcicoles and calcifuges some of them with strict calcicoles such as dwarf sedge (*Carex humilis*), burnt-tip orchid (*Orchis ustulata*) and field flea-wort (*Senecio integrifolius*).

In 1978 when the reserve was purchased most of these chalk heaths were in very poor condition with heather (*Calluna vulgaris*) becoming tall through lack of grazing. This had led to the loss of the intimate mixture and also to the acidification of soils beneath the heather making it unlikely that the calcicoles would be able to re-establish here when the area was grazed or mowed. Trials showed that if the areas were grazed to reinstate a short turf and then kept like this, there would be a gradual regeneration of heather from the seed bank, although nearly all the mature heather would die. In the past few years there has been a welcome increase in the areas of new heather in intimate mixtures with calcicoles. Chalk heath is also found on land which was returned to grassland from arable in 1957 and it has been very interesting to see the development of these areas under the grazing regime.

The results of the past 15 years at Martin Down demonstrate the possibility of getting neglected grasslands back to something approaching their state before management ceased, how this can be done using sheep alone and how a wide variety of grazing regimes can be used either on their own or together to achieve the conservation aims of a chalk grassland site.

APPENDIX 1

Short herb-rich grassland

Site: Martin Down NNR   Compartment: 4a

Description: in 1979 this was rank *Bromus erectus* with large patches of *Brachypodium pinnatum*. Since then grazing has reduced *Bromus erectus* and a much richer turf has developed between patches of *Brachypodium pinnatum*, but this latter species is spreading and becoming dominant over a large part of the compartment.

Compartment 4a

Year	Months	Sheep /ha/a year	No. of days	Sheep days /ha/a year	Sheep /ha/a year
1979/80	April/May	50	18		
	Jun./Jul.	70	6	1650	4.5
	Jan./Feb.	10	33		
1980/81	Jun/Jul.	50	24		
	Dec./Jan.	10	42	1620	4.4
1981/82	Mar./Apr.	30	21		
	Nov./Dec.	10	30	1065	2.9
	Jan.	15	9		
1982/83	Mar./Apr.	10	33		
	Aug.	15	24	690	1.9
1983/84	Jul./Sep.	10	60		
	Jan./Feb.	20	48	1860	5.1
	Feb./Mar.	10	30		
1984/85	Oct./Dec.	25	66	1650	4.5
1985/86	Apr.	20	15		
		10	6	1005	2.8
	Jul./Aug.	25	21		
1986/87	Mar/Apr.	10	27		
	Oct./Nov.	50	33	1920	5.3
1987/88	Jul.	60	45		
	Oct./Nov.	40	22	3930	10.7
	Nov.	24	14		
1988/89	Oct.	55	11		
	Oct./Nov.	33	19	1232	3.4
1989/90	Oct./Nov.	32	39	1248	3.4
				Average	4.3

APPENDIX 2

Medium length grassland
Site: Martin Down NNR   Compartment: 5b
Description: in 1979 this was rank *Bromus erectus* grassland. Since 1982 it has been grazed in early winter at about 40 sheep per ha for 2 -3 weeks and then again in spring to remove the first flush of *Bromus erectus*. The objective is to keep a fairly open herb-rich sward with long grass and tussocks, good for dark-green fritillary and marbled white butterflies in particular.

Compartment 5b

Year	Months	Sheep /ha	No. of days	Sheep days /ha	Sheep /ha/a
1979/80	Dec.	20	9		
	Jan./Feb.	10	39	570	1.6
1980/81	May.	50	9	450	1.2
1981/82	Nov./Dec.	45	18	810	2.2
1982/83	Nov./Dec.	40	12		
	Mar./Apr.	10	27	750	2.1
1983/84	Nov.	45	18		
	Apr.	20	9	990	2.7
1984/85	Oct.	40	12		
	Mar./Apr.	20	21	900	2.5
1985/86	Oct./Nov.	35	15		
	May.	20	12	765	2.1
1986/87	Nov.	35	12		
	Apr.	8	16	650	1.8
1987/88	Oct./Nov.	45	12		
	Apr.	20	19	820	2.2
1988/89	Oct.	50	15		
	Apr.	19	12	980	2.7
1989/90	Oct.	50	12		
	Apr.	20	12	840	2.3
				Average	2.2

APPENDIX 3

Reverting arable

Site: Martin Down NNR   Compartment: 11a

Description: arable from 1943 to 1957 and then re-seeded. This compartment was rank *Bromus erectus/Arrhenathrum elatius* grassland in 1979 when organised grazing was re-started, but there were even then many areas of shorter turf within the compartment. This is now a mosaic of *Bromus erectus*, *Arrhenathrum elatius* and short turf. The sward is quite open and increasingly herb-rich. Horseshoe Vetch (*Hippocrepis comosa*) and Kidney Vetch (*Anthyllis vulneraria*) are becoming abundant in places. Pyramid Orchids (*Anacamptis pyramidalis*) are frequent and abundant in parts. Burnt-tip Orchids (*Orchis ustulata*) have also colonised the area.

Compartment 11a

Year	Months	Sheep /ha	No of days	Sheep days /ha	Sheep /ha/a
1979/80	March	30	21	630	1.7
1980/81	Feb.	25	21	525	1.4
1981/82	May/Jun.	10	24		
	Sep.	20	27	780	2.1
1982/83	July/Aug.	25	21		
	Feb.	20	24	1005	2.8
1983/84	Aug.	30	18		
	Jan/Feb.	30	15	990	2.7
1984/85	Aug.	30	27	510	1.4
1985/86	April	25	15		
	Dec.	25	12	765	2.1
	Mar.	10	9		
1986/87	May.	15	15		
	Aug/Sep.	40	21	1065	2.9
1987/88	April/May.	26	11	286	0.8
1988/89	April	36	14	504	1.4
				Average	1.9

Landscape Ecology and Grassland Conservation

J. BAUDRY, C. THENAIL, D. LE COEUR[1], F. BUREL[1] AND D. ALARD[2]
Institut National de la Recherche Agronomique, 65, rue de Saint-Brieuc,
35042 Rennes Cedex, France
[1]Centre National de la Recherche Scientifique, Université de Rennes 1,
35042 Rennes Cedex, France
[2]Université de Rouen, 10, Bd de Broglie, BP 118, 76134 Mont-Saint-Aignan
Cedex, France

ABSTRACT

The goal of landscape ecology is to describe spatial ecological patterns and to relate them to processes. The spatial patterns are grassland types and species distribution, size of individual patches, connections among and between patch types, relationships with the physical environment and the farming systems. Two major processes are related to human activities: land use changes and changes in agricultural practices. Among the ecological processes involved in grassland dynamics are species movement (colonization, succession), seed survival, population dynamics and nutrient fluxes.

INTRODUCTION

Meadows and pasture are not isolated ecosystems, they are part of a mosaic made of similar or different grassland types and/or other land uses that may affect their ecological functioning. Research at the field level reveals gradients of factors responsible for the diversity of grassland types as a result of interactions between the physical environment, the management practices and plant (or animal) populations. The central paradigm of landscape ecology is that the distribution of the different types of grassland also depends on the proximity of species in grassland boundaries or in adjacent grassland.

Landscape ecology focuses on spatial ecological patterns and the processes that make them change over time (Zonneveld and Forman, 1989). The main patterns under consideration are habitats and species distribution; the processes can be ecological processes (e.g. species dispersal, succession) or processes that shape landscapes (e.g. human activities). This approach is now well developed for the study of species composition of forest, hedgerow networks and prairie habitats. It has barely been used to understand ecological patterns in temperate grassland. The purpose of this paper is to present the main landscape ecological concepts and how they may be used to study the conservation biology of grassland. Examples are drawn from ecological studies in the Pays d'Auge, central Normandy, France.

We first consider spatial patterns, since they are starting points for most studies. Then, we identify the relevant processes. Finally, applications for policies and conservation are outlined.

157

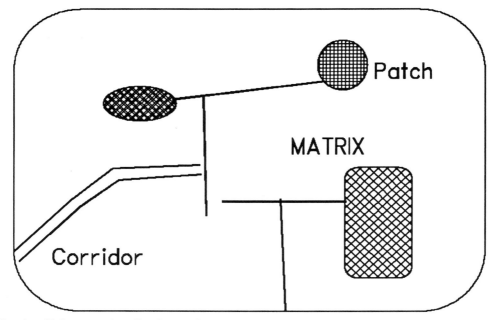

Fig. 1. Main categories of landscape elements.

Spatial patterns

Changing the scale of observation from quadrats to landscape is a way to deal with processes such as fluxes of species, information or nutrient that affect the species composition of quadrats.

The main spatial pattern concepts are: matrix, patch, corridor, connection, heterogeneity, metapopulation (Forman and Godron, 1985) (Fig.1). The **matrix** is the dominant type of land cover in a landscape, while **patches** are other types of landscape elements. Patches are characterized by their species composition, size, shape and degree of isolation from patches of similar or different type. As the study of interactions among landscape elements is the "core of landscape ecology", the recognition of landscape features that enhance or inhibit species movement is very important. In landscape ecology "species movement" applies to plants as well as to animals, "plant movement" being their dispersal. "Connectivity" is the ecological process by which species actually move from one patch to another and permits populations have genetics exchanges.

In heterogeneous landscapes some local populations installed in small landscape elements can be linked by individual dispersers, their demography being controlled at the landscape level in a metapopulation (Levins, 1970).

Ecological processes and landscape patterns

Several hypotheses have been developed in landscape ecology to relate patterns and processes and to explain differences or changes in species composition:

1)   A size effect Small patches contain less species than large patches according to Island Biogeography Theory (MacArthur and Wilson, 1967). In grassland this may apply to birds, although this is not well documented. Landscape ecologists have focused mainly on "natural habitats" (e.g. woodlots). We hypothesize that grassland fragmentation has a negative impact on conservation, as occurs in forest conservation (Saunders *et al.*, 1991). The interactions with other types of landscape elements (e.g. crops, highways) permit entry of harmful pesticides and nutrients. Populations of plants and animals thereby become smaller and thus more prone to extinction with a lesser probability of recolonization.

In prairie grassland, Coffin and Lauenroth (1989) have shown that large gaps created by disturbance recover more slowly than small gaps.

2)   Interactions among patches and fluxes of species (sources and sinks, Fig. 2). Most studies on changes in species composition leave out the problem of species sources, concentrating more on changes in the physical environment or the management practices (Balent, 1986; Losvik, 1988). Research on grassland establishment following crops have involved studies on seed banks (Graham and Hutchings, 1988) but investigation on other sources, such as other grassland fields or field margins, are scarce.

The importance of field margins as sources of species invading fields has been demonstrated for cropland (Marshall, 1989). Field margins are also important when cropland is converted to grassland or when management practices such as fertilization are relaxed. Casual observations show that species sensitive to fertilization or heavy trampling (e.g. *Centaurea sp.*, *Crepis capillaris*, *Festuca rubra*, and *Leucanthemum vulgare*) are

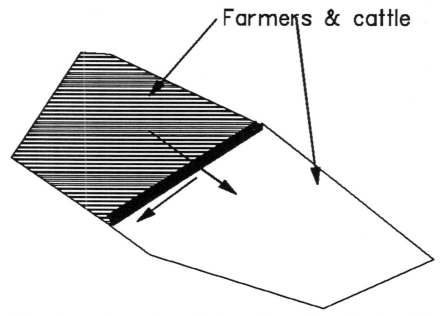

Fig. 2.   Fluxes of species, from patch to patch, along corridors and through farming activities.

still present under fencelines even when absent from the adjacent meadow or pasture. One of us (D. Alard) is conducting an experiment on the recolonization of former arable land from road verges.

The case of undergrazing exemplifies fluxes of species from adjacent elements into grassland. In pastures surrounded by hedgerows, ungrazed patches (patches of *Rubus spp.*) are only colonized by plant species present in adjacent hedgerows (Buttenschon, 1988; Burel and Baudry, 1990; Baudry, 1989). The ungrazed patches are colonized by "forest" ground beetles only if connected to hedgerows (Burel and Baudry, 1993 a). Both plants and carabids use hedgerows as corridors to move in landscapes (Burel and Baudry, 1993 b). Thus changes in species composition do not only depend on soil conditions and grazing pressure but also on their position in the landscape and available seed sources. In contrast, very mobile species such as spiders react very rapidly to any change in vegetation structure and do not exhibit distance or size effect in colonization (Asselin and Baudry, 1989).

Farmers are also responsible for various fluxes of seeds. Seeds can move from one field to another in manure or if hay is distributed outdoors to cattle. Farmers also directly select and utilize seed mixtures of grasses and legumes. Cattle transport seeds, whilst dung deposits act as important seed sources. Many grasses can be transported this way and dung may help their establishment by killing former vegetation and providing nutrients (Welch, 1985).

Fluxes of species are not always desirable. For instance, high connectivity of grassland may cause pest outbreaks, as in the case of *Microtus arvalis* (Delattre *et al.*, 1992).

Changes in landscape patterns

Landscapes are dynamics. Changes in patch types are due not only to changes in species composition but also to disturbances (e.g. fire, pests) and human activities. Normandy, renowned for its permanent grassland, was mostly cropland in the 19th century. For example, the Manche "département" had 20% permanent grassland in 1882 but almost 75% in 1965. In this region, hedgerows are numerous, with earth banks covered by well maintained herb layers harbouring many grassland species that may have acted as sources of species to complement seeds spreading from hay barns on pastures and meadows.

Landscape patterns and farm functioning

The diversity of grassland and the ecological dynamics that underline this diversity will only be sustained in large tracks of grassland over a wide zone. This implies that farmers are "responsible" for grassland biodiversity. They act on it in two ways: 1) by changing the proportions of permanent grassland in their system and 2) by their management practices (e.g. fertilization, grazing, haying) (Hopkins *et al.*, 1988; Vivier, 1990).

In the Pays d'Auge, 115 farms have been surveyed for land use. The farm sample was representative of the farming systems of the region. We obtained 8 categories of farms as described in Table 1. This survey indicates the mosaic of land use, the mosaic

Table 1. Types of farming systems.

Specialized meat production	Mixed production	Specialized milk production
M1: Small suckling cows or beef stockfarm, part time	**DM1:** Small traditional dairy and beef stockfarm	**D1:** Specialized average dairy stockfarm.
M2: Suckling cows and beef stockfarm, high rate	**DM2:** Large dairy and beef stockfarm only grassland	**D2:** Highly productive specialized dairy stockfarm
M3: Large beef stockfarm, low stocking rate	**DM3:** Dairy and meat stockfarm with cash and forage crops	

of management practices in grassland, including levels of inputs (Baudry and Thenail, 1993) and the relationships between practices and farming systems which are the driving factors of changes in the grassland mosaic. Table 2 gives a summary of the different management strategies in terms of inputs. Other management techniques are usually correlated, for example silage making with input of mineral nitrogen and high stocking rate.

Table 2.   Relationships between management of grassland (1 = no input; 2 = manure; 3 = fertilisers) and farming systems.

Practices	M1	M2	M3	DM1	DM2	DM3	D1	D2
1	59	13	32	65	29	21	15	7
2	23	0	8	15	8	1	0	5
3	44	20	36	67	85	157	91	54
TOTAL	126	33	76	147	122	179	106	66

For **M1** etc, see Table 1

A more detailed survey of the 115 farms having different types of production systems was then carried out to understand the within - and between - farms grassland management diversity (Thenail, 1992). The main conclusions are that the management regimes are a function of both farm productivity level and farm production diversity. In the most intensive farms, high inputs are on cropland (maize silage for dairy cattle). In these farms, grasslands which cannot be ploughed are used by beef cattle as a "secondary" production. From a landscape management and conservation point of view, it is worth noting that this meat production does not, in itself, provide a good income to the farmers. However, associated with dairy cattle, it permits farmers to avoid the abandonment of non-arable grassland. This is the reason why on farms with the most cropland, grasslands receive little, if any, fertiliser.

The pattern of "main" versus "secondary" production is found in almost every farm. In farms where no fertiliser is used, the differences in management practices are differences in stocking rate and mowing of ungrazed swards. Three main types of management regimes have been differentiated, along a gradient of management intensity: no input, manure only, chemical fertilisers.

The localization of the different types of management regimes is an important factor of the organization of the landscape mosaic. If at a global scale the physical constraints do not play a major role, they may be important determining factors within farms. Within each farm the most intensive management regime is localized on the most favourable soils (less slope and/or humidity and/or stoniness).

The current mosaic of grasslands composed of chalk grassland (*Brachypodium pinnatum, Sanguisorba minor, Cirsium acaule*), wet pastures (*Juncus spp., Scirpus palustris, Scorzonera humilis*), mesic unfertilised meadows (*Agrostis sp., Potentilla erecta, Anthoxantum odoratum*) and nutrient-rich meadows and pasture (*Lolium perenne, Alopecurus pratensis*) will be maintained in the near future.

Most of the time, chalk grasslands only exist as small patches in larger pastures; in this case the grazing pressure is heavier than in large spots, because cattle size is adapted to the mesic grassland. The species diversity is generally lower than in large patches where it may be over 100 species. Large tracts of chalk grasslands are threatened by abandonment and fertilization, for instance by the spreading of pig slurry.

Wet pastures are threatened by a lack of ditch management that leads to a dominance of *Juncus sp., Mentha sp.* and the disappearance of species such as *Lychnis flos-coculis*. Unfertilised mesic grasslands are being fragmented by ploughing and fertilization. Nevertheless as they represent the majority of grassland and since the farms are large (according to French standards), patches of several hectares still persist.

The map of one municipality constructed from land classes and the survey of practices (Table 3) permits a measure of landscape organization. We use a map that enables the proportion of the different grassland classes to be calculated, together with the probability that cells (0.25 ha) of one class be next to a cell of the same class if distributed randomly. This can be compared to the actual probability in the landscape. The ratio of actual/random probability of vicinity gives a measure of the spatial organization of the grassland classes (Table 4). If it is always higher than one, the clases are not randomly distributed.

Landscape pattern, grassland diversity and farming systems: a general model of grassland dynamics at the landscape level

Patch dynamics and fluxes of species are central to a landscape ecological approach. Until now these two aspects have been treated separately. Fluxes of species have been studied in wooded corridors, whilst studies of between-patch fluxes are still at the the-

Table 3. Type of grassland classes combining land classes and management practices.

Class 1	:	arable land, no input
Class 2	:	arable land, manure
Class 3	:	arable land, fertiliser
Class 4	:	non arable, no input
Class 5	:	non arable, manure
Class 6	:	non arable, fertiliser
Class 7	:	non arable, no machine, no input
Class 8	:	non arable, no machine, manure

Table 4. Spatial patterns of grassland classes. **p(n)** = frequency; **landscape** = actual probability of one class being next to a cell of the same class; **random** = probability in a random pattern; **organization** = ratio of actual to random.

Class	p(n)	Landscape	Random	Organization
1	0.163	0.124	0.026	4.702
2	0.023	0.013	0.001	24.675
3	0.081	0.054	0.007	8.313
4	0.199	0.146	0.040	3.671
5	0.017	0.010	0.000	35.223
6	0.111	0.082	0.012	3.672
7	0.036	0.018	0.001	13.558
8	0.014	0.007	0.000	34.487

oretical model stage (Milne, 1991). Patch dynamics studies are well developed for forests (Shugart, 1984) and more generally for land use. Grassland studies provide opportunities to merge both aspects. There are still methodological difficulties in sampling (scale of sampling) and data analysis (samples are neither independent nor normal).

This preliminary paper stresses that the biodiversity of grassland can be seen at two different scales: the patch and the landscape. Clearly, the maintenance of species richness requires management at the two scales. Some patches may have less species than others but, nevertheless, they participate in the global richness, because they harbor species not found elsewhere. Thus it is important to understand not only why different patches have different species, with different abundance, but also to understand why and how the grassland mosaic change.

The two scales can be combined in a model. A first entry point is the field. At the quadrat scale, ecologists study the factors differentiating grassland species composition including the effect of soil and management practices (Alard *et al.*, 1973). This can only be done on a limited number of fields. The set of farms covering a landscape is the second entry point, giving the combination of the physical environment and practices as well as their potential evolution. This kind of study must provide an exhaustive survey over the area of interest. The landscape as a mosaic and associated corridors is the third entry point that allows study of ecological interactions. This can be done on characteristic subsets of landscapes (Baudry, 1989; Burel and Baudry, 1993 a).

Spatial patterns in temperate grasslands have been mostly investigated within fields (Mahdi and Law, 1987; Thörhallsdttir, 1990). Within the studied range of scale, species interactions and clonal growth are responsible for the observed patterns that deviate from random patterns in both cases. Chaneton and Facelli (1991) assessed the effects of disturbances (grazing and flooding) at two different scales: patches and clusters of patches of about 1 ha. They found that changes in species diversity are scale dependent. Collins and Glenn (1990) studied the distribution patterns of prairie grassland species over a wide range of scale and found that they were similar and dependent on fine scale processes. This is certainly not the case in temperate grassland as agricultural practices are major factors of patterning at the landscape scale.

Landscape ecological principles emphazise the role of field boundaries in vegetation dynamics and as refuge for oligotrophic species during high input phases of management. They also provide an understanding of how the grassland mosaic is organized and how it could change if farming systems change. The landscape approach facilitate links with landscape architects and amenity studies (Green, 1990), although a common language is not always easy to find.

ACKNOWLEDGEMENTS
We thank the Fondation LIMAGRAIN whose financial support made possible the cooperation among the authors.

REFERENCES
ALARD D., BANCE J. F. and Frileux P. N. (1973) Grassland vegetation as indicator of the main agro-ecological factors in a rural landscape: consequences for biodiversity and wildlife conservation in Central Normandy. *Journal of Environmental Management* (in press).

ASSELIN A. and BAUDRY J. (1989) Les araneides dans un espace agricole en mutation. *Acta Oecologica Oecologia Applicata*, **10**, 143-156.

BALENT G. (1986) Modélisation de l'évolution des surfaces pastorales dans les Pyrénées Centrales. Mise au point d'un référentiel micro-régional de diagnostic au niveau de la parcelle. *Cahiers de la Recherche-Développement*, **9/10**, 92-99.

BAUDRY J. (1989) Colonization of grassland under extensification by hedgerow species. *Proceedings Brighton Crop Protection Conference, Weeds-1989*, 765-774

BAUDRY J. (1989) Interactions between agricultural and ecological systems at the landscape level. *Agriculture, Ecosystem and Environment*, **27**, 119-130.

BAUDRY J. and THENAIL C. (1993) Agricultural input/output and landscape patterns. *In: Fluxes in landscapes*. EUROMAB-INTECOL Seminar. Polish Academy of Sciences (in press).

164

BUREL F. and BAUDRY J. (1989) Hedgerow network patterns and process in France. *In:* Zonneveld I.S. and Forman R.T.T. (eds.) - *Changing landscapes: an ecological Perspective*. Springer Verlag, New-York, pp 99-120.

BUREL F. and BAUDRY J. (1993 a) Control of biodiversity in hedgerow network landscapes in Western France. *In: Hedgerow Management and Nature Conservation*. Wye University Press, (in press).

BUREL F. and BAUDRY J. (1993 b) Reaction of ground beetles to vegetation changes following grassland deriliction. *Acta Oecologica* (in press).

BUREL F. and BAUDRY J. (1990) Hedgerow networks as habitats for colonization of abandonned agricultural land. *In:* Bunce, R.H.G. and Howard, D.C. (eds.) *Species dispersal in agricultural environments*, pp 238-255 Lymington: Belhaven Press.

BUTTENSCHON J. (1988) The establishment of woody species in grassland conservation areas. *Aspects of Applied Biology*, **16**, 373-381.

CHANETON E.J. and FACELLI J.M. (1991) Disturbance effects on plant community diversity: spatial scales and dominant hierarchies. *Vegetatio*, **93**, 143-155.

COFFIN D.P. and LAUENROTH W.K. (1989) Disturbances and gap dynamics in a semiarid grassland: a landscape level approach. *Landscape Ecology* 3: 19-27.

COLLINS S.L. and GLENN S.M. (1990) A hierarchical analysis of species' abundance patterns in grassland vegetation. *American Naturalist*, **135**: 633-648.

DELATTRE P., GIRAUDOUX P., BAUDRY J. (1992). Land use patterns and types of common vole (*Microtus arvalis*) population kinetics. *Agriculture, Ecosystems and Environment*, **39**, 153-169.

FORMAN R.T.T. and GODRON M. (1985) *Landscape Ecology*. John Wiley and sons.

GRAHAM D.J. and HUTCHINGS M.J. (1988) Estimation of the seed bank of a chalk grassland ley established on former arable land. *Journal of Applied Ecology*, **25**, 241-252.

GREEN B.H. (1990) Agricultural intensification and the loss of habitat, species and amenity in British grasslands: a review of historical change and assessment of future prospects. *Grass and Forage Science*, **45**, 365-372.

HOPKINS A., WAINWRIGHT J., MURRAY P.J., BOWLING J.P. and WEBB M. (1988) 1986 survey of upland grassland in England and Wales: changes in age structure and botanical composition since 1970-72 in relation to grassland management and physical features. *Grass and Forage Science*, **43**, 185-198.

LEVINS R. (1970) Extinctions in some mathemetical questions in biology. *Lectures on mathematics in the life sciences*, **2**, 77-107. American Mathematical Society, Providence, Rhode Island.

LOSVIK M.H. (1988) Phytosocioloy and ecology of old hay meadows in Hordaland, western Norway in relation to management. *Vegetatio*, **78**, 157-187.

MACARTHUR R.H. and WILSON E. O. (1967) *The theory of island biogeography*, Princeton, New-Jersey: Princeton University Press.

MAHDI A. and LAW R. (1987) On the spatial organization of plant species in a limestone grassland community. *Journal of Ecology*, **75**, 459-478.

MARSHALL E.J.P. (1989) Distribution patterns of plants associated with arable field edges. *Journal of Applied Ecology*, **26**, 247-258.

MILNE B.T. (1991) The utility of fractal geometry in landscape design. *Landscape and urban planning*, **21**, 81-90.

SAUNDERS D.A., HOBBS R.J. and MARGULES C.R. (1991) Biological consequences of ecosystem fragmentation: a review. *Conservation Biology*, **5**, 18-32.

SHUGART H. (1984) *A theory of forest dynamics*. New York: Springer-Verlag.

THENAIL C. (1992) *Fonctionnement des exploitations agricoles du Pays d'Auge et Utilisation des prairies permanentes*. DAA INA-PG, INRA-SAD Normandie, unpublished report.

THORHALLSDOTTIR T.E. (1990) The dynamics of a grassland community: a simultaneous investigation of spatial and temporal heterogeneity at various scales. *Journal of Ecology*, **78**, 884-909.

TURNER M.G. and GARDNER R.H. (1991) *Quantitative methods in landscape ecology*. Springer Verlag.

VIVIER M. (1990) Les prairies et les pratiques d'exploitation. Eléments et réflexions pour un diagnostic. *Fourrages*, **124**, 337-356.

WELCH D. (1985) Studies in the grazing of heather moorland in north-east Scotland. IV Seed dispersal and plant establishment in dung. *Journal of Applied Ecology*, **22**, 461-472.

ZONNEVELD I.S. and FORMAN R.T.T. (Eds.) (1989) *Changing Landscapes: an ecological perspective*. New York: Springer-Verlag.

Possible Policy Options and their Implications for Conservation

D. BALDOCK
Institute for European Environmental Policy
158 Buckingham Palace Road, London SW1W 9TR

ABSTRACT

Grassland management in Europe is influenced by several different policies, with the Common Agricultural Policy being of particular importance. The implications of some recent changes in this policy are considered, with particular reference to the livestock sector. Future options for integrating conservation objectives more fully into agricultural policy include additional environmental incentive payments, the greater use of cross-compliance, increased support for extensive pastoral systems, reform of policies for the Less Favoured Areas and the introduction of special aids for shepherding.

INTRODUCTION

Relatively little grassland in Europe is managed for purposes other than agricultural production and most of the policy options considered in this paper are in the agriculture or agri-environment sphere. Nonetheless, there is a variety of other policies which influence the management of grassland, including forestry policy, environmental policy, controls over land use planning and taxation regimes.

The conservation and appropriate management of grassland in Europe cannot be attained simply by policies seeking to influence farm practice. For example, there are areas where the principal threat to grassland lies in pressures such as urbanization, the development of infrastructure, afforestation and other changes in land use. In others, the pressure takes the form of pollution, for example acid deposition, contamination with heavy metals and, in parts of Central and Eastern Europe especially, pollution by ionising radiation. Specific policies are required to address such problems.

Agricultural policy historically has been rather little concerned with conservation objectives. Until recently, there has been only localized concern about the drastic reduction in the area of semi-natural grassland. Increasing output and productivity have been dominant themes in agricultural policy, less attention has been paid to the deterioration of the grassland resource. EC policy on sheep production, for example, has encouraged a rapid increase in stock numbers in Britain and Ireland, leading to overgrazing over significant areas, sometimes accompanied by poor vegetation management.

Over the last five years, however, environmental concerns have become more prominent in agricultural policy. At the time of agreeing the MacSharry reforms to the CAP in May 1992 the Agriculture Council declared its commitment to pursuing the requirements of environmental protection as an integral part of the CAP. Given this, and the necessity to constrain or reduce production of several agricultural commodities, including milk and beef, there should be opportunities within the Community to strike a new balance between agricultural and environmental objectives for grassland. Lower stocking densities, coupled with appropriate sward and field margin management, could contribute to conservation objectives in many parts of Europe. At the same time, there are substantial areas where the reintroduction of stock or increased grazing intensity is necessary for the maintenance or enhancement of valued semi-natural habitats.

THE REFORM OF THE COMMON AGRICULTURAL POLICY

European agricultural policy entered a new phase with the agreement in May 1992 to reform the Common Agricultural Policy (CAP). Although this reform is not as far-reaching as it is sometimes portrayed to be, it introduced new limitations on the arable sector and increased restraints on both beef and sheep production. The full programme of reform is intended to be implemented in a series of stages and it is entirely possible that some elements will be modified before they have been put into place. Should the Uruguay round of the GATT negotiations be concluded within the next six months, some amendments to the MacSharry plans may become necessary for example.

In their present form, the new CAP arable and livestock regimes are likely to influence the extent and management of grassland in several different ways. It is worth considering the implication of these policies before attempting to identify new options.

One characteristic of the new support regime for cereals, oilseeds and protein crops is that farmers will be compensated for lower prices by means of direct support payments per hectare, known in the UK as area payments. These payments will be available only on land which already was producing the relevant crops on 31 December 1991 or earlier. Payments are available on temporary grassland which was part of an arable rotation, provided the grass was newly planted on or after 1 January 1987. In principle, this rule will create an incentive for some farmers to plough up grass leys planted since January 1987 in order to claim arable area payments. On larger farms where part of the arable area must be put into set-aside in order to be eligible for the area payment there may be a further incentive to reduce the acreage of previous grass leys in order to accommodate set-aside within a modified rotation.

On the other hand, the new regime should reduce the incentive for farmers to convert permanent grassland to arable production because they will be unable to claim area payments on newly converted land. Similarly, there should be less pressure to convert old orchards and other agricultural land uses with a grassland component into arable production. It is difficult to tell how effectively the rules on area payments will be enforced in every Member State and there are informal reports of some ploughing up of permanent grassland taking place after December 1991. Nonetheless, the rules should prevent the further ploughing up of permanent grassland on any significant scale.

168

Conversely, new barriers to the conversion of arable land to permanent grass have been erected. Farmers will lose the right to arable area payments on such land and will not gain an equivalent payment for grassland. Furthermore, with strict limitations now imposed on the number of stock eligible for livestock headage payments of different kinds, few farmers will find it economically attractive to increase their stock numbers and so will have little requirement for additional grassland.

Alongside these structural changes in agricultural policy are more specific initiatives, including the three "accompanying measures" which were agreed with the main package of MacSharry reforms. One of these is the EC agri-environment Regulation 2078/92 which requires Member States to introduce a range of voluntary incentive schemes for farmers. It has not yet been fully implemented, since Member States were to submit schemes for Community approval by the end of July 1993 and very few have been approved yet. One of the group of measures, which Member States are strongly encouraged but not absolutely obliged to introduce under the Regulation, is long term set-aside for environmental purposes. Such land must be taken out of production for at least 20 years. This scheme may cause small areas of arable land to be converted to grassland and the adoption of conservation management on limited areas of intensive grassland.

In England, MAFF has proposed to respond to this obligation by introducing a new "Habitats Scheme" which is expected to be launched in 1994. Farmers will be offered payments to create three new categories of habitat - inter-tidal habitats, particularly saltmarsh, water-fringe habitats alongside lakes and water courses in small pilot areas and particularly valuable habitats established under the now obsolete EC five year set-aside scheme. Where such habitats are created on arable or temporary grass, the payments offered will range from £275 to £525/ha. The total budget proposed for the period up to 1995/96 is £3 million.

Many, but not all, Member States are proposing to introduce long-term set-aside schemes. Generally these will be on a small scale within strictly defined areas, as in the current proposals from France and Ireland. Some, but not all, of this land will be within arable rotations.

However, the uptake of long-term set-aside schemes on arable land is likely to be limited severely by the ruling that such land withdrawal must be additional to any set-aside obligations that a farmer may have under the arable support scheme - known in Britain as the Arable Area Payments Scheme. Long-term set-aside is most likely to appeal to larger arable farmers who are subject to an obligation to set aside at least 15 per cent of their eligible arable area if they wish to claim area payments. In the UK, such farmers choosing the new non-rotational set-aside option will have to set aside 18 per cent of their eligible area, while in other Member States the figure will be 20 per cent. It seems unlikely that many farmers will wish to enter land into long-term conservation set-aside in addition to these shorter term obligations.

Consequently, the British government, supported by many NGOs, has been pressing for the long-term set-aside obligation to count towards the shorter term requirement. At the time of writing, it seemed unlikely that this request would be accepted, partly because of concern within the Commission that it would prove difficult adequately to monitor and control the simultaneous application of two different kinds of set-aside.

In principle, the growing emphasis on production restraints and set-aside within the reformed CAP should provide new opportunities for creating new habitats, including permanent grassland. However, the refusal to amend EC rules to allow long-term habitat creation to count towards set-aside under the arable support scheme is a severe impediment, both to participation by farmers in existing schemes and to the development of new schemes. In England, MAFF has suggested that the new "Habitats Scheme" might be expanded to provide incentives for the creation of lowland damp grassland and lowland heath, but only if the EC rules are amended.

The MacSharry reforms will affect the distribution and management of livestock within the Community, and therefore the pattern of grazing, as well as the overall area of grassland. The reforms affect sheep and beef producers much more than the dairy sector.

For sheep producers, one of the principal innovations of the reforms is the introduction of additional restrictions on the number of ewes qualifying for Sheep Annual Premium (SAP). Payments are limited to the total number of ewes held on a farm in a base year, which is 1991 in the UK. Farmers will be permitted to keep larger numbers of ewes than their total "reference flock" but these will not qualify for SAP. The new ceiling is in addition to the previous rules restricting full SAP payments to 1,000 ewes in the LFA and 500 elsewhere. Effectively, the right to an SAP has become a form of quota and has acquired a value. Regulations restrict the transfer of this quota out of "sensitive areas", which in the UK have been defined as the Less Favoured Areas (LFA). Whilst a new national reserve of quota has been established, this has been insufficient to meet the demands of special cases, such as new entrants to sheep farming and those taking over traditionally grazed land without any current quota.

Since these changes are relatively recent, their full implications are not yet clear. However, a greater rigidity has been introduced into the sheep sector. New factors will influence the movements of stock between holdings and the incentives to build up numbers on holdings without a quota, or only a small quota, are much reduced. The movement of sheep from the LFAs down to the lowlands in the UK and other Member States will be constrained. One effect of this is that the cost of moving stock from overgrazed to undergrazed areas has been increased. It may be difficult or expensive to obtain a quota for keeping sheep on semi-natural habitats in the lowlands where grazing is required but sheep were not kept in 1991. Equally, farmers whose stock numbers have been built up to the level where severe overgrazing is taking place have been rewarded by obtaining a quota for this number and have an incentive to retain an excessive number of stock.

Alterations in the CAP beef and veal support regime also have implications for grassland management. A farmer's eligibility for Suckler Cow Premium (SCP) is now limited not only to 90 animals per holding, but also to the farm's "reference herd", defined in most Member States as the number of cows held on the farm in 1992. The

Beef Special Premium Scheme (BSPS) is subject to a new system of "regional reference herds" which effectively are regional quotas on the right to premium. Where claims for premium within a region exceed the reference herd, there will be a *pro rata* cut in the level of premium paid on each animal.

Both the BSPS and the SCP are now subject to stocking density limitations, derived from calculations of the "forage hectares" on a holding. In 1993 payments will be limited to 3.5 livestock units (LUs) per hectare, taking account of dairy cattle and sheep on the holding, as well as beef animals. In 1994 the limit will be reduced to 3.0 LU/ha and by 1996 onwards it will be set at 2.0 LU/ha. It is intended that this limitation on stocking density will reduce the number of cattle eligible for headage payments and provide some relative advantage for those with lower stocking densities. However, it is recognized that more intensive beef producers are likely to benefit from lower cereal prices following the MacSharry reforms. To compensate, producers with a stocking rate of less than 1.4 LU/ha will be eligible for an additional premium of 30 ECU (about £27) per head under both the SCP and BSPS schemes.

As with the sheep regime, the new arrangements for supporting beef production introduce a greater element of rigidity and will discourage producers without beef cattle at present from starting up a beef enterprise. This is a restraint on a return to mixed farming in arable areas and may limit the options of some farmers considering conversion to organic production. The stocking density limits are expected to result in a decline in intensive beef production in some parts of the Community but it is less clear whether extensive forms of beef production will remain competitive, particularly in view of the large structural surplus in the beef sector.

The stocking density limits apply throughout the Community and so are a very crude mechanism for matching stock numbers more precisely to ecological as well as agronomic conditions. The ceiling of 2.0 LU/ha has not been set in response to any specific environmental policy goals and there is no allowance for varying it according to regional conditions. Furthermore, farmers may exceed the stocking density limitations without any penalty other than losing the premium on those stock above the threshold. Originally, the Commission had proposed that no headage payments would be made at all on farms where stocking density limits were exceeded.

NEW POLICY OPTIONS

The changing climate for agricultural policy has resulted in discussion of a growing number of different policy options for integrating farming, environmental and rural development objectives in Europe. Some of these are particularly applicable to the goal of improving grassland management. For the purposes of this paper, the main focus will be on policy options for the livestock sector.

a) **Safeguarding sustainable extensive livestock systems**
There are large areas of Europe where extensive forms of pastoral agriculture survive, often under traditional management systems. Extensive farming systems are the primary form of management for many semi-natural habitats of high conservation value,

including alpine grassland, lowland hay meadows and several categories of dry grassland. From the evidence available, it appears that these systems are subject to decline in most parts of Europe and many observers expect this trend to continue (Bignal and McCracken, 1992).

The main reasons for the decline in this form of farm management are abandonment and intensification (Baldock, 1990). In many Northern European countries a range of new incentive schemes is being introduced to provide farmers with stronger incentives to maintain such systems. The "Environmentally Sensitive Areas" schemes in Britain and Denmark, the recent Article 19 scheme in France, the Management Agreement Regulation (RBO) in the Netherlands and the growing array of landscape and nature management schemes in Germany are all examples of this approach.

However, all these schemes are on a relatively small scale. There is some information available about public expenditure on the most prominent schemes of this kind in 1991 or 1992. In Denmark it was less than ECU 4,000,000, in the UK it was around ECU 18,000,000, in France about ECU 5,000,000 and the RBO programme in the Netherlands involved expenditure of just under ECU 10,000,000. Larger sums were devoted to such schemes in Germany - the Bavarian Landscape Management Programme involved expenditure of about ECU 42,000,000 for example (Baldock, 1992).

Expenditure on this scale is dwarfed by the total CAP budget which is now close to ECU 35 billion annually. Even when the new EC agri-environment programme, Regulation 2078/92, is implemented fully, annual expenditure by the Community is expected by the Commission to average only about ECU 400,000,000 per annum, little more than one per cent of the total CAP budget. This total includes funds for schemes concerned with pollution control, extensification, the management of abandoned land, long term set-aside, the preservation of rare breeds and other measures in addition to those akin to the present generation of ESA schemes.

The expansion and improvement of ESA schemes clearly is one means of improving the economic viability of farms and farming systems where grazing management is compatible with conservation requirements. Voluntary incentive payments of this kind appear acceptable to most members of the farming community and are sufficiently flexible to be tailored to local conditions and priorities. Regulation 2078/92 allows for considerable variation between regions and Member States in the way that schemes are designed and implemented. "Zonal programmes" tailored to local conditions are envisaged in the Regulation. To a considerable degree, Member States are free to initiate their own national and regional incentive schemes in addition to those permitted under 2078/92, as has occurred in many German Länder and in other countries - Tir Cymen in Wales would be a further example.

Nonetheless, there are limitations on the extent to which these schemes can be expanded. There are uncertainties over the scale of the budget available at Community level and under Regulation 2078/92 national authorities must contribute between 25-50 per cent of the cost of implementing schemes. In many countries, including the UK, there are severe budgetary limitations on the funds available for environmental schemes of this kind, especially since the cost of the CAP is increasing relatively rapidly. Furthermore, many of the southern Member States have had little experience of offering such schemes in the past and need to build up appropriate systems of training and education, and institutions equipped to design and put into practice workable schemes. In the southern Member States particularly there are large areas of extensively farmed land which are not in private ownership and many of the holdings are very small. In these conditions, the type of management agreements offered in northern Europe may not be appropriate and it may take some years to develop effective schemes.

b) **Cross-compliance**
The term cross-compliance has come to be used in a loose sense to apply to any set of environmental conditions attached to agricultural support payments. This approach is used in the United States in order to require arable farmers in areas subject to severe soil erosion to draw up and comply with conservation plans. The same principle could be utilized within the CAP, for example to require farmers receiving livestock headage payments to comply with maximum stocking densities or codes of practice concerning grassland management.

Some modest steps towards adopting this approach have been taken already. Member States now are empowered to apply environmental conditions to applicants for the Suckler Cow Premium although none appear to have done so to date. The Commission is expected to issue proposals to allow a similar form of optional cross-compliance to apply to the BSPS and the Sheep Annual Premium schemes.

One advantage of cross-compliance is that it offers a route towards improved environmental management on farms without the need to increase public expenditure to any marked degree. A simple form of cross-compliance might involve a code of practice covering issues such as drainage, irrigation, input use, cutting dates in sensitive areas, management of field margins and on-farm habitats, etc. More sophisticated forms of cross-compliance could introduce maxima on stocking densities or other stipulations regarding livestock management, such as the removal of stock from sensitive areas during the winter.

At present, few European governments are in favour of introducing cross-compliance to the main CAP market support instruments. It would be unpopular with farmers, at least initially, and would introduce new administrative procedures and costs. Nonetheless, if environmental conditions are attached to the increasingly costly direct payments to farmers, there might be greater public support for the continuation of these subsidies in future.

c) **Reforming the CAP livestock support systems**
As suggested above, the new CAP policies for supporting beef, sheep and goat production are likely to inhibit the redistribution of livestock between farms and between regions. From a conservation perspective, a more flexible approach allowing stock to be transferred without the requirement to purchase quota would be preferable. Several different mechanisms can be envisaged for this purpose. For example, within the

173

sheep regime Member States could be obliged to draw up schedules of appropriate stocking densities in different regions taking account of ecological as well as agronomic considerations.

On this basis, "sensitive areas" for the purposes of SAP quota could be redefined and new mechanisms introduced to encourage the movement of stock from overgrazed to undergrazed areas. Such mechanisms might include a larger national reserve, a significant proportion of which could be devoted to making quota available to areas which are undergrazed, including semi-natural grassland in the British lowlands where grazing has been abandoned.

More fundamentally, the sheep and beef headage payment systems could be replaced by area payments made per hectare, irrespective of the number of stock carried. These area payments could be set in accordance with the appropriate, rather than the historical, stocking density. Although some farmers would suffer reduced incomes as a result of this approach, it could be introduced over a period of time and special compensatory measures could be offered to farmers in areas where total subsidy per hectare fell sharply, which might occur in parts of mid Wales for example. It is also possible to consider a hybrid system whereby livestock farmers receive some subsidy in the form of a headage payment and some in the form of an area payment. In cooperation with the Moorland Associations the National Farmers' Union (NFU) has proposed a scheme of this kind whereby farmers would be able to qualify for area payments in return for voluntarily suspending part of their sheep quota. This would allow stocking densities to fall without any increase in public expenditure (NFU, 1993).

This scheme could result in an overall reduction in lamb production in the UK and any other Member State that adopted it, unless it was possible to increase sheep numbers on other farms without benefit of SAP. If this fall in production proved undesirable, then farmers should be allowed to run sheep on some set-aside land without benefit of SAP and with some control on overall numbers, possibly achieved by a form of "B" quota.

d) Amending the LFA support scheme

Livestock numbers within the LFA have been maintained partly because of the level of support offered under the sheep and beef regimes and partly because of additional premiums available within the LFA, supported by more generous investment aid than available elsewhere. At present, the stocking density limitation is 1.4 LU/ha, which is not sufficiently low to prevent overgrazing in some parts of the Community. Furthermore, investment aid has been available for ploughing, reseeding and other forms of grassland improvement even in areas where this is environmentally damaging and not productive agriculturally.

Consequently, there is scope for introducing a stronger environmental element into the LFA scheme. Investment aid could be confined to appropriate areas and forms of farm improvement which are not damaging environmentally. Similarly, stocking density limitations could be refined and matched more closely to regional conditions. This might result in some decline in livestock numbers within the LFA but farm incomes would not necessarily decline commensurately, because gross margins per animal may increase and there may be scope for rebalancing subsidies, as discussed earlier.

e) New incentives for shepherding

One reason for the decline in grassland management in some areas grazed by sheep, such as parts of the British uplands and the Spanish dehesas, is the abandonment of traditional forms of shepherding because of their high cost or the lack of labour willing to undertake this work. For example, the tendency for flocks to roam more freely often leads to undergrazing and abandonment in certain areas and trampling and over-grazing in others.

It would be possible to provide direct aid to farmers for shepherding in the form of a labour subsidy, rather than a headage subsidy. Such an approach could be experimented with in pilot areas with the costs being divided between the Community and individual Member States.

f) Extensification

Hitherto, livestock extensification schemes within the EC have had limited take-up. However, it would be possible to adopt different approaches to extensification, for example by offering special aid to areas with major problems of overgrazing. Rather than insisting on a fixed target for lower production, the scheme could be aimed at meeting new target stocking densities over a period of years. Such an incentive scheme could be introduced in advance of policies applying more stringent environmental conditions to CAP support payments. In this way, voluntary schemes could pave the way for a more mandatory approach.

g) Other approaches

In addition to those alterations in agricultural policy discussed here, there is a range of other options, including increased incentives for farmers converting to organic production and special schemes to encourage those retaining regionally distinct and environmentally sustainable systems, such as transhumance in Central Spain, Greece and Italy. In addition, there is the possibility of introducing taxes or controls on the inputs of fertilizers and agrochemicals on grassland. Outside agricultural policy, there are further options, including the strengthening of land use planning and environmental regulations. In several Member States, implementation of the EC "Habitats" Directive should lead to stronger protection for those categories of grassland listed in the annexes, although additional financial resources may be required to ensure that they are managed appropriately.

REFERENCES

BALDOCK D. and PIANTANIDA A. (1990) *Agriculture and Habitat Loss in Europe*, WWF International CAP Discussion Paper No 3, Gland, Switzerland.

BALDOCK D. (1992) *A Summary of Incentives for Countryside Management in Denmark, Germany, France, the Netherlands and the UK*, background paper for Countryside Commission seminar, Yorkshire, October 1992.

BIGNAL E. and MCCRACKEN D. (1992) *Prospects for Nature Conservation in European Pastoral Farming Systems*, Joint Nature Conservation Committee, Peterborough.

NATIONAL FARMERS UNION (1993) *Response to MAFF Consultation Paper - Agriculture and England's Environment*.

THEATRE PAPERS

Pennine Dales ESA: Grassland Management and Nature Conservation Interest

D. R. ASKEW

ADAS Leeds Statutory Centre, Otley Road, Leeds LS16 5PY

ABSTRACT

Botanical and field management data have been analysed for a sample of fields in the Pennine Dales ESA. A series of CHAID analyses have been carried out to identify management variables associated with high conservation interest. A number of aspects of traditional management as encouraged by the ESA have been identified as important, including; fertiliser rates, hay making regimes, grazing patterns and liming practices.

INTRODUCTION

The Pennine Dales Environmentally Sensitive Area (ESA) was designated in March 1987 as one of the first 6 ESAs in England and Wales under Section 18 of the Agriculture Act 1986. Background information to the ESA schemes is published elsewhere (MAFF, 1989). Within the [Pennine Dales] ESA annual payments are made to participating farmers in return to their agreeing to farm according to specific ESA management prescriptions designed to protect the landscape, historical features and nature conservation interest of the area.

The area now designated covers some 46,500 ha in the upper reaches of 25 valleys (dales) in the mid and north Pennines. Mean altitude is 326m and the upland climate can be harsh with high rainfall (mean annual total of 1305mm) and a short growing season. Agriculture is based on hill sheep but also suckler cattle and some dairying. The majority of the ESA is enclosed grassland used either for pasture (grazing only) or meadow (stock removed prior to cutting for hay or silage in early summer). These grasslands created by traditional low-input farming are of central interest to the ESA representing a unique and extensive reserve of botanically rich communities of national importance. It is one of the few remaining areas of the country with good numbers of flower-rich, generally mesotrophic, traditionally managed hay meadows. Pastures, particularly calcareous ones, also support very diverse swards with many attractive species such as bird's-eye primrose (*Primula farinosa*) and common rock-rose (*Helianthemum nummularium*). These grasslands are also of significant ornothological interest with associated species such as lapwing (*Vanellus vanellus*) and curlew (*Numerius arquata*) in pastures and yellow wagtails (*Motacilla flava flavissima*) in meadows.

The national loss of grassland of nature conservation interest is well documented and the Dales have not been immune from these changes with agricultural improvement of grassland seen particularly in the lower dales. There has been a steady loss of meadowland, with for example a decline from 15,000 ac in Wensleydale in the 1930's to less than 10,000 by the 1970's (Fieldhouse, 1980). Even in the remoter ESA dales changes have continued on land not entered into the scheme with 33 ha (approximately 1%) of semi-improved grassland improved in the period 1987-1990 (MAFF, 1991).

To address these changes the ESA seeks to re-establish or maintain traditional grassland management. This paper gives the results of an initial analysis relating botanical composition of grasslands to management within the Pennine Dales ESA.

METHODS AND DATA COLLECTION

Data were collected between 1987 and 1989 from 307 fields (151 meadows and 156 pastures) as part of the environmental monitoring programme established in 1987 by ADAS (MAFF, 1991). All fields were randomly selected from those under ESA agreement, except 25 fields whose selection was dependent upon the co-operation of farmers who were not in the scheme. For each field, management data was obtained by questionnaire and botanical data derived from five, 1 x 1m quadrats per field as described in MAFF (1991).

The questionnaire data were used to characterise the management regime at the time of ESA designation and the botanical data to characterise the associated conservation interest. Data for 20 management variables were collected and reduced to nominal or ordinal scales. The botanical data can be treated in a number of ways to yield indices reflecting conservation interest. The analysis uses the field mean percentage of species per quadrat classified as stress-tolerant (or borderline stress-tolerant) following the functional model developed by Grime *et al.*, (1988). These species are characteristic of the more interesting and diverse swards in the Dales. They include for example, lady's mantle (*Alchemilla vulgaris agg.*), northern marsh orchid (*Dactylorhiza purpurella*) and marsh marigold (*Caltha palustris*). Analysis was also based on the presence of particular species known to be of interest such as wood cranesbill (*Geranium sylvaticum*), a characteristic species of traditional Dales hay meadows.

The method of analysis used is the CHAID (Chi-squared Automatic Intercation Detector) segmentation technique (Magidson, 1989). It is essentially an exploratory technique based on Chi-squared analysis of categorical data. The end result of the analysis is a hierarchy of significant (P) management variables identifying the management associated with high or low conservation interest. CHAID reduces the number of categories used for predictor variables where possible.

RESULTS

Results are presented in the form of tree-diagrams with each cell containing the management variable and category, the total number of fields in the group, and the percentage of these fields defined as being of conservation interest. Moving down the tree, variables are identified in decending order of priority. Fig. 1 and 2 show the results from analyses using a specified percentage of stress-tolerators to categorise fields

180

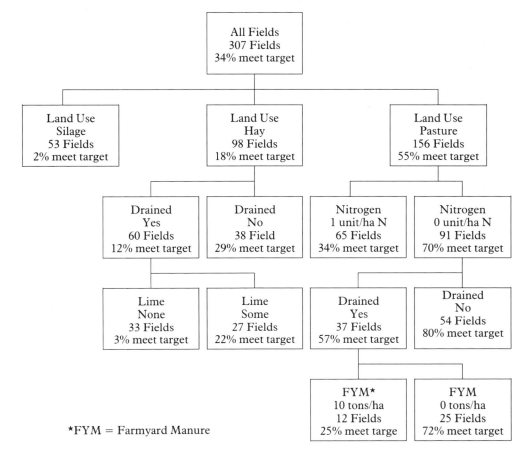

Fig. 1. CHAID analysis of all fields; Target = fields with more than 15% stress-tolerators.

as having high or low conservation interest. These percentage cut-offs have been selected to ensure a reasonable split of fields between high and low interest.

Land use is identified as the best overall predictor, with pastures most often meeting the target level of stress-tolerators and silage fields least often. For pastures, organic or inorganic fertiliser inputs are associated with reduced interest. Drainage has a similar effect in both hay meadows and pastures, with more undrained fields being of conservation interest. For drained hay meadows, fields that have received some lime are likely to have more stress-tolerant species than fields which have not. The target level of stress-tolerators is reduced in meadows to account for the lower frequency of these species. For undrained meadows a small group of fields cut late in the year all have the target level of interest. Earlier cut fields not receiving slurry and grazed for longer over winter also all meet the target. Liming again appears as an important management variable with most interest being associated with infrequent applications (ie before 1980) as opposed to recent or no applications.

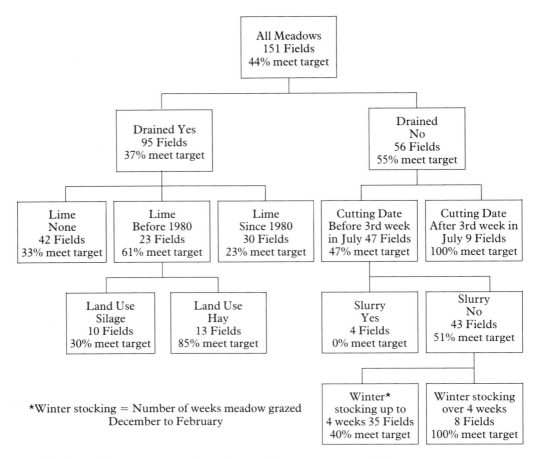

Fig. 2. CHAID analysis of meadows; Target=fields with more than 8% stress-tolerators.

Wood crane's-bill is strongly associated with meadows and in particular those grazed for up to 9 weeks in spring and grazed over a longer period in winter (Fig. 3). No other variables are identified as significant. Analysis of the distribution of yellow rattle (*Rhinanthus minor*) showed it to be also associated with meadows and in particular those not receiving herbicide treatments or recent lime as well as fields cut later where lime has been applied recently.

DISCUSSION

The analyses presented here should be regarded as preliminary. There are a number of potentially confounding effects in the data. In practise cutting dates and fertiliser inputs for example are clearly linked. The data does not cover important physical environmental variables that obviously have an influence such as soil type. Overall however, the association between the many individual management practices that

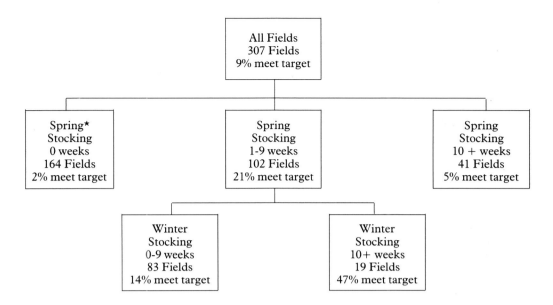

*Spring stocking = Number of weeks meadows grazed March to May. 0 weeks indicates Pasture or Meadow not grazed in spring.

Fig. 3.   CHAID analysis of all fields; Target = fields with wood crane's-bill recorded.

make up 'traditional management' and conservation interest can be seen. The distinction between grassland used as pasture or meadow is an important one, with overall more stress-tolerant species associated with pastures (but not higher species richness). Hay making as opposed to silage making emerges as an important factor in distinguishing meadows with convervation interest. This may be related to the higher fertiliser inputs or earlier cutting associated with silage making. Other factors inherent in the silage making process may be important such as the reduced opportunity for vegetation to shed seed with less turning of the cut crop. Lack of drainage and lower fertiliser input also appear to have a significant overall influence. It is axiomatic that meadows must be managed as meadows to maintain their interest. In this context it is interesting to note that with regard to liming, a feature of management in the Dales since the nineteenth century, the greatest interest is associated with some lime application rather than none. In the Pennine Dales ESA, although lime applications are prescribed against, in practise, after field inspection moderate applications have generally been permitted on meadow land.

With regard to individual species it is clear that even for two species characteristic of hay meadows the particular aspects of management they are associated with differ. It has been suggested that the grazing regime of meadows (Smith, 1988) is an important element of management either by reducing competition or providing germination

183

sites. For wood crane's-bill, the meadow grazing regime is identified as the factor most significantly associated with its presence; particularly a long winter and moderate spring grazing period. Yellow rattle is a relatively early flowing annual and it may be more susceptible to early cutting (Smith and Jones, 1991). Later cutting is identified as a significant factor but after herbicide use and lime application in importance.

CONCLUSIONS
The continuation of meadow management, encouragement of hay making instead of silage making, control of drainage works, reduced fertiliser inputs and, to a lesser extent no herbicide applications and later cutting dates all appear to be associated with greater conservation interest. Lime applications can be beneficial to botanical interest in meadows and therefore need to be considered on merit. Some meadow species are also associated with management regimes which include a significant period of winter grazing.

ACKNOWLEDGEMENT
This work is funded by MAFF as part of a full monitoring programme assessing the environmental impact of ESAs.

REFERENCES
FIELDHOUSE R.T. (1980) Agriculture in Wensleydale from 1600 to the present day. *Northern History*, vol. *XVI*, 169 - 195.

GRIME J P., HODGSON J. E. and HUNT. R. (1988) *Comparative Plant Ecology.* Unwin Hyman Ltd.

Ministry of Agriculture, Fisheries and Food (1991) *The Pennine Dales; Report of Monitoring 1991* London: (MAFF Publications).

Ministry of Agriculture, Fisheries and Food (1989) *Environmentally Sensitive Areas. (First Report).* London (HMSO).

MAGIDSON. J. (1989) CHAID, LOGIT and Log-Linear modelling. *Marketing Information Systems.* Report 11-130, Deltran N.J: Datapro Research Corporation.

SMITH R. S. and JONES L. (1991) The Phenology of mesotrophic grassland in the Pennine Dales, Northern England: historic hay cutting dates, vegetation variation and plant species phenologies. *Journal of Applied Ecology*, **28**, 42-59.

SMITH R.S. (1988) Farming and the conservation of traditional meadowland in the Pennine Dales Environmentally Sensitive Area. *Special Publication Number 7.* The British Ecological Society.

Grassland Management and its Effect on the Wildlife Value of Field Margins

A. C. BELL, T. HENRY AND J.H. McADAM
Department of Agriculture for Northern Ireland
Newforge Lane, Belfast BT9 5PX

ABSTRACT

Four distinct management strategies were applied to grass field margins incorporating well-maintained hawthorn hedges. Analysis of flora and fauna by TWINSPAN and DECO-RANA showed that sheep grazing had profound effects on the habitat. The results indicate that protection from intensive grazing is necessary if the wildlife value of grass field margins is to be conserved.

INTRODUCTION

The agricultural land area of Northern Ireland is approximately 1M ha of which 70% is grassland based. Family farms are small (average 35.1 ha) and the small field size (average 1.8 ha) results in a landscape characterised by 150,000 km of predominantly hawthorn hedges. While some research has been conducted on the conservation value of arable field margins (Way and Greig-Smith, 1987), there is relatively little information for grass field margins.

Thomas *et al.* (1991) state that, for arable crops, the hedge is relatively unimportant as a reservoir for polyphagous invertebrate predators. The nature of the ground flora and the physical structure of the hedge or boundary base is of greater importance. Pollard (1968) showed that complete removal of the bottom flora of a hawthorn hedge by spraying with herbicide reduced the abundance of many carabid species. This was attributed to marked changes in microclimate. It has also been demonstrated that management practices have a profound effect on the carabid and spider fauna of grassland (Luff *et al.*, 1990; Rushton *et al.*, 1989). Many species found on unimproved sites were not present after pasture improvement.

Virtually all grass field margins in Northern Ireland are subject to the same management as the remainder of the field, i.e. fertilised and cut for silage and/or grazed. This paper reports the effects of four different grassland management practices on the flora and fauna of grass field boundaries with the aim of recommending the best strategy for maximising wildlife value.

MATERIALS AND METHODS
Treatments
Three well-maintained, mature, predominantly hawthorn (*Crataegus monogyna*) hedges separating paired grass fields formed the blocks for the study set up in 1990.

Within a block, 4 treatments, each 30 m long, were randomly arranged across the hedge extending 10 m into the fields. The treatments were:

(1) Fertilise/graze. Plots were fertilised (100 kg N/ha) and rotationally grazed with sheep.

(2) Plough/game cover. A 2 m strip adjacent to the hedge was ploughed and sown initially with a game cover crop of kale, mustard and quinoa; the remaining 8 m was fertilised (150 kg N/ha) and two cuts of silage taken. In March 1993 Jerusalem artichokes were planted as the game cover crop.

(3) Plough/unmanaged. This was similar to the previous treatment except that the 2 m strip was left unseeded and allowed to be colonised naturally.

(4) Unmanaged control. These plots received no fertiliser or management treatments.

Flora and fauna recording

Plant species presence and percentage cover were recorded in July 1991 and August 1993 in permanent quadrats in the hedge and hedge base, and at 0.5, 2, 6 and 9 m into the field. Quadrats were placed along three randomly arranged line transects on both sides of the hedge. Carabid beetle species were trapped in each plot using three pitfall traps placed 1-2 m ("margin" sample) and 8-10 m ("field" sample) either side of the hedge. Monthly catches were taken in March, May, July and September of each year.

Data analysis

The floristic data for each set of three quadrats at a particular distance from the hedge were added together giving a total of 144 samples for each sampling session. The resultant data matrix was subjected to classification and ordination using TWINSPAN (Hill, 1979a) and DECORANA (Hill, 1979b) respectively.

The catches for each set of three pitfall traps were combined to produce a total of 48 samples. The number of each species occurring in each sample was counted and submitted to ANOVA. Species presence data was analysed using TWINSPAN and DECORANA for each trapping month, and for the same months over the three years, 1991 - 1993.

Recording of air and soil temperatures was conducted in all treatments in May and July 1993. Probes were placed both in the margin and field zones of each plot and hourly readings collected using a Squirrel data logger.

RESULTS

Floristic data

An analysis of variance of plant species diversity of the 1991 data revealed no significant differences among treatments. The highest species diversity was found at 0.5 m from the hedge over all treatments (Henry *et al.*, 1992). TWINSPAN analysis of the 1991 data demonstrated a clear separation of the hedge samples, but failed to distinguish between the remainder of the treatments. In 1993 there was a clearer distinction between the hedge group and the other data. Hedges could be classified clearly as those bordering ungrazed plots, and those which were at the edge of grazed plots. This split was on the basis of more gaps occurring in the grazed treatments. The remainder of the samples were grouped as either margin (0.5 m) or field samples (9 m). The exception to this grouping was the presence of the fertilised/grazed 0.5 m samples within the field grouping. DECORANA demonstrated this distribution of samples (Fig. 1).

Carabid data

There were no significant differences among treatments in species richness in any trapping month, the highest number of species occurring in May. TWINSPAN revealed the presence of two distinct habitat groups, margin and field. No distinction was found between the margin treatments that were ploughed and the unmanaged control. The fertilise/graze treatment at the margin was consistently grouped with the field habitats in May and July over the three years. This clustering was clearly demonstrated by a DECORANA plot of the data (Fig. 2). The analysis of variance for margin and field beetle species supported this classification of treatments.

Air temperatures at 10 cm above ground were extremely variable in all treatments. However, soil temperature ranges were significantly ($P<0.05$) greater in the grazed margins compared to those in the same zones of the other treatments.

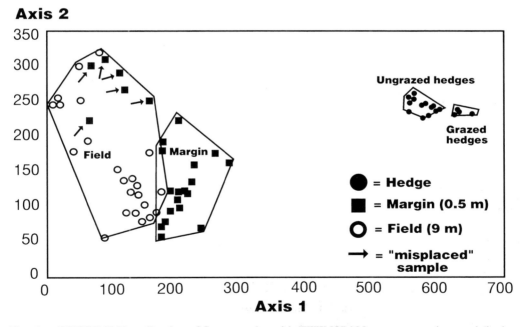

Fig. 1. DECORANA ordination of flora samples with TWINSPAN groups superimposed (hedge base, 2 m and 6 m samples have been omitted for clarity). The "misplaced" fertilise/graze margin samples are indicated.

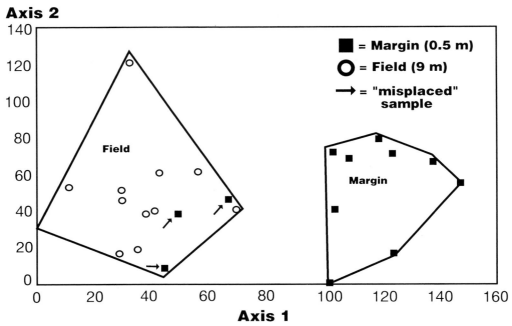

Fig. 2. DECORANA ordination of carabid samples with TWINSPAN groups superimposed. The "misplaced" fertilise/graze margin samples are indicated.

In 1993 difficulties were experienced in establishing a successful game cover crop. The emergent shoots of virtually all the Jerusalem artichokes planted were grazed by slugs.

DISCUSSION

The results of this study clearly demonstrate the impact of sheep grazing on both the flora and fauna of field margins. Samples of flora and carabids from the fertilised/grazed plots bordering the hedgerow were consistently classified with samples from open field. This is probably due to the close cropping of vegetation, and a further effect of this was the wider soil temperature fluctuation recorded in the grazed margins. The associated change in microclimate may well be an important element in modifying the carabid communities in these areas, an effect referred to by Pollard (1968).

No clear differences in the margin flora and fauna emerged among the three treatments, plough/game cover, plough/unmanaged and unmanaged control. Differences in flora may be expected as soil fertility declines, a long-term process. In addition, problems have been experienced in establishing a successful game cover crop. The failure of the Jerusalem artichokes was due to a combination of a wet, cold period of weather following planting, combined with high slug activity in the plots following shoot emergence.

The results from the present study indicate that protection of the field margin from intensive grazing is necessary if the wildlife value is to be conserved. This work is a long-term trial and monitoring will continue for several years to follow the effects of the management regimes imposed.

REFERENCES

HENRY T., McADAM J. and BELL A. (1992) The effect of grassland management practices on the conservation value of grass field boundaries. *Proceedings Third BGS Research Conference*, British Grassland Society, 1992, pp159-160.

HILL M.O. (1979a) TWINSPAN: a FORTRAN programme for arranging multivariate data in an ordered two-way table by classification of the individuals and attributes. *Cornell University, Ithaca, New York.*

HILL M.O. (1979b) DECORANA: a FORTRAN programme for detrended correspondence analysis and reciprocal averaging. *Cornell University, Ithaca, New York.*

LUFF M.L., EYRE M.D. and RUSHTON S.P. (1990) Grassland management practices and the ground beetle fauna. *Proceedings Second BGS Research Conference*, British Grassland Society, 1990, pp 19-20.

RUSHTON S.P., LUFF M.L. and EYRE M.D. (1989) Effects of pasture improvement and management on the ground beetle and spider communities of upland grasslands. *Journal of Applied Ecology*, **26**, 489-503.

THOMAS M.B., WRATTEN S.D. and SOTHERTON N.W. (1991) Creation of 'island' habitats in farmland to manipulate populations of beneficial arthropods: predator densities and emigration. *Journal of Applied Ecology*, **28**, 906-917.

WAY J.M. and GREIG-SMITH P.W. (1987) Field margins. *BCPC Monograph No. 35. London,: British Crop Protection Council.*

Species-rich Hay Meadows and their Relationship to the Socio-economic Status of Farmers

M.R. EAKIN AND A. COOPER

Department of Environmental Studies, University of Ulster,
Coleraine, Northern Ireland BT52 1SA

ABSTRACT

County Fermanagh is one of the most botanically rich wetland areas in the British Isles and has the greatest concentration of species-rich hay meadows in Northern Ireland. Traditional farming methods in the county have persisted so that semi-natural vegetation communities are still commonplace. A vegetation survey of hay meadows in 1991 established the main grassland types which are associated with varying degrees of intensity of farm management. A questionnaire survey subsequently carried out in 1992 sought to characterise the main socio-economic characteristics of traditional farm managers compared to their more intensive counterparts. This approach provided quantitative information to test anecdotal evidence that related species-rich meadows to older, bachelor farmers living on small, uneconomic farm holdings. With such knowledge, conservation managers will have a better understanding of the reasons for the persistence of semi-natural vegetation communities throughout a period of agricultural intensification. Predictions of changes in the farming community can be made and allied to consequent land use change within a region recently designated an Environmentally Sensitive Area (ESA).

INTRODUCTION

Heavy textured soils and poor land drainage have meant that the farming economy of Co. Fermanagh has always been dominated by grasslands (Symons, 1963). Traditional farming methods have carried on alongside more modern, intensive management regimes so that a range of grassland communities can be recognised. These vary from higher yielding species-poor types to less productive species-rich types (Eakin, 1992).

Part of the grassland survey fieldwork involved obtaining preliminary information on the agricultural management of land. In meeting farmers it was evident that many of the best meadows belonged to older, bachelor farmers operating relatively traditional farm management. Conversely, some of the most species-poor, more productive meadows were managed by younger married farmers with children. It was considered necessary to describe, in a more quantitative manner, the relationship between the grassland communities and the socio-economic status of the farm managers.

190

METHODS

A TWINSPAN classification (Hill, 1979) of the botanical data grouped the grassland types into two broad categories. The Group 1 category includes species-poor, intensively-managed grassland types with a mean number of taxa per $2m^2$ quadrat (N) less than 15. Group 2 comprises species-rich grassland communities with N20. For each of the field parcels surveyed for its botanical composition in 1991 a return visit was made and the farm owner interviewed and a questionnaire completed. Each questionnaire included questions about the area of land farmed, the number of livestock, the age of the farmer, the family composition of the farm household and off-farm income. Farm size and Farm Business Size (FBS) are grouped into categories published in the Annual Farm Census Results (DANI, 1991). The FBS is an indirect measure of farm income and is determined by calculating the Standard Gross Margin (SGM) of each farm. The SGM (measured in European Currency Units (ECU)) is calculated from stock numbers and crop areas. Minor holdings (SGM <2,000 ECU) are excluded from the DANI agricultural censuses but were included in the questionnaire analysis.

The Empty Nest households refers to couples living alone and whose children are no longer living in the family house. The non-family household category includes households where the farmowner has no spouse but is living with family of the same generation, with or without parents. The bachelor/spinster category are unmarried farm owners living alone.

RESULTS

Farm Size

A Chi-squared test indicated a significant relationship between the number of quadrats from each grassland type and the three farm size categories (Table 1). Eighty-one percent of all the quadrats occurring in the smallest farm size category (<14.9 hectares) belonged to Group 2 grassland types. The two larger categories displayed small or no differences in the number of quadrats belonging to either grassland group.

Table 1. The number of quadrats from species-poor (Group 1) and species-rich (Group 2) grasslands associated with farm size categories. $\chi^2 = 15.7$, P<0.01

Farm size (ha)	Grassland type		
	Group 1	Group 2	Total
0.0 - 14.9	12	52	64
15.0 - 49.9	51	57	108
50.0+	15	15	30

Farm Business Size (FBS)

Twenty-six percent of all holdings were minor holdings (Table 2) which agricultural economists regard as economically unviable farm businesses (DANI, 1991). Of these, only one quadrat belonged to the Group 1 grassland type. The very small holdings were fairly evenly distributed between the grassland types while 77% of the quadrats in the small category belonged to the species-poor group.

Table 2. The number of quadrats from species-poor (Group 1) and species-rich (Group 2) grasslands, associated with Farm Business Size categories. $\chi^2=55.8$, P<0.01

| Farm business size (ECU) | Grassland type | | |
	Group 1	Group 2	Total
Minor holdings <2,000	1	53	54
Very small 2,000-8,000	40	54	94
Small 8,000-32,000	37	14	51

Farmer Age and Grassland Type

Over 50% of all quadrats belonged to farmers older than 56 years (Table 3). Within the species-poor grassland group, 80% of quadrats were on land owned by farmers between 36 and 65 years. In the species-rich grassland group, 33% were on land owned by farmers aged 65 and over. A further 30% were on land owned by farmers aged between 56 and 65 and the remaining 37% were owned by the younger farmers (7). Seventy-seven per cent of grassland types owned by farmers over 65 were species-rich.

Table 3. The number of quadrats from species-poor (Group 1) and species-rich (Group 2) grasslands, associated with farmer age. $\chi^2=11.1$, P=0.01

| Farm owner age | Grassland type | | |
	Group 1	Group 2	Totals
Under 45	23	34	57
46 - 55	19	14	33
56 - 65	26	40	66
Over 65	13	44	57

Household Composition

Table 4 shows the distribution of the grassland groups within household units. Seventy-seven per cent of all holdings owned by the bachelor/spinster household category were associated with Group 2 grassland types. Similarly, non-family households had 4 times more Group 2 quadrats than Group 1. The households with children had a more equal number of quadrats in each grassland group.

Table 4. The number of quadrats from species-poor (Group 1) and species-rich (Group 2) grasslands, associated with household composition.

Household composition	Group 1	Group 2	Totals
Bachelor/spinster	11	37	48
Non-family household	3	12	15
Couple living alone ('Empty nest')	7	11	18
Couple/widow(er) & children (>15)	31	24	55
Couple/widow(er) & children (<15)	32	46	78

DISCUSSION

In economic terms, an association between smaller farms or farm businesses and species-rich grassland communities has been shown. Also, there is a lack of other forms of farm income, except welfare benefit, among those family household units (bachelors/spinsters and non-family households) associated with species-rich grassland types. Two socio-characteristics of farm owners have been related to grassland types. Species-rich grassland types are particularly common in farms owned by older farmers and by family units where there is, or has been, no marital connection.

Bachelor/spinster and non-household families have no children and so they lack an obvious successor to the farm holding. Potter and Lobley (1992) showed that elderly farmers without successors lack the incentive and motivation to continue expanding the business and accumulating capital into old age. This grassland study confirms this relationship between older farmers lacking sibling successors and less intensive farm management beneficial to wildlife conservation.

The recent Fermanagh ESA designation (DANI, 1993) is an excellent opportunity for DANI (Department of Agriculture for Northern Ireland) to target incentives at groups of farmers in most need of financial support and at the best conservation sites (Potter, 1990). But can it address the problem of abandonment and the loss of flower-rich meadows which is evident in much of this peripheral region and which is bound to continue as the last generation of traditional farm managers passes on?

REFERENCES

DANI (1991) *Farm Census Results.* Department of Agriculture Economics and Statistics Division, Belfast.

DANI (1993) *West Fermanagh and Erne Lakeland Environmentally Sensitive Area.* Department of Agriculture for Northern Ireland, Belfast.

EAKIN M.R. (1992) *A Botanical Survey of Conserved Grassland in Co. Fermanagh* Report to the Countryside and Wildlife Branch of the Department of the Environment for Northern Ireland.

HILL M.O. (1979) *TWINSPAN - a FORTRAN program for arranging multivariate data in an ordered two-way table by classification of the individuals and attributes.* Cornell University, New York.

POTTER C. and LOBLEY M. (1992) Ageing and succession on family farms. *Sociologia Ruralis,* **32**, 317-334.

POTTER C. (1990) Conservation under a European farm survival policy. *Journal of Rural Studies,* **4**, 365-375.

SYMONS L. (1963) *Land Use in Northern Ireland: The General Report of the Land Utilisation Survey.* London: University of London Press.

Effects of Seed Mixture, Cutting/Grazing and Slurry on Yield and Composition of Sown Pastures

G.E.J. FISHER, L.J. BAKER AND D.A. ROBERTSON
Scottish Agricultural College, Auchincruive, Ayr KA6 5HW

ABSTRACT

Small plot and field-scale experiments were devised to study the effects of flower growth habit, clover, cutting/grazing regimes and slurry applications on herbage yield and quality, and the presence and abundance of wildflowers in sown extensively managed pastures. A small plot experiment demonstrated that seed mixtures with rosette type flowers, no clover and a simulated one-cut for hay management produced the most favourable balance of high DM yield and high flower content. Results from field-scale experiments suggested that applications of slurry markedly reduced the abundance and diversity of flower species, while a two-cut system improved the ME and CP contents of cut herbage and maintained the diversity of flowers. Grazing in spring to reduce the competitive ability of grasses improved the quality of cut herbage, but reduced flower content.

INTRODUCTION

Pressure for the reduction of inputs into grassland-based agriculture has stimulated research on the use of extensive grassland systems. There has been little work on species-rich pastures for production systems, although some management guidelines are available (Ash *et al.*, 1992). The objectives of this work were to: 1. Use a small-plot experiment to investigate the effects of wildflower growth habit, white clover and cutting regime on yield and botanical composition of herbage cut from sown extensively managed swards, and 2. Study the effects of cutting/grazing management and slurry application on sown extensive pastures on a field-scale.

MATERIALS AND METHODS

Small-plot experiment

An experiment was established in 1990 on free draining sandy-loam soil at Auchincruive. All plots were sown with red fescue (*Festuca rubra*) and meadow fescue (*Festuca pratensis*) and with or without white clover (*Trifolium repens*). The wildflower mixtures used were either erect (E) or rosette (R) types. The E flowers sown were knapweed (*Centaurea nigra*), scabious (*Knautia arvensis*), ragged robin (*Lychnis flos-cuculi*), red campion (*Silene dioica*), oxeye daisy (*Leucanthemum vulgare*), burnet (*Sanguisorba officinalis*) and tufted vetch (*Vicia cracca*). The R flowers sown were kidney vetch (*Anthyllis vulneraria*), chicory (*Cichorium intybus*), hawkbit (*Leontodon autumnalis*), dandelion (*Taraxacum officinale*), thyme (*Thymus serpyllum*), bird's-foot trefoil (*Lotus corniculatus*), plantain (*Plantago lanceolata*), and yarrow (*Achillea millefolium*). The flowers were sown as R or E, or R & E. The plots were 6 x 2 m and were cut with a Haldrup to 3 cm to simulate grazing (G), hay (H) or silage (S) cutting. Three cutting treatments were employed to simulate (a) hay cut and aftermath grazing (-/-/H/G/G/G), (b) spring grazing, hay cut and aftermath grazing (G/-/-/H/G/G) and (c) two silage cuts and aftermath grazing (-/S/-S/G/G). Therefore, there were 18 treatment combinations (3 growth habit x 3 management x 2 white clover) and each was replicated three times (total of 54 plots). The plots did not receive fertilisers.

Field-scale experiments

Experiments commenced in 1989 and 1990 on extensive pastures at Crichton Royal Farm, Dumfries. Fields were sown with a mixture of 16 flowers, 5 grasses (cocksfoot, *Dactylis glomerata*; timothy, *Phleum pratense*; crested dog's-tail, *Cynosurus cristatus*, meadow fescue and red fescue) and 2 clovers (white clover and red clover, *Trifolium pratense*). Of the flowers sown, those which established successfully were plantain, yarrow, oxeye daisy, chicory, red campion, ragged robin, knapweed, hawkbit, scabious, burnet, bird's-foot trefoil and tufted vetch. The basic management of the swards was nil fertilisation, cut for hay or big bale silage in July, graze the aftermath with dairy youngstock and graze overwinter with sheep.

Three experiments were established: 1. SLURRY APPLICATION; the effects of applying cattle slurry in winter equivalent to 100 kg N/ha/year ("with slurry") was compared to nil slurry applications ("without slurry") on two adjacent 1 ha paddocks. One conservation cut was taken in July every year from each sward. 2. CUTTING REGIME; the effects of taking one conservation cut per year in July ("one-cut") was compared with taking two cuts in May and July ("two-cut") on two adjacent 0.6 ha paddocks. 3. GRAZING/CUTTING MANAGEMENT; the effects of making one conservation cut in July and grazing the aftermath (C/G) was compared to the same treatment with an additional three to four weeks grazing in May of each year (G/C/G) at 6.4 L.U./ha with dairy youngstock. Total DM yield and herbage metabolisable energy (ME) and crude protein (CP) contents were recorded for each treatment. In April of each year the ground cover of species was estimated using a 10-point quadrat. At least 30 random quadrats per treatment were used in each year, recording all hits to ground level.

RESULTS AND DISCUSSION

In the small-plot experiment, the simulated hay management produced the highest DM yields of total herbage and flowers ($P<0.01$), while the simulated silage management gave the highest yields of clover DM (Table 1). The use of R type flowers increased DM yields of total herbage and flowers ($P<0.01$), compared to plots with E and R & E types. Yield of grasses was highest where only E flowers were used. Adding white clover to the plots increased total ($P<0.001$) and grass ($P<0.01$) DM yields.

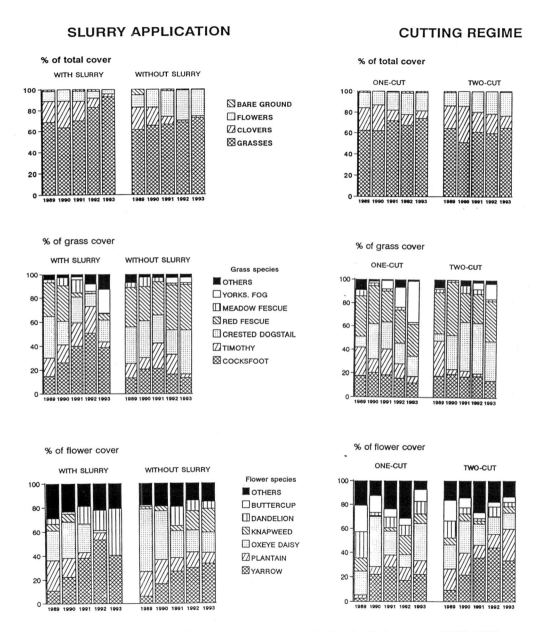

Fig. 1. Botanical composition from point quadrats recorded in April of each year (1989-1993).

Table 1. DM yields of cut herbage (t DM/ha) in second harvest year of small-plot experiment.

Treatment	Total	Yield of Grasses	Yield of Flowers	Yield of Clover
Hay	7.8	2.6	3.9	1.3
Late hay	6.1	2.0	2.6	1.5
Silage	6.7	2.5	2.2	2.1
±sed	0.89	0.40	0.46	0.65
R	7.4	2.1	3.7	1.6
E	6.6	2.7	2.1	1.8
R & E	6.6	2.2	2.8	1.6
±sed	0.95	0.40	0.50	0.67
- Clover	5.4	1.7	3.2	0.5
+ Clover	8.4	2.9	2.6	2.9
±sed	0.46	0.22	0.45	0.21

In the field-scale experiments, slurry applications increased DM yield by 30% and yield of energy and CP per ha, compared to the adjacent sward which did not receive slurry (Table 2). However, the use of slurry reduced the abundance and diversity of flowers according to ground cover data (Fig. 1) and encouraged the growth of cocksfoot and Yorkshire fog (*Holcus lanatus*). The two-cut system did not markedly affect DM yield (Table 2) but produced higher covers of clovers over the period of study (Fig. 1) and herbage of superior ME and CP content, compared to the one-cut system.

Table 2. Average DM yields and ME and CP contents and yields from herbage cut for conservation in 1989 to 1992.

Treatment	DM yield (t/ha)	ME (MJ/kg DM)	CP (g/kg DM)	ME yield (GJ/ha)	CP yield (kg/ha)
With slurry	6.77	8.1	83	55	562
Without slurry	5.19	7.8	70	40	363
One-cut	6.66	8.3	69	55	460
Two-cut 1st	4.65	11.1	139	66	939
Two-cut 2nd	1.45	10.1	202		
*C,G	6.07	8.8	68	53	413
*G,C,G	4.44	9.4	144	42	639

* 1990 to 1992 only

This resulted in 20% more ME and 104% more CP being harvested on average from the two-cut sward (Table 2). The two-cut system did not lead to reductions in the abundance and diversity of flowers in ground cover (as might have been expected) but it did eliminate timothy from cover measurements. Imposing a spring grazing in the G/C/G treatment reduced average DM yield by 27% but improved herbage ME and CP contents (Table 2), compared to the C/G treatment. The G/C/G treatment also increased the clover content and reduced the flower content of cut herbage (Frame *et al.*, 1993).

CONCLUSIONS

1. In a small plot experiment on sown extensive pastures, sowing rosette type flowers, imposing a hay cut and not using clover in the mixture produced the most favourable balance of herbage yield and flower content.

2. Field-scale experiments demonstrated that: (a) The use of slurry increased DM yield of herbage, but reduced flower content; (b) A two-cut system improved herbage ME and CP contents and did not affect the diversity and abundance of flowers; (c) Imposing high stocking rates in early season encouraged the growth of clover, reduced yield of herbage cut for hay and increased herbage ME and CP contents.

REFERENCES

ASH H.J., BENNET R. and SCOTT R. (1992) *Flowers in the Grass. Creating and Managing Grasslands with Wildflowers*. Peterborough: English Nature.
FRAME J., FISHER G.E.J. and TILEY G.E.D. (1993) Wildflowers in grassland systems. In: Haggar, R.J. and Peel, S. (eds.). *Occasional Symposium of the British Grassland Society* No. 28 (in press).

Lowland Grassland In England: Conservation of a Declining Resource in Worcestershire

R.G. JEFFERSON, H.J. ROBERTSON, J. MARSDEN[1], AND A.J.L. FRASER[2]

English Nature, Science Directorate, Northminster House, Peterborough PE1 1UA
[1]English Nature, West Midlands Region, Masefield House, Wells Road, Malvern Wells, Worcestershire WR14 4PA
[2]The Worcestershire Nature Conservation Trust Ltd, Lower Smite Farm, Smite Hill, Hindlip, Worcester WR3 8SZ

ABSTRACT

Dry neutral grasslands conforming to the National Vegetation type MG5 Cynosurus cristatus - Centaurea nigra *have only been described by phytosociologists from the British Isles. In England these semi-natural grasslands are now a scarce resource and it has been estimated that less than 4,000 ha now remain. Worcestershire has a particular concentration of MG5 grassland estimated to be 12% of the national resource. Loss rates of neutral grassland between 1980 and 1991 were estimated to be 3% per annum and market research has shown that of a sample of neutral grasslands, only 35% are currently under management likely to sustain their nature conservation value.*

INTRODUCTION

Semi-natural lowland grasslands whilst probably widespread in Europe at the turn of this century are now a scarce and declining resource (Van Dijk, 1991). Permanent grassland occurring on neutral brown soils in the British lowlands has been classified systematically by Rodwell (1992). On dry, largely free-draining soils, the main semi-natural grassland type is the crested dog's tail *Cynosurus cristatus* - common knapweed *Centaurea nigra* grassland (MG5) (Rodwell, 1992). This grassland type is valued for nature conservation as it is composed of native grasses and dicotyledenous herbs, is species-rich per unit area and is normally associated with a long history of hay cropping and aftermath grazing with no fertiliser inputs apart from occasional light dressings of farmyard manure.

It has become increasingly rare as a result of agricultural improvement over the last 50 years, and it is now a scarce and still declining resource in Great Britain (Rodwell, 1992). The lowland plain of the old County of Worcestershire is known to have a particular concentration of MG5 grassland (Stephen, 1993) and this paper examines the distribution and extent of the MG5 resource, threats to its maintenance and enhancement and how its conservation might be effected.

DISTRIBUTION AND EXTENT IN ENGLAND

To date very few surveys have been undertaken to find the precise extent of *Cynosurus cristatus - Centaurea nigra* grassland in any defined geographical area in England. Despite this, it is possible, using the data from the few surveys that have been undertaken (Palmer and Blake, 1991) and data on the extent of this grassland type in the Site of Special Scientific Interest (SSSI) series, to make a rough estimate of the current extent of the resource. Extrapolating this data, Jefferson and Robertson (in prep) estimated that less than 4,000 ha of MG5 grassland now remain in England. Such grassland is usually widely scattered and often occurs as small isolated fields or small groups of fields (NCC, 1989). Porley and Ulf-Hansen (1991) estimated that 50% of all neutral grassland in Dorset occurred as fragments of less than 5 ha in extent and 71% of sites were less than 10 ha in extent.

NEUTRAL GRASSLAND IN WORCESTERSHIRE

Distribution and extent

The area referred to in this paper is the old County of Worcestershire prior to Local Government reorganisation in 1974 and comprises an area of c 174,277 ha.

A high proportion of the MG5 neutral grassland community occurs on the loams and clays of the central Worcestershire Plain, particularly the *Lathyrus pratensis* and *Galium verum* sub-communities (Stephen, 1993).

It was not until the early 1970s that it was realised that Worcestershire might be especially rich in unimproved neutral grassland. A few neutral grasslands were notified as Sites of Special Scientific Interest (SSSI) as early as 1971 and initial survey work by the Worcestershire Trust commenced in 1972. During 1991 and 1992, English Nature undertook surveys of semi-natural neutral grasslands in Worcestershire which proceeded in three phases (Fraser, 1991, 1992; Stephen, 1993). The survey covered all types of neutral grassland and a few sites were surveyed which supported National Vegetation Classification grassland communities other than MG5, such as the MG4 meadow foxtail *Alopecurus pratensis* - great burnet *Sanguisorba officinalis* grassland (Rodwell, 1992). Sites were surveyed using the standard Nature Conservancy Council Phase II grassland survey method which is described fully in Smith *et al* (1985) and utilises the National Vegetation Classification. Of 623 fields visited (1,273 ha), 386 fields totalling 500 ha were MG5 *Cynosurus cristatus - Centaurea nigra* grassland. This is likely to be an underestimate of the Worcestershire resource as some fields which were likely to be MG5 were not surveyed (Fraser, 1992; Stephen, 1993). All 3 sub-communities of MG5 were present with the *Danthonia decumbens* sub-community (MG5c) being largely restricted to the north of the area on the Sandstones and Coal Measures. The *Galium verum* sub-community (MG5b) principally occurred on the Calcareous Lias Clays in the south and east whilst the *Lathyrus pratensis* sub-community (MG5a) showed no particular pattern in relation to geology and soils (Stephen, 1993). Using the national estimate of MG5 grassland, Worcestershire currently has a minimum of 12% of the English resource of this grassland type.

Losses

Comparison of the 1991/92 surveys with the survey undertaken by the Worcestershire Trust in 1980 revealed a 37% loss over the period equating to a c 3% loss rate per annum of semi-natural neutral grassland over the period. Most losses (83%) were the result of agricultural improvement including ploughing and re-seeding with high yielding ryegrass or conversion to arable.

Over and above this figure it was estimated that a further 28% of neutral grasslands were damaged or were under management inappropriate to maintaining their nature conservation value. This was caused by a number of factors including lack of hay cutting, intensive horse grazing and partial agricultural improvement. Since the 1992 survey, of 59 sites revisited by English Nature, one had been destroyed, 4 had suffered long-term damage due to the use of slurry or fertiliser, whilst 9 had not been subject to recent hay cutting or grazing management (J. Bingham, English Nature personal communication).

Whilst loss rates in Worcestershire have been high, a study by Porley and Ulf-Hansen (1991) showed an even higher loss per annum (10%) of neutral grasslands in Dorset between 1982 and 1988.

Tenure and management

A research project undertaken by ADAS (ADAS 1992) for English Nature and the Countryside Commission investigated the tenure and management of Worcestershire neutral grasslands. The survey aimed to collect data from 10% of owners, 10% of the estimated number of fields and 10% of the area of unimproved neutral grassland identified by Fraser (1992). The total sample consisted of 57 owners or occupiers managing a total land holding of 1,518 ha and 110 individual neutral grassland fields covering 245 ha.

ADAS (1992) concluded that of the total area of semi-natural neutral grassland in the survey only 35% is currently under a management system likely to maintain its nature conservation interest - that is extensive management of hay cutting followed by aftermath grazing with sheep or cattle. It follows that 65% is potentially under threat. Key threats include agricultural intensification and inappropriate management, such as horse grazing. The ownership profile is such that 29% of the resource is owned or managed by full-time farmers, 14% by part-time farmers with much of the remainder (46%) being owned or managed by non-agricultural owners including equestrian businesses. Managers over 60 own 46% of the grassland of which 35 ha (14%) is grassland currently in beneficial management. A high proportion of this resource is thus likely to change ownership in the medium term. In terms of the actual management type, 21% of the resource is used for horse grazing. The implications of these findings are that a large proportion of the remaining neutral grassland resource is under threat from inappropriate management which could lead to a degradation of its nature conservation value.

One particular problem is posed by horse grazing which can lead to a decline in the species-richness of MG5 grassland through nutrient enrichment. This results from horses establishing latrine areas which are subsequently not used for grazing (Odberg and Francis-Smith, 1977). This effect is particularly pronounced in small enclosed fields. Also annual species such as yellow-rattle (*Rhinanthus minor*) can be lost under heavy spring/summer grazing regimes because seed formation is prevented. In addition, supplementary feeding of horses, particularly in autumn and winter, can result in mechanical damage to the sward.

The possibility of changing management from horse grazing to a more appropriate management system is limited for a number of reasons. Firstly, in many cases horse owners do not have alternative land on which to keep horses even if willing and in the event that this was possible, many do not have the agricultural infrastructure necessary to re-instate hay cutting and grazing management. This latter situation would also apply to other non-agricultural owners and occupiers of neutral grasslands.

NATURE CONSERVATION STRATEGY

Conservation of the remaining areas of unimproved neutral grassland in Worcestershire is clearly a priority for those organisations whose function it is to conserve and maintain important wildlife habitats in the rural landscape. There are a range of mechanisms currently potentially available to conserve the neutral grassland resource. Firstly, sites can be notified by English Nature as Sites of Special Scientific Interest under Section 28 of the Wildlife and Countryside Act 1981. Currently 21 sites in Worcestershire are notified primarily for their neutral grassland interest and contain 104 ha of MG5 grassland (15% of the County resource). Further notification of MG5 grassland sites is planned in 1993/4 following on from the survey work (Fraser, 1991, 1992; Stephen, 1993). The conclusion of Management Agreements under Section 15 of the 1968 Countryside Act with owners and occupiers on SSSIs is one method of encouraging appropriate management. A possibility for the future is the inclusion of Worcestershire neutral grassland SSSIs into English Nature's Wildlife Enhancement Scheme which provides standardised payments for positive management.

Other voluntary mechanisms include Countryside Stewardship Scheme Agreements with the Countryside Commission under the Hereford and Worcester old meadow and pasture option (by 30 March 1992, 21 Agreements had been concluded over 135 ha) and Management Agreements with Hereford and Worcester County Council under Section 39 of the Wildlife and Countryside Act 1981. Finally, further sites could be purchased by the Worcestershire Nature Conservation Trust. The Trust already manages ten neutral grassland sites and is currently engaged in a meadows campaign of which acquisition is a principal element.

Clearly, conservation of neutral grassland requires an integrated effort by conservation organisations, planners and policy makers utilising the full range of legislative and management incentive mechanisms.

ACKNOWLEDGEMENTS
We thank John Bingham, Pauline Homer and Dr Peter Holmes of English Nature for their invaluable assistance.

203

REFERENCES

ADAS (1992) *Report and results of research into the ownership and management of Worcestershire semi-natural neutral grasslands*. Contract report to English Nature and the Countryside Commission.

DIJK G VAN (1991) The status of semi-natural grasslands in Europe. In: Goriup, P. D., Batten, L. A. and Norton, J. A. (eds.). *The conservation of lowland dry grassland birds in Europe*, pp.15-36, Joint Nature Conservation Committee, Peterborough.

FRASER A. J. L. (1991) *Worcestershire grasslands 1991. Report of Botanical Survey*. Contract Report to English Nature. Worcestershire Nature Conservation Trust Ltd, Hindlip, Worcester.

FRASER A. J. L. (1992) *Worcestershire Grasslands 1992. Provisional Resource Inventory*. Contract Report to English Nature. Worcestershire Nature Conservation Trust Ltd, Hindlip, Worcester.

NATURE CONSERVANCY COUNCIL (1989) *Guidelines for the selection of biological SSSIs*. Nature Conservancy Council, Peterborough.

ODBERG F. O. and FRANCIS-SMITH K. (1977) Studies on the formation of ungrazed eliminative areas in fields used by horses. *Applied Animal Ethology*, **3**, 27-34.

PALMER M. and BLAKE C. (1991) *Review of the extent of grassland survey in England*. England Field Unit Project No 101. Nature Conservancy Council, Peterborough.

PORLEY R. D. and ULF-HANSEN P. F. (1991) Unimproved neutral grassland in Dorset : survey and conservation. *Proceedings of the Dorset Natural History and Archaeological Society*, **113**, 161-165.

RODWELL J. S. (ed.) (1992) *British Plant Communities 3 : Grassland and Montane Communities*. Cambridge University Press, Cambridge.

SMITH I. R., WELLS D. A., WELSH P. (1985) *Botanical survey and monitoring methods for grasslands*. Focus on Nature Conservation No 10. Nature Conservancy Council, Peterborough.

STEPHEN K. (1993) *Worcestershire Grasslands 1992. Report of Botanical survey for English Nature*. English Nature, West Midlands Region, Malvern.

Rotational Management of Grasslands and Invertebrate Diversity

M.G. MORRIS AND W.E. RISPIN

NERC Institute of Terrestrial Ecology, Furzebrook Research Station,
Wareham, Dorset BH20 5AS

ABSTRACT

A rotational grazing trial at Old Winchester Hill National Nature Reserve is briefly described. Hemiptera were sampled from each of 11 plots from 1982 to 1985. There were differences in abundance generally, and of individual species, between years, between positions on the hillside and between plots. There were also differences due to the grazing treatments, with the abundances of many species positively correlated with vegetation height. The results are discussed in relation to wildlife conservation aims and management. When aims include maintenance of invertebrate diversity, rotational management is recommended.

INTRODUCTION

Grassland is conserved and maintained by management, yet all methods of management have deleterious effects on most species of invertebrate animals. Consequently, rotational management, in which tall and short grassland are maintained continuously in time though not in space, has been advocated as a system of management (Morris, 1971; Bacon, 1990) for the conservation of faunal diversity on nature reserves and other protected areas (Morris, 1991).

In this paper the success of a rotational grazing system in conserving invertebrates, particularly Hemiptera, is described.

SITE AND METHODS

A rotational sheep-grazing trial was established on the south-facing slope of the Old Winchester Hill National Nature Reserve in 1981. Nine paddocks were established using flexi-netting and these were grazed for about two months in a 9 year cycle, with grazing in successive years being at a later period in the year. Two of three additional, permanently-fenced paddocks were maintained as grassland by the periodic removal of scrub and were included in the invertebrate sampling programme.

From 1982 to 1985 invertebrates were sampled on the site using a variety of methods. This paper concentrates on vacuum-net sampling in summer. In the 4 years of sampling 7 samples from about 2.2 m^2 were taken in each year at 2-3 week intervals from May to October. The catch was killed in the field, stored in a cold room and sorted and identified at a later date.

On each sampling occasion the height of the vegetation was recorded by placing a ruler upright in the sward and averaging 4 measurements. During later analysis these measurements were averaged as Height 1 (May-June) and Height 2 (July-September).

As the grazing trial was not a formal experiment statistical analyses were based on the total numbers of species and individuals found each year in each of the plots, which were treated as "plot-year" observations. As the same number of plots were grazed for the same combination of months in each year any apparent overall differences in fauna between years were independent of, and not influenced by, effects of the grazing regime. Influences of position on the hillside were assessed by nested analysis of variance (ANOVAR).

The main aspects of the effects of the grazing regime which were assessed were:

(1) Grazing any time in the current year.
(2) Differences between early (March-July) and late (July-December) grazing.
(3) Residual effect of grazing in the previous year.

As grazing clearly reduces the height of the vegetation, the direct relationship between invertebrates and sward structure (mean Heights 1 and 2) was assessed by separate multiple regression.

All ANOVAs were made simultaneously using a multiple regression approach, based on the log $(n+1)$ data. An arbitrary standard (100 or more individuals taken during the four years of sampling) was adopted. The numbers of species (S) and total abundance (N) were also analysed for major taxonomic groups.

Fuller details of the analytical approach and procedures will be published elsewhere.

Table 1. Heteroptera (vacuum net samples). Significance of effects recorded for abundant species (>100 individuals) ★, ★★, ★★★ denote significance at the 5%, 1% and 0.1% probability levels respectively; NS, not significant.

Species	Effect of: Years	Hillside position (Top, Middle Bottom)	Plots within hillside position	Grazing this year	Grazing last year when this year is Grazed	Not grazed	Early vs Late Grazing
S	★★★	NS	NS	★★	NS	NS	★★
N	★★★	★★★	★★	★★	NS	NS	★
Stygnocoris pedestris	★★★	NS	NS	★★	NS	★	NS
Berytinus clavipes	★★★	NS	NS	NS	★	NS	NS
Berytinus signoreti	★★★	NS	★★★	★★	NS	★	NS
Campylosteira verna	★★★	★★★	★★	NS	NS	NS	NS
Acalypta parvula	★★★	★★	★★★	NS	NS	NS	NS
Catoplatus fabricii	★★★	★	NS	NS	NS	NS	NS
Agramma laeta	★★★	★★★	★★	★	NS	NS	★
Nabis ferus	★★★	NS	NS	★	NS	★★	NS
Hallodapus rufescens	NS	NS	★	★	NS	NS	NS
Orthocephalus saltator	★★★	NS	★	★★	NS	NS	NS
Phytocoris varipes	★★★	NS	★★	NS	NS	NS	★★
Leptopterna ferrugata	★★★	NS	★★	★★★	NS	NS	★

RESULTS
Heteroptera
Twelve species of plant bugs occurred as 100 or more individuals. All except one, together with species number (S) and total abundance of individuals were affected by years (Table 1). Four species (all Tingidae) were affected by position on the hillside, with the top, middle and bottom positions most favourable to at least one species. Seven species, and S and N, were affected by grazing in the year of sampling. Grazing was deleterious to S and to all species except the small tingid *Agramma laeta*. N, because of the great abundance of *A. laeta*, was positively affected by grazing. Only a

Table 2. Auchenorhyncha (vacuum net samples). Significance of effects recorded for abundant species (>100 individuals)★, ★★, ★★★ denote significance at the 5%, 1% and 0.1% probability levels respectively; NS, not significant.

Species	Effect of: Years	Hillside position (Top, Middle Bottom)	Plots within hillside position	Grazing this year	Grazing last year when this year is Grazed	Not grazed	Early vs Late Grazing
S	★★★	★★★	★	★★	★	NS	★★★
N	★★★	★	NS	★★★	NS	NS	★★
Neophilaenus exclamationis	NS	★★★	★★★	NS	NS	NS	NS
Ulopa trivia	★★★	★★	★	NS	★	NS	★
Agallia venosa	★★★	★★	★★★	NS	NS	NS	NS
Eupelix cuspidata	NS	NS	NS	NS	NS	NS	NS
Aphrodes albifrons	★★★	★	NS	NS	NS	NS	NS
Aphrodes bicinctus	★★★	★	NS	NS	NS	NS	NS
Arocephalus punctum	★★	★★★	★★★	★★	NS	NS	NS
Turrutus socialis	★★	NS	★	NS	NS	NS	NS
Rhytistylus proceps	★	NS	★★	★★	NS	NS	NS
Paluda adumbrata	★	★★★	★★★	NS	NS	NS	NS
Mocydia crocea	★	NS	★★★	NS	NS	NS	NS
Mocydiopsis attenuata	★★	NS	NS	★★	NS	NS	NS
Macrosteles laevis	★★★	NS	★	NS	NS	NS	★
Macrosteles sexnotatus	★★★	NS	NS	NS	NS	NS	NS
Macrosteles (females)	★★	NS	NS	★	NS	NS	NS
Eupteryx notata	★★★	NS	★	★★★	NS	NS	★
Zyginidia scutellaris	★★★	★★★	★★★	★★	NS	★★	NS
Arboridia parvula	★★★	★	★★★	★	NS	NS	NS
Kelisia guttata	★★★	★★	★★	★★★	NS	★	NS
Kelisia vittipennis	★★★	★	★★★	★★	NS	★	NS
Delphacinus mesomelas NS	★★★	★	NS	NS	★	NS	
Hyledelphax elegantulus ★	★★★	★	NS	NS	NS	NS	
Javesella pellucida	★★★	NS	★	NS	NS	NS	NS
Kosswigianella exigua	★	NS	★★★	NS	NS	NS	NS

few species were influenced by a residual effect of grazing in the year preceding sampling, or by early, as opposed to late, grazing (Table 1). S and the abundance of 6 species was significantly, and positively, correlated with both Height 1 and Height 2.

Auchenorhyncha
Twenty-three species of leaf- and frog-hoppers were taken as 100 or more individuals. N, S and 21 species were affected by years, and N, S and 13 species by position on the hillside (Table 2). Ten of the last occurred on the top of the slope. However, the vegetation was tallest there (Table 3).

Grazing in the year of sampling affected N, S and 9 species significantly. The residual effect of grazing in the year previous to sampling was significant for only S and 5 species. N, S and three species were significantly affected by early grazing (Table 2).

N, S and the abundance of 18 species was significantly correlated with vegetation height, in most cases with both Height 1 and Height 2. All the correlations were positive, except *Macrosteles laevis*, a well-known species of disturbed and short swards.

DISCUSSION

Most previous work on the effects of management on invertebrates has involved formal field experiments and has emphasised the effects of methods (rather than systems) of management. In contrast to previous work, differences between years, between plots and between positions on the hillside turned out to be important at Old Winchester Hill, although Morris (1990) showed that site characteristics were the main influence distinguishing year-samples of Auchenorhyncha, on calcareous grasslands. Differences between years and individual differences between plots are largely outside the control of site managers. The same is partly true of hillside position, although in appropriate circumstances this position can be selected for the conservation of biodiversity of invertebrates. However, the association of many species with the top of the slope rather than the two other positions is likely to be related to the taller vegetation there (Table 3).

Table 3. Mean height of vegetation (cm) in plots at top, middle and bottom of the hillside, with S.E. of the mean; Height 1 before end June, Height 2 July-September. *** = p<0.001

	Height 1	Height 2
Significance of difference	***	***
Top	11.6 ± 3.8	14.6 ± 3.7
Middle	7.1 ± 3.8	8.2 ± 3.7
Bottom	6.1 ± 3.8	8.1 ± 4.5

The Old Winchester Hill study confirms much previous work which shows the importance of tall grassland for the conservation of invertebrates (Morris, 1991). Seventeen species were favoured by tall grassland and only one by short turf. The importance of rotational systems is that they provide a means whereby a grassland site may be maintained to provide conditions for plants and animals characteristic of swards of several structural types. Although other systems may be appropriate where there are different aims of management, rotational management is indicated where such aims include maintenance of invertebrate diversity.

ACKNOWLEDGEMENTS
We thank Mr Ralph Clarke for statistical help and analysis and John Bacon for practical assistance and useful discussion. English Nature (South Region) gave continual encouragement and financial support to complete the study.

REFERENCES
BACON J.C. (1990) The use of livestock in calcareous grassland management. In: Hillier, S.H., Walton, D.W.H. and Wells, D.A. (eds.) *Calcareous Grasslands - Ecology and Management*, pp. 121-7. Huntingdon, Bluntisham Books.

MORRIS, M.G. (1971) Differences between the invertebrate faunas of grazed and ungrazed chalk grassland. IV. Abundance and diversity of Homoptera-Auchenorhyncha. *Journal of Applied Ecology*, **8**, 37-52.

MORRIS, M.G. (1990) The Hemiptera of two sown calcareous grasslands. III. Comparisons with the Auchenorhyncha faunas of other grasslands. *Journal of Applied Ecology*, **27**, 394-409.

MORRIS M.G. (1991) The management of reserves and protected areas. *The Scientific Management of Temperate Communities for Conservation*. In: Spellerberg, I.H., Goldsmith, F.B. and Morris, M.G. (eds.) *31st Symposium British Ecological Society*, Blackwell, Oxford, pp. 323-47.

Integration of Nature Conservation Management with Low Input Livestock Production

J. R. TREWEEK AND T. A. WATT[1]

ITE Monks Wood, Abbots Ripton, Huntingdon, Cambridgeshire
[1]Wye College, University of London, Wye, Ashford, Kent.

ABSTRACT

Sheep grazing is often used on British nature reserves to enhance the wildlife conservation value of pastures, but sheep production has rarely been monitored in these systems. It is therefore unclear whether effective nature conservation management can be combined with commercially viable, low-input livestock production. This paper describes aspects of a grazing trial established on a nature reserve to study the effects of sheep grazing at different times of year, and at different intensities, on both botanical change and sheep production. Sheep performed better in summer when grazing swards which had been grazed the previous winter or spring. This also increased the total number of plant species recorded, suggesting potential for successful integration of nature conservation and sheep production.

INTRODUCTION

Agricultural intensification has been a major factor in the decline of species-rich, semi-natural grasslands in the British countryside, and remaining species-rich meadows and pastures are now valued highly for nature conservation. As pressure to de-intensify the agricultural industry grows, new opportunities have arisen for integrating farming with positive management for nature conservation, and it has become increasingly important to consider how farming and wildlife management can be combined effectively.

In some studies, loss of botanical interest due to agricultural intensification has been reversed by combining grazing by livestock with cessation of fertiliser applications. Sheep are frequently used for grassland management on British nature reserves, but their effectiveness in enhancing the species richness and nature conservation value of lowland grasslands on some of the more nutrient-rich soils likely to be found on land taken out of intensive production is unclear (Treweek, 1990). There is also little information available on the levels of performance which can be expected (Large and King, 1978; McLaren, 1987). It has been suggested that many livestock enterprises used in nature conservation management of grasslands run at a loss (Thiele-Wittig, 1974; Green, 1989).

This paper describes part of a study set up to explore scope for combining commercially viable low-input sheep production with grazing to enhance the species richness of lowland grassland recently taken out of intensive use. The effects of sheep grazing at different times of year, and at different intensities, were tested in relation to both botanical change and sheep production. The trial was run as a low-input system, with sheep grazing unfertilised swards and receiving no supplementary feeding.

METHODS
Study area and experimental design
The experiment was set up at Little Wittenham Nature Reserve, Oxfordshire, in March 1986, on grassland which had been managed intensively until two years previously, when fertiliser applications ceased. Soils were calcareous clay loams with an average pH of 7.5 and high residual fertility (Treweek, 1990). The sward was dominated by perennial grasses, notably *Lolium perenne*, *Agrostis stolonifera* and *Poa* spp, with very few 'wildflowers' present.

The experiment had a 2x2x2 factorial structure, eight treatments being assigned at random to paddocks of 50x50m in each of two blocks. For each main grazing period (winter: November 1 to March 21, spring: March 21 to May 21 and summer: May 21 to November 1) there were two levels of grazing, with sheep present or absent in the winter, present or absent in the spring and grazing to two different target sward heights of 3cm (short) and 6cm (tall) in the summer. The eight treatments are summarised in Table 1.

Table 1. Summary of treatments.

Treatment	Summer	Winter	Spring
A	Short (3cm)	-	-
B	Short (3cm)	-	+
C	Short (3cm)	+	-
D	Short (3cm)	+	+
E	Tall (6cm)	-	-
F	Tall (6cm)	-	+
G	Tall (6cm)	+	-
H	Tall (6cm)	+	+

+ represents sheep present and - represents sheep absent

Grazing management
Suffolk x Mule ewes purchased in the spring were allocated at random to the eight treatment paddocks within each block. Winter- and spring-grazed paddocks were grazed at the basal stocking rate of 8 sheep/ha. In summer, a core group of animals was designated for each paddock, which was always returned to that paddock after weighing. Additional animals were used on a 'put and take' basis to achieve an 'adjusted set-stocking' system of continuous grazing in relation to target sward heights of

3cm ('short') and 6cm ('tall'). Core groups consisted of 6 and 4 sheep, giving minimum summer stocking rates of 20 and 16 sheep/ha on 'short' and 'tall' paddocks respectively

Monitoring

Impacts of grazing were assessed in relation to botanical composition and the performance of sheep in terms of liveweight change. Sheep were weighed weekly to assess their relative performance under the eight grazing treatments. As figures for average weight gain or loss over the summer grazing period were likely to conceal shorter term fluctuations in weight due to changes in forage quality throughout the summer, the SAS General Linear Model (GLM) procedure for repeated measurements (SAS Institute Inc., 1985) was used to analyse the linear and quadratic components of the pattern of liveweight change over time for the 1987 data.

Botanical sampling was carried out in two permanent quadrats of $1m^2$, situated at the corners of a central square of 10x10m in each paddock. The species present were recorded in spring (March), summer (June) and autumn (September/October). Factorial analysis of variance was carried out on the total number of species recorded in each paddock.

RESULTS

Mean changes in weight per sheep over the whole experiment are summarised in Table 2. Sheep always gained weight during the spring and summer grazing periods and lost weight during the winter, but there was considerable variation between years. Analysis of trends over time for liveweight data from 1987 showed that there were significant differences between grazing treatments in linear and quadratic trends of liveweight change throughout the summer.

Table 2. Mean weight per sheep (kg).

Grazing period		Start weight (kg)	Finish weight (kg)	Gain/Loss (kg)
1986	Summer	44.2	50.7	+6.5
	Winter	53.9	47.3	−6.6
	Spring	52.5	65.1	+12.6
1987	Summer	45.4	49.2	+3.8
	Winter	48.6	43.1	−5.5
	Spring	52.4	53.3	+0.85
1988	Summer	53.8	63.5	+9.74
	Winter	66.1	65.9	−0.16

There were significantly different linear trends for winter-grazed paddocks and for those not winter-grazed ($P<0.05$, Figure 1) and also for spring-grazed paddocks and

those not spring-grazed (P<0.05, Figure 2). Grazing in either winter or spring resulted in maintenance of higher sheep weights during the subsequent summer and
autumn. The linear trends for paddocks grazed short or tall in the summer were also
different (P<0.001, Figure 3), with swards grazed to a target height of 6cm resulting
in better maintenance of liveweight during summer and autumn. When liveweights
were averaged across all eight grazing treatments, there was also a general quadratic

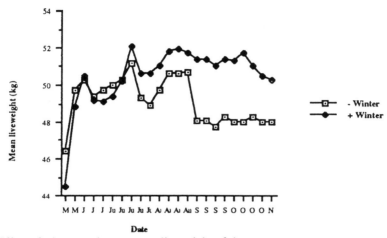

Fig. 1. Effect of wintergrazing on mean liveweight of sheep.

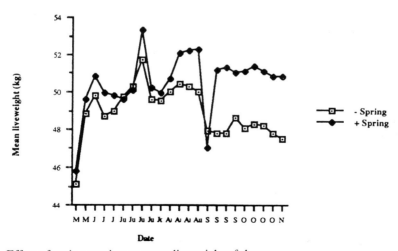

Fig. 2. Effect of spring grazing on mean liveweight of sheep.

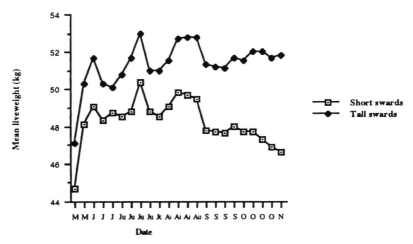

Fig. 3. Effect of summer grazing on mean liveweight of sheep.

trend in liveweight change throughout the summer (P<0.001). This trend differed significantly between paddocks grazed in winter and those not winter-grazed (P<0.01, Figure 1), with sheep on winter-grazed swards maintaining weight in the autumn (September to November) better than sheep grazing swards which were not winter-grazed.

Botanical assessment: total number of species per paddock

At the start of the experiment there were no significant differences between paddocks in the numbers of species recorded or their relative proportions. By the autumn of the second year (1987), the total number of higher plant species recorded was greater in spring-grazed paddocks (a mean of 8.6 species) than in paddocks not grazed in spring (6.8 species) (P<0.05; s.e.d = 0.57). Grazing in other seasons also had a positive effect (Table 3). The lowest number of species was recorded in the least-grazed paddocks,

Table 3. Interaction between effects of summer, winter and spring grazing on the total numbers of species recorded inside the quadrats in each paddock: autumn 1987.

Summer	Winter	- Spring	+ Spring
Short	-	8.3	6.8
	+	6.6	9.1
Tall	-	5.0	9.4
	+	7.4	9.1

P<0.05; s.e.d 2.28

which had received grazing in neither winter nor spring, and had tall swards in the summer. If paddocks were winter-grazed, summer sward height made no difference to the number of species recorded (9.1 for both tall and short swards), but if they were spring-grazed the average number of species recorded was higher on paddocks with tall swards in summer (9.4 species) than on those with short swards (6.8 species).

There were also significant effects of grazing in different seasons, on the frequencies of individual grass species, which are discussed in more depth elsewhere (Treweek, 1990).

DISCUSSION
Analysis of trends over time for sheep liveweight data showed that the performance of sheep in summer was influenced by the effects of grazing in previous seasons as well as by summer grazing treatment. Grazing in either the winter or the spring appeared to enhance sheep performance in the latter part of the summer grazing period. Sheep grazing short swards in summer were lighter than sheep grazing the taller swards on all dates. All animals lost weight at the end of August; but whereas sheep on tall swards began to gain weight again in the middle of September, those sheep grazing short swards showed only a brief recovery in weight before declining in weight again throughout October.

Sheep performance, as measured by liveweight gain, benefitted from grazing in the winter or spring, or both seasons, followed by grazing to a relatively tall sward height of 6cm throughout the summer. Species richness of the sward was enhanced by grazing in the spring or winter, but if spring-grazing was used, it was important that swards were not grazed too heavily in the following summer. This did not appear to affect the outcome for winter-grazed treatments.

The results of this study suggested that the need to maintain sheep liveweight gains on mixed species swards receiving no fertiliser could be reconciled with the objective of increasing the species-richness of pastures, by combining winter- or spring-grazing with summer grazing to a relatively tall sward height.

ACKNOWLEDGEMENTS
This work was funded by a postgraduate research studentship from the SERC and by the Northmoor Trust. We thank all the staff of Little Wittenham Nature Reserve, and in particular, Fiona Woolmer and John Sargent for all their help.

REFERENCES
GREEN B. H. (1989) *Countryside Conservation. Resource Management Series 3*. London: George, Allen and Unwin.
LARGE R.V. and KING N. (1978) The integrated use of land for agricultural and amenity purposes. Lamb production from Soay sheep used to control scrub and improve the grass cover of chalk downland. *Technical Report 25*. Hurley: Grassland Research Institute.

McLAREN D.P. (1987) *Chalk grassland: a review of management experience.* M.Sc. thesis, Wye College, University of London.

THIELE-WITTIG H.C. (1974) Maintenance of previously cultivated land not now used for agriculture. *Agriculture and the Environment*, **1**, 129-137.

TREWEEK J.R. (1990) *The ecology of sheep grazing: its use in nature conservation management of lowland neutral grassland.* D. Phil. thesis, University of Oxford.

Effect of Extensification on Yield and Botanical Composition of Grassland on Dry Sandy Soil

K. WIND, J.H NEUTEBOOM AND L.'t MANNETJE

Wageningen Agricultural University, Department of Agronomy
Haarweg 333, 6709 RZ Wageningen, The Netherlands

ABSTRACT

An area of grassland was sown to perennial ryegrass (Lolium perenne)*, timothy grass* (Phleum pratense)*, white clover* (Trifolium repens) *and smooth meadow grass* (Poa pratensis) *in 1966 and fertilised with 300 kg N/ha/annum and P and K at required levels for 5 years. In 1971 the area was subdivided into areas without further fertilisation (0-treatment) and with only moderate levels of P and K (PK-treatment). The 0-treatment was further subdivided into a hay (0-hay) and grazing (0-pasture) treatment, whilst the PK-treatment was set stocked. Annual dry-matter yields declined within 5 to 10 years from 10 to less than 4 t/ha on 0-pasture and to less than 1 t/ha on 0-hay. In the PK-treatment the dry-matter yields oscillated around 4.5 t/ha/annum. The sown species declined to low proportions in all treatments. Perennial ryegrass was maintained in the PK-treatment only at around 10% of the total dry weight and occurred mainly in old dung and urine patches sand in white clover patches. Rapidly establishing volunteer species were common bent* (Agrostis capillaris) *and Yorkshire-fog* (Holcus lanatus)*. Red fescue* (Festuca rubra) *as one of the main components of the original grassland before 1966 hardly increased in the grazed treatments until 1993. It was concluded that 0-hay does not constitute an agriculturally interesting proposition and that even after 23 years of extensification the sward had not reached a stable botanical composition. It is recommended that special attention should be given to the heterogeneity caused by dung and urine patches in studies of population dynamics in grazed areas.*

INTRODUCTION

Dutch government policy aims to increase the area of farmed grassland for nature conservation by offering financial compensation for reduced yield and quality as a result of reduced N fertilisation and delayed first cutting date. This paper presents data on changes in dry-matter yield and botanical composition of newly sown grassland, which was intensively managed for 5 years and then subjected to different forms of extensification during a period of 25 years.

217

MATERIAL AND METHODS

In 1966 an area of 0.82 ha of grassland was sown on a dry sandy soil on the University experimental farm (Meenthoeve) near Wageningen. A seed mixture (30 kg/ha) consisting of 54% perennial ryegrass (*Lolium perenne*), 26% timothy (*Phleum pratense*), 13% white clover (*Trifolium repens*) and 7% smooth meadow grass (*Poa pratensis*) was used. Many species of the original red fescue (*Festuca rubra*) - common bent (*Agrostis capillaris*) sward were still present along ditches and road sides in the immediate vicinity. The area was fertilised with 300 kg N/ha and adequate P and K according to soil analysis and grazed for 5 years. In 1971 the area was divided into the following treatments without replication: 1) 0: no fertiliser 2) PK: 20 kg/ha P_2O_5 and 40 kg/ha K_2O per annum. The 0-treatment (0.26 ha) was divided into an area that was intermittently grazed as part of a simulated rotational grazing system (0-pasture) and an area that was mown for hay in June and October each year (0-hay). The PK-treatment (0.56 ha) was set stocked with 5 steers/ha for 4 years and 3 steers/ha thereafter. The yield of the 0-hay plot was estimated by weighing the hay as it was removed from the paddock. The dry-matter yield of the 0-pasture and PK-treatment was estimated every 3 or 4 years by harvesting grass under cages in June and at the end of October. In autumn of 1968, 1979 and 1991 soil samples (0-5 cm) were analyzed for pH (KCl), organic matter, P_2O_5 and K_2O (mg/100 g soil). Botanical composition was estimated in early May of 1967, '68, '69, '71, '75, '77, '84, '85, '91 and 1993 by hand sorting 100 handfuls of grass per plot for dry weight proportions (DW%) and/or by taking 100 cores of 0.25 dm^2 for presence frequencies (F% on leaf basis). In addition, presence frequencies and dry weight proportions, using the Dry Weight Rank Method ('t Mannetje and Haydock, 1963) were estimated using 1 dm^2 quadrats inside and in a border of 20 cm around old dung and urine patches and also in white clover patches and in the interpatch background area. Complete species lists were made in each plot every 3 to 4 years.

RESULTS AND DISCUSSION

Annual dry-matter yields decreased rapidly in all treatments after N fertilization had ceased (Fig. 1), oscillating around 4.5 t/ha on the PK-treatment and stabilizing to just under 4 and 1 t/ha on the 0-pasture and the 0-hay treatments, respectively. Although N would have been the main limiting factor for yield in all treatments from the beginning of extensification, P and K supplies may have become limiting on the 0-treatments later. The P_2O_5 and K_2O concentrations in the soil of the 0-treatments decreased from 14 and 22, respectively, in 1968 to 8 and 9 on 0-pasture and 5 and 8 on 0-hay, respectively in 1991. In the PK-treatment soil P and K values in 1991 were still approximately at the same level (P a little higher) of 1968 (20 and 21, respectively). Over the same period, pH had changed from 4.7 to 4.3 and organic matter percentage from 4.3 to 6.3 in all treatments. The total number of plant species increased from 19 in 1969 to 37 in 1977 on all treatments but then decreased to below 25 in 1991 in the 0-treatments (Fig.1). This ultimate decrease probably also indicates that soil fertility levels are becoming too low for high species diversity. All sown species decreased after

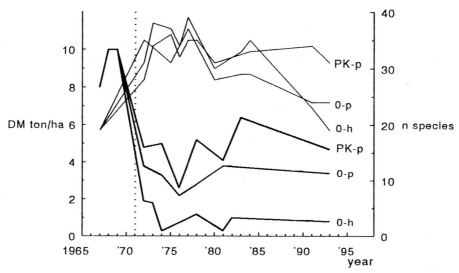

Fig. 1. Annual dry-matter yields (———) and number of plant species (———) in time of PK-pasture (PK-p),) 0-pasture (0-p) and 0-hay (0-h). Treatments were imposed in 1971.

Table 1. Presence frequencies (F%, leaf frequency) and DW% in 1dm^2 sampling quadrats of perennial ryegrass (*Lp*) and white clover (*Tr*) within and in between old dung, old urine and white clover patches in PK-pasture. Soil P$_2$O$_5$ (P-Al), K$_2$O and within brackets total cover of the 3 patch types and remaining area are also given.

| | Botanical analysis | | | | Soil analysis | |
| | *Lp* | | *Tr* | | mg/100 g soil | |
Patch type (cover %)	F%	DW%	F%	DW%	P$_2$O$_5$	K$_2$O
Old dung (8)	53	10.1	18	4.0	54	20
Old urine scorch (3)	41	8.1	9	1.4	39	102
White clover (5)	66	3.5	100	65.3	28	17
Remaining area (84)	17	1.2	8	1.6	21	14

N fertilisation had ceased (Fig.3), as did typical weed species characteristic of intensive grassland (data not shown), such as couch (*Elymus repens*), chickweed (*Stellaria media*), annual meadow-grass (*Poa annua*) and knotgrass (*Polygonum aviculare*). Perennial ryegrass was only maintained in the PK-treatment (10% DW) in 1991 but it occurred mainly around old dung and urine patches and in white clover patches (Table 1). Dung and urine patches also showed higher soil fertility, coinciding with the higher fertility requirements of perennial ryegrass. The size and very regular shape of the white clover patches suggest that these also originated in dung or urine patches. This agrees with observations of Weeda (1967) that white clover, because of its stoloniferous habit, establishes easily in dung patches. This is further supported by the higher F% and higher DW% of white clover in old dung patches in the present study (Table 1). Dominant grass species in 1991 were common bent and Yorkshire-fog (*Holcus lanatus*) in all treatments, sweet vernal grass (*Anthoxantum odoratum*) in both 0-treatments and red fescue in the 0-hay treatment. It is surprising that red fescue, one of the main components of the original pasture before 1966, established in the 0-hay treatment in 1976 but was still only present at low frequencies (F% ≤2) in the 0-pasture and the PK-treatment in 1993. This is in keeping with Morisson (1978), who placed red fescue at the end of the succession from sown to old permanent grassland as a volunteer species that usually does not increase substantially in the first 20 years.

With the commencement of extensification, a number of dicotyledonous species increased in all treatments, as is illustrated for the PK-treatment in Fig. 2. Two botanical changes occurring after 1985 are illustrative for the change to lower soil fertility status: (1) dandelion (*Taraxacum vulgare*) and autumnal hawkbit (*Leontodon autumnalis*) were replaced by cat's-ear (*Hypochaeris radicata*) and (2) common mouse-ear chickweed (*Cerastium fontanum*) was replaced by little mouse-ear chickweed (*C. semidecandrum*). According to data of Kruijne *et al.* (1967) cat's-ear and little mouse-ear chickweed are correlated with poor soil fertility conditions. The reason for continuing a moderate P and K fertilisation (PK-treatment) was to stimulate legumes in order to maintain some production. However, white clover steadily decreased, while suckling clover (*T. dubium*) only increased temporarily (Fig.3). Nevertheless, drymatter production was maintained at a higher level compared to the 0-treatments. In

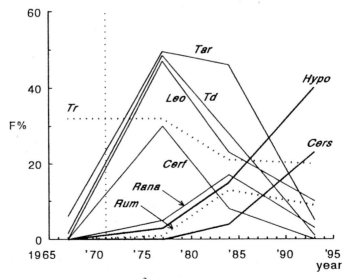

Fig. 2. Presence frequencies (F%) in $^1/_4$dm^2 cores in time of the main dicot species in PK-pasture.

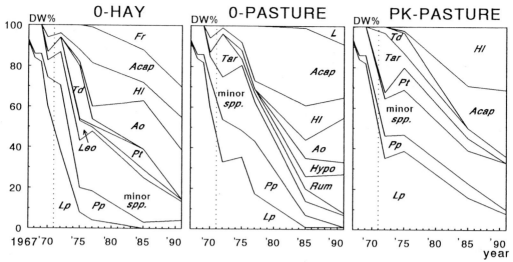

Fig. 3. Dry weight proportions (DW%) in time of the main plant species in 0-hay, 0-pasture and PK-pasture.

List of abbreviations and species names used in Figures 2 and 3

Acap	:*Agrostis capillaris*	*Hypo*	:*Hypochaeris radicata*	*Rana*	:*Ranunculus acris*
Ao	:*Anthoxanthum odoratum*	*L*	:*Luzula campestris*	*Rum*	:*Rumex acetosa*
Cerf	:*Cerastium fontanum*	*Leo*	:*Leontodon autumnalis*	*Tar*	:*Taraxacum vulgare*
Cers	:*Cerastium semidecandrum*	*Lp*	:*Lolium perenne*	*Td*	:*Trifolium dubium*
Fr	:*Festuca rubra*	*Pp*	:*Poa pratensis*	*Tr*	:*Trifolium repens*
Hl	:*Holcus lanatus*	*Pt*	:*Poa trivialis*		

conclusion, it is evident that the 0-hay treatment cannot seriously be considered of agricultural value any more. Further, it is clear that, since red fescue, cat's-ear and sweet vernal grass are still systematically increasing after more than 25 years at more or less stabilized dry-matter yields, the sward still has not arrived at a stable botanical composition. In studying vegetation dynamics of grazed areas, special attention should be paid to the heterogeneity caused by dung and urine patches.

REFERENCES

KRUIJNE A.A., DE VRIES D.M. and MOOI H. (1977) Bijdrage tot de oecologie van Nederlandse graslandplanten (Contribution to the ecology of the Dutch grassland plants). *Verslagen van Landbouwkundige Onderzoekingen*, No. 696. PUDOC, Wageningen.

't MANNETJE L. and HAYDOCK K.P. (1963) The dry-weight-rank method for the botanical analysis of pasture. *Journal of the British Grassland Society*, **18**, 268-275.

MORISSON J. (1978) Botanical changes in agricultural grassland in Britain. In: Charles, A. H. and Haggar, R.J. (eds.) *Changes in sward composition and productivity*. *Occasional Symposium of the British Grassland Society*, No. 10, pp.5-10.

WEEDA W.C. (1967) The effects of cattle dung patches on pasture growth, botanical composition and pasture utilization. *New Zealand Journal of Agricultural Research*, **10**, 150-157.

POSTER PRESENTATIONS

Long-term effects of applications of sewage sludge on the distribution of metals in grassland soils.

M. N. AITKEN, D. W. MERRILEES AND T. H. W. BROMILOW, Scottish
Agricultural College (SAC), Ayr, Scotland

INTRODUCTION

Sewage sludge when applied to farmland contributes useful amounts of plant nutrients and organic matter. In the UK, 42% of the 1.2 million tonnes (expressed as dry solids) of sewage sludge produced annually is applied to agricultural land. This figure will increase due to recent regulations regarding the cessation of sea disposal by 1998 and tighter restrictions on direct discharges of partially treated sludge. The heavy metal content of sewage sludge is variable and may be very high from some sources, particularly from industrial areas. These metals can persist in the soil long after sewage has been applied. High concentrations of soil metals may be toxic to grazing animals (Thornton, 1974) or may adversely affect the soil microbial biomass (Brookes and McGarth, 1984)or may cause changes to plant species/cultivar populations (Baker, 1987). As a result of EC directive 86/278/CEC, UK legislation has been passed to protect soils from heavy metals (Statutory Instrument, 1989). The purpose of this research is to determine the long-term environmental effects of sludge metals applied to grassland.

MATERIALS AND METHODS

Three experimental sites were established on contrasting soils on grassland farms in 1985. The soil types for the 2 sites reported here are Watsonfoot (WF), clay loam and Garrionhaugh (GH), sandy loam. A Latin Square design with 4 replicates was used to compare the effects of 3 annual rates of sludge (67, 135 and 270 m^3/ha) with a control receiving inorganic fertiliser only. A split plot design was used to compare the effects of maintaining the soil pH at 5.5 or 6.5.

RESULTS AND DISCUSSION

After 4 years the total addition of sludge solids applied to the plots with the highest rate was 33.8 t/ha (on dry weight basis) and individual metal values (kg/ha) as follows: Zn (27.5); Ni (1.78); Cd (0.11); Cu (15.30); Pb (12.76) and Cr (3.60).

Total soil concentrations of metals following these additions are shown in Table 1.

225

Table 1. Soil profile metals concentrations (mg/kg) at site GH for pH 5.5 treatments (pH 6.5 treatments in brackets).

Soil depth (mm)	Zinc (SED ± 13.83)		Copper (SED ± 2.548)	
	Control	Sludge	Control	Sludge
		($270 \, m^3/ha/yr$)		($270 \, m^3/ha/yr$)
0-25	70 (73)	102 (102)	19 (19)	39 (38)
25-50	74 (78)	84 (91)	21 (21)	30 (30)
50-100	75 (76)	85 (84)	20 (20)	26 (25)
100-150	77 (77)	82 (80)	22 (21)	24 (23)
150-200	75 (75)	77 (77)	21 (21)	25 (22)
200-400	72 (67)	73 (71)	20 (20)	21 (20)

There was no significant effect of soil pH on the distribution of Zn or Cu within the profile. There was an increase in metal concentration above controls down to a depth of 150-200 mm. The greatest increase occurred in the top 0-25 mm. Metal movement down the soil profile could have occurred due to physical movement of sludge particles during heavy rainfall or transport by soil fauna. By 1992, the sludge applications resulted in a significant decrease in ground cover of *Lolium perenne* (perennial ryegrass) and an increase in *Agrostis stolonifera* (creeping bent grass) as shown in Table 2.

Table 2. Changes in herbage composition (% species cover) after seven years of sewage sludge treatment at Watsonfoot.

Species cover	0	Sludge rate ($m^3/ha/yr$) 67 (SED ± 7.216)	135	270
Lolium perenne	88.8	86.9	68.2	43.2
Agrostis stolonifera	11.2	13.1	31.8	56.8

CONCLUSIONS
Sewage sludge use on grassland resulted in an increase in soil metal concentrations. Increases in Zn and Cu were found to a depth of 150-200 mm with a maximum increase in the top 0-25 mm. The annual sludge rates of 130 m^3/ha and 270 m^3/ha significantly reduced the % cover of perennial ryegrass. The area previously occupied by this species was recolonised by bent grasses.

REFERENCES
Baker A. J. M. (1987) Metal tolerance. *New Phytologist*, **106**, 93-111.

Brookes P. C. and McGarth S. P. (1984) Effect of metals toxicity on the size of the soil microbial biomass - *Journal of Soil Science*, **35**, 341-344.

Field A. C. and Purves D. (1964) The intake of soil by grazing sheep. *Proceedings of Nutrition Society*, **23**, 24-25.

Statutory Instrument (1989) The Sludge (Use in Agriculture) Regulations, HMSO London.

Effects of Cessation of Fertiliser Inputs, Liming and Grazing on Microbial Activity in Upland Soil

R.D. BARDGETT

AFRC Institute of Grassland and Environmental Research, Plas Gogerddan, Aberystwyth, Dyfed SY23 3EB

INTRODUCTION

Intensification of sheep farming in the uplands has caused concern in terms of over-production and nature conservation. Changes in agricultural policy reflecting this concern are likely to result in reduced management intensity of upland grasslands. This study examines the effects of changes in grassland management on the biomass and activity of microorganisms involved in the processes of organic matter decomposition and nutrient turnover in a reseeded upland grassland soil.

MATERIALS AND METHODS

Five grassland treatments in a randomized complete block design with three replicate plots, located at Bronydd Mawr, South Wales (370-390m altitude) were sampled. Four of the treatments had been grazed for two growing seasons to a standard sward surface height of 4 cm, and were as follows: 1) CaNPK: fertiliser applications in line with current practice (N input 150 kg/ha), 2) CaPK: as for 1 but no N applied, 3) Ca only, 4) Nil inputs. The fifth treatment received nil inputs and was ungrazed. The soil was sampled in November 1992 by taking 10 random soil cores (3.5 cm diameter, 15 cm deep) from each treatment replicate plot. Soil cores from individual treatment replicate plots were bulked, sieved (<6mm) and measurements of soil basal respiration (CO_2 production), microbial biomass C and N, ATP content, dehydrogenase and urease activity were made on triplicate samples using standard techniques. All results are expressed on an oven-dry weight basis.

RESULTS AND DISCUSSION

The cessation of fertiliser applications and liming, with and without grazing (treatment 4 and 5, respectively), resulted in significant reductions in both microbial biomass-C ($P<0.05$ and $P<0.001$, respectively) and dehydrogenase activity ($P<0.01$ and $P<0.001$, respectively), the latter being an index of total soil microbial activity (Table 1). Similarly, the removal of fertiliser inputs, liming and grazing (treament 5) resulted in significant reductions in urease activity ($P<0.05$), microbial respiration ($P<0.05$), and microbial biomass-N ($P<0.05$) (Table 1). These effects are likely to be a result of changes in soil pH, particularly of the removal of sheep grazing (Table 1). A significant negative linear relationship ($r^2 = 0.97$, $P < 0.01$) was shown between increasing soil acidity and dehydrogenase activity. Where liming and grazing were maintained, the removal of fertiliser N and NPK (treatment 2 and 3, respectively) had no effect on microbial biomass or activity. Soil ATP content, a measure of active microbial biomass, was unaffected by changes in management.

Table 1. Effects of removing fertiliser applications, liming, and grazing on microbial characteristics and pH of an upland grassland soil.

Treatment	ATP (μgATP g^{-1} soil)	Microbial biomass-C (μg N g^{-1} soil)	Microbial biomass-N (μg N g^{-1} soil)	Basal respiration (μgCO$_2$. C g^{-1} soil h^1)	Dehydrogenase (nmol INTF g^{-1} soil 2h^{-1})	Urease (μg NH4 $^\pm$N g^{-1} soil h^{-1})	Soil pH (1:2.5w:v)
1. Ca NPK	3.44±0.48	1035±197	104±7	0.54±0.04	890±140	6.67±1.42	5.4
2. CaPK	3.87±0.71	931±148	103±9	0.55±0.07	840±148	5.75±1.13	5.2
3. Ca	4.02±1.58	1105±190	106±15	0.60±0.10	844±79	6.09±1.11	5.1
4. Nil/Grazed	3.35±0.57	847±173	102±14	0.51±0.07	708±49	6.70±0.64	4.7
5. Nil/Ungrazed	2.84±0.67	579±258	93±9	0.46±0.04	616±101	5.50±1.26	4.5

CONCLUSION

The cessation of fertiliser inputs and liming on an upland grassland has been shown to result in reductions in both microbial biomass and activity. Greater reductions in microbial biomass and activity have been shown to occur following the removal of grazing. These effects are likely to be related to increases in soil acidity following the cessation of liming and grazing. In conclusion, changes in management resulting in reductions in soil microbial biomass and activity are likely to have a profound influence on processes of organic matter decomposition and nutrient turnover, and hence sward composition and productivity in upland grasslands.

Extensification of Milk Production using White Clover

J. A. BAX AND I. BROWNE[1]

Scottish Agricultural College, Crichton Royal Farm, Dumfries DG1 4SZ

[1] Milk Marketing Board, Westmere Drive, Crewe CW1 1ZD

INTRODUCTION

Since the introduction of milk quotas which imposed a ceiling on output, the profitability of a dairy enterprise has been governed to a greater extent by the variable costs of production. One of the responses to this has been an increased interest in more extensive systems of production which offer an opportunity to reduce the levels of inputs. The basis for extensive systems of milk production in the UK is grassland and the cheapest method of producing grass is to use white clover-rich swards. Both the management techniques and the varieties of white clover now available have been refined and improved, so that grass/white clover swards can be productive and persistent (Bax and Thomas, 1992). However, there is still a perception that white clover is a specialist crop for grassland enthusiasts despite evidence that profitable and sustainable dairying systems can be based upon mixed swards (Thomas and Bax, 1993). The following paper describes a project, which aims to investigate the potential for extensification of milk production on commercial farms, using grass/white clover swards.

Table 1. Soil texture, height above sea level (m), and annual rainfall (mm) of the participating farms.

Farm No.	1	2	3	4	5
Soil texture	clay	silty loam	sandy/clay	clay loam	clay loam
Height above sea level (m)	180-190	60-122	90-137	135-230	15
Rainfall (mm)	1574	1298	1110	1378	1102

MATERIALS AND METHODS

Five commercial farms were selected on which the performance of grass/white clover swards could be monitored. The farms provided a range of climatic conditions, soil textures, herd size and farm management systems. They were located in 1: Devon; 2: Somerset; 3: Shropshire; 4 and 5: Yorkshire. Two separate dairy herds were managed on the farm in Somerset. Representative swards on each farm were monitored to provide data on herbage yields, botanical and chemical composition of the herbage. Grazing and fertiliser applications were recorded and dairy herd performance was monitored.

RESULTS AND DISCUSSION
At the start of the monitoring period, (April 1992) the proportion of the grassland managed for white clover ranged from nil to 100% on the farms (See table 2).

Table 2. Participating farm details.

Farm No.	1	2		3	4	5
Herd size (No.cows)	86	124	185	93	61	99
Stocking rate (cows/ha)	1.49	1.56	1.51	1.83	1.9	2.12
Proportion of grassland managed for white clover	0.27	1.0	1.0	0.33	0	0
Mineral N fertiliser use (kg/N/annum)	227	0	0	124	220	332

Farm 2 relied upon grass/white clover swards to provide all of the grazing and the majority of its winter forage. By contrast farms 4 and 5 relied entirely upon mineral N fertilised swards, with none managed specifically for clover.

For the first year of the project, reseeding to establish clover-rich swards was carried out on four of the five farms. On farm 1, a direct reseed was carried out in Autumn 1991. The reseed was sprayed with a clover safe herbicide in Spring 1992 and 75 kg N/ha applied, before it was cut for first cut silage. The mean clover content of the reseed in August 1992 was 0.3% (% clover in the total herbage DM). On farm 2, grass and white clover was undersown to a barley/pea crop in Spring 1992. No mineral N fertiliser or herbicides were applied. The mean clover content was 41% by August 1992. A direct reseed was carried out on farm 4 in Spring 1992, with no inputs of nitrogen fertiliser or herbicide, and a mean clover content of 45% was achieved by August 1992. A different approach was adopted on farm 5 where an established sward was oversown with white clover after second cut silage. By August, the clover content had risen from 7.4% to 38.6%. Silage cuts were taken from grass/clover swards on three of the farms at first cut. On farm 1, a yield of 2.9t DM/ha was recorded on the grass/clover swards which received no mineral N fertilizer, which was 75% of the yield where 150kg N/ha was applied. The yield of silage on farm 2 was 5.8t DM/ha on 20 May. No mineral N fertilizer was applied and the mean clover content of the herbage was 15.3%. On farm 3, following an application of 87kg N/ha, the yield of silage was 3.8t DM/ha with a mean clover content of 8.3%.

The proportion of clover in the mixed swards increased during the growing season at all the sites. By August 1992, the mean clover contents were 14.7, 50.9, 39.9, 45.5 and 38.6% respectively. On farms 1, 2 and 3 where mixed swards were already established, the D-values and CP (g/kg DM) content of the herbage in early season (April) were 74.1, 151; 75.7, 186; and 75.5, 258 respectively. The values for mid-season (June) were 66.0, 154; 68.3, 150.8 and 71.4, 186. By late season (August) the D-values and Crude Protein (CP) (g/kg DM) contents were 56.4, 188; 59.8, 220 and 68.1, 201 respectively. The results demonstrated that grass/white clover swards can be successfully integrated into commercial dairying enterprises under a wide range of conditions. With appropriate management satisfactory clover contents were maintained throughout the growing season.

ACKNOWLEDGMENT

The authors are grateful to the Milk Marketing Board (England and Wales) for financial sponsorship.

REFERENCES

BAX J. A. and THOMAS C. (1992) Developments in legume use for milk production. In: Hopkins, A. (ed), *Grass on the move, Occasional Symposium of the British Grassland Society*, No. 26, pp. 40-53.

THOMAS C. and BAX J. (1993) Milk production from extensive systems based on swards of perennial ryegrass and white clover. *Proceedings of the VII World Conference on Animal Production*, Edmonton, 1993. (in-press).

The Response of Weed Species to Sheep Grazing in an Early Successional Calcareous Grassland

H.L. BILLINGTON, J.A. HOLLIER[1] AND V.K. BROWN[1]

Division of Environmental Science, Coventry University, Priory Street, Coventry CV1 5FB

[1] Department of Biology, Imperial College at Silwood Park, Ascot, Berks SL5 7PY

INTRODUCTION

Grazing by sheep can change the relative abundance of plant species in early successional plant communities (Gibson *et al.*, 1987). Grazing promotes plant species diversity by reducing the growth of perennial grasses and can therefore enable weed species to persist in grasslands by both reducing competition and creating regeneration sites. This experiment and analysis tests the hypothesis that disturbance of the ground by grazing animals at the time of peak germination is the most important factor controlling population size of three weed species; *Bromus sterilis*, *Vicia sativa* and *Senecio jacobaea*.

METHODS

The grazing experiment took place in a 10ha field abandoned from agriculture in 1982. Treatments were; grazed by three sheep for 14 days in autumn; for 10 days in spring, ungrazed; grazed by approximately five sheep per hectare from April to November or from late August to November.

Densities (m^{-2}) of the weed species in each management treatment were determined by direct count of individuals. In each treatment, 25 plants of each species were marked and their performance and number of neighbours were monitored throughout the 1990 growing season. Seedling recruitment in an area of 0.2m^2 centered on each marked plant was measured in November 1990 (*V.sativa*) and May 1991 (*B.sterilis* and *S.jacobaea*).

RESULTS

The densities of the three species (Table 1) support the hypothesis that disturbance by grazing animals around the time of peak germination increases abundance. *B.sterilis* and *V.sativa* were most abundant in autumn grazed treatments and *S.jacobaea* was most abundant in spring, and spring and autumn grazed treatments. Seed number per plant, seed weight, seed viability and the number of neighbours were all correlated with the number of seedlings around each marked plant in the subsequent year. The predicted and observed seedling numbers around each marked plant (Table 2) showed that for *B.sterilis* and *S.jacobaea* autumn grazing produced more seedlings than ex-

233

pected. For *V.sativa*, more seedlings that expected were found in the ungrazed controls. In both *V.sativa* and *S.jacobaea* fewer seedlings than expected were recruited into the population in the areas subjected to longer periods of grazing.

CONCLUSIONS

1. For *B.sterilis* and *S.jacobaea*, disturbance caused by grazing at the time of peak germination increases the recruitment of seedlings, allowing these weed species to persist in early successional grasslands. Therefore, altering the timing of grazing or leaving the field ungrazed can minimise seedling recruitment in *B.sterilis* and *S.jacobaea*.

2. In addition, for *V.sativa* and *S.jacobaea*, seedling recruitment can be reduced to less than predicted by prolonging the period of grazing.

REFERENCE

GIBSON C.W.D., WATT T.A. and BROWN, V.K. (1987) The use of sheep grazing to recreate species-rich grassland from abandoned arable land. *Biological Conservation*, **42**, 165-183.

Table 1. Density (m^{-2}) of *Bromus sterilis*, *Vicia sativa* and *Senecio jacobaea* under different management regimes.

Grazing	*B.sterilis*	*V.sativa*	*S.jacobaea*
Nil	14.4	8.0	2.9
Spring	5.1	13.4	7.6
Autumn	156.8	25.4	4.1
Aug.-Nov.	67.0	27.9	1.0
April-Nov.	12.2	0.1	6.6
ANOVA	★★★	★★★	★★★
LSD	55.4	8.4	3.0

Table 2. Predicted (and observed) number of seedlings of *Bromus sterilis*, *Vicia sativa* and *Senecio jacobaea* per 0.2m^2.

Grazing	*B.sterilis*	*V.sativa*	*S.jacobaea*
Nil	16.4 (12.8)	10.8 (15.7)★	2.3 (2.2)
Spring	13.9 (13.1)	12.7 (11.0)	1.8 (1.8)
Autumn	35.9 (33.5)	10.4 (11.8)	1.6 (2.4)★
Aug.-Nov.	39.1 (48.9)★	14.6 (9.5)★	1.4 (0.6)★
April-Nov.	5.8 (3.0)	5.3 (1.0)★	1.2 (0.2)★

★ = significant at $P > 0.05$

Discrimination between Unimproved Pastures by Multivariate Analysis of Coleopteran Assemblages

SHONA BLAKE AND G.N. FOSTER

Environmental Sciences Department

The Scottish Agricultural College, Auchincruive, Ayr KA6 5HW

INTRODUCTION

It is possible to classify grassland habitats by multivariate analysis of their ground beetle (Coleoptera: Carabidae) assemblages (Rushton *et al.*, 1989, 1991; Eyre and Luff, 1990). Sampling is normally by pitfall trapping over a season, but it should be possible to obtain valid results by sampling over a more limited period. Rove beetles (Staphylinidae) are caught in large numbers but have not been utilized for habitat classification to the same extent as ground beetles.

METHODS

Beetle populations were sampled by pitfall trapping at five unimproved grassland sites in Ayrshire from April to October, 1990. Four or six lines of traps were set at various locations within each site. Annual and monthly catch data for both ground and rove beetles were analysed by detrended correspondence analysis (DECORANA - Hill, 1979). DECORANA orders the sites on two or more axes according to differences in their beetle assemblages. The positions of the sites on each axis can then be correlated to measured environmental variables.

RESULTS

Ordination of the annual ground beetle data gave a good separation of the five sites (Figure 1a). An equally good separation was achieved using the data for June and July alone (Figure 1b). Soil moisture was found to be the most important variable in June and July, with a Spearman's correlation coefficient (r_s) between Axis 1 position and soil moisture of -0.523, n = 24 and p < 0.01. For rove beetle assemblages, the separation obtained during May alone (Figure 1d) was very similar to that for the whole season (Figure 1c). In this case, Axis 2 was significantly correlated to soil moisture, with $r_s = 0.457$, p < 0.05.

CONCLUSIONS

It may be possible to obtain good grassland classifications from data collected over a limited season in early summer rather than trapping throughout the year. The interpretation of catches can only be undertaken satisfactorily with a sound knowledge of the species sampled; given this, it is possible that equally good, or better, habitat classifications may be obtained from rove beetle data as from ground beetle data. Soil moisture content is an important environmental variable affecting beetle assemblages in these unimproved grassland sites.

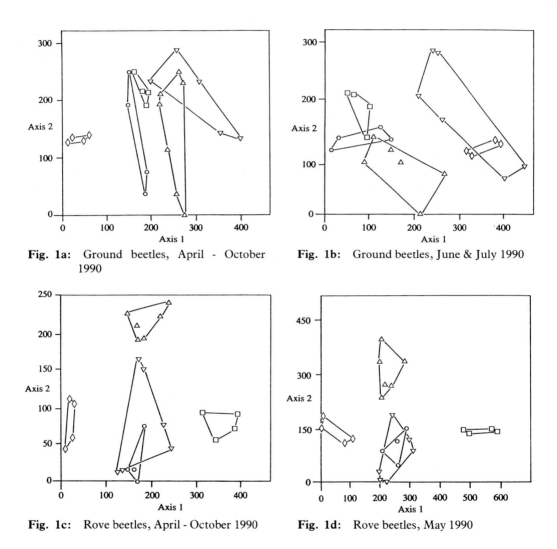

Fig. 1a: Ground beetles, April - October 1990

Fig. 1b: Ground beetles, June & July 1990

Fig. 1c: Rove beetles, April - October 1990

Fig. 1d: Rove beetles, May 1990

Fig. 1. DECORANA ordinations of beetle assemblages at five Ayrshire sites. Polygons include the site scores for all trapping locations at each site. O: Auchalton meadows, NS 3303. Δ: Cairn Hill, NX 1793. □: Feoch meadows, NX 2682. ◊: Macawston farm, NS 2104. ▽: Shewalton sandpits, NS 3237.

ACKNOWLEDGEMENTS

The Scottish Agricultural College receives financial support from the Scottish Office Agriculture and Fisheries Department. We wish to acknowledge help with identification from Dr M L Luff and Dr M D Eyre, of the University of Newcastle upon Tyne. We are also indebted to land owners and occupiers, in particular the Scottish Wildlife Trust, for permission to operate traps. The then Nature Conservancy Council (replaced by Scottish Natural Heritage within Scotland) gave permission for trapping to take place on Sites of Special Scientific Interest.

REFERENCES

EYRE M.D. and LUFF M.L. (1990) The ground beetle (Coleoptera: Carabidae) assemblages of British grasslands. *Entomologist's Gazette*, **41**, 197 - 208.

HILL M.O. (1979) *DECORANA: a FORTRAN program for detrended correspondence analysis and reciprocal averaging*. New York: Ecology and Systematics, Cornell University.

RUSHTON S.P., LUFF M.L. and EYRE M.D. (1989) Effects of pasture improvement and management on the ground beetle and spider communities of upland grasslands. *Journal of Applied Ecology*, **26**, 489 - 503.

RUSHTON S.P., LUFF M.L. and EYRE M.D. (1991) Habitat characteristics of grassland *Pterostichus* species (Coleoptera, Carabidae). *Ecological Entomology*, **16**, 91-104.

Survival and Spread of Pot-grown Wildflowers Inserted into a Perennial Ryegrass Ley

D. BOYCE

ADAS Wolverhampton, Woodthorne, Wolverhampton WV6 8TQ

INTRODUCTION

This experiment assessed a transplanting method of increasing plant diversity within species-poor former agricultural grassland, which avoided disturbing the existing sward, the soil, or the soil seed-bank. Nineteen species of typical grassland and woodland-edge wildflowers, inserted as pot-grown plants within a species-poor perennial ryegrass ley retained as a wide ride within new farm-woodland, were monitored for survival and spread. Soils were calcareous clays (pH 7.8) which varied in depth and proneness to drought.

METHODS

Pot-grown (7 cm) wildflowers were randomly planted, during July 1988, at 1m spacings within 8 plots. Each plot contained 210 plants (19 species).

Treatments, replicated 4 times, comprised cutting and removing the vegetation from each plot at either the end of July or the beginning of October. Two unplanted control plots were similarly maintained.

Survival was assessed from counts of plants (or offspring) which continued to occupy their original planted positions. Local spread was estimated from presence or absence within fifty 100 mm x 100 mm squares of a sub-divided 1m x 0.5m quadrat placed centrally over the original planted positions of a sample of each species.

Data analysis used contingency table chi-square analysis for survival data and Mann-Whitney U-test and Kruskal-Wallis test for spread data.

RESULTS

After 5 years there were no significant overall differences in survival or spread, for all species combined, between the planted treatments ($p > 0.05$).

Mean overall survival was 76.4%, but survival was significantly ($p < 0.001$) reduced within three of the plots by competition from white clover, which had increased from within the existing sward. Local spread of the planted species was also significantly ($p < 0.001$) reduced within clover-dominated plots. Rates of survival and spread (Table 1) varied significantly ($p < 0.001$) between species.

There was no evidence of spontaneous development of the planted species within the unplanted controls.

DISCUSSION

The degeneration of perennial ryegrass which followed the withdrawal of fertiliser inputs on this site gave rise to an open sward, with little competition for the introduced wildflowers and gaps for subsequent vegetative spread and seedling colonisation.

Rates of survival and spread suggest that considerably wider planting spacings than those used here would suffice to increase species-diversity within some types of formerly intensively-managed agricultural grassland.

However, white clover apparently needs to be eliminated before plant introduction commences.

Table 1. Mean survival and local spread within all plots, 5 years after planting.

Species	Survival (%)	Local Spread (Median value out of 50)
Cowslip (*Primula veris*)	30.0	2.0
Cuckooflower (*Cardamine pratensis*)	37.5	2.0
Ragged Robin (*Lychnis flos-cuculi*)	47.5	5.0
Small Scabious (*Scabiosa columbaria*)	52.3	5.5
Red Clover (*Trifolium pratense*)	59.1	20.5
Agrimony (*Agrimonia eupatoria*)	70.8	7.0
Perforate St. John's-wort (*Hypericum perforatum*)	73.8	8.0
Self-heal (*Prunella vulgaris*)	77.1	25.5
Bird's-foot Trefoil (*Lotus corniculatus*)	79.2	26.5
Hairy St. John's-wort(*Hypericum hirsutum*)	79.5	3.5
Meadow Crane's-bill (*Geranium pratense*)	85.9	8.5
Devil's-bit Scabious(*Succisa pratensis*)	88.5	6.5
Rough Hawkbit(*Leontodon hispidus*)	89.6	20.0
Betony (*Stachys officinalis*)	90.6	6.5
Bugle (*Ajuga reptans*)	91.7	50.0
Meadow Buttercup (*Ranunculus acris*)	93.8	45.0
Oxeye Daisy (*Leucanthemum vulgare*)	93.8	40.5
Yarrow (*Achillea millefolium*)	97.2	44.0
Common Knapweed (*Centaurea nigra*)	99.0	26.5

ACKNOWLEDGEMENTS

This work was funded by the Ministry of Agriculture, Fisheries and Food, and was carried out at ADAS Drayton, Warwickshire. Statistical advice was provided by Mr. S M C Poulton, ADAS Wolverhampton.

Nature, Extent and Management of Grassland within Golf-related Sites of Special Scientific Interest

A-M. BRENNAN
The Durrell Institute of Conservation and Ecology,
The University, Canterbury, Kent CT2 7NX

INTRODUCTION

Golf has a high degree of land redundancy: tees, greens and fairways comprise the playing area accounting for a third of the average course, whilst the rest, predominantly grassland, is out of play and has potential as a wildlife resource (Nature Conservancy Council, 1989). Using available Phase 1 habitat survey data it was possible to examine the extent of the habitats, particularly grassland, which occur on golf-related Sites of Special Scientific Interest (SSSIs).

The extent of the grassland resource and its management

Of the 83107 ha of grassland habitat mapped and recorded for golf-related SSSIs, the largest area is occupied by dune grassland (49%), [Fig. 1], followed by acid grass-

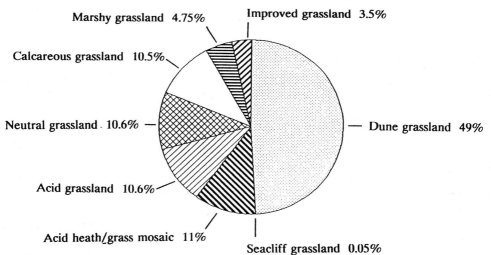

Fig. 1.   Grassland habitats occurring within golf-related SSSIs.

land/heath mosaic which accounts for 11%. Acid, neutral, calcareous, marshy, improved and seacliff grassland are also represented.

Management of grassland on golf courses offers a number of options and despite courses being in active use, grazing still does take place on a number of sites. This can either be free-range sheep grazing on Scottish coastal links, or more directly targeted in the form of enclosed grazing of calcareous grassland within steep-sided west country coombes. Where grazing is impracticable, mowing regimes mimic either pasture or meadow management by the cutting and removal of material (Brennan, 1992), with many clubs having both human and technical resources to undertake this kind of work.

As with other areas of conservation, the twin threats to the grassland habitats consist of mismanagement or neglect. In golf-related SSSIs the former is avoided through statutory site-safeguard. Lack of management remains a more insidious problem as scrub/bracken encroachment and build-up of grass litter can lead to eutrophication and invasion by coarse grass species such as Yorkshire-fog (*Holcus lanatus*). Where this occurs near the playing area, action is undertaken as part of standard greenkeeping procedure. However, on more distant parts of the course the management imperative for clubs may be less urgent. This resulted in the former Nature Conservancy Council producing a document outlining the principles of management planning (Nature Conservancy Council, 1990) to encourage positive management of the entire course.

CONCLUSIONS

Of the designated habitats occurring within golf-related sites, grassland represents a significant conservation resource, especially as previous estimates (for SSSIs on English courses) suggest that the bulk of the grassland component of golf-related SSSIs tends to lie within the golf course (Dair and Schofield, 1990). This, along with the management potential and the availability of resources, makes the continued conservation of such areas an achievable objective.

ACKNOWLEDGEMENTS

I would like to thank staff within Countryside Council for Wales, English Nature and Scottish Natural Heritage for their assistance in allowing me access to site-related data.

REFERENCES

BRENNAN A-M. (1992) The management of golf courses as potential nature reserves. *Aspects of Applied Biology*, **29**, 241-248.
DAIR I. and SCHOFIELD J.M. (1990) Nature conservation and the management of golf courses in Great Britain. In: Cochran, A.J. (ed.) *Science and Golf*. pp. 330-335. London: Spon.
NATURE CONSERVANCY COUNCIL (1989) *On Course Conservation: Managing Golf's Natural Heritage*. Nature Conservancy Council: Peterborough.
NATURE CONSERVANCY COUNCIL (1990) *Your Course... Preparing a conservation management plan*. Nature Conservancy Council: Peterborough.

Factors Associated with the Survival of Semi-Natural Grassland in the Lowlands of Leinster

C. BYRNE
School of Botany, Trinity College, Dublin

INTRODUCTION

Leinster is the eastern province of Ireland comprising of 12 counties and measuring approximately 200 km by 150 km. Lowland Leinster (land below 300 m) covers about 90% of the province. The climate, topography and soil parent material of Leinster are eminently suitable for grass growth (O'Sullivan, 1982) and grassland under agricultural management predominates. There is no-up-to date information in the Republic on the area occupied by semi-natural grasslands of conservation interest nor on their current status.

METHODS

For the purpose of this study semi-natural grassland was defined as historic grassland or grassland of long standing. Road and rail verges were excluded as were areas liable to flooding. A non-random method of site selection was adopted using a data base of suitable sites stored with the Irish Wildlife Service. Thirty sites were selected for investigation. The sampling intensity was three 2 × 2 m releves per site. A releve is a description, including a species list, of a homogenous stand of vegetation. Environmental and management information were also collected for each releve.

RESULTS AND DISCUSSION

Six sites were found to have disappeared and a further 7 sites were found to occupy smaller areas than previously recorded. The average species density per releve was 33 species but the figures for calcareous and species-rich wet grassland were as high as 589 species per releve.

On preliminary analysis of management data for 26 of the 30 sites, a number of overlapping factors appear to be associated with the survival of semi-natural grassland in lowland Leinster (Table 1 and Figure 1). The majority of releves (77%) have severe agricultural impediments for grassland production as defined by the National Soil Survey of Ireland (Finch et al., 1983). The implication is that semi-natural grassland in lowland Leinster persists mainly in conditions unsuited to intensive agriculture. The term "protected" is used in a broad sense to include grasslands owned by the Government or Military, commonage and areas associated with racecourses and quarries. Such lands comprised a relatively small proportion of the releve (29%) considering that 49% of the sites are in Areas of Scientific Interest. The factor of semi-abandonment (24%) was almost always associated with one of the other two factors. It occurred where grazing by trespassing livestock and/or wild herbivores maintained species diversity and where land had recently been taken out of active agricultural management. Such sites were under threat from dereliction. The remaining 8% of the releves could not be explained in terms of the factors mentioned and may be accounted for by socio-economic reasons which are to be subsequently explored.

Table 1. Interacting factors considered to be associated with survival of semi-natural grassland in lowland Leinster (total number of releves = 76).

Factor	No. of releves	%
Severe impediments to agriculture	60	77
Protected	23	29
Semi-abandoned	19	24
None of the above	6	8

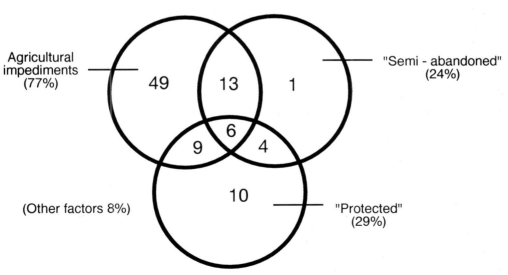

Fig. 1. Percentage overlap between factors associated with the survival of semi-natural grassland in lowland Leinster.

CONCLUSIONS
The data suggest that we are dealing with a very threatened resource and that suitable management guidelines and/or Government legislation is urgently required. At least three factors appear to promote survival of semi-natural grassland in lowland Leinster: severe impediments to agriculture, "protection" and "semi-abandonment".

ACKNOWLEDGEMENTS
My thanks to my supervisors, Dr. D.W. Jeffrey and Dr. D.L. Kelly and my sponsors Timotei Ltd. and the Office of Public Works.

REFERENCES
FINCH T.F., GARDINER A., COMEY A. and RADFORD T. (1983) National soil survey of Ireland. Soils of Co. Meath. In: *Soil Survey Bulletin*, No. 37, pp 62-67.
O'SULLIVAN A.M. (1982) The lowland grasslands of Ireland. *Journal of the Life Sciences Royal Dublin Society*, **3**, 131-142.

Effects of Reduced Stocking on Semi Natural Vegetation in Northumberland and Mid Wales

J.P. BYRNE, J. WILDIG[1] AND S.P. RUSHTON [2]

ADAS Redesdale, Rochester, Otterburn, Newcastle upon Tyne NE19 1SB

[1]ADAS Pwllpeiran, Cwmystwyth, Aberystwyth, Dyfed

[2]University of Newcastle upon Tyne, Newcastle

INTRODUCTION

Dwarf shrub heath communities dominated by *Calluna* are of particular interest ecologically in upland Semi Natural Rough Grazings (SNRG). However, nationally between 1947 and 1984, 20% of *Calluna* cover has been lost through land improvement, afforestation and a marked increase in sheep numbers arising from national/EC policies.

The ecological quality of much of the remaining *Calluna* is continuing to decline through overgrazing, with grass and moss coming in at the expense of *Calluna* and *Vaccinium*.

Measures to ensure the long-term survival of *Calluna* and a reversal of the trend towards grass and moss, must therefore focus on the need to reduce stocking. There would appear to have been few studies undertaken which provide comparative data of flocks under reduced stocking regimes. The 1989/90 ADAS Hills and Uplands project set out to redress this with farm unit comparisons of a 30% reduction in stocking on two contrasting centres—Redesdale in the Northumberland National Park and Pwllpeiran in the Cambrian Mountains ESA in mid Wales.

MATERIALS AND METHODS

a) **Redesdale.** A complete heft of 117 ha was allocated to the work. Ewe numbers rose by over 50% from 1973 to 1987. Output of weaned lamb rose at the expense of individual performance and *Calluna* cover was reduced. In October 1989, a complex division taking account of the disposition of 7 plant communities took place. A control flock of 115 ewes and 31 hoggs stocked at 2.1 ewes/ha was created along with a treatment of 93 ewes and 24 hoggs stocked 30% less at 1.48 ewes/ha. Management of the two flocks thereafter has been the same.

b) **Pwllpeiran.** The work at Pwllpeiran has been orientated to the Cambrian Mountains ESA which was set up in 1987 with the objective of safeguarding the large areas of SNRG which were under threat from land improvement and overgrazing. Two stocking rates are being compared—the ESA prescription for manage-

245

ment agreements and a 30% reduction. A mountain unit with 90% of the land over 400 m above sea level was made available.

The land resources ranges from dry grassy heath to rank mature *Calluna* on wet and dry heath. Splitting this into two was extremely difficulty and the two units were set up with each having 16-17% improved middle hill and 5 paddocks of SNRG reflecting the range of vegetation types. *Each paddock was individually surveyed for its stocking.* Some 556 ewes plus followers utilise 300 ha of land.

The ESA unit consists of 150 ha of which 130 ha is SNRG stocked at 1.74 sheep/ha and the −30% unit 149 ha of which 127 ha is SNRG stocked 30% below the ESA prescription at 1.16 sheep/ha. Taking into account the improved land, actual stocking of the ESA unit in 1992/93 was 2.01 sheep/ha and of the −30% unit 1.80 sheep/ha.

RESULTS AND DISCUSSION

a) **Redesdale.** Output of weaned lamb/ha is lower on the lower stocking rate and costs are somewhat higher but there are only relatively small differences in physical performance.

Table 1. Comparative physical and financial performance of flocks stocked at 1.48 and 2.1 ewes per hectare (per 100 ewes).

Ewes/ha	1.48			2.1		
	Year			Year		
	1	2	3	1	2	3
Weaning, %	116	117	126	108	125	123
Lamb weaning wt, kg	31.9	31.4	32.0	32.3	32.2	31.7
Output of weaned lamb, kg/ha	55.4	54.6	59.7	72.7	83.7	74.9
Gross output, £/ewe	48.95	54.50	65.94	46.12	57.19	63.52
Less variable costs, £/ewe	13.85	17.42	15.77	123.26	16.79	15.14
Gross margin, £/ewe	35.10	36.98	50.17	32.86	40.40	48.37
Gross margin, £/ha	52.28	55.08	74.73	68.21	83.86	102.40

b) **Pwllpeiran.** Although the SNRG on the paddocks of each unit has been grazed to ESA prescription or 30% below since the spring of 1990, the way in which the grazing animals were utilised has varied. Moreover, within the Cambrian Mountains ESA stock displayed by management agreements for SNRG can be retained on the improved middle hill which is not subject to agreement and is consequently grazed harder. This aspect of farming in the ESA was incorporated in the 1991/92 sheep year.

Table 2. Overall flock results for 1991/92 sheep year and output of weaned lamb from SNRG 1991 and 1992.

	ESA Flock		−30% Flock	
	1991	1992	1991	1992
Ewes to tup		292		264
Weaning %		101		96
Lamb weaning weight, kg		22.1		23.1
Kg of weaned lamb/ha		42.9		40.5
Gross output/ha, £		123.50		120.50
Gross margin/ha, £		52.92		55.82
Thin ewes (CS < 2) at weaning	84	44	33	21
Area of SNRG	130.2	130.2	124.0	124.0
Lambs weaned off SNG	212	191	102	99
Lambs weaning weight, kg	22.5	22.5	23.1	23.9
Output of weaned lamb/ha, kg	35.5	33.0	19.0	19.1

CONCLUSIONS
Results from both centres suggest that although there have been some differences in individual performance and in the financial performance of the flocks, overall performance has been satisfactory with the notable result being the reduced output of weaned lamb/ha off SNRG and lower Gross Margin/ha from the treatment flock at Redesdale. Of concern at Pwllpeiran has been the relatively high numbers of thin ewes at weaning.

ACKNOWLEDGEMENTS
Funding for this work from MAFF (LUCC Group) is gratefully acknowledged.

The Influence of Legumes on the Ecology of a Species-Rich Meadow Established on a Restored Site

R. CHAPMAN AND A. YOUNGER

The University of Newcastle upon Tyne, Newcastle upon Tyne NE1 7RU

INTRODUCTION

In recent years there has been a growing interest in the establishment of species-rich grasslands that have high ecological and amenity values (Wells, 1989). The objective of any such excersise is to establish a stable community with high levels of both species richness and diversity. This paper reports on the observed influence of pasture legumes on the species richness and diversity of such a grassland established on a site restored after opencast coal mining in Northumberland.

MATERIALS AND METHODS

A species-rich grassland community was established in 1988 from a commercial seed mixture. From 1989 until 1991, management consisted of a mid July hay cut with spring and aftermath grazing. Spring fertilizer was applied at a rate of 115 kg/ha of 22:11:11 $N:P_2O_5:K_2O$. Prior to each hay cut, species presence and abundance were determined in 15 quadrats each $1m^2$. Grass, forb and legume ground cover were determined and values for species richness and Simpsons diversity index were calculated.

RESULTS AND DISCUSSION

Legume ground cover increased significantly over successive seasons while ground cover of the grasses and forbs declined (Table 1). This was associated with a simultaneous and significant reduction in diversity. These observations imply that aggresssive growth by the legumes was suppressing the growth of their grass and forb companion species and thus reducing the diversity of the community. This may be attributed to the legume's N fixing ability. It has been argued that an unusually low soil N supply is a principle factor inhibiting plant growth on restored sites (Chapman *et al.*, 1994). Legumes, with their independent N supply, will be unaffected by this, and therefore have higher growth rates than their non-leguminous companion species. Thus legumes became increasingly dominant in the community, and reduced its diversity.

Species richness showed an initial increase between 1989 and 1990 due to both the recruitment of additional species into the community and to the proliferation of species already present. Between 1990 and 1991, species richness showed a slight but significant decline as aggressive legume growth eliminated some of the less aggressive companion species.

These results suggest that aggressive legume growth in species-rich grassland established on restored opencast coal sites may suppress non-leguminous companion species thus reducing the community's diversity and species richness.

Table 1. Values for grass, forb and legume component ground cover (%) Simpsons diversity index and species richness, 1989-1991.

Year	Ground cover			Diversity	Species richness
	Grass	Forb	Legumes		
1989	75.0	61.7	34.0	13.5	20.3
1990	63.0	60.0	75.3	10.7	23.5
1991	56.3	51.3	90.7	9.5	21.8
SED	2.2	1.5	3.3	0.493	0.325
Sig.	★	★	★★★	★	★

ACKNOWLEDGEMENTS
The technical assisstance of Mr P. Shotton and Mr W. Hewison is acknowledged. This work was supported by British Coal Opencast Executive.

REFERENCES
CHAPMAN R., YOUNGER A. and DAVIES R. (1994) The influence of soil factors on the growth of a grass/clover sward on a restored Opencast site in Northumberland. *Grass and Forage Science* (in press).

WELLS T.C.E. (1989) The re-creation of grassland habitats. *The Entomologist*, **108**, 97-108.

Recruitment of Non-Sown Species into a Species-Rich Grassland Established on a Restored Site

R. CHAPMAN AND A. YOUNGER

The University of Newcastle upon Tyne, Newcastle upon Tyne NE1 7RU

INTRODUCTION

The botanical composition of an established species-rich grassland will be the product of the establishment of sown species and the natural recruitment of unsown species. Natural recruitment may represent a low-cost scource of species for such a community. A study was therefore undertaken with the twin aims of i) assessing the contribution to total S (species/m^2) made by species recruitment, and ii) to identify the likely origin of the unsown species in a species-rich grassland established on land restored after opencast coal mining.

MATERIALS AND METHODS

Details concerning the establishment and management of this grassland are given elsewhere (Chapman and Younger, 1993). Four years after establishment, S (species/m^2) was determined in 15 quadrats, each 1 m^2. S was then partitioned between the sown and recruited grass, forb and legume components. The likely origin of the non-sown species was identified using details of their comparative biology (Grime et al., 1988).

RESULTS AND DISCUSSION

The mean observed S was 22.4 species/m^2. Sown species accounted for the greater part of S (Table 1). Contributions within this fraction were in the order grasses>forbs>legumes. However, total S was augmented considerably by the recruitment of unsown species, and contributions within this fraction were in the order legumes>forbs>grasses.

A persistent seed bank is a likely scource for 8 of the recruited species (*Cirsium arvense, Cerastium holosteoides, Lotus corniculatus, Ranunculus repens, Trifolium dubium, Trifolium pratense, Trifolium repens, Ulex europeus*), making this the greatest scource of unsown species. Two species may have established following wind dispersal of seed (*Cirsium arvense, Taraxacum officinale*). Two grasses (*Bromus hordeaceus, Lolium perenne*) may have been imported on machinery managing the crop. *Lolium perenne* may also have survived as a volunteer persisting from a previously established cover crop. Details on the comparative biology of the two remaining recruited species (*Geranium dissectum, Lathyrus pratensis*) are not available but the biology of closely related species suggests that recruitment from a persistent seed bank may also have been possible.

These results therefore show that the recruitment of unsown species made a substantial contribution to the S of an artificially established grassland. The species recruited will, however, be largely dependent upon the characteristics of the soil seed bank.

Table 1. The partitioning of S (species/m^2) between sown and unsown grasses, forbs and legumes.

Fraction	% of total S	% of recruited S
All species	100.0	-
Sown grasses	36.7	-
Sown forbs	28.6	-
Sown legumes	4.2	-
Sown species	68.9	-
Unsown grasses	6.8	21.8
Unsown forbs	9.8	31.4
Unsown legumes	14.6	46.8
Unsown species	31.2	100.0

Acknowledgements

This work was suppoerted by British Coal Opencast Executive.

REFERENCES

CHAPMAN R. and YOUNGER A. (1993) The influence of legumes on the ecology of a species rich grassland established on a restored site. This volume.

GRIME J.P., HODGSON J.G. and HUNT R. (1988) Comparative Plant Ecology. London: Unwin Hyman.

The Effect of Slugs, Sward Conditions and Sheep Grazing on Seedling Emergence

B.H. CLEAR HILL AND J. SILVERTOWN[1]

Oxford Research Unit, Open University, Boars Hill, Oxford OX1 5HR

[1]Open University, Walton Hall, Milton Keynes MK7 6AA

INTRODUCTION

Work in a sheep grazing experiment at Little Wittenham Nature Reserve near Abingdon, Oxfordshire has shown that the sward is very resistant to invasion by dicot. species (Bullock et al., 1994a). This may be due to various factors such as a lack of germination sites (Bullock et al., 1994b) or the inability to withstand herbivore attacks (Harper, 1977). The experiment, which was set up in 1986, consists of a 2x2 fully factorial and replicated combination of two seasonal grazing treatments: summer and winter (see Treweek, 1990 for more details). The grassland was intensively farmed until 1984 when it became part of the nature reserve. Since then it has received no artificial fertilisers or chemicals. An experiment was carried out to assess the effect of slug herbivory on seedling emergence in the sward.

METHODS

Seeds of five common grassland dicot. species:*Cerastium fontanum* (in autumn 1992), *Leucanthemum vulgare*, *Lotus corniculatus*, *Plantago lanceolata* and *Achillea millefolium* (all spring 1993) were sown into relocatable positions in the sward. In each of the 8 paddocks two slug treatments were applied in which the sowing areas were either protected from, or exposed to, slugs (*Derocerus reticulatum*) by the use of modified defined-area traps (DAT's). These, by their use of galvanised iron above and below ground, prevent slugs from moving in or out of a defined area (Ferguson et al., 1989). Seedling emergence was monitored and related to slug presence or absence and to grazing treatment. Sward conditions were monitored at each sowing point. The presence/absence of a leaf canopy and the presence/absence of ground cover were determined.

RESULTS

All 5 species gave similar results. In all paddocks the exclusion of slugs significantly increased seedling emergence. Total emergence was greatest in bare soil or areas with no leaf canopy, ie.'gaps'. These gaps were most numerous in the winter grazed paddocks. Emergence, in the absence of slugs, was increased in bare soil. If slugs were present then ground cover did not affect emergence levels. There was a significant interaction between winter grazing and slug presence (p<0.001), the benefit of winter grazing being removed by the presence of slugs (Table 1).

Table 1. The effect of slugs on seedling emergence; combined numbers of species emerging per trap under winter grazing.

Slugs	Winter grazing	
	Minus	Plus
Absent	2.31	4.44
Present	1.44	1.63
s.e.d.	1.218	

CONCLUSION

This work shows that slug damage can be a significant factor in preventing the establishment of dicots. in a sward. Grazing aided establishment by creating gaps but only if slugs were excluded.

Acknowledgements

We thank the Northmoor Trust and the Open University for funding for this project and the staff of Little Wittenham Nature Reserve for all their help.

References

BULLOCK J.M., CLEAR HILL B.H. and SILVERTOWN J. (1994a) Demography of *Cirsium vulgare* in a grazing experiment. *Journal of Ecology* (in press.)

BULLOCK J.M., CLEAR HILL B.H., DALE M.P and SILVERTOWN J. (1994b) An experimental study of vegetation change due to grazing in a species-poor grassland and the role of the seedbank. *Journal of Applied Ecology* (in press.)

FERGUSON C.M., BARRATT B.I.P. and JONES P.A. (1989) A new technique for estimating density of the field slug *Derocerus reticulatum* (Muller). *British Crop Protection Council Monograph No.41. Slugs and Snails in World Agriculture.* pp331-336.

HARPER J.L. (1977) *Population Biology of Plants*, pp435-456. London: Academic Press.

TREWEEK J.R. (1990) *The ecology of sheep grazing: Its use in nature conservation management of lowland neutral grassland.* D.Phil.Thesis University of Oxford.

Biological Monitoring of Grasslands in Environmentally Sensitive Areas in England and Wales

C.N.R. CRITCHLEY AND S.M.C. POULTON[1]

ADAS Newcastle, Kenton Bar, Newcastle upon Tyne NE1 2YA

[1]ADAS Wolverhampton, "Woodthorne", Wergs Road, Wolverhampton WV6 8TQ

INTRODUCTION

Biological monitoring of grasslands in 19 ESAs is being undertaken by ADAS, as part of a wider evaluation of the effectiveness of ESA designations in England and Wales. The project started in 1987, and expanded with the introduction of further ESAs in 1988 and 1993.

ESA MONITORING STRATEGY

The aim is to assess the success of the scheme in preserving existing wildlife conservation value of grasslands threatened by agricultural practices, and in enhancing the value of degraded grasslands. Surveillance and monitoring schemes as defined by Hellawell (1991) have been used. Surveillance is based on random sampling from the whole ESA. Its objectives are to record changes in grassland vegetation within the ESA boundaries, including those which may be attributable to unpredictable and uncontrollable factors such as weather. Prescription monitoring is based on targeted locations. Its objectives are to test specific hypotheses of the intended effects on grassland vegetation of ESA prescribed management.

FIELD RECORDING METHODS

The first ESA monitoring schemes followed the recommendations of Smith *et al.* (1985), and are based on estimates of cover of plant species on the Domin scale within fixed quadrats. Preliminary results of a replicated, blocked trial undertaken at 14 sites in 1992 have shown that observer consistency is better for presence/absence records from nested quadrats than for abundance estimates from other techniques in common use. An improved field recording method has therefore been developed for the more recent ESA monitoring, based on a system of nested quadrats similar to those described by Hodgson *et al.* (in prep).

ANALYSIS OF SHORT-TERM CHANGE

Vegetation monitoring must be of long duration to enable the separation of short-term cycles from long-term trends (Usher, 1991), but the detection of short-term changes in grassland can give an early indication of whether the desired outcome of the ESA is likely to occur.

As an example, one component of the Broads ESA management prescriptions is the maintenance of high water levels to benefit grassland vegetation and bird communities. The conservation objectives for grassland vegetation in the Broads include the enhancement of agriculturally improved grassland and the maintenance of semi-improved mesotrophic grassland. Data for 1987 and 1990 from the prescription monitoring programme for each of these grassland types have been analysed to test null hypotheses relating to these objectives. Criteria for selection of species for analysis were (i) categorised as common in and characteristic of wetland or largely absent from wetland (Grime *et al.*, 1988) and (ii) minimum of 6 occurrences. In semi-improved grassland, analysis of 18 wetland species showed no evidence of deterioration as would be indicated by a decrease in their abundance ($P = 0.1$), and there was some limited evidence of an increase in abundance of wetland species ($P < 0.05$). No changes were detected in improved grassland except creeping thistle (*Cirsium arvense*) which increased in cover ($P < 0.05$). The problem of thistle control in ESAs is being addressed.

ACKNOWLEDGEMENTS
Many colleagues organised and carried out fieldwork. The work is funded by MAFF.

REFERENCES
GRIME J. P., HODGSON J.G. and HUNT R. (1988) *Comparative Plant Ecology*. London: Unwin Hyman.

HELLAWELL J.M. (1991) Development of a rationale for monitoring. In: Goldsmith, F.B. (ed.) *Monitoring for Conservation and Ecology*, pp. 1-14, London: Chapman and Hall.

HODGSON J.G., COLASANT R., PHILIPSON P., LEACH S., MONTGOMERY S., DIXON M., HEWSON R. and HUNT R. (in preparation). A simple method for monitoring grassland vegetation.

SMITH I.R., WELLS D.A. and WELSH P. (1985) *Botanical Survey and Monitoring Methods for Grasslands*. Peterborough: Nature Conservancy Council.

USHER M.B. (1991) Scientific requirements of a monitoring programme. In: Goldsmith, F.B. (ed.) *Monitoring for Conservation and Ecology*, pp 15-32, London: Chapman and Hall.

Effect of Reducing Nutrient Input on Productivity and Botanical Composition of an Upland Sward

D.A. DAVIES, M. FOTHERGILL AND C.T. MORGAN

AFRC Institute of Grassland and Environmental Research
Plas Gogerddan, Aberystwyth, Dyfed SY23 3EB

INTRODUCTION

Current agricultural policy aims to counteract over-production. However, there is also a commitment to maintaining viable rural communities in the uplands. Increasingly, financial incentives are offered to farmers to manage land with the objectives of meeting the needs of nature conservation and maintaining the aesthetic value of the landscape. To maintain profitability, upland farmers are likely to overcome restrictions on stocking rates, coupled with lower prices for the end product, by reducing input costs. This could result in a reduction in use of lime and fertilizers. Little is known of the consequences of a reduction in nutrient input on sward dynamics and productivity of permanent pastures. Hence, a study was initiated in autumn 1990 at Bronydd Mawr Research Station in south Powys. Results obtained during 1991 and 1992 are presented.

MATERIAL AND METHODS

The experiment was established on a 25-year old perennial ryegrass/bent (*Lolium perenne/Agrostis capillaris*) dominant permanent pasture at 370-390 m above sea level. The effects of elimination of a) N, b) N, P, and K, and c) N, P, K and Ca were compared with a treatment which received all four nutrients. Lime was applied at 5 t/ha in September 1990. During 1991 and 1992, 150 kg N/ha, 25 kg P/ha and 50 kg K/ha were applied each year to the appropriate treatments.

Individual plots, which were 0.4 ha and replicated three times, were continuously stocked with Brecknock Cheviot ewes and their single purebred lambs from early May until weaning in early August, and thereafter with the ewes only until the end of October. Sward surface height was maintained at 4 ± 0.5 cm by regular adjustments of animal numbers on individual plots.

In two further treatments (plot size 0.2 ha), the effects on biodiversity of the cessation of both nutrient application and grazing is being studied. One of these treatments is defoliated mechanically in mid-July every year and the cut herbage removed.

Plant population densities are monitored during spring and autumn by lifting and dissecting twenty 5 cm diameter cores from every plot.

RESULTS AND DISCUSSION

Mean ewe stocking rates on the 4 grazed treatments in 1991 and 1992 are given in Table 1. In both years, the stock carrying capacity of the CaPKN treated pasture was higher than those of the other 3 pastures. During 1992, the carrying capacity of the nil-input pasture was also lower than that of the CaPK pasture. In year 2, the stocking rate on the nil-input pasture was only 50% of that on the pasture which received all 4 nutrients.

Table 1. Mean stocking rate (ewes/ha) during 1991 and 1992.

Year	Treatment				s.e.m.	significance
	CaPKN	CaPK	Ca	Nil		
1991	31.4	24.1	23.7	20.8	1.55	*
1992	30.8	21.9	19.4	15.4	1.73	**

A detailed account of the changes in grass tiller numbers and white clover (*Trifolium repens*) stolon length per unit area of ground during the first 2 years was published earlier (Fothergill *et al.*, 1993). Elimination of nutrient input resulted in a reduction in perennial ryegrass and an increase in bent density under grazing. By May 1992, ryegrass tiller number in the nil-input sward was only $4070/m^2$ compared to $13067/m^2$ in the CaPKN sward. Corresponding bent tiller number was $14942/m^2$ and $5666/m^2$ respectively. White clover stolon density in the CaPKN sward at $11.4 m/m^2$ was only one third of that in the CaPK sward. In the uncut treatment, Yorkshire-fog (*Holcus lanatus*) accounted for 43% of total grass tiller density ($5769/m^2$), with perennial ryegrass and white clover completely absent by December 1992.

The results highlight the substantial and rapid reductions in pasture productivity after elimination of nutrient input, coupled with associated changes in sward composition.

REFERENCE

FOTHERGILL M., DAVIES D.A., DANIEL G.J. and MORGAN C.T. (1993) Early botanical changes associated with extensification of grazing. In: Hopkins, A. (ed.) *Forward with Grass into Europe. Occasional Symposium of the British Grassland Society*, No. 27, pp. 144-146.

Grass Production from Meadowlands managed in an Extensive and Environment-friendly Way

K.K. DEBOSZ AND A.L. NIELSEN
The Danish Institute of Plant and Soil Science,
Research Centre Foulum, DK-8830 Tjele, Denmark

INTRODUCTION

Hay meadows, with a high content of organic matter, are often reseeded at intervals of a few years to optimize yield and crop quality. This reseeding may have unfortunate consequenses, e.g. an increased loss of organic matter and nutrients, plus a lowering of floral diversity. An acceptable production without reseeding, by applying different utilization strategies on meadowlands, is evaluated in this project. The change in floral composition, production and quality of the crop as well as potential N mineralization and N leaching are studied.

MATERIALS AND RESULTS

The project started in 1992 at Gislum, Denmark, on a 5-year old meadow. Typical management during the previous years included the addition of 200-250 kg N/ha, 30 kg P/ha and 70 kg K/ha, plus one or two cuts followed by grazing. Soil characteristics of the upper 20 cm in spring 1992 were: pH 5.6, organic C 40%, total N 2.2%, P 6 mg/kg and exch. K 28 mg/kg. The experimental treatments were cutting, cutting followed by grazing and grazing at fertilization with 0, 100 or 200 kg N/ha as well as 20 kg P/h and 105 kg K/ha. Also grazing and cutting without fertilization with N, P and K are included in the treatments.

Under cutting, yields were more related to P and K than to N fertilization (Table 1). Protein concentration was higher in the second than in the first cut. IVOMD varied only a little by the treatments. In the grazed sward crude protein content and digestibility varied more through the season than as a response to fertilization (Table 2).

After a year with the different experimental treatments the botanical composition seemed more influenced by the type of use than to N-fertilization. There was a big drop in perennial ryegrass under cutting in 1993 (Table 3). The content of total mineral N ($TN=NH_4^+ +NO_3^-$) in four horizons below the cut sward indicates an accumulation of N in the soil profile in autumn (Table 4).

DISCUSSION

The high yields obtained by cutting without N fertilization may be caused by a high mineralization in the soil. The variation in crude protein and IVOMD in the grazed sward may be caused by the very dry summer in Denmark in 1992. The botanical composition being more related to the type of use than to fertilization is in agreement with long term recordings on clay soil by Elberse *et al.* (1983). The drought may be the cause of an increase of species with offshoots, such as smooth meadow grass and couch. Also the accummulation of N in the soil profile in autumn may be due to the dry summer.

Table 1. Average yields, crude protein and IVOMD under cutting, 1992.

Treatment	DM[1] t/ha	CP % of DM	IVOMD
N-P-K kg/ha[2]			
0 - 0 - 0	6.5	14	63
0 - 20 - 105	7.8	13	64
100 - 20 - 105	8.5	15	65
200 - 20 - 105	8.8	18	66
Time of cutting[3]			
18 June	5.5	13	64
30 September	2.4	20	66

[1] For the fertilization treatments LSD.95 = 1.1.
[2] CP and IVOMD as % of total production from the two cuts.
[3] Average of fertilizer treatments.

Table 2. Crude protein and IVOMD of the sward grazed by heifers, average of 0, 100 and 200 kg N/ha 1992.

Time of sampling	CP % of DM	IVOMD
25 May	21	78
21 July	15	60
18 Sep	21	65

Table 3. Botanical composition on dry-matter percentage basis, averaged from areas fertilized with 0, 100 and 200 kg N/ha.

Treatment[1]	*Lolium perenne* 1992	1993	*Poa pratensis* 1992	1993	*Elytrigia repens* 1992	1993
(A) Cut	62	28	8	15	5	34
(B) Cut + graze	61	49	5	10	6	11
(C) Graze	43	52	5	8	10	5
LSD.95	18	10	n.s.	3	n.s.	11

Table 4. Content of total mineral nitrogen $(TN=NH_4^+ + NO_3^-)$ in soil profiles under cut swards ★g/g dry soil

	0 - 20	20 - 40	40 - 70	70 - 100 cm
Spring[1]	22	33	51	33
Autumn[2]				
0 N	44	29	20	30
200 N	122	132	66	93

[1] Before experiment started in 1992 sward was fertilized with 200-250 kg N/annum.
[2] After the second cut.

REFERENCES

ELBERSE W.TH., BERG J.P. VAN DEN and DIRVEN J.G.P. (1983) Effect of use and mineral supply on the botanical composition and yield of old grassland on heavy-clay soil. *Netherland Journal of Agricultural Science*, **31**, 63-88.

Biodiversity, Land Use and Management: the Role of the Farm Household

N.E. ELLIS AND O.W.HEAL

Institute of Terrestrial Ecology, Bush Estate, Penicuik, Midlothian EH26 OQB

INTRODUCTION

In 1991, a socio-economic survey of Grampian farm households revealed that farms earning non-agricultural income, i.e. 'pluriactive' farms (Dent, 1993), have trebled in number since 1980. Pluriactive farms were grouped into three types: farms earning extra income exclusively 'OFF-FARM', farms earning non-agricultural income exclusively 'ON-FARM' (e.g. Bed and Breakfast) and farms earning non-agricultural income 'BOTH' off-farm and on-farm. This study was designed to assess the effect of type of pluriactivity on land use and plant species diversity. A vegetation survey was carried out on seventy-one farms which were stratified by type of pluriactivity and by the Institute of Terrestrial Ecology (ITE)'s Land Classification system, which takes into account the physical characteristics of the land (Bunce and Heal, 1984).

METHOD

Occupier interviews provided details for 694 grass fields: whether the field was permanent grass or in arable rotation, its current use, year of last reseed and rate of inorganic nitrogen application. The extent of grassland was obtained by producing habitat maps of each farm at 1:10 000. Species data were collected from 414 grass fields using 10 randomly-placed 2 x 2m quadrats per farm. The proportion of grassland and of grass fields within each land use/management category and the mean number of species per field quadrat were compared between the type of pluriactivity and non-pluriactive farms using analyses of variance.

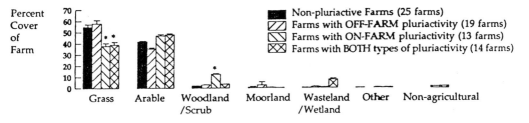

Fig. 1. Pluriactivity and land use as represented by the proportion of each habitat
Bars indicate s.e. about the mean. $\star P < 0.05$ significance between type of pluriactivity and non-pluriactive farms.

RESULTS

ON-FARM and BOTH had proportionally less grass ($P<0.05$) than non-pluriactive farms (Fig. 1) and OFF-FARM had less grass in arable rotation ($P<0.05$).

OFF-FARM and BOTH had a greater proportion of fields classified as 'sheep' and 'sheep with cattle' ($P<0.05$) whilst ON-FARM had the least number of fields with livestock. There was a tendency for OFF-FARM and BOTH to have older grass swards and ON-FARM to have most grass under four years. All pluriactive farms tended to use less inorganic nitrogen. Even when the same use is applied to a field, plant species diversity was generally greater within OFF-FARM and least within non-pluriactive and ON-FARM (Fig. 2). Farms with BOTH types of pluriactivity were found to have significantly ($P<0.05$) more weed species.

The socio-economic survey revealed that farmers within non-pluriactive farms were older than those from pluriactive farms ($P<0.05$) whilst farmers within OFF-FARM were older than other pluriactive farmers ($P<0.05$). Sixty percent of household members working off-farm (OFF-FARM and BOTH) were *not* the farmer although 54% of household members involved in ON-FARM pluriactivity were the farmer and were well educated.

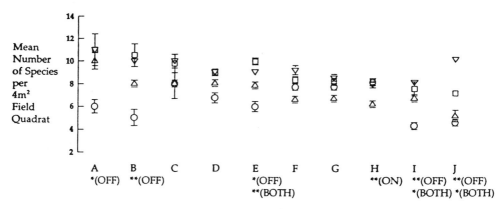

MAIN FIELD USE

A = Horse; B = 'other' grazing, i.e. pigs, goats *etc.*; C = empty; D = sheep; E = empty after a cut; F = sheep with cattle; G = one cut (mostly silage); H = cattle; I = two cut (silage); J = cut following grazing earlier in the year.

      o Non-pluriactive Farms   △ Farms with ON-FARM pluriactivity
       ∇ Farms with OFF-FARM pluriactivity   □ Farms with BOTH types of pluriactivity

Fig. 2. Plant species diversity in relation to pluriactivity and grassland use shown by the mean number of species within the grass field quadrats.

CONCLUSIONS

Differences in farmland ecology and the type of pluriactivity taken up are attributed to the socio-economic characteristics of the household. Farmers with the most extensive and species-rich grasslands appear to have few successors to continue farm management with off-farm work appearing to be more attractive than a future on the farm. The younger farmers appear to be reducing the extent of grassland and either managing grass fields more intensively, which reduces species diversity, or with less diligence, increasing weed populations.

ACKNOWLEDGEMENTS

This project was funded by the Economic and Social Research Council as part of the Joint Agriculture and Environment Programme (JAEP).

REFERENCES

BUNCE R.G.H. and HEAL O.W. (1984) Landscape evaluation and the impact of changing land use on the rural environment: the problem and an approach. In: Roberts R. D. and Roberts, T. M. (eds) *Planning and Ecology*, pp.164-188. Chapman and Hall.

DENT J.B. (1993) *Pluriactivity in the Agricultural Sector, Scotland*. JAEP Final Report to the Economic and Social Research Council.

Meadows Rich in Species and their Traditional Management in the Central Spanish Pyrenees

F. FILLAT, C. CHOCARRO AND R. FANLO[1]

Instituto Pirenaico de Ecologia (CSIC),

Apdo.64. 22700 JACA. Espana.

[1]Universitat de Lleida, Rovira Roure 177. 25006 Lleida. Espana.

INTRODUCTION

Most lowland meadows are young (about 20 years). They contain species arising from different sources, eg woodlands, wet lands, cornfields, paths, etc (Ellenberg, 1988). Because they are managed with low external inputs, the resulting plant communities are rich in species.

In the mountains, variations in climate, soil and management result in a patchwork of different meadow types. The aim of this study is to report on the floristic composition of this grassland and its associated spring production.

MATERIALS AND METHODS

The study was sited on Fragen meadowland in the Broto Valley, situated on the southern slopes of the Pyrenees, at over 1100m a.s.l., with an annual rainfall of 1165mm. Three meadow types were identified: (1) pastured meadows ("panares"), 44% of the total, situated at some distance from the village and with poor access, (2) non-irrigated meadows ("secanos"), comprising 40% of the total, (3) irrigated and intensively managed meadows("regadios"), amounting to about 15% of the total meadowland. From each meadow type 4 samples (0.5 x 0.5m) were cut at the end of spring. Each sample was separated into species, dried at 80°C for 24h and weighed. Management operations on these meadows (Fig. 1) were recorded.

RESULTS AND DISCUSSION

In Fig. 2 two large groups can be distinguished: (i) pasture meadows with 53-70% of "other species" and a high legume contribution (16-39%), and (ii) hay meadows with 60-90% of grasses and few legumes.

The species richness and the production for each type of meadow was found to be: (1) pastured meadows: 40 species/m^2 and 0.3-2.6 t/ha; (2) non-irrigated meadows: 27 species/m^2 and 2.1-5.8 t/ha; (3) irrigated meadows: 28 species/m^2 and 3.6-5.6 t/ha. We can corroborate that in the meadows the reduction of species richness is a result of intensive management (Bakker, 1989) and that production is made up by good forage

264

plants. For instance an increase in management favours *Dactylis glomerata* and *Festuca pratensis*, whereas *Arrhenatherum elatius* and *Trisetum flavescens* have similar values in hay meadows and decrease in pastured ones. The high percentage of *Bromus hordeaceus* (25%) in non-irrigated meadows suggests open habitats and moderately fertile soils (Grime *et al.*, 1988). Legumes tended to decrease with increase in management intensity.

CONCLUSIONS
Livestock management over the last 20 years in mountain areas, with minimal external inputs, has enabled the restoration of grassland communities with acceptable productions and rich specific plant diversity. It also contributes to the upkeep of landscape diversity.

REFERENCES
BAKKER J.P. (1989) *Nature Management by grazing and cutting*. Dordrecht Kluwer Academic Publishers.

ELLENBER H. (1988) *Vegetation Ecology of Central Europe*. Cambridge: Cambridge University Press.

GRIME, J.P., HODGSON J.G. and HUNT R. (1988) *Comparative Plant Ecology*. Unwin Hyman.

Preferential Grazing by Goats and Sheep on Semi-natural Hill Pastures

G.E.J. FISHER, S. SCANLAN AND A. WATERHOUSE
Scottish Agricultural College, Auchincruive, Ayr KA6 5HW

INTRODUCTION

Cashmere production from goats has been seen as a possible enterprise for hill and up-land farmers. For systems to succeed, emphasis needs to be placed on grazing semi-natural hill pastures as well as sown in-bye swards. This is particularly the case in cool, wet western regions where landscape and wildlife conservation values are high. The objectives of this work were to investigate the effects of goat and sheep grazing on semi-natural pastures to enable the consequences of this diversification on sites of wildlife conservation value to be assessed.

MATERIALS AND METHODS

An experiment was established in August 1991 on hill pasture at Auchtertyre farm, Crianlarich, west Perthshire. Three grazing treatments were used each having a 2.9 ha fenced paddock. These were: **S** - sheep only; **GS** - goats and sheep and **G** - goats only. Swards were set-stocked with the same liveweight between May and December.

Plant communities were identified in each paddock, characterised by: 1. herb-rich *Festuca/Agrostis*; 2. *Nardus stricta*; 3. *Juncus* spp.; 4. *Trichophorum cespitosum*; 5. *Calluna vulgaris*; 6. *Myrica gale* and 7. *Molinia caerulea*. The height of each of these main species was recorded in each paddock every 10 days using an HFRO swardstick. At the start of the experiment, 4 permanent 1 m² quadrats were set up in each community of each paddock. These were randomly placed within the communities, with the communities being balanced for aspect, topography and altitude. Each quadrat was subdivided into 25 squares and all species were recorded in each square along with a ground cover score of the main species. The data from this baseline botanical survey were analysed using detrended correspondents analysis (DECORANA) and two-way indicator species analysis (TWINSPAN).

RESULTS AND DISCUSSION

Specific herbage height measurements, presented in Figure 1, suggested that goats in treatments G and GS preferentially grazed *Juncus* spp., *Myrica gale* and *Molinia caerulea*, in comparison with sheep in treatment S. In the GS treatment, grazing of *Myrica* by goats seemed to be delayed in 1992 until the end of July, compared to where goats grazed alone in the G treatment. The herbage height results from the start of 1993 for *Calluna vulgaris* suggested that sheep, whether grazed alone (S) or in combination with goats (GS) grazed this species to a lower height than goats. There were no indications of differences between treatments in the grazing of *Trichophorum cespitosum*, *Festuca/Agrostis* or *Nardus stricta*.

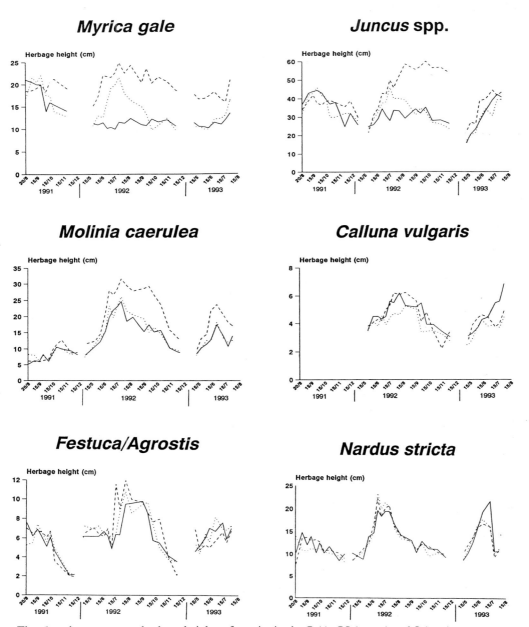

Fig. 1. Average green herbage heights of species in the G (-), GS (.......) and S (-----) treatments.

TWINSPAN analysis of data records from the permanent quadrats recorded in 1991 gave indicator species for the communities being studied. These are shown in Table 1. Data recorded from these quadrats in 1994 will be similarly analysed and compared in terms of species presence and abundance in order to detect the effects of treatments on the persistence of species.

Table 1. Species and communities recorded in 1991.

SPECIES	Festuca/Agrostis	Nardus	Juncus	Calluna	Tricophorum	Molinia	Myrica
				COMMUNITY			
Agrostis carina			★			★	
Agrostis capillaris	★	★					
Anthoxanthum odoratum	★	★					
Calluna vulgaris			★				
Carex pilulifera	★	★				★	
Carex panicea	★	★	★			★	★
Danthonia decumbens	★	★					
Erica tetralix					★		
Eriphorum angustifolium				★		★	
Festuca ovina	★	★				★	
Galium saxatile	★	★					
Juncus acutiflorus			★				
Juncus bulbosus			★				
Molina caerulea			★	★	★	ʻ★	★
Myrica gale							★
Nardus stricta		★		★	★	★	★
Narthecium ossifragum			★	★	★	★	★
Potentilla erecta	★	★	★	★		★	★
Trichophorum cespitosum				★	★	★	★
Violaceae palustris		★					

Extensification and Botanical Change in Semi-Natural Hill Pastures

G.E.J. FISHER, A. WATERHOUSE, J.T.B. WYLLIE AND D.A. ROBERTSON

Scottish Agricultural College, Auchincruive, Ayr KA6 5HW

INTRODUCTION

European Community subsidies and financial support from central government are the main source of income for hill sheep farming. The level of income which can be expected from the market is uncertain. One response to these issues at the farm level may be to reduce inputs and sheep numbers (extensify) in an attempt to maintain economic viability, perhaps with specific payments to encourage this change. The objectives of this work were to monitor the changes which occurred in the vegetation of semi-natural hill pastures as a consequence of extensification policy.

MATERIALS AND METHODS

The experiment covers 2,160 ha of Kirkton and Auchtertyre farms, Crianlarich, west Perthshire. Botanical assessment started in April 1990 and will continue, at least, to 1995. The two production systems in which the flora are being studied are: *i) Moderate input system (control)* - This is the existing system with a high level of management input and sheep numbers (1.1 ewes/ha) with supplementary feeding of ewes according to age and foetal load; *ii) Extensified system* - Sheep numbers were reduced to 0.7 ewes/ha in this system and all inputs, including supplementary feed and labour, are reduced to a minimum. Within both systems (adjacent glens) seven major plant communities were identified, characterised by: 1. herb-rich *Festuca/Agrostis;* 2. Matgrass (*Nardus stricta*); 3. Rushes (*Juncus* spp.); 4. Deergrass (*Trichophorum cespitosum*); 5. Cottongrass (*Eriophorum angustifolium*); 6. Blaeberry (*Vaccinium myrtillus*) and 7. Heather (*Calluna vulgaris*).

Species specific and non-specific green herbage heights were recorded in each community at the beginning, middle and end of each season using an HFRO swardstick. Biomass was measured at the beginning and end of each season in each community by cutting three 0.33 m^2 quadrats to ground level in each community of both glens using electric shears. A 10 m^2 sheep exclosure area was also established in the extensified system to determine the effects of eliminating sheep grazing between October and April on the characteristics of heather and associated species.

RESULTS AND DISCUSSION

There was a general increase in herbage height in the communities which were monitored in the extensified system, compared to those in the control (Table 1). This increase was statistically significant for *Trichophorum* and *Vaccinium* species and non-specific herbage in all communities. On 25 May 1993, the height of *Vaccinium myrtillus*, *Nardus stricta*, *Trichophorum cespitosum* and *Calluna vulgaris* in the exclosure area were 7.2, 10.7, 11.7 and 10.7 cm respectively. This indicated that exclusion of sheep grazing over winter in the extensified glen had resulted in further increases in the herbage height of *Nardus*, *Trichophorum* and particularly *Calluna*, beyond that resulting from reduction in sheep numbers.

Table 1. Herbage heights recorded on 29/7/92 and 25/5/93.

Community	1992			1993		
	Control	Extensified	±sed	Control	Extensified	±sed
Herb-rich	3.3[a]	4.3[a]	0.64	4.1[a]	4.4[a]	0.86
Nardus	11.8[a]	12.3[a]	1.30	9.6[a]	9.6[a]	1.32
Juncus	39.7[a]	28.4[b]	2.04	20.1[a]	15.2[b]	2.29
Trichophorum	11.2[a]	13.1[a]	1.34	7.8[a]	10.2[b]	0.73
Eriophorum	10.3[a]	11.2[a]	1.02	12.3[a]	14.4[a]	1.75
Vaccinium	6.7[a]	8.1[b]	0.72	4.8[a]	7.2[b]	0.78
Calluna	4.5[a]	5.0[a]	0.64	-	4.7	
Non-specific herbage in all communities	4.7[a]	6.9[b]	0.46	3.7[a]	5.9[b]	0.54

Means with different superscripts were significantly different by at least $P < 0.05$

Biomass measurements recorded over 4 years are presented in Fig. 1. These show a general increase in biomass in communities dominated by *Nardus*, *Trichophorum*, *Vaccinium* and *Eriophorum* in the extensified treatment, compared to the control. The standard errors of difference for biomass data were very large and the differences shown in Fig. 1 were not statistically significant. There has been no indication of an increase in biomass resulting from extensification in any other of the community types being studied. Further, there is no evidence as yet of any effect of extensification on the proportion of live and dead material, or chemical composition, of biomass samples.

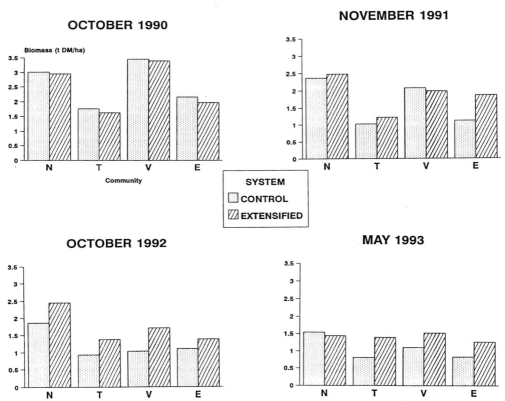

Fig. 1. Mean biomass in communities dominated by *Nardus* (N), *Trichophorum* (T), *Vaccinium* (V) and *Eriophorum* (E) on the Control and Extensified treatments.

271

Soil Seed Banks and Vegetation of Limestone Grassland Patches in Wytham Woods, Oxford

A. D. FOWLER

16 Taverner Place, New Marston, Oxford OX3 0LF

INTRODUCTION

Variations in geology/soils, patch age, size and management may all influence the composition and structure of grassland vegetation. These factors may also affect the size and composition of both the soil 'seed bank' and seedling populations. The aims of this research were four-fold:

i) To relate differences in the composition, structure and diversity of the vegetation between patches to variations in soil, patch age, size or management.

ii) To relate differences in vegetation structure between the grassland patches to seedling emergence.

iii) To assess to what extent the soil 'seed bank' varies between the patches and reflects the aboveground vegetation.

iv) To examine the effects of altering vegetation structure by cutting on species composition, diversity and seedling emergence.

STUDY SITES

Wytham Woods once contained large areas of calcareous grassland but myxomatosis, forestry and agriculture have reduced these to a series of small patches. The richest patches consist of a *Bromus erectus* (upright brome)/*Brachypodium pinnatum* (tor grass) grassland *Hieracium* (hawkweed) subcommunity. The present study examines the vegetation of six of the limestone grassland patches. Of these Upper (USR) and Lower Seeds Reserves (LSR) are 25-30 years old, Lords Common (LC) and the Quarry (Q) are at least 100 years old and Rough Common (RC) and The Dell (D) are at least 170 years old. In terms of management treatments Q and RC are cut regularly, LC and D are cut intermittently and USR and LSR are left alone.

METHODS

A series of 1 m^2 quadrats was located as follows: 6 in LC, USR and Q and 12 in RC, LSR and D. In the latter three patches for six randomly selected quadrats the vegetation was cut to 2 cm in late October and late April. Recordings were made in late May and late July 1992 using a quadrat wired to give twenty five 20×20 cm cells. The abundance of seedlings and established plants of all dicotyledonous species were recorded in terms of presence/absence in the 25 cells. Vegetation structure was assessed by recording touches of litter, moss, grasses and dicots on a 3 mm quadrat pin. Soil depth was recorded using a 1.6 mm pin pushed in to the ground. A single soil core of volume 375 cm³ was analysed for pH and organic content. For seed bank assessment another four cores were removed from the quadrats in February 1992. These were spread out in seed trays containing potting compost and watered regularly. Two recordings were made in late March and early May 1992. Seedlings which emerged were identified, scored and removed and the soil was then stirred.

RESULTS AND DISCUSSION

i) Patches with the deepest, most organic soils of lowest pH were generally the oldest (RC and D). Highest pH values occurred in LC and Q which had the thinnest, least organic soils. The grassland patches were broadly similar in composition but they differed mainly in terms of the relative abundance of species. Stress-tolerant species, e.g. *Helianthemum nummularium* (common rockrose) and *Sanguisbora minor* (salad burnet), were more common in the patches on very thin soil (LC and Q). More ruderal species, e.g. *Linum catharaticum* (purging flax) and *Medicago lupulina* (black medick), were associated with patches where the soil was moderately thin or the vegetation subject to disturbance (USR and LSR). The only common herbs in the patches on the deeper soil or with infrequent management (RC and D) were competitive species more typical or hedgerows, e.g. *Glechoma hederacea* (ground ivy) and *Rubus fructicosus* (bramble). Species number and density was highest in USR due to the greater abundance of more ruderal species which establish from seed.

ii) Litter height and accumulation was greatest in the patches on deeper soils (RC) or those that were unmanaged (USR and LSR) and least on the intensively managed patches (Q and D). Grass height and abundance was less related to management than to soil differences being greatest in all the patches on deeper soil (RC, LSR, D) and least in those on very thin soil (LC and Q). Seedling emergence was greatest in the shorter vegetation on the thinnest soils (LC and Q) and least on the deeper soils (RC and D). It was significantly negatively related to quantities of litter ($p<0.005$) and grass ($p<0.001$).

iii) The seed bank was more diverse in the patches that were older or occurred on deeper soil (RC, LSR and D, 18-21 species) than in those on very thin soil (LC, Q and USR, 10-13 species). Most of the species present in the seed bank also occurred in the aboveground vegetation and the abundance of many in both was strongly correlated. This is proposed to be the result of frequent and unpredictable disturbance which permits species to establish from the seed bank. Weaker correlations occur for species that reproduce mainly by vegetative means.

iv) Compared to uncut controls cut quadrats had significantly less litter and grass ($p<0.001$) and significantly higher species density ($p<0.01$) and seedling emergence ($p<0.01$). Prior to treatment, cut and uncut quadrats did not differ greatly in terms of composition, soil properties or the seed bank.

CONCLUSIONS

i) Variable soil depth influenced the species composition, diversity and structure of the vegetation and explained differences in the frequency of management.

ii) Differences in vegetation structure (i.e. litter and grass) determined levels of seedling emergence. Patches that were managed or on thin soil contained more seedlings.

iii) The species composition of the seed bank was correlated with that of the above-ground vegetation. The seed bank was more diverse in the patches on deeper soil.

iv) Cutting modified vegetation structure creating gaps and reducing grass and litter interference. This markedly increased seedling emergence and species diversity.

v) More intensive management (e.g. grazing) would reduce grass dominance, thus increasing the abundance of species which regenerate from seed and the diversity of the grasslands.

Diet of Goats, Red Deer and South American Camelids Grazing Sown and Indigenous Vegetation

M. D. FRASER AND I. J. GORDON

Macaulay Land Use Research Institute, Craigiebuckler, Aberdeen AB9 2QJ

INTRODUCTION

An understanding of the foraging strategies of sheep and cattle can now be used to predict the impact of these species on vegetation dynamics (Hodgson, 1985). There is, however, a lack of information regarding the foraging strategy of other species of domestic and semi-domesticated ruminant such as goats (*Capra hircus*), red deer (*Cervus elaphus*) and South American camelids on semi-natural vegetation communities in the UK. This lack of information limits the ability to manage and utilise alternative species to achieve both agricultural and conservation objectives in these ecosystems.

The aim of this study was to determine and compare the diet composition of goats, red deer and guanacos (*Lama guanicoe*) grazing a sown sward and communities indigenous to the Scottish hills and uplands.

METHOD

Dietary composition was determined for the three species of animal when grazing three contrasting vegetation communities: an established sown sward (*Lolium perenne* dominated); an indigenous grassland community (*Nardus stricta* dominated); and a dwarf-shrub community (*Calluna vulgaris* dominated). During the growing season of 1992 experimental sites were grazed and each vegetation community was sampled during the spring (May/June) and summer (August/September). Two plots of each community were grazed in successive 6-day periods. The first was to allow the animals to gain preliminary experience of the vegetation community. Subsequently the animals were moved to the measurement plot. To prevent the presence of one species of animal influencing the behaviour of another this second plot was subdivided into three subplots. On the *Nardus* and *Calluna* dominated communities each of these subplots were 1 ha in size, while on the *Lolium* dominated sward they were 0.3 ha. At each site prior to the animals being introduced botanical composition and canopy structure of the vegetation communities were characterized using a point-quadrat inclined at 35 degrees (Grant *et al.*, 1985). Samples of the diet selected by 5 mature castrated oesophageal-fistulated goats, red deer and guanacos were subsequently collected for each of the three measurement plots. Both vegetation and dietary components were subsequently grouped, taking into account dietary importance, ecological significance and ease of identification.

RESULTS

On all three vegetation communities each species of animal selected a diet which was significantly different from the composition of the sward. The degree of selectivity was proportional to the heterogeneity of the sward and occurred at a number of levels. On the *Nardus* sward, for example, it was found that irrespective of season there was selection for green material in preference to dead (e.g. August percentage frequency of green material: Sward: 67%; Diet: goat = 91%; red deer = 86%; guanaco = 86%). More specifically, all three species of animal exhibited strong selection for the leaves of broad-leaved grasses (Sward: 14%; Diet: goat = 80%; red deer = 69%; guanaco = 49%). Despite these broad similarities substantial differences could be identified in the diet selected by the three species of animal. For example, during May the contribution of *Luzula* spp. and *Juncus* spp. to the goat diet was high despite the proportion in the diets of the other two species remaining low (Sward: 1%; Diet: goat = 22%; red deer = 0%; guanaco = 2%). Similarly, in August the guanacos were found to exhibit a strong preference for grass flowerheads (Sward: 7%; Diet: goat = 4%; red deer = 2%; guanaco = 29%).

When grazing the *Calluna* community all three species of animal exhibited strong selection for the limited quantity of grass available, particularly in spring when grass digestibility is high and heather digestibility is low (Sward: 5%; Diet: goat = 48%; red deer = 55%; guanaco = 46%). While grass continued to be the main component in the camelid diet in September (Sward: 5%; Diet: goat = 18%; red deer = 19%; guanaco = 33%) dicotyledonous plants (dicots) made an increased contribution to the diets of the goats and deer. In particular the consumption of heather shoots by the deer increased significantly (Sward: 26%; Diet: goat = 15%; red deer = 44%, guanaco = 10%).

The avoidance of browse by the camelids while grazing the *Calluna* community is mirrored in their diet selection on the *Lolium* sward. Irrespective of season their consumption of clover and other dicots was minimal (Total dicot frequency in August - Sward: 12%; Diet: goat = 18%; red deer = 20%; guanaco = 4%).

CONCLUSIONS

Goats, red deer and guanacos were found to be selective feeders on all three contrasting vegetation types. Guanacos were principally grazers while goats and red deer were intermediate feeders selecting browse as well as grass. The variations identified in the diet composition on a given community are of particular importance since they will result in differences in the impact of each of the three species on the vegetation communities. Consequently, careful consideration must be given to the possibility of using novel species for the implementation of management regimes on a range of vegetation communities of conservation importance in the UK.

REFERENCES

GRANT S.A., SUCKLING D.E., SMITH H.K., TORVELL L., FORBES T.D.A. and HODGSON J. (1985) Comparative studies of diet selection by sheep and cattle: the hill grasslands. *Journal of Ecology*, **73**, 987-1004

HODGSON J. (1985) Grazing and its influence on hill vegetation. In: *Vegetation Management in Northern Britain. Proceedings of a BCPC/COSAC Symposium, Peebles*, British Crop Protection Council Monograph No. 30, pp.21-31

Conservation on Grassland Farms in South West Scotland

G.E.D. TILEY AND R.F. GOODING

South West Scotland Grassland Society, Auchincruive, Ayr KA6 5HW

INTRODUCTION

A combination of climatic suitability and good grassland and stock management has resulted in high performance levels of grass production and utilisation in south west Scotland. Current trends, however, are moving away from maximising food production in the direction of environmental care and conservation of wildlife. In tune with this change, the local South West Scotland Grassland Society (SWSGS) introduced a Grassland Environmental Competition in 1989, to encourage farmers to think about care for the environment while carrying out their grassland management.

The aims of the competition are:
1. To encourage an increased sympathy for the environment when carrying out grassland management.
2. To commend farmers who can identify aspects on their farm which contribute to wildlife and to enhancement of the environment.
3. To identify farmers who can do this alongside good commercial management of grassland and livestock.

METHODS

Entry. Entrants are asked to briefly note any activities on their farm which are helping to improve the environment, under the following headings: hedgerows and boundaries, tree planting and landscaping, watercourses and ponds, old grassland and wildflowers, effluents and wastes, buildings and steading, rubbish disposal and plastic, other. Entry forms are circulated to all Society members and to any interested non-members in the spring. Press and radio publicity, together with encouragement from Scottish Agricultural College (SAC) and Farming and Wildlife Advisory Group (FWAG) advisers are used to attract potential entrants.

Judging and prizes. A short list of 3-5 farms for judging in the autumn is drawn up by the Society's Executive Committee. The judges are a local farmer with an interest in conservation (the previous year's winner) and a representative of a local conservation organisation, such as FWAG or Scottish Natural Heritage (SNH). The prizes (first and second) are donated by Forum Chemicals Limited, who are sponsors of the competition. The winner is awarded the Society's Grassland Environmental Trophy. Candidates must also show high standards of commercial grassland and stock management. Winning farmers are invited to hold farm visits to publicise and demonstrate their wildlife conservation.

RESULTS

Conservation features which have been most frequently entered during the first four years of the competition, and which have attracted comment by the judges are indicated in Table 1.

Table 1. Conservation features on prize winning farms (1st and 2nd) in the SWSGS Environmental Competition, 1989 - 1993. Total farms: 8; Dairy: 6; Beef-Sheep: 2.

Conservation feature	No. of farms	Conservation feature	No. of farms
Effluents and wastes	8	Plastic recycling	5
Tree planting	7	Wetland management	4
Hedge planting	7	Protection of burns	4
Dyke (stone wall) rebuilding	6	Old buildings restoration	4
Bird interest	6	Clover/reduced N	4
Old grassland management	5	Landscaping	3
Pond construction	5		

To date a total of 17 farms have been entered in the environmental competition, including 2 from non-members. The degree of conservation interest varied widely from farm to farm according to 1) farm geography and history and 2) farmer interest and enthusiasm. Particular account of the latter was taken during judging.

Planting of trees and hedges and attention to effluent control were the most frequent conservation activities mentioned. Many entrants had taken advantage of ESA and other grants available and were also seeking advice on the integration of conservation with commercial farming.

DISCUSSION

Most farmers have, by tradition, combined efficient farming with sympathy and care for the countryside. Opportunities now exist for more positive measures, many of which attract grant aided support. The need to maintain and develop an attractive countryside for the benefit of future generations has constantly been articulated during the first 4 years of the Grassland Environmental Competition in south west Scotland. Tree and hedge planting and dyke maintenance were very visible improvements which featured regularly on the prize winning farms. Effluent control is now a legal necessity but farmers' knowledge and interest in conservation is increasing. Key elements are: (1) the farm enterprise must first of all be profitable to allow conservation activities to take place; (2) advice from FWAG, SNH and SAC is very worthwhile at the planning stage.

ACKNOWLEDGEMENTS

Support from the local FWAG advisers, Forum Chemicals Limited and SAC, which is partly funded by the Scottish Office Agriculture and Fisheries Department, is acknowledged.

Soil Nutrient Availability of Culm and Species-poor Grassland

JANE GOODWIN

Seale-Hayne Faculty, University Of Plymouth, Newton Abbot, Devon TQ12 6NQ

INTRODUCTION

Culm grassland is a species-rich semi-natural grassland with succession to woodland arrested by management. Traditional management involves cattle grazing in the summer and winter burning or topping to prevent *Molina* becoming too strong and to maintain species-richness. However, little research has been conducted on the effects of different management strategies on plant communities and particularly soil conditions which support them.

Since the beginning of this century 92% of the Culm grassland has been lost. The remainder may be found in North Devon and North-East Cornwall. Agricultural improvements involving drainage and increased use of artificial fertilisers are responsible for 87% of the loss. The surviving area is highly fragmented; 3000 ha are in Devon spread over 450 sites, with SSSIs making a large contribution. Abandonment, with ensuing scrub invasion, and inappropriate management account for the remaining 13%.

Culm 'grassland' embraces a complex of wet, acid grassland, wet heath, fen and mire communities. Culm may be referred to as a molinietum due to the dominance of purple-moor grass (*Molinia caerulea*) which contributes to 50% or more of the vegetation cover. The community encompasses rushes, sedges, ericaceous shrubs, bryophytes and grasses. Flowers present include meadow thistle, bitter vetchling, heath spotted orchid and devils bit scabious.

These unique communities are associated with the Culm Measures, deposited during the Carboniferous period which give rise to soil of poor drainage and structure. Soil conditions are further exacerbated by a high, mean annual rainfall of 1150 mm for North Devon. To investigate the influence of these soil conditions a comparison of species-rich and species-poor grassland was conducted.

EXPERIMENTAL DESIGN AND METHODS

A Culm grassland site was selected near Okehampton, North Devon called Staddon Moor which is an SSSI and has been grazed by store cattle and topped in the autumn for about 40 years. Adjacent to Staddon Moor an improved (species-poor) grassland field provided an ideal opportunity for comparisons.

279

Soil nutrient availability was investigated on both of these sites by employing a random stratified sampling regime, and analysing the soil for the major extractable plant nutrients.

RESULTS OF SOIL NUTRIENT STATUS

Table 1. Soil nutrient availability of Culm and species-poor grassland in mid-April, mg/kg at 0.05m depth.

	Culm grassland		Species-poor grassland	
	Average of 15 samples	Standard error	Average of 15 samples	Standard error
pH	4.46	0.08	5.26	0.12
Phospate-phosphorous	4.74	0.16	27.17	1.78
Ammonium-nitrogen	5.21	0.57	3.23	0.21
Nitrate-nitrogen	0.94	0.26	0.41	0.10
Potassium	344.10	14.90	344.50	26.60

CONCLUSIONS

From the results in Table 1, it is apparent that there are variations between a species-rich and improved grassland which exist on the same soil type but subjected to different management. These differences are manifested in detected levels of phosphate-phosphorous which merit further study to gain a fuller understanding of plant uptake on a community and individual species level.

REFERENCES

GOUGH M.W. and MARRS R.H. (1990) A comparison of soil fertility between semi-natural and agricultural plant communities: implications for the creation of species-rich grassland on abandoned agricultural land. *Biological Conservation*, **51**, 83-96.
NATURE CONSERVANCY COUNCIL AND DEVON WILDLIFE TRUST (1989) *Culm Grassland resource pilot survey—an assessment of the loss of species-rich grassland in North Devon.*

Medium Scale Surveys of Grassland for Landscape and Conservation Purposes

R. L. GULLIVER

The Schoolhouse, Isle of Colonsay, Argyll PA61 7YR

MEDIUM SCALE RECORDING IN CENTRAL LEICESTERSHIRE

A survey of the grasslands of a study area of 5x5km in central Leicestershire at the medium scale, i.e. the field level, was carried out in 1966-70 and repeated at intervals thereafter. Species-rich permanent grassland (SRPG) was detected by the presence of four non-improvement indicator species. The quantity of SRPG has declined markedly since 1966-70, with only 18% of the original 60.4 ha now remaining.

Table 1 shows the increase of species detected by the use of progressively larger quadrat sizes. Greig-Smith (1983) concluded that effective community classification could be achieved over a wide range of quadrat sizes and shapes. Field scale recording, however, ensures that all rare and/or indicator species are included in the records, and can therefore be used for subsequent conservation evaluation.

Table 1. Plant species number in quadrats of different sizes on unimproved, farmed canal banks at seven sites in central Leicestershire in 1983.

	Quadrat			Entire site	$4m^2$ values,	Entire site,
	$1m^2$	$4m^2$	$25m^2$	1983	% entire site	all dates
Mean	27	31	41	45	69	57
Range	21-32	25-34	36-51	40-55	62-76	52-58

The presence of a farmed canal embankment along one edge of some of the fields served as a demonstration of the impact of modern grassland management. Four of these had not been drained, limed, effectively fertilised, or reseeded and contained a mean species richness of 41 compared with 22 for the rest of the field: (single visit data). Four others had been partly improved, with a species richness of 28 compared with 23 for their associated field. Canal embankments did, however, have less humic and more freely drained soils than the body of the field.

The numbers and patterns of distribution of the ant-hills of the yellow field ant (*Lasius flavus*) are also best recorded at the field scale (Table 2). The ant-hills indicate an absence of sward improvement by any tractor powered operation, including mechanical haymaking. They are also valuable wildlife features in their own right, see Gulliver (1983), Woodell and King (1991, pp. 522-523). Colonisation of the fields is likely to have taken place from adjacent railway embankments or canal towpaths, indicating the importance of the management and use of the surrounding land parcels.

Table 2. Characteristics of fields with ant-hills (produced by the yellow field ant: *Lasius flavus*) in a 5 x 5km area of central Leicestershire.

Field code no.	No. of ant-hills	Distribution of ant-hills	Adjacent land parcel	Survival in 1993
W598	2593E	A	R	I
W596	1034E	A	R+C	El*
W614	773E	A	C	I*
W555	30	SG	R+C	El*
W605(N)	29	A	R	S
W520	16	M	R+C	S
WW5	NR	SG	C	El
W514	5	M	R	S
WW142	2	M	R	S

E = estimated based on sample 100m^2 plots
NR = number not recorded pre-elimination
A = all over
M = margins only
SG = small group
R = railway
C = canal (sources of colonisation)
S = Surviving
El = eliminated
I = intermediate: (ant-hills flattened but some colonies surviving).

*1 marginal ant-hill survives at W596, 4 at W614 and 3 at W555.

HETEROGENOUS GRASSLAND SITES

In many parts of Britain fields contain a mosaic of plant communities, including wetlands and shrub stands, as well as mesotrophic grassland communities. Typical examples include stands of *Juncus* species, *Pteridium aquilinum*, ericaceous species, *Ulex europaeus*, *Crataegus monogyna* and willow species (e.g. *Salix cinerea* or *aurita*). Each of these stands/communities has its own wildlife complement and visual qualities which can usefully be recorded by mapping, using the field boundary as a frame. Multiple visits are, however, necessary to record and appreciate the full range of communities at their optimal attractiveness, as these occur at different times of the year, as do the associated animal populations.

CONCLUSIONS AND WIDER CONSIDERATIONS

The use of the field as the site study unit (medium scale surveying) therefore allows the ready compilation and presentation of data on a) plant species richness and presence of rare/interesting plant species for conservation assessment, b) plant community designation(s), c) long-term changes, d) intensification studies, e) the analysis of visual and textual qualities of grassland landscapes; as well as possessing other useful attributes. Furthermore it provides a framework for recording further important features of the environment in the widest sense, including i) the surrounding and nearby habitats; ii) archaeological information; and iii) historic features for example field barns.

REFERENCES

GREIG-SMITH P. (1983) *Quantitative Plant Ecology*, third edition. Oxford: Blackwell Scientific Publications.

GULLIVER R. L. (1983) Making a mound of an anthill. *The Field*, 22 October, p.898.

WOODELL S. R. J. and KING T. J. (1991) The influence of mound building ants on British lowland vegetation. In: Huxley, C. R. and Cutler, D. J. (eds.) *Ant-Plant Interactions*, pp. 521-535, Oxford: Oxford University Press.

Botanical Changes In Upland Pasture Induced By Withdrawl of Nutrients

M.J. HAYES AND E.D. WILLIAMS

ARFC Institute of Grassland and Environmental Research, Plas Gogerddan, Aberystwyth, Dyfed SY23 3EB

INTRODUCTION

Current agricultural trends suggest that improved upland pastures will receive less fertiliser in the future than during preceding decades. Although surveys have indicated broad patterns of botanical change in ageing swards there are few detailed assessments of successional changes in specific swards undergoing extensification and of subsequent floristic diversity.

A detailed study was, therefore, initiated in 1991 to ascertain the effects of withholding specific nutrients under two contrasting frequencies of defoliation on botanical changes in turves taken from an upland sward at Bronydd Mawr Research Station, Powys. This paper summarises results after two seasons.

MATERIALS AND METHODS

In spring 1991, 60 turves (each 46 × 30 × 14 cm deep) were obtained from a 25-year old *Lolium perenne*-dominated pasture and maintained in plastic boxes. The turves were arranged in 5 blocks of 12 (6 turves being defoliated 3 weeks and 6 turves being defoliated every 9 weeks). Within each defoliation regime, turves were subjected to one of the following nutrient treatments:

(1) Lime (Ca) + Nitrogen (N) + Phosphorus (P) + Potassium (K);
(2) CaPK; (3) CaK; (4) CaP; (5) Ca; (6) Nil. After an initial application of 5 t/ha of lime, turves were given 150 kg N, 80 kg P and 160 kg K/ha annually. Botanical composition was assessed as the % contribution of each species to dry weight yields, every 9 weeks throughout the 1991-93 growing season.

RESULTS AND DISCUSSION

With reduced nutrients, swards had differentiated significantly by October 1992; after 2 years (June 1993) *Lolium perenne* had decreased from 76% to less than 25% (Table 1).

Conversely, *Agrostis capillaris* and *Cynosurus cristatus* together had increased from a total of 5% to 15-30%. Omission of N resulted in *Trifolium repens* increasing in most treatments except where K was also witheld. These changes occurred with both defoliation frequencies, although with the less frequent defoliation *Agrostis* increased only without any applied nutrients. Dicotyledonous species (mainly *Cerastium fontanum,*

Table 1. Effects of reduced nutrients inputs on botanical composition of permanent pasture as % contribution of dry weight yield.

	Lolium	Poa	Agrostis	Cynosurus	Other	T. repens	Dicots.
June '91	76	3	4	1	7	6	4
June '93 Treatment			*Three-weekly defoliation*				
CaNPK	50	10	4	4	5	14	13
CaPK	23	8	9	10	6	22	22
CaK	18	1	18	11	4	19	29
CaP	12	8	25	9	4	3	40
Ca	11	3	9	12	3	10	53
Nil	2	2	26	6	2	14	49
			Nine-weekly defoliation				
CaNPK	64	16	0.1	2	4	4	11
CaPK	24	28	0.1	21	5	18	4
CaK	25	6	3	28	11	11	17
CaP	24	17	0.4	33	2	2	22
Ca	23	12	0.2	25	4	5	32
Nil	10	1	19	16	14	12	28

Veronica serpyllifolia, Ranunculus repens, Sagina procumbens, Taraxacum officinale and *Bellis perennis*) increased greatly in all treatments where some nutrients were witheld and particularly where all nutrients except lime were withheld. The most pronounced change and greatest equitability in botanical composition were achieved with both defoliation frequencies when all nutrients were withheld.

These results support the thesis that lowering nutrient inputs can soon enhance at least some aspects of floristic diversity.

A Simple Method for Monitoring Grassland Vegetation

J. G. HODGSON, R. COLASANTI, P. PHILLIPSON[1], S. LEACH[1], S. MONTGOMERY[2] AND R. HUNT

NERC Unit of Comparative Plant Ecology, The University, Sheffield,
[1]English Nature, South West Region, Taunton, Somerset, UK
[2]Peak Park Planning Board, Bakewell, Derbyshire

INTRODUCTION

The agricultural processes that created the grasslands of conservational importance are not the same as those currently employed on site nor are other features of the environment identical to past conditions. Thus, if the conservational interest of grassland is to be maintained, monitoring procedures must both detect vegetational change early and understand the reasons for it. However, (a) a very large number of sites need monitoring, (b) the financial provision for monitoring work is small, (c) the methods of monitoring currently in use are time-consuming and hence expensive, (d) other types of (often less expensive) activity have greater impact on public relations and (e) while a high level taxonomic competence is essential for a reliable end product, promotion of the best field botanists leaves recording to less experienced, but cheaper personnel. A research programme has therefore been carried out by NERC Unit of Comparative Plant Ecology on behalf of and in collaboration with Peak Park Planning Board and English Nature to develop practical methods of grassland monitoring that will work despite the practical constraints that currently exist.

METHODS

A diagrammatic representation of the proposed method of monitoring is presented as Fig. 1. Within this scheme the following procedures are particularly important.

(a) How to sample

The use of a large quadrats for monitoring, so that a majority of species are recorded, would require accurate, time consuming, quantitative measurements. A method has therefore been devised to provide equivalent data using rapid presence/absence records. This involves a 'nested quadrat' form of sample recording where, if a species is not found in the smallest cell of the quadrat, it is then looked for in a succession of progressively larger cells within the quadrat. We use a $1m^2$ quadrat and search successively in 10 x 10, 20 x 20, 30 x 30, 40 x 40, 50 x 50 100 x 100 cm cells. Common species are mainly detected at the smaller cell sizes (10 x 10 and 20 x 20 cm) while less common ones may not be found until the cell size is large. Cumulative frequency of individual species can be plotted against cell size. The extent to which a species has

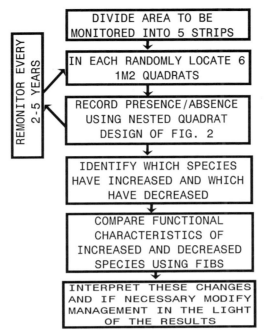

Fig. 1. Flow diagram illustrating the proposed monitoring protocol.

increased or decreased can then be estimated either subjectively or by fitting a hyperbolic function.

Quadrats are positioned randomly because relocation of permanent quadrats is prohibitively time consuming and data are captured in the field on a hand held computer.

(b) What to sample

Ideally everything is sampled. However, preliminary studies suggest that recording only herbs, ferns and woody species is sufficient provided that the dominant grasses, sedges and rushes are also recorded. This procedure both minimises taxonomic errors and saves a disproportionate amount of time; graminoids tend to be both more difficult to identify and to locate. This is nevertheless a retrograde step stemming from both qualitative and quantitative inadequacies in the resources available for monitoring.

(c) How often to sample

We assert that most current monitoring schemes record vegetation too frequently. Species of unproductive grasslands, unlike those of modern productive agriculture, are inherently slow-growing (Grime and Hunt, 1975) and some are very long-lived. Such vegetation will tend to change slowly and frequent recording is unnecessary. Assuming that floristic change will be most rapid where plants are fast-growing or short-lived or both a protocol for how frequently to monitor can tentatively be suggested (Table 1).

Table 1. How frequently to monitor.

We provisionally estimate that a high, moderate and low frequency constitute sampling every two, three and five years respectively

Commonest strategy, Grime (1974)	Optimal interval between sampling
Stress tolerators > 50%	Very low
Stress tolerators < 50%	Low
CSR strategists (with % of S + SR + SC>R + CR + C)	Low - moderate
CSR strategists (with % of S + SR + SC<R + CR + C)	Moderate
Competitors, ruderals, competitive ruderals and stress tolerant ruderals	

(d) How to interpret data

In the event of vegetational change monitoring provides lists of increased and of decreased species. The ecological attributes of the two groups are compared and interpreted by means of an ecological rule base similar to that described in Hodgson (1989, 1991). However the calculations have become more automated as a result of the computer analysis program FIBS (Functional Interpretation of Botanical Surveys).

REFERENCES
GRIME J.P. (1974) Vegetation classification by reference to strategies. *Nature*, **242**, 344-347.

GRIME J.P. and HUNT R. (1975) Relative growth-rate: its range and adaptive significance in a local flora. *Journal of Ecology*, **63**, 393-422.

HODGSON J.G. (1989) The use of autecological information for selecting and managing plant materials used in habitat construction and the creation of species-rich vegetation. In: Buckley G. P. (ed.) *Habitat reconstruction, transplantation and repair*, pp. 45-67, London: Bellhaven Press.

HODGSON J.G. (1991) The use of ecological theory and autecological datasets in studies of endangered plant and animal species and communities. *Pirineos*, **138**, 3-28.

Grassland Turf Transplantation: An Assessment of Their Nature Conservation Value

P. J. HORTON AND P. R. BENYON

Humphries Rowell Associates, Prince William Road, Loughborough,
Leicestershire LE12 0GU

INTRODUCTION AND METHODS

Considerable debate has occurred in recent years regarding both the ethical and practical aspects of schemes to move species-rich turf of ecological value from sites threatened by development. The study carried out between 1991 and 1993 involved the monitoring and assessment of a number of such transplantation schemes, all of which had already been implemented. Where possible, the vegetation existing at the time of the study was compared with that prior to transfer.

The current paper describes changes in floristic structure of four of the sites investigated. All four transfers involved turf from existing or proposed SSSIs. The sites described are situated in Devon, West Midlands, Cambridgeshire and Berkshire, and involved three examples of NVC MG5 *Cynosurus cristatus - Centaurea nigra* mesotrophic grassland (Rodwell, 1992) and one example of NVC M24 *Molinia caerulea - Cirsium dissectum* fen meadow (Rodwell, 1991). The sites are referred to as Sites A to D respectively. Turf from Site B was taken to two receptor Sites Bi and Bii. Site Bii had a soil profile which was both wetter and deeper than the donor site. In all other examples, the physical conditions of the donor site were similar to those of the receptor area.

RESULTS

The results of the fieldwork are set out in Tables 1 and 2. Species selected for Table 1 are considered typical of, and in most cases are constants of, the NVC type originally present. Species considered of nature conservation value are shown in Table 2.

DISCUSSION

It will be noted from Table 1 that species showing the most consistent increase are the grasses, tufted hairgrass (*Deschampsia cespitosa*) and Yorkshire-fog (*Holcus lanatus*), along with the forb common sorrel (*Rumex acetosa*). Many of the other species appear to have maintained their frequency, although a decrease is apparent for some sites, especially Sites Bii and C. These are the two sites which have received no management since transfer. In addition Bii was physically different from the donor site. A similar trend is apparent with the species considered of nature conservation value (Table 2),

Table 1. Changes in frequency of selected constant species.

	Site				
Species	A	Bi	Bii	C	D
Anthoxanthum odoratum	o	o	o	o	o
Arrhenatherum elatius	np	np	np	+	np
Deschampsia cespitosa	np	o	+	+	+
Cynosurus cristatus	o	o	o	o	np
Holcus lanatus	+	o	+	+	+
Centaurea nigra	o	o	o	o	o
Plantago lanceolata	o	o	-	-	np
Rumex acetosa	o	+	+	+	o
Trifolium pratense	o	o	-	-	o
Years since transfer	3	4	4	2	3
Management	Cut	Cut	None	None	Grazed

Table 2. Changes in frequency of species of nature conservation value.

	Site				
Species	A	Bi	Bii	C	D
Cirsium dissectum	np	o	-	np	o
Genista tinctoria	np	-	-	np	np
Oenanthe pimpinelloides	o	np	np	np	np
Sanguisorba officinalis	np	o	o	-	np
Serratula tinctoria	np	o	-	np	np
Silaum silaus	np	+	-	-	np

Key to Tables 1 & 2
+   = increase
o   = no significant change
-    = decline
np   = not present in donor turf

with populations maintained where physical conditions and management have been maintained. Great burnet (*Sanguisorba officinalis*) has however maintained itself at Site Bii, where it appears to be competing with the vigorous growth of tufted hairgrass. At the time of our study, none of the selected species had disappeared entirely from this site. At Site C, where false oat-grass (*Arrhenatherum elatius*) has become dominant, great burnet appears to be declining. In terms of the NVC types present, increases of both tufted hairgrass and Yorkshire-fog are shifting the community towards MG9 *Holcus lanatus - Deschampsia cespitosa* grassland (Sites Bii and D). Where false oat-grass is increasing (Site C), MG1 *Arrhenatherum elatius* grassland is developing. These types are considered of generally low botanical interest unless rare plant species are present. A number of authors have noted similar changes in grassland type caused by cessation of grazing and/or deterioration in drainage (Rodwell, 1992).

CONCLUSIONS

The general conclusion of the study is that, at least for the first few years after transplantation, the main floral elements of species-rich turf can be maintained provided the donor site is not significantly different from the receptor area, and that management continues. Those planning turf transplantation in the future must ensure that these criteria are met. It is also essential that the physical condition of the turves when relaid allows them to be cut mechanically, with cut material removed, and wherever possible subsequently grazed.

REFERENCES

RODWELL J.S. (1991) *British Plant Communities - Vol. 2: Mires & Heaths*. Cambridge: Cambridge University Press.

RODWELL J.S. (1992) *British Plant Communities - Vol. 3: Grasslands & Montane Communities*. Cambridge: Cambridge University Press.

ACKNOWLEDGEMENTS

The authors wish to thank British Coal Opencast Headquarters for funding this project, the staff of English Nature for their help and advice, and landowners for access permission.

Effects of Mixed Grazing by Sheep and Cattle on *Nardus stricta* Dominated Grassland.

C.L. HOWARD AND I.A. WRIGHT

Macaulay Land Use Research Institute, Craigiebuckler, Aberdeen AB9 2QJ

INTRODUCTION

Nardus stricta is avoided by grazing sheep and tends to increase in abundance in areas grazed exclusively by sheep (Chadwick, 1960). However cattle will consume *Nardus stricta*, the proportion in their diets increasing with grazing pressure (Grant *et al.*, 1985). This suggests that complementarity of sheep and cattle may exist and that mixed grazing may be a viable management strategy for the indigenous grassland communities that are dominated by *Nardus stricta*.

EXPERIMENTAL DESIGN

A replicated experiment was conducted to investigate the effects of grazing pressure and mixed or mono-species grazing of a *Nardus stricta* dominated sward on animal performance and sward composition. Over three successive summers Cheviot ewes and single lambs grazed from early June to late September either with cattle (Charolais X Blue Grey steers) or alone. The steers were present from early June until the end of July. Two grazing pressures were imposed; inter-tussock sward heights of 4-5 cm (high) or 6-7 cm (low).

Animal live-weights, herbage intake and diet selection (using oesphageal fistulated animals) were estimated. The botanical composition of the sward was monitored at the beginning and end of every grazing season and *Nardus stricta* utilization was assessed twice during the season in July and September.

RESULTS

Results are presented for the first two years. The level of utilization of *Nardus stricta* was greater (p<0.001) at the high grazing pressure in both years (Table 1) and tended to be higher on mixed-species plots in July (p<0.069). Utilization in September tended to be lower than in July.

Both sheep and cattle diets consisted mainly of species from the vegetation between *Nardus stricta* tussocks, the leaf lamina of the broad leaved grasses forming the main component of the diet (46.3%) although this component represented less than 25% of the sward. In both years the percentage of *Nardus stricta* in the diet of the sheep grazed alone at the high grazing pressure increased over time, reaching 15% in year 1, but remained below 5% on the other treatments. The percentage in the cattle diets was 13% and 5% on the high and low treatments respectively in year 1, but less than 5% on

Table 1. Utilization of *Nardus stricta* measured as the percentage of green leaves grazed.

Inter tussock sward height (cm)		Sheep alone		Sheep and cattle	
		4-5	6-7	4-5	6-7
Year 1	July	26.1	17.5	39.0	14.4
	September	29.2	8.5	21.2	4.7
Year 2	July	17.5	18.1	17.6	24.6
	September	14.4	12.9	20.7	11.3

both treatments in year 2. The cattle diets contained a lower proportion (7.5%) of fine leaved grass lamina than the sheep diets (20.2%) in both years.

There was enhanced performance for both ewes and lambs under mixed grazing at both grazing pressures in both years (Table 2). At the lower grazing pressure on the mixed-species plots average lamb weaning weight was 5kg greater in year 1 ($p<0.001$) and 2 kg greater in year 2 ($p<0.05$). Although ewe performance was generally lower in year 2, the same trends were apparent in both years. Pre-weaning there was a loss in live-weight for both sheep-only treatments whereas for the mixed grazing treatments overall live-weight loss only occurred at the high grazing pressure in the second year. The live-weight performance of the steers reflected the different grazing pressures and were similar in both years.

Table 2. Sheep and cattle live-weight changes (g/day).

Inter tussock sward height (cm)	Sheep alone		Sheep and cattle	
	4-5	6-7	4-5	6-7
Year 1 (1991)				
Ewe: Pre-weaning (June-Aug)	−72 ± 17	−6 ± 15	−16 ± 17	69 ± 17
Ewe: Post-weaning (Aug-Sept)	−80 ± 34	5 ± 17	−13 ± 27	43 ± 20
Lamb: (June-Aug)	83 ± 4	143 ± 8	139 ± 8	217 ± 7
Steer: (June-July)	—	—	318 ± 166	613 ± 108
Year 2 (1992)				
Ewe: Pre-weaning (June-Aug)	−102 ± 12	−72 ± 10	−83 ± 11	2 ± 8
Ewe: Post-weaning (Aug-Sept)	−10 ± 31	72 ± 20	17 ± 24	36 ± 29
Lamb: (June-Aug)	100 ± 9	160 ± 6	119 ± 8	174 ± 9
Steer: (June-July)	—	—	322 ± 177	698 ± 54

CONCLUSIONS

These results suggest management of *Nardus stricta* swards by mixed grazing produces short term benefits in terms of the enhanced performance of sheep under these conditions. Long term benefits may arise from the increased utilization of *Nardus stricta* under mixed grazing resulting in a reduction of the dominance of this species thus creating the opportunity for greater species diversity within these communities.

REFERENCES

CHADWICK M.J. (1960) *Nardus stricta. Journal of Ecology*, **48**, 255-268.

GRANT S.A., SUCKLING D.E., SMITH H.K. TORVELL L., FORBES T.D.A. and HODGSON J. (1985). Comparative studies of diet selection by sheep and cattle: The hill grasslands. *Journal of Ecology*, **73**, 987-1004.

Field-margins as Sources of Wildflower Propagules in Grassland Extensification for Diversity

A. T. JONES AND R. J. HAGGAR

AFRC Institute of Grassland and Environmental Research, Plas Gogerddan,
Aberystwyth, Dyfed SY23 3EB

INTRODUCTION

Within ESA and grant-aided extensification schemes, the recreation of diverse grass-lands is a high priority. However, many such grasslands, particularly overgrazed up-land sheep pastures within wire fenced boundaries, are unlikely to develop a diverse sward in the short term. This is because wildflower populations are non-existent or patchy and the potential for colonisation is therefore limited.

The use of commercially obtained wildflower seed-mixtures to enhance diversity is extremely inappropriate as the species composition, the ecotypes and provenances will not match that required by the recipient site. Furthermore, these mixtures are often prohibitively expensive. A more realistic method is introduction via hay harvested from nearby grassland SSSI's or old meadows, though this may require heavy manage-ment inputs. Alternatively, where field-margins retain reasonable levels of diversity, it may be hypothesized that with appropriate management, wildflowers may be encour-aged to colonise adjacent fields which are within the extensification process.

This paper reports on a survey of the vegetation and associated soil seed-banks of 5 field-margins on acid/neutral soils at low/mid altitudes and adjacent to intensively managed silage crops. Four sites are on separate farms within 10km of Aberystwyth and one is near Trecastle, Brecon.

METHODS

At each of the 5 sites, a 30m strip of field-margin bank was randomly chosen. Within this all plant species were recorded and 10 quadrats of 0.5x0.5m were randomly situ-ated along the strip and percent cover of each species was measured. Four additional quadrats of the same size were also placed along each strip and 4 soil cores taken to a depth of 6cm at the corners of each quadrat. Estimates of seed-bank composition were made from seedlings emerging from these cores over 18 months. For this estimate, cores were spread over compost in seedtrays and were kept well watered in a cool glasshouse. Data of vegetation and seed-banks has been combined for the purposes of this presentation.

RESULTS AND DISCUSSION

The results indicate the relatively diverse nature of field margins in this area (Table 1) and their potential for use in the restoration of herb-rich grassland. Seedbank samples, by comparison, were much less rich in herb species, indicating that field-margin habitats should be managed carefully, otherwise diversity will be lost. However, even the poorest field-margin had sufficient levels of wildflower diversity and appropriate species to provide a basis for progressing to a semi-natural meadow, providing seed production, dispersal and seedling recruitment can be encouraged.

Table 1. Species diversity (total number) of vegetation and seed-banks within five 30m field margin sites.

	(a) Vegetation					
Sites:	1	2	3	4	5	Means
Meadow forb species	23	10	9	12	8	12.4
Perennial grass species	8	5	8	10	8	7.8
Ruderal/weed species	1	4	3	3	3	2.8
	(b) Seedbanks					
Sites:	1	2	3	4	5	Means
Meadow forb species	10	3	3	1	0	3.4
Perennial grass species	4	3	1	2	2	2.4
Ruderal/weed species	3	6	3	2	2	3.2

The commonest forbs found in the survey were *Centaurea nigra*, *Achillea millefolium*, *Plantago lanceolata*, *Rumex acetosa* and *Stellaria graminea*. There were, however, weed species such as *Cirsium arvense* and *Urtica dioica* present in many of the field-margins so that in promoting dispersal of seed, there has to be careful management of resulting swards to avoid a build up of these unwanted species.

ACKNOWLEDGEMENT

The authors wish to thank the Ministry of Agriculture, Fisheries and Food for funding this work.

Effect of Grazing on the Persistency of a Newly Sown Forb-rich Sward

D. JONES AND R. J. HAGGAR

AFRC Institute of Grassland and Environmental Research
Plas Gogerddan, Aberystwyth, Dyfed SY23 3EB

INTRODUCTION

The present trend towards reducing fertiliser inputs allows scope for creating species-rich swards. Good persistency and productivity of conventionally-sown forbs can be achieved under cutting regimes (Haggar and Jones, 1989; Frame and Tiley, 1993). However, under grazing, the outcome may be quite different. A simulated grazing experiment was carried out to determine how components of grazing, *viz:* defoliation, treading and urine deposition, affects establishment and persistency of four species which are widely used in seed mixtures for creating species-rich grassland.

MATERIALS AND METHODS

A forb mixture containing yarrow (*Achillea millefolium*), chicory (*Cichorium intybus*), salad burnet (*Sanguisorba minor*) and ribwort plantain (*Plantago lanceolata*) was sown at 0.03, 0.11, 0.22 and 0.5 g/m^2 respectively with S.23 perennial ryegrass (*Lolium perenne*) at 2.4 g/m^2 in shallow boxes containing low fertility soil at pH 6.5.

The following treatments were applied 6 weeks after sowing (treatments 1 to 3 = low stocking; treatments 4-6 = high stocking): (1) lax defoliation to 7 cm after reaching 15 cm; (2) as (1) plus light treading (hoof pressure of 0.1 megapascals/80 cm^2, equivalent to 0.15 livestock units); (3) as (2) plus low urine (150 cm^3, representing a single urination from 0.15 livestock units); (4) close defoliation (3 cm from 15 cm); (5) as (4) plus heavy treading ($\times$ 3 of treatment 2); (6) as (5) plus high urine ($\times$ 3 of treatment 3).

Regular counting of populations of each forb species was carried out up to 100 days after application of treatments.

RESULTS AND DISCUSSIONS

In general, forb establishment was adversely affected by the treatments in the following order: defoliation < treading < urination, although individual species responded differentially to treatments (Table 1).

For instance, chicory was found to be severely damaged by treading but was least affected by urine. Conversely, yarrow, while being fairly resistant to treading was completely eradicated by high urine, as was salad burnet. Ribwort plantain was relatively resistant to both defoliation and treading, being able to quickly produce new growth from below ground level. However, it too proved very susceptible to urine damage.

Table 1. Forb populations 100 days after treatment (% of original population).

	Low stocking			High Stocking				
	Lax cut	Plus light tread	Plus low urine	Close cut	Plus heavy tread	Plus high urine	Mean	s.e. diff.
Yarrow	111	123	30	100	92	0	76	15.9
Chicory	127	72	44	139	59	21	77	23.7
Burnet	17	72	15	89	62	0	59	14.7
Plantain	267	232	83	331	530	83	254	61.6
Mean	130	124	43	164	185	26		

It therefore seems that early introduction of grazing animals, particularly at high stocking rates, can be damaging to most non-graminaceous species establishing in forb-rich swards. Hence, mechanical defoliation, rather than animal grazing would seem the preferred means of regulating grass growth and controlling annual weeds during the first few weeks of establishment. Field based experiments are currently in progress to confirm the findings of this study, and to measure the impact of components of grazing on the persistency of individual species within a well-established species-rich sward.

REFERENCES
FRAME J. and TILEY G. E. D. (1993). The performance of wildflower mixtures with grass under hay and silage cutting managements. *Proceedings of the 17th International Grassland Congress* (in press).
HAGGAR R. J. and JONES D. (1989) Increasing flora diversity in grassland swards. *Proceedings of the 16th International Grassland Congress*, 1633-1634.

Effects of Land-use Changes on the Luznice Floodplain Grasslands in the Czech Republic

C.B. JOYCE

International Centre of Landscape Ecology, Loughborough University,
Loughborough, Leictershire LE11 3TU

INTRODUCTION

Botanically diverse river floodplain grasslands are a diminishing ecological resource in Europe. In the Czech Republic, their loss has been accelerated by changes in land use and research is needed to ensure appropriate management of the remnants and to find ways for rehabilitation.

This case study explores the vegetation dynamics of a complex of floodplain grasslands along the Luznice river in southern Bohemia in the Czech Republic.

The study area was once characterised by botanically diverse floodplain meadows, but for 40 years has been subject to a range of agricultural practices due to Communist policies. This resulted in dramatic changes in meadow management, often with a decrease in the intensity of mowing and substantial inputs of both organic and inorganic fertilizers. Some meadows were also drained. Other parts of the floodplain were part of an 'Iron Curtain' exclusion zone and were abandoned. Consequently, many diverse meadows have been replaced by species-poor plant communities.

METHODS

A successional gradient of floodplain grasslands, from regularly mown meadows to unmanaged grasslands, was sampled in August 1992 using 2 x 2 m quadrats. Sampling included an identification of all species present and the percentage cover of each species. The management history, nutrient status and soil moisture level of each sample was also determined.

The data were analysed by means of TWINSPAN classification.

RESULTS AND DISCUSSION

TWINSPAN enabled a diagrammatic model of vegetation change to be developed (Fig. 1). This was based on an original by Prach (1991). Sampled grassland communities were examined in relation to the main influencing land-use factors, namely frequency of mowing, nutrient status and soil moisture levels.

A gradation of grassland communities, each with their characteristic species (Fig. 1), existed. Plant species diversity was generally higher in drier, regularly mown meadows that had received a low level of nutrients. They were not dominated by a single species and contained a number of relatively rare plants. These grasslands were

299

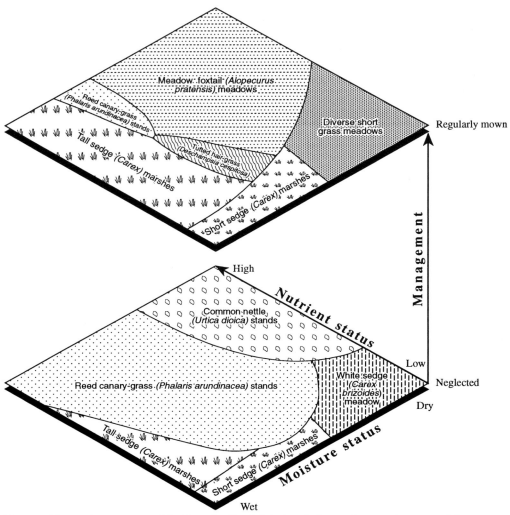

Fig. 1. Vegetation patterns of the Luznice floodplain in relation to three environmental factors.

once characteristic of the Luznice floodplain and are considered to be of high nature conservation value. An increase in nutrient input lead to the development of meadows dominated by meadow foxtail (*Alopecurus pratensis*), whilst an absence of management and a low nutrient level favoured communities dominated by sedges (*Carex* spp.). Both of these were typically of intermediate or low species diversity. Neglect and eutrophication promoted stands of just a few robust and competitive species, usually common nettle (*Urtica dioica*) and, especially in wetter locations, reed canary-grass (*Phalaris arundinacea*).

This case study has shown that rehabilitation of the characteristic, botanically diverse Luznice floodplain grasslands should be possible by reducing the amount of fertilizers used in the catchment and reinstating regular mowing.

REFERENCE

PRACH K. (1991) Grasslands in the Luznice river floodplain. In: Czechoslovak Academy of Sciences *Hydrobotany Report 1987-1990*, pp. 14-15, Trebon: Institute of Botany, Section of Plant Ecology.

Vegetation Management to Manipulate Field Vole Populations in Grassy Plantations

H.J. MACVICKER AND R.C. TROUT

Central Science Laboratory, MAFF, Tangley Place, Worplesdon, Guildford GU3 3LQ

INTRODUCTION

In the UK, government grants encourage landowners to turn agricultural land over to woodland. Ex-agricultural land is often rich in nutrients and so the vegetation between the trees is lush. Small mammals, including field vole (*Microtus agrestis*), invade the new plantations because of the food and cover available (Fig. 1). Voles, however, remove the bark of young trees and can cut through the smaller stems and roots. Damage can reach unacceptable levels (Gill, 1992) and tree shelters are ineffective against voles if the ground cracks in summer.

One option for preventing tree damage would be to reduce the vegetation biomass to discourage voles. As alternatives to a complete burn-off with herbicide, which is often unacceptable ecologically, trials were set up to test the effects of mowing and a paint-on repellant on vole abundance and tree damage.

The work was done under funding from the Land Use, Conservation and Countryside Group, MAFF.

METHOD

Six plots on a grassland site near Cambridge were assessed for small mammals in autumn 1991. Forty eight ash trees were then planted in each plot in March 1992. Three of the plots were mown and three were left unmown. Within each plot, tree shelters were placed around half of the trees. Mowing was done in March, June and September 1992. A repellent was painted onto 100 trees in unmown plots nearby with 100 controls.

Assessments of damage for both trials, to note evidence of bark removal, were made every two months through until March 1993. Vole abundance was found by recording evidence of vole signs in the vegetation. This involved throwing a quadrat at random 16 times within each plot and noting the presence of vole runs, cuttings and droppings.

RESULTS

In the mown plots, vole damage was very much lower than in the unmown plots (F value with 1,34 d.f. $= 177.36$ p$<$0.001), reaching only 3% by the end of the trial (Fig. 2). Voles, which were formerly abundant in all the plots, became scarce in the mown areas (Fig. 3). Tree shelters significantly reduced the damage (from 96% to 68%) in the unmown plots. Despite this, the damage level was still unacceptable. The repellent was very effective for at least a year (Fig. 4) reducing damage from 95% to 5%.

DISCUSSION

Repeated mowing of farm woodland plantations to exclude voles will have strong ecological repercussions for flora, invertebrates and vertebrates. As an alternative, the repellent effectively stopped vole damage for at least a year. This option could be used in preference to vegetation management where the conservation value of a plantation is important.

REFERENCES

GILL R.M.A. (1992) A review of damage by mammals in northern temperate forests: 2 Small mammals. *Forestry*, **65**, 281-308.

MacVICKER H.J. & TROUT R.C. 1993. Preventing voles damaging young trees in plantations. *International Union of Game Biologists 22nd congress*; Halifax. August 1993. In press.

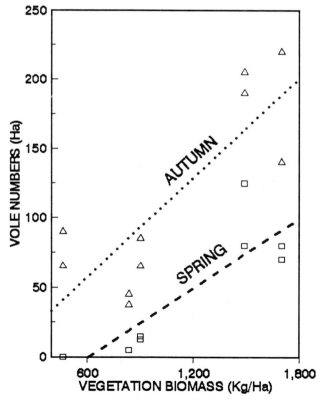

Fig. 1. The relationship between vegetation biomass and vole density.

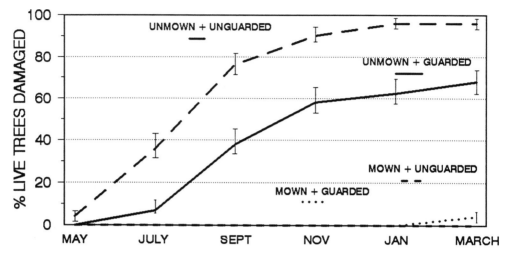

Fig. 2. Vole damage to ash trees in mown and unmown farm woodland plantations (F_{mow} with 1,34 d.f. =177.36, p<0.001; F_{guard} with 1,12 d.f. =42.20, p<0.001).

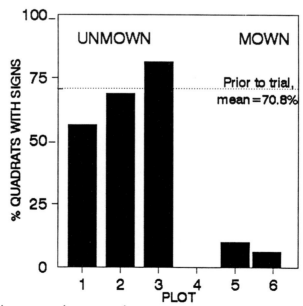

Fig. 3. Vole signs in mown and unmown plots.

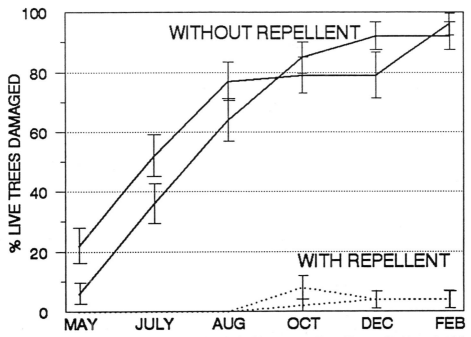

Fig. 4. Progressive vole damage to trees with and without a repellent ($F_{3,12} = 59.41$, $p < 0.001$).

Restoration Strategies for Overgrown Hawthorn Hedges along Grass Fields

J.H. McADAM, A.C. BELL AND T. HENRY
Department of Agriculture for Northern Ireland, Newforge Lane,
Belfast BT9 5PX

INTRODUCTION

In Northern Ireland small (mean 1.8 ha) enclosed fields are a significant feature of the largely pastoral landscape. There were estimated to be 150,000 km of hedgerow in 1979 (Graham, 1979). Broadleaved tree cover is approximately 1% with 60% of broadleaved trees found in hedgerows (Carlisle, 1990). Many hedges are poorly maintained and managed and have become 'straggling' and 'gappy' (Cooper et al., 1991). Such hedges fail to provide stockproof barriers and are of limited conservation value. Hence an experiment was set up to compare the effect of restoration strategies on the flora and microfauna of overgrown, hawthorn-dominated hedges bordering grass fields.

MATERIALS AND METHODS

In 1990 and 1991 a randomised block experiment was set up in 14 hawthorn-dominated, uniform, overgrown and unmanaged hedges at 10 sites throughout Northern Ireland.

The following treatments were imposed on 25 m lengths of hedge: (i) Control - hedge unmanaged; (ii) Laid - stems partially severed and woven into the hedge; (iii) Pollard - cut to 1.5 m high with stem bases nicked to encourage sprouting; (iv) Coppiced and gaps planted with hawthorn; (v) Coppiced and gaps planted with hawthorn, beech, hazel, blackthorn and holly. Hedges were fenced and trimmed to 1.5 m after three years. Plant-species in the whole plot-length were recorded in 1992. Invertebrates were trapped using shelter traps placed in the hedge canopy during May and the results initially presented to the level of invertebrate order. Differences among treatments were analysed using ANOVA.

RESULTS

Although all restoration treatments increased numbers of plant species, only the two coppiced treatments had significantly (p $\leqslant$0.05) more species than the control (Table 1). There were significantly (p $\leqslant$0.05) more invertebrate orders associated with the laid treatment compared to the control (Table 1). None of the other treatments differed significantly from the control though there were considerably fewer invertebrate orders found in the control plots compared to the other treatments.

Table 1. Mean total number of higher plant species and invertebrate orders recorded per treatment plot in 1992 (N = 14).

Treatment	Control	Lay	Pollard	Coppice	Coppice (mixed sp.)	s.e.m.
Plant species	25.8	27.2	8.6	30.7	31.3	1.04
Invertebrate orders	2.6	4.1	3.2	3.6	3.8	0.37

DISCUSSION

It should be noted that the data represents the early stages of a long-term trial. However, it is interesting that even after one or two years, definite trends are emerging. Both coppiced treatments had significantly more plant species than the control, probably due to more light reaching the hedge bottom. Conversely, the laid treatment had a more diverse insect fauna compared to the control, probably because a denser structure was created, providing a better habitat for a wide range of fauna. As the hedges develop this situation may well change, the coppice treatments will 'thicken up' and become more suitable as a habitat for insect groups, though less suitable for some plant species. As the invertebrate fauna and flora of a hedge increase it is likely that the hedge will be colonised by a wider range of bird species.

The relatively rapid response of flora and fauna to the treatments indicates the dynamic nature of hedgerow ecology and the impact which positive restoration can make on the wildlife value of hedgerows around grass fields.

REFERENCES

CARLISLE E. (1990) A hedgerow code of practice. Agriculture in Northern Ireland, 5, 19-20.

COOPER A., MURRAY R. and McCANN T. (1991) Land use and ecological change in Areas of Outstanding Natural Beauty. In : Jeffrey, D.W. and Madden, B. (eds.) *Bioindicators and Environmental Management*, pp 207-224, London : Academic Press.

GRAHAM T. (1979) *Private woodland inventory of Northern Ireland* Forest Service, Department of Agriculture for Northern Ireland.

The Role of Aftermath Grazing in a Flood-meadow Community

A.W. MCDONALD

Oxford University Department of Plant Sciences, South Parks Road, Oxford OX1 3RA

INTRODUCTION

A long-term experiment to create a now rare great burnet/meadow foxtail (*Sanguisorba officinalis-Alopecurus pratensis*) association in Somerford Mead, Oxford University Field Station, Wytham, was begun in 1986 (McDonald, 1993). 'Normal' succession was advanced by sowing seed harvested from Oxey Mead Site of Special Scientific Interest. By 1989 success was attributed to matching the land-use history of the seed-source site to that of the experimental site and to following, as far as possible, traditional management practices (McDonald, 1992). The effect of aftermath grazing by cattle and sheep on the established flood-meadow community and its consequent implications for management for species-diversity are being examined.

METHODS

1. Somerford Mead is cut for hay at the end of June each year. In October 1989 it was divided by temporary, electric-fencing into 9 stratified random plots (c.0.6ha each) with 3 replicates of 3 treatments: sheep grazing (10 in each of 3 plots), cow grazing (2 in each of 3 plots) and no grazing (control). The grazing animals are removed after 4 weeks when the sward is approximately 5cm high.

2. In May 1991 soil samples were taken and within two months tested for pH, adenosine tri-phosphate (ATP) and dehydrogenase (DHA) activity.

3. In June 1991 and 1992 species-composition was recorded in a 10 x 10m permanent stand in the centre of each plot. Ten $1m^2$ quadrats/stand were each divided into 9 sub-units and the frequency of higher plant species in each sub-unit was recorded. The data from the sub-units were combined to provide scores/m^2 quadrat for principal component analysis (PCA).

4. In May 1992 the sward-surface height was recorded with a sward-stick at the rate of 250/plot. Flowering culms were ignored.

5. In May 1992 250 measurements of phytomass/plot were made with a rising-plate meter, measuring 30.5 x 30.5 cm and exerting a pressure of 4.62 kg/m^2.

RESULTS

1. Soil analysis showed a trend in water holding capacity, pH, DHA (microbial activity), ATP (microbial biomass (C_{micr})) and the C_{micr}/C_{org} ratio which increased from cow-grazed to sheep-grazed to the ungrazed treatments (T. Hill, pers. comm.).

2. PCA eigen values for the first two components of the 1991 botanical data were very low, suggesting uniformity and no clustering of samples due to treatments

(Ben Morgan pers. com.). PCA of the 1992 data showed some diversity within treatments and a significant difference between grazed and ungrazed plots.
3.   In 1992 the height of the herbage in each of the treatments showed a mosaic of taller and shorter vegetation which was, nevertheless, significantly different from each other. The ungrazed plots were the tallest, the cow-grazed plots the shortest.
4.   The productivity in each of the treatments in 1992 was also significantly different from each other. The ungrazed plots were the most and the cow-grazed plots the least productive.

DISCUSSION

In 1989, at the beginning of this experiment, the vegetation in Somerford Mead showed some variation due to environmental factors but was otherwise uniform. Differences in the heterogeneity of the sward due to the different dunging and grazing behaviour of the cows and sheep were expected and were first observed in spring 1990 but were masked as the sward height increased during the season. Eighteen months and a second episode of 4 weeks of grazing later, soil analysis clearly showed that the soil in the ungrazed plots had become the most fertile and the cow grazed plots the least fertile (T. Hill, pers. comm.) and, within another year, analysis of the herbage structure showed that this fertility was significantly affecting plant growth, particularly in the ungrazed plots. Most of the species sown in Somerford Mead are long-lived perennials with a transient seed bank, changes in botanical composition of the sward is expected to be slow and dependent upon niches becoming available for colonisation from the seed bank and seed rain. Whilst the botanical data showed no difference between treatments in 1991, by 1992 there was a significant difference between grazed and ungrazed plots and a slight trend in species-diversity from ungrazed ($n = 34$) and sheep-grazed ($n = 34$) to cows-grazed ($n = 37$).

Analysis of the herbage height and mass data did not pick up the greater mosaic effect in the cow-grazed plots which is likely to be a response to poaching and defecation. Nevertheless, when considering the management of meadow restoration projects it is safe to say that cutting for hay without aftermath grazing can produce a higher yielding crop and that the lower fertility inherent in aftermath grazing by cows may in time result in higher species diversity.

REFERENCES

McDONALD A.W. (1993) The role of seedbank and sown-seeds in the restoration of an English flood-meadow. *Journal of Vegetation Science*, **4**, 395-400.
McDONALD A.W. (1992) Succession in a three-year-old flood-meadow near Oxford. *Aspects of Applied Biology*, **29**, 345-351.

ACKNOWLEDGEMENTS

Thanks to Professor C.J. Leaver and Dr. R.H. Hall, Department of Plant Sciences, Oxford University, and the Oxford University Chest for research facilities; the British Ecological Society and the Hamamalis Trust for grants; M.Gibb, D. Sharp, T. Hill, B. Morgan and many volunteers for help and advice.

Seeds Mixtures for Chalk Downland

S. PEEL, G. SWASH[1] AND S. McKENZIE[2],
ADAS, Coley Park, Reading, Berkshire RG1 6DE
[1]ADAS, Cromwell House, Andover Road, Winchester, Hampshire SO21 1AP
[2]ADAS, Medwyn House, Mountfield Road, Lewes, E. Sussex BN7 2XJ

INTRODUCTION

Since 1987 some 5000 ha of the South Downs ESA has been converted from arable to grassland using predominantly perennial ryegrass and white clover seed. This grassland is still dominated by these species despite no fertiliser use. The current payment to farmers entering this option is £200/ha. A new option was introduced in 1992, to encourage the establishment of species more typical of chalk downland. The payment is £240/ha and mixtures must contain at least 5 grass species from a list of 10. A new component has been added to the ESA monitoring programme to evaluate and improve this option. This project aims to identify the most appropriate seed mixtures to sow on land previously under arable cropping, on soils of initially high P and K status, which will produce a sward resembling chalk downland under sheep grazing.

METHODS

Plots 4.2 × 10m were sown on 27 August 1992 within a field previously under oilseed rape with a long history of arable cropping and a high nutrient status (P index 2/3 and K index 4). The plots are not fenced and are grazed by sheep. Long-term changes in the swards are being monitored. The following mixtures were sown at two rates; 15 and 30 kg/ha:

1   Chewings fescue (*Festuca rubra* ssp. *commutata* cv. Banner)
2   Strong creeping red fescue (*F. rubra* ssp. *rubra* cv. Boreal)
3   Equal parts (1) and (2)
4   'Commercial mix' (30% *F. rubra* ssp. *commutata*; 30% *Cynosurus cristatus*; 30% *Poa pratensis*, 5% *F. ovina*, 5% *Phleum pratense*)
5   'Commercial mix', with 15% legumes (as (4) but reduce main components to 25% and add 7.5% *Lotus corniculatus* cv. Empire, 7.5% *Medicago lupulina* cv. Virgo Pajberg)
6   'Diverse mix' (Equal seed numbers of all 10 of the permitted grass species*)
7   'Diverse mix', with 20% wildflowers (as (6), replacing 20% with six flower species**)
8   No seeds sown

* The 10 grass species are: *F. rubra* spp. *commutata*: *F. ovina*; *C. Cristatus*; *P. pratense* spp. *bertolonii*; *Agrostis capillaris*; *P. pratensis*; *Anthoxanthum odoratum*; *Trisetum flavescens*; *Briza media*; *Bromus ertectus*.

**The 6 wildflower species are: *Gallium verum*; *Plantago lanceolata*; *Prunella vulgaris*; *Sanguisorba minor*; *Scabiosa columbaria*; *Dancus carota*.

310

RESULTS

Ground cover was assessed in March 1993 (6.5 months after sowing) following intermittent grazing by sheep. The percentage cover was 27% on low seed rate and 34% on high seed rate treatments (SED 1.4). This is judged to represent successful establishment. A further 15% of the ground was covered by ruderal species (e.g. *Bromus sterilis*, *Poa annua*, *Stellaria media* and *Veronica* spp.) but these had declined by July 1993.

To examine the productive potential of the 'commercial' mixtures 4 and 5, exclosure cages were laid on 12 March 1993. Herbage accumulated was cut to a 5 cm stubble height on 17 June 1993. The yields, shown in Table 2, represent a light but worthwhile hay crop.

Samples of herbage from the high seed rate plots were analysed. Herbage quality was significantly increased by inclusion of legumes. The higher ash % is indicative of higher mineral status.

A detailed botanical assessment made in June/July 1993 shows that all species sown have established. Assessments have also been made of other fields sown under the new option. Initial observations are that the *Festuca* spp., *Cynosurus* and *Phleum* establish quickly, whereas *Poa pratensis*, *Agrostis* spp. and *Bromus erectus* are relatively slow. The 'commercial' *Medicago lupulina* grows rapidly. Of the wildflowers, *Daucus carota* and *Sanguisorba minor* are particularly conspicuous.

Table 1. Herbage production on 17 June of 'commercial' mixtures with and without legumes.

		Herbage yield (kg DM/ha)	
		Low seed rate	High seed rate
Mix. 4	Grasses only	3500	3750
Mix. 5	Grasses plus legumes	3870	4120

SED mixture 254, seed rate 254

Table 2. Nutritive value on 17 June of 'commercial' mixtures with and without legumes.

		Digestibility NCDG	Nitrogen (%)	Ash (%)
Mix. 4	Grasses only	50.1	1.39	7.67
Mix. 5	Grasses plus legumes	54.2	1.76	8.97
	SED	1.62	0.194	0.153

PRELIMINARY CONCLUSIONS

All species sown can establish and survive for 10 months on a fertile site under sheep grazing.

311

Seed rates as low as 15 kg/ha can give satisfactory cover - the benefit from doubling this rate is small.

Both subspecies of *Festuca rubra* are cheap and quick to establish.

Herbage production in the first harvest year was surprisingly good (note 1993 was a wet year).

The inclusion of legumes, particularly 'commercial' *Medicago lupulina*, increases digestibility and mineral content.

ACKNOWLEDGEMENT

This work is funded by the Ministry of Agriculture, Fisheries and Food.

Botanically Diverse Pastures and Lamb Production

R.I.W.A. RICHARDS AND D.E. EVANS

ADAS Pwllpeiran, Cwm Ystwyth, Aberystwyth, Dyfed SY23 4AB

INTRODUCTION

Re-creation and management of florally rich hay meadows is one of three main objectives of the Cambrian Mountains Environmentally Sensitive Area (ESA) scheme, which extends to 76,500 ha in mid Wales. Within this area there exists a range of unimproved meadows, ranging from acidic hill pastures at the moorland edge to traditional hay meadows and marshy grassland in the valleys. These botanically diverse meadows enhance wildlife value, by creating suitable environments for native plants and insects which contribute to the food chain of birds and small animals.

METHOD AND RESULTS

6.5 ha of grassland, south facing, lying between 70-122 m above sea level on moderately well drained, brown silty loam over clay loam was divided equally into two treatment areas. Each area was subdivided into 5×0.44 ha grazing paddocks and 1×1.05 ha paddock where silage or hay could safely be conserved. The whole area was ploughed in mid August 1990 and two seeds mixtures (botanically diverse and conventional) were sown on 30 August.

Each year, two mini flocks of Hardy Speckleface ewes and their lambs were allocated to treatments on a liveweight and age basis. Within each mini flock, "core" animals were identified which would remain on their specific plots up to weaning in mid August. The rest of the mini flocks acted as "flexible" animals to supplement grazing on plots within treatments. Stock movements were dependant on weekly sward height measurements, aimed at maintaining a sward height of 4-6 cm throughout the grazing period.

Annually, 100 kg N/ha of fertiliser was applied in two dressings to the 5 grazing paddocks of the conventional sward treatment (60 kg N/ha in April and 40 kg N/ha in early July). In early May, 144 kg N/ha was applied to the conservation area of the conventional sward treatment, with a further 190 kg/ha of complete fertiliser (20:10:10) applied in early July. No fertiliser was applied to the diverse sward treatment.

Herbage was conserved as big bale silage with yields recorded for both treatments. Two cuts were taken on the conventional sward (June and August) and one cut on the diverse sward (any time after 15 July).

A standardised grassland monitoring methodology, devised for use on hay meadows within the ESA, was applied to each paddock. Within each paddock, 5 stratified point quadrats were established along a diagonal transect. At each fixed point all species were identified and recorded within a 1 × 1 m quadrat with each species being allocated an individual score on the DOMIN scale (Botanical Dominance Indicator).

Table 1. Results (Mean of 1991 and 1992).

	Conventional	Diverse	Difference,%
Sheep grazing days:			
Pre weaning	5390	4148	30.0
Post weaning	7727	5708	35.6
Annual	13117	9856	33.1
Weight gain to weaning:			
Ewes (kg)	2.0	−1.0	
Lambs (kg)	21.7	19.1	13.6
DLWG of lambs (g)	215	202	6.3
Herbage yields:			
Yield of silage, kg DM/ha	8475	4703	80.2
Gross margin/ha (£)	1266	937	35.0

No health or welfare problems were experienced in animals on either sward treatments.

Daily liveweight gain of lambs grazing diverse swards up to weaning was 6.3% less than those on conventional swards and this was achieved not only at the expense of greater ewe body weight loss but also at lower stocking rates (30% less sheep grazing days). Conventional swards produced 80.2% more silage dry matter per ha.

The monetary value of this extra fodder increased gross margin/ha for the conventional sward treatment from 24.5% (produced from improved lamb production) to an overall 35.0%. Differences in botanical composition within both sward types is becoming less pronounced with time, and the maintenance of the diversity within a sward could be dependant on the management imposed upon it.

One Farmers' Ideas Over the Last Thirty Years

M. WALL

Rackleigh Farm, East Worlington, Crediton, Devon EX17 4SW

A BRIEF HISTORY OF THE CONSERVATION AREA

The conservation area at Rackleigh consists basically of three fields, 840, 844 and 845 on the Ordanance Survey Map. Field 840 contains some good grazing and lies adjacent to the wet Field 844 which is dominated by rushes, (*Juncus* spp.). Field 845 provides a rich and varied habitat from dry heath to wet bog and contains good culm grassland with indicator plants common, for example, meadow thistle and heath spotted orchid. Within the site are areas of gorse, abundant with insect life and suitable for the smaller nesting birds. The area is surrounded by trees which have proved excellent for larger perching birds. It has been my policy during my lifetime to maintain the site and strive to educate and encourage others to do so. My philosophy is to achieve an overall balance of plants, birds and insects, especially butterflies, spiders and small mammals and amphibians. For details of Rackleigh Farm, see Table 1.

Table 1. Details Of Rackleigh Farm.

		N	P	K
Total area of holding:		93.4 ha		
Area of Rackleigh:		61.5 ha		
Rackleigh Moors (conservation area)		6.9 ha		
Altitude:		200 m above sea level		
Annual rainfall 30 y average:		1053 mm		
Soil type:		Culm measures clay, poorly draining, over shillet		
Stock:		125 dairy cows plus 75 followers		
Grassland:		All permanent pasture		
Fertiliser:	Grazing	325	57	0
(kg/ha)	Silage	312	57	225

The project began in 1963 when the Ministry of Agriculture approved drainage, liming, bulldozing out trees and shrubs, ploughing and re-seeding the moors. At this time the basic boundary ditches were excavated. In May 1964 a three hour survey was undertaken by Mrs. Parkinson of Devon TNC. This revealed 108 different plant species and Mrs. Parkinson stated that it would be criminal to reclaim the moors. We made a conscious decision following this to retain the moorland area by intensive fertilising of existing grassland, cutting out cereal crops and kale. We sought to purchase further land to reduce the pressure on Rackleigh.

Between 1965 and 1992 the moorland was grazed by a group of in-calf dry cows to keep the grass under control; the numbers of the cattle depending on the season. No stock was kept on field 845 until after the orchids had flowered and seed pods formed.

We won the Devon FWAG Wildflower Award sponsored by The South West Electricity Board in 1992.

In 1993 we entered into a Management agreement with the Countryside Commission but have mixed thoughts on the efficacy of this scheme.

THE DIFFICULTIES

Getting the grazing balance correct is a problem because every season is different. If the number of cows grazing is too few in a year of good growth then there is excess un-eaten vegetation; conversely in a wet year there is heavy poaching.

Encouraging species such as petty whin (*Genista anglica*) and the lesser butterfly orchid (*Platanthera bifolia*) is difficult because their habitat is always under pressure.

Species such as marsh ragwort (*Senecio aquaticus*), marsh thistle (*Cirsium palustre*) and creeping buttercup (*Ranunculus repens*) can become dominant for a season. Fortunately, natural balance keeps them under control.

Maintaining species favourable to butterflies is not easy. Identification of the habitat of the host plants is the first priority. Ladies smock (*Cardamine pratensis*), bog violet (*Viola palustris*), saw-wort (*Serratula tinctoria*), devil's bit (*Succisa pratensis*), alder buckthorn (*Frangula Alnus*), sneezewort (*Achillea ptarmica*) and hardheads (*Centaurea nigra*) all need to be protected.

Finally, ecouraging bog pimpernel (*Anagallis tenella*) and bog St. Johns wort (*Hypericum elodes*) is a must, on a site with many dominant species.

THE CHANGES OVER 30 YEARS

We have seen many changes in 30 years, too many to detail in the space allowed, but among the most important are:

1. Most of the Culm Measures grassland in the area has gone (especially in the last ten years) thus increasing the ecological pressure on this site.
2. For observed changes in the bird population see Table 2.
3. The number of butterflies has not increased over the years but we now commonly see: ringlet, meadow brown, marbled white, orange tip, marsh fritillary and silver washed fritillary.

CONCLUSIONS

1. It is difficult to maintain Culm grassland and sustain all the plant species.
2. The introduction of milk quotas gave economic incentive to re-seed the Culm pastures and increasing reclamation is putting pressures on the remaining wet grasslands.

316

3. Agricultural Colleges need to stimulate students' awareness and concern for wildlife.
4. It would assist if there was more detailed knowledge available of the life histories of plants and butterflies e.g. the complicated cycle of the silver washed fritillary.
5. Looking at your wildlife habitats as a hobby is cheaper than a round of golf!
6. The rewards are worth the years of slog. In 1993 we found southern marsh orchid (*Dactylorhiza* sp.) for the first time. This was a moment of joy and celebration.
7. By close observation we discover one or more new species of plant most years.

Table 2. Observed Changes In Bird Population.

	1963	1993
Curlew	Common	Rare
Lapwing, golden plover	Common	Very rare
Buzzard	Always present	No change
Barn owl	Frequent	Occasional
Cuckoo	Frequent	Rare
Willow warbler	Common	Fewer Number
Grasshopper warbler	Regular Migrant	Rare
Tree pipit, woodlark, skylark	Common	None

Potential for Restoration of Species-Rich Grasslands on Set-Aside Arable Land

P.J. WILSON

The Game Conservancy Trust, Fordingbridge, Hampshire SP6 1EF

INTRODUCTION

Recent decades have seen worldwide overproduction of cereals. The farming methods resulting in this have caused environmental degradation, and costs of storing the surpluses are huge. The chief method proposed in Europe for the reduction of surpluses has been the withdrawal of land from arable production. Although such set-aside schemes are at the mercy of short-term market changes, they may offer considerable potential for the restoration of some features of farmland ecology.

METHODS

The vegetation of 63 set-aside fields on 23 farms in the south of England was surveyed between 1989 and 1992. Only fields in which vegetation had been allowed to develop naturally were included. The only management permitted was cutting during the summer. The data was analysed using canonical correspondence analysis with respect to number of years since the last harvest and a range of other environmental variables.

Species were divided into three categories: (1) annual seed-bank forming species and other weeds of arable fields, (2) species of disturbed habitats but not arable fields, (3) species typical of stable habitats (Clapham *et al.*, 1987; Grime *et al.*, 1988). The proportions of these were analysed by analysis of variance with respect to number of years since setting-aside.

RESULTS and DISCUSSION

The most important factors ($P<0.01$) affecting the composition of the vegetation were found to be the number of years since setting-aside, soil texture, presence of limestone in the soil and the presence of adjacent semi-natural grassland and woodland.

Set-aside presents ideal opportunities for colonisation, and after setting-aside, vegetation is in rapid flux. Of species recorded in the first year, 46% were in category 1 (see above), declining to 20% by year four, while species in category 2 increased from 25% to 44%, and category 3 species increased from 23% to 36%. 30% of the area of the fields was unvegetated in the first year, declining to 5% by year two ($P<0.001$).

Many species typical of established habitats were recorded, especially where fields were adjacent to areas of semi-natural grassland. Such grassland was present at 18 of the 63 sites, and woodland at 28. The developing vegetation in several fields was clearly related to NVC grassland types (Rodwell, 1992).

Zonation of species was marked, and colonisation appeared to proceed from the field edge in most cases (Rew *et al.*, 1992). Some grassland species were present at considerable distances from their most likely source. Regeneration of species-rich grassland was also observed where no adjacent habitat was present and where it could only have developed from the seed-bank remaining from grassland ploughed for arable crops in the past.

Where adjacent habitats are present, or where a seed resource remains in the soil, species-rich grasslands can develop on set-aside land where conditions are suitable. This succession can be rapid and there are many examples in Britain, especially on chalk soils, where grasslands of conservation importance have developed on abandoned arable land (Gibson and Brown, 1991).

Essential management for the establishment of species-rich grasslands involves grazing (Gibson and Brown, 1992) or cutting, preventing dominance by competitive species and helping to maintain a low nutrient status. In the pilot set-aside scheme, only very limited grazing was allowed and plant litter was not removed after cutting. It is to be hoped that future schemes will give greater priority to the management of set-aside for the natural establishment of species-rich grasslands.

REFERENCES

CLAPHAM A.R., TUTIN T.G. and MOORE D.M. (1987) *Flora of the British Isles*. Cambridge: Cambridge University Press.

GIBSON C.W.D and BROWN V.K. (1991) The nature and rate of development of calcareous grassland in southern Britain. *Biological Conservation*, **58**, 297-316.

GIBSON C.W.D. and BROWN V.K. (1992) Grazing and vegetation change: deflected or modified succession? *Journal of Applied Ecology*, **29**, 120-131.

GRIME J.P., HODGSON J.G and HUNT R. (1988) *Comparative Plant Ecology*. London: Unwin Hyman.

REW L., WILSON P.J., BOATMAN N.D. and FROUD-WILLIAMS R.J. (1992) Changes in vegetation composition and distribution in set-aside land. In: *Set-Aside*, Ed. J. Clarke. BCPC Monograph No. 50, 79-84.

RODWELL J. (1992) *British Plant Communities; II Grasslands*. Cambridge: Cambridge University Press.

Conservation of the Culm Grasslands of South-West England

R. J. WOLTON

English Nature, 37 North Street, Okehampton, Devon

INTRODUCTION

In the mid 1980s conservationists in south-west England became aware of the existence of numerous sites of a distinctive type of species-rich grassland concentrated on the Culm Measures of Cornwall and Devon. Since this habitat did not fit within any existing terminology the name Culm Grassland was coined. Subsequently a strong similarity with what is known in Wales as Rhos Pasture was noted, and it is this latter term that is gaining generic acceptance.

The Culm Measures are a broad band of slates and shales covering about 2,800km^2 bounded by the river Exe, the Atlantic, Dartmoor and Exmoor. They have poorly-drained acidic soils and it is these, together with the oceanic climate, that provide suitable conditions for the development of Rhos Pasture. Elsewhere in Europe the habitat is known from Galicia in Spain, Brittany in France (Wolton and Trowbridge, 1990, 1992) and Dyfed-Powys in Wales (Fowles, in press). It is also probable that it occurs in Dumfries and Galloway in Scotland and western Ireland. All these localities are along the Atlantic seaboard, reflecting the need for high rainfall, warm winters and cool summers.

CHARACTERISTIC FLORA AND FAUNA

Botanically Culm Grasslands consist of a range of wet heath, fen meadow, rush pasture and mire communities, usually in close proximity to one another. It is this mosaic effect, together with patches of willow (*Salix*) or birch (*Betula*) scrub, which gives the habitat its distinctive appearance. The predominant communities are M16b, M23a, M24c and M25 (Rodwell, 1992). M16b and M24c are nationally scarce habitats of high conservation significance.

Characteristic plants of special interest include wavy St. John's-wort (*Hypericum undulatum*), whorled caraway (*Carum verticillatum*) and lesser butterfly orchid (*Platanthera bifolia*). Culm Grasslands are a stronghold for the internationally threatened marsh fritillary butterfly (*Eurodryas aurinia*). Other insects of note include the narrow-bordered bee hawkmoth (*Hemaris tityus*), the flies *Urophora spoliata* and *Microdon mutabilis* and the beetle *Trachys troglodytes*. Typical birds are breeding curlew (*Numenius arquata*) and grasshopper warbler (*Locustella naevia*), wintering snipe (*Gallinago gallinago*) and foraging barn owl (*Tyto alba*).

MANAGEMENT

Traditionally Culm Grasslands are used as rough summer grazing for suckler or store cattle, supplemented as necessary by autumn topping of rushes (*Juncus* spp.) or winter burning of purple moor-grass (*Molinia caerulea*) (Wolton, 1992). Such a simple regime enables the characteristic wildlife to survive and often to thrive, and is near optimal for conservation purposes. Hardy cattle breeds such as the local Devon are best suited to the ground, but other beef or dairy-beef animals will at least maintain condition if previously habituated to the sward.

LOSS AND FRAGMENTATION

Full surveys carried out by the Devon Wildlife Trust (DWT, 1992) in 1990/1, confirmed that Culm Grassland has, like other species-rich grasslands, experienced heavy rates of loss and fragmentation. 62% of sites and 48% of the total area recorded in 1984 was lost by 1990/91. It is estimated that only 12% of that existing in about 1900 survives. Nevertheless some 510 sites remain covering 3,600ha, representing one of the greatest concentrations of species-rich grasslands now in Britain. In addition numerous semi-improved fields persist which, although relatively species poor, are of some conservation value.

The predominant cause of loss during the 1980s was agricultural improvement which accounted for 76% of site loss or damage (DWT, 1992). Scrub invasion (12%), pond creation (3%) and tree planting (3%) were of minor importance. Scrub invasion due to lack of grazing is a growing threat as beef enterprises become more orientated towards single species leys of high productivity.

CURRENT PROTECTION

In the late 1980s the DWT, together with the Nature Conservancy Council (now English Nature(EN)) spearheaded a campaign to protect Culm Grasslands from further loss and to encourage sympathetic management. This campaign has already achieved considerable success.

Twenty seven sites, covering 1,100ha, have been notified as Sites of Special Scientific Interest. Most (978ha) of this land is now being managed under EN's new Wildlife Enhancement Scheme (EN,1991). A further 61 sites, covering 554ha, are under the Countryside Commission's Countryside Stewardship scheme (CC,1993) and another 16 (161ha) under Devon County Council's Environmental Land Management Scheme. Parishes containing clusters of sites have been especially targeted to benefit species with metapopulations such as the marsh fritillary.

Together with other protected sites 51% of the total area of Culm Grassland is now under favourable management. However, since this represents only 23% of sites, the conservation effort continues.

REFERENCES

COUNTRYSIDE COMMISSION (1993) *Handbook for Countryside Stewardship*. Countryside Commission, Cheltenhan.

DEVON WILDLIFE TRUST (1992) *Devon Culm Grassland*. DWT, Exeter.

English Nature (1991) *Wildlife Enhancement Scheme*. EN, Peterborough.

FOWLES A. (In press) Lowland grasslands in Dyfed-Powys. *Invertebrates In Wales*. Joint Nature Conservation Committee, Peterborough.

RODWELL J. (1992) *British Plant Communities*. Volume 2: Mires and Heaths. Cambridge: Cambridge University Press.

WOLTON R. J. and Trowbridge B. J. (1990) *The occurence of acidic, wet, oceanic grasslands (Rhos Pastures) in Brittany, France*. EN, Okehampton, Devon.

WOLTON R. J. and Trowbridge B. J. (1992) *The occurence of Rhos Pasture in Galicia, Spain*. EN, Okehampton, Devon.

WOLTON R. J. (1992) *Management guidelines for Culm Grassland*. EN, Okehampton, Devon.

Effect of Agricultural Practices on Floral Development of Machair Pasture in the Outer Hebrides

D. YOUNIE, J. ANDERSON, M. ELLIOTT[1] and A. BUCHANAN[2]
Scottish Agricultural College, 581 King Street, Aberdeen AB9 1UD
[1]Scottish Natural Heritage, Mamore House, The Parade, Fort William PH33 6BA
[2]SAC Advisory Service, Balivanich, Benbecula PA88 5LA

INTRODUCTION

The machair plain on the western coasts of the Outer Hebrides is an area of land formed from raised beach and blown sand deposits. The sandy soil is characterised by a pH of between 7 and 8 and organic matter content of 3-4%. It provides a unique habitat for a wide range of flora, fauna and bird life, and was designated an Environmentally Sensitive Area in 1988. However, because it is flat, stone-free and easily cultivated, it also provides the major area of cultivable land available to crofters. Crofters find themselves under pressure on the one hand to intensify production of home grown forage because of increased feed costs and, on the other hand, to farm in an environmentally benign way.

The natural climax vegetation on the machair plain is herb-rich grassland. The traditional crop rotation is two spring cereals (*Avena strigosa* and/or *Secale cereale*) (harvested by binder for feeding whole to cattle) followed by two years fallow, although some crofters replace the fallow period with a grass ley, normally undersown with the second cereal. This paper describes a field trial carried out at two sites to assess the effects of a range of agricultural practices (fertiliser nitrogen, herbicide, reseeding) on flora development of machair pasture.

MATERIALS AND METHODS

Trials were undertaken at Drimsdale, South Uist (Site A), a very dry site, and at Griminish, Benbecula (Site B), which has a relatively high water table and is less prone to drought. The same trial was established at both sites. Fertiliser nitrogen (40 kg N/ha; 80 kg N/ha), herbicide (H+; H-), and undersowing (U+; U-) treatments were imposed on a spring cereal crop (oats/rye mixture) in 1991 and, in the following year, fertiliser N (30 kg N/ha; 60 kg N/ha) was applied to the pasture as an additional treatment in a split plot layout. The experiments were analysed as 2^3 factorials in 1991 and 2^4 factorials in 1992. There were three replicates at each site. The herbicide used was bentazone + MCPA + MCPB (product Acumen) applied to the cereal at 6.5 l/ha. The seed mixture used in undersowing treatments was a perennial ryegrass/cocksfoot/white clover mixture sown at 35 kg/ha.

323

Dry-matter yield of the whole crop cereal mixture was measured in September 1991 and the grass hay yield in July 1992. Botanical composition was assessed by point quadrat in late October in 1991 and again in 1992. In addition to point quadrat assessments, the presence of all species occurring in each plot was recorded.

RESULTS AND DISCUSSION

The major component in these pastures in October 1992, 18 months after sowing, was unsown grass. Most machair soils are colonised by rhizomatous grasses such as *Festuca rubra* and *Elymus repens*. Even in reseeded plots these species together made up 55-58% ground cover whilst in fallow (non-reseeded) plots they comprised 71-76%. Because of the presence of these aggressive native species, coupled with the very infertile and dry soil type, sown species made up only 29-32% ground cover. There were between 4 and 11 unsown broad-leaved species per plot in October 1992 with an average of 8.7 species at Site A and 7.5 species at Site B. The effects of treatments on the presence of broad-leaved species is shown in Table 1.

Table 1. Effect of treatments on forage DM yield and presence of broad-leaved species in machair pasture.

	Site	Forage DM yield (t/ha)		No of broad-leaved spp per plot		% ground cover broad-leaved spp	
		A	B	A	B	A	B
Year 1: Year of sowing							
Fertiliser	40	4.39	4.30	6.5	6.8	7.0	12.8
	80	5.18	4.86	7.0	5.8	8.1	8.9
Reseeding	+	4.79	4.75	6.4	5.5	6.4	8.2
	-	4.78	4.41	7.1	7.1	8.7	13.5
Herbicide	+	4.97	4.54	6.0	5.2	4.7	5.8
	-	4.60	4.62	7.5	7.4	10.4	15.9
	LSD 5%	0.556	0.589	1.53	2.00	2.60	4.04
Year 2 First year ley							
Fertiliser	30	-*	0.56	8.8	7.5	11.5	18.0
	60	-	0.72	8.6	7.6	11.9	15.3
Reseeding	+	-	0.73	8.1	6.8	9.0	14.4
	-	-	0.56	9.3	8.2	14.4	18.9
Herbicide	+	-	0.64	8.1	7.7	9.2	12.9
	-	-	0.64	9.3	7.4	14.2	20.4
	LSD 5%	-	0.136	1.02	0.86	3.84	4.77

*No sample possible because of drought conditions

Increasing fertiliser N application had a significant effect on yield, both of the cereal crop and of the subsequent grass crop, but had no significant adverse effect on the proportion of broad-leaved species in the sward (although its potential effect in pasture may have been masked by the dry weather which restricted grass growth in 1992).

In contrast, herbicide had little effect on yield but, as expected, a significant adverse effect on the presence of broad-leaved species. This effect persisted into the second year. Reseeding also had a significant adverse effect on broad-leaved species after 18 months.

These trials suggest that there is considerable scope for increased N use as a means of improving forage production on machair without seriously reducing floral diversity. In contrast, the use of herbicide does not appear to be justified. The value of reseeding also needs to be re-examined in terms of its production and its effect on botanical diversity. Given that the cereal species traditionally used on machair are better adapted to the dry soil conditions than most grass species, it may be that the double objectives of satisfactory forage production and diverse flora are best achieved by a policy of more intensively fertilised whole crop cereals coupled with a fallow period. The implications of such a policy need further study.

LIST OF DELEGATES

Mr M Aitken
Environmental Science Unit
SAC
Auchincruive
Ayr
KA6 5HW

Mrs P Anderson
52 Lower Lane
Chinley
Stockport
SK12 6BD

Mr H Armstrong
Fellows Hall
Killylea
Co. Armagh
Northern Ireland

Mr D Askew
ADAS Leeds
Lawnswood
Otley Road
Leeds
LS16 5PY

Mr M Ausden
43 Melrose Road
Norwich
Cheshire
NR4 7PT

Dr J P Bakker
Laboratory of Plant Ecology
University of Groningen
PO Box 14
NL 9750, AA Haren
The Netherlands

Mr D Baldock
IEEP
158 Buckingham Palace Road
London
SW1W 9TR

Dr S F L Ball
Dept. of Field Crops &
Grassland
CABI
Wallingford
OX10 8DE

Dr R Bardgett
AFRC IGER
Plas Gogerddan
Aberystwyth
Dyfed
SY23 3EB

Ms H Barrett-Mold
Robertswood Cottage
Kings Ash
The Lee
Great Missenden
HP16 9NP

Mr S Bates
English Nature
44 Bond Street
Wakefield
West Yorkshire
WF1 2QP

Mr J Bax
Crichton Royal Farm
Mid Park
Bankend Road
Dumfries
DG1 4SZ

Dr A C Bell
Agricultural Zoology Research
Division
DANI
Newforge Lane
Belfast
BT9 5PX

Dr F F Bermudez
CSIC
Consejo Superior de
Investigaciones Cientificas
Estacion Agricola Experimental
Apdo. 788 - 24080 Leon
Spain

Dr H Billington
Div. of Environmental Science
NES
University of Coventry
Priory St.
Coventry, CV1 5FB

Dr C Birch
MLURI
Craigiebuckler
Aberdeen
AB9 2QJ

Ms L Blainey
Yorkshire Wildlife Trust
10 Toft Green
York
YO1 1JT

Dr T Blair
Phosyn plc.
Manor Place
The Airfield
Pocklington
York
YO4 2NR

Ms S Blake
Environmental Science Dept.
SAC
Auchincruive
Ayr
KA6 5HW

Dr A Bonis
Dept. of Plant Sciences
University of Cambridge
Downing Street
Cambridge
CB2 3EA

Mr D Boyce
ADAS Wolverhampton
Woodthorne
Wergs Road
Wolverhampton
WV6 8TQ

Mr D Braine
13 Ashmead Close
Walderslade
Chatham
Kent
ME5 8NY

Dr A-M Brennan
130 Westbrook Avenue
Margate
Thanet
Kent
CT9 5HH

Ms F Burch
Environment Section
Wye College
Wye
Ashford
Kent
TN25 5AH

Dr E Burstedt
Kungsangens Research Station
75323 Uppsala
Sweden

Dr R Buxton
Little Wittenham Nature
Reserve
Manor House
Little Wittenham
Abingdon
OX11 0EX

Ms C Byrne
School of Botany
Trinity College
Dublin 2
The Republic of Ireland

Dr J Byrne
ADAS Redesdale
Rochester
Otterburn
Northumberland
NE19 1SB

Dr E Carlisle
Countryside Management
Division
DANI
Room 554 Dundonald House
Upper Newtownards Road
Belfast, BT4 3SB

Mr A Cathersides
English Heritage
Room 621 Keysign House
429 Oxford Street
London
W1X 2HD

Dr R Chapman
Dept of Agriculture
The University
Newcastle upon Tyne
NE1 7RU

Mr P A Christensen
Kingston Hill Farm
Kingston Bagpuize
Abingdon
Oxfordshire
OX13 5HY

Mr D Clayden
Institute for Applied Biology
The University of York
York
YO1 5DD

Mrs B Clearhill
ORU Open University
Foxcombe Hall
Boars Hill
Oxford
OX1 5HR

Mr R Cooke
English Nature
Coldharbour Farm
Wye
Kent
TN25 5DB

Mr A J Corrall
BGS Secretary
No.1 Earley Gate
University of Reading
Reading, RG6 2AT

Mr C N R Critchley
ADAS Newcastle
Kenton Bar
Newcastle upon Tyne
NE1 2YA

Mrs J M Crichton
BGS Admin Secretary
No.1 Earley Gate
University of Reading
Reading, RG6 2AT

Ms A Crofts
RSNC
The Green
Witham Park
Waterside South
Lincoln
LN5 7JR

Dr M Currie
Ross & Cromarty District
Council
Council Offices
Dingwall
IV15 9QN

Mr G Danielsson
Berghult
360 52 Kosta
Sweden

Mr D A Davies
AFRC IGER
Plas Gogerddan
Aberystwyth
Dyfed
SY23 3EB

Mr T Dixon
Institute for Applied Biology
The University of York
York
YO1 5DD

Ms J Drage
21 Eaton Road
Handbridge
Cheshire
CH4 7EN

Mr M Eakin
c/o Dept. of Environmental
Studies
University of Ulster
Coleraine
Co. Derry
BT52 1SA

Dr J Edmunds
Mill House
Mill Lane
Goosnargh
Preston
PR3 2JX

Miss N E Ellis
Institute of Terrestrial Ecology
Bush Estate
Penicuik
Midlothian
EH26 0QB

Mr M J Emery
1 Dacre Road
Herstmonceux
Near Hailsham
East Sussex
BN27 4LP

Mr F Fillat
Instituto Pirenaico de Ecologia
(CSIC)
Apdo. 64. 22770-Jaca
Spain

Dr G E J Fisher
Grassland & Ruminant Science
Dept.
SAC
Auchincruive
Ayr
KA6 5HW

Mr N Fisher
Institute for Applied Biology
The University of York
York
YO1 5DD

Mr M Fothergill
AFRC IGER
Plas Gogerddan
Aberystwyth
Dyfed
SY23 3EB

Mr A D Fowler
16 Taverner Place
New Marston
Oxford
OX3 0LF

Dr J Frame
Ard Choille
13 St Vincent Crescent
Alloway
Ayr
KA7 4QW

Ms M Fraser
MLURI
Craigiebuckler
Aberdeen
AB9 2QJ

A Garcia
CSIC
Consejo Superior de
Investigaciones Cientificas
Estacion Agricola Experimental
Apdo. 788 - 24080 Leon
Spain

Dr C Gibson
Bioscan Ltd
The Stable Block
Bagley Croft
Hinksey Hill
Oxford
OX1 5BD

Mr D I Gillies
110 Manygates Lane
Sandal
Wakefield
West Yorkshire
WF2 7DP

Miss J Goodwin
Seale-Hayne Faculty
University of Plymouth
Newton Abbot
TQ12 6NQ

Dr I Gordon
MLURI
Bucksburn
Craigiebuckler
Aberdeen
AB2 9SB

Dr D J G Gowing
Silsoe College
Silsoe
Bedford
MK45 4DT

Dr R Gulliver
The Schoolhouse
Kilchattan
Isle of Colonsay
Argyll
PA61 7YR

Prof. R J Haggar
AFRC IGER
Plas Gogerddan
Aberystwyth
Dyfed
SY23 3EB

Ms C J Hallam
ITE Merlewood
Windermere Road
Grange over Sands
Cumbria
LA11 6JU

Mr D M Harding
Court Lodge Farm
Wartling
Near Hailsham
East Sussex
BN27 1RY

Mrs M Harding
Court Lodge Farm
Wartling
Near Hailsham
East Sussex
BN27 1RY

Dr H J Harvey
National Trust
33 Sheep Street
Cirencester
GL7 1QW

Mr M Hayes
Plant Ecology Dept.
AFRC IGER,
Plas Gogerddan
Aberystwyth
Dyfed
SY23 3EB

Dr S Head
Little Wittenham Nature
Reserve
Little Wittenham
Abingdon
OX14 4RA

Dr T Henry
Agricultural Technology
Division
Greenmount College
Antrim
BT41 4PU

Mr J Hodgson
Unit of Comparative Plant
Ecology
The University of Sheffield
Sheffield
S10 2TN

Mr A Hopkins
AFRC IGER
North Wyke Research Station
Okehampton
Devon
EX20 2SB

Dr J Hopkins
JNCC
Monkstone House
City Road
Peterborough
PE1 1JY

Mr P Horton
Humphries Rowell Associates
Prince William Road
Loughborough
LE11 0GU

Ms J Houghton
43 Dongola Road
London
N17 6EB

Dr C Howard
8 Redmoss Terrace
Nigg
Aberdeen
AB1 4TU

Mr D P Hughes
52 Lower Lane
Chinley
Stockport
SK12 6BD

Dr S C Jarvis
AFRC IGER
North Wyke Research Station
Okehampton
Devon
EX20 2SB

Dr R G Jefferson
English Nature
Northminster House
Peterborough
Cambridgeshire
PE1 1UD

Dr I Johnson
Beds & Cambs Wildlife Trust
Enterprise House
Maris Lane
Trumpington
Cambs
CB2 2LE

Mr J Johnson
46 Denton Road
Ilkley
West Yorkshire

Ms B Jones
Countryside Council for Wales
Plas Penrhos
Ffordd Penrhos
Bangor
Gwynedd, LL57 2LQ

Mr D Jones
Plant Ecology Dept.
AFRC IGER
Plas Gogerddan
Aberystwyth
Dyfed
SY23 3EB

Mr G W Jones
Pembrokeshire Coast National
Park
County Offices
St Thomas' Green
Haverfordwest
SA61 1QZ

Mr C Joyce
ICOLE
Dept. of Geography
Loughborough University
Leicestershire
LE11 3TU

Mr F W Kirkham
AFRC IGER
North Wyke Research Station
Okehampton
Devon
EX20 2SB

Ms D Leach
Institute for Applied Biology
The University of York
York
YO1 5DD

M. D Le Coeur
CNRS
Université de Rennes 1
Laboratoire d'Evolution des
Systèmes
Campus de Beaulieu
35042 Rennes Cedex
France

Mr D MacIntyre
Terrington Court
Terrington St Clement
Kings Lynn
Norfolk ,PE34 4NT

Ms E J Mackintosh
Scottish Natural Heritage
2 Anderson Place
Edinburgh
EH6 5NP

Ms J Manley
English Nature
Northminster House
Peterborough
PE1 1JY

Mr W Manley
Royal Agricultural College
Cirencester
Gloucestershire
GL7 6JS

Prof. L't Mannetje
Dept. of Agronomy
Haarweg 333
6709 RZ Wageningen
The Netherlands

Dr C Matthew
c/o AFRC IGER
Plas Gogerddan
Aberystwyth
Dyfed
SY23 3EB

Dr J H McAdam
Agric. Botany Research
Division
DANI
Newforge Lane
Belfast
BT9 5PX

Dr A W McDonald
1 Osborne Close
Upper Wolvercote
Oxford
OX2 8BQ

Mrs R McLaren
ADAS Worcester
Whittenham Road
Worcester
WR5 2LQ

Mr B Mercer
English Nature
Thornborough Hall
Leyburn
North Yorkshire

Dr J A Milne
MLURI
Craigiebuckler
Aberdeen
AB9 2QJ

Dr J Mitchley
Environment Section
Wye College
Wye
Ashford
Kent
TN25 5AH

Mr C Morgan
AFRC IGER
Bronydd Mawr
Trecastle
Brecon
Powys
LD3 8RD

Mr S Mortimer
Dept. of Biology
Imperial College
Silwood Park
Ascot
Berkshire
SL5 7PY

Mr J O Mountford
ITE Monks Wood
Abbots Ripton
Huntingdon
PE17 2LS

Mr J M M Munro
AFRC IGER
Bronydd Mawr
Trecastle
Brecon
Powys
LD3 8RD

Ms S Nicholson
Countryside Commission
110 Hills Road
Cambridge

Dr A L Nielsen
Dept. of Forage Crops &
Potatoes
Research Centre
Foulum PO Box 21
DK-8830 Tjele
Denmark

Prof. J Nösberger
Dept. of Plant Sciences
Swiss Federal Inst. of
Technology
CH-8092 Zurich
Switzerland

Prof. I Noy-Meir
Dept. of Evolution
Systematics & Ecology
Hebrew University
Jerusalem
Israel 91907

Dr S E Pattinson
Kirkton Farm
Crianlarich
Perthshire
FK20 8RU

Miss S Payne
39 Pound Lane
Marlow
Bucks
SL7 2AZ

Mr S Peel
ADAS Coley Park
Reading
Berkshire
RG1 6DE

Dr D J Pope
Dept. of Landscape
Manchester Metropolitan
University
All Saints
Manchester, M15 6HA

Mr S M C Poulton
ADAS Wolverhampton
Woodthorne
Wolverhampton
WV6 8TQ

Mr J Power
University of Ulster at
Coleraine
Faculty of Science &
Technology
Coleraine
Co. Londonderry
Northern Ireland, BT52 1SA

Mr S Pullan
20 Holystone Drive
Holystone
Newcastle upon Tyne
NE27 0DH

Mr C R Ratcliffe
Hill Farm
Sound
Nantwich
Cheshire, CW5 8AE

Mr P Rawlings
ADAS Rosemaund
Preston Wynne
Hereford
HR1 3PG

Miss S Rees
The Old Vicarage
Bondgate
Helmsley
North Yorkshire
YO6 5BP

Mr R W Richards
ADAS Pwllpeiran
Cwmystwyth
Aberystwyth
Dyfed

Mr W E Rispin
Furzebrook Research Station
Near Wareham
Dorset
BH20 5AJ

Dr H Robinson
English Nature
Northminster House
Peterborough
Cambridgeshire
PE1 1UA

Miss L Roger
SAC Rural Centre
West Mains
Ingliston
Newbridge
Midlothian
EH28 8N2

Mr P G Rooney
c/o Ashton Court Visitor Centre
Ashton Court
Long Ashton
Bristol
BS18 9JN

Dr I D Rotherham
Sheffield City Ecology Unit
City Museum
Weston Park
Sheffield
S10 2TP

Mr J Shildrick
3 Ferrands Park Way
Harden
Bingley
West Yorkshire
BD16 1HZ

Mr R J W Slack
Ryedale
Ryehills Road
Skinburness
Carlisle
Cumbria

Mr J T Slater
New House
Thomas Close
Calthwaite
Penrith
Cumbria
CA11 9QF

Dr R S Smith
Dept. of Agricultural &
Environmental Sciences
Faculty of Agriculture
The University
Newcastle upon Tyne
NE1 7RU

Mr M Street
Milton Keynes Parks Trust
25 Erica Road
Stacey Bushes
Milton Keynes
MK12 6LD

Dr C Studholme
Dulverton Building
Robinswood Hill Country Park
Reservoir Road
Gloucester

Mrs G D Swash
ADAS Reading
Coley Park
Reading
Berkshire
RG1 6DE

Mr J R B Tallowin
AFRC IGER
North Wyke Research Station
Okehampton
Devon
EX20 2SB

Mr S Taylor
British Seed Houses
Bewsey Industrial Estate
Pitt Street
Warrington
Cheshire

Ms D Thenail
INRA
Département de Recherche sur
les Systèmes Agraires et le
Développment
65 rue de Saint-Brieuc
35042 Rennes Cedex
France

Dr C Thomas
SAC Auchincruive
Auchincruive
Ayr
KA6 5HW

Mr J Thompson
Rose Cottage
Condover
Shrewsbury
SY5 7AA

Dr G E D Tiley
SAC
Auchincruive
Ayr
KA6 5HW

Dr P Toynton
English Nature
The Limes
High Street
Damerham
Fordingbridge
SP6 3EU

Dr J R Treweek
ITE Monkswood
Abbots Ripton
Huntingdon
Cambs.
PE17 2LS

Dr R C Trout
CSL Worplesdon
MAFF
Tangley Place
Worplesdon
Guildford
GU3 3LQ

Miss P Twigg
Maes Helyg
Capel Dewi
Aberystwyth
Dyfed
SY23 3EB

Mr T N Twiggs
c/o Ashton Court Visitor Centre
Ashton Court
Long Ashton
Bristol
BS18 9JN

Mr K C Tyson
AFRC IGER
North Wyke Research Station
Okehampton
Devon
EX20 2SB

Mr M Wall
Rackleigh Farm
East Worlington
Crediton
Devon
EX1Y 4SW

Dr A Waterhouse
SAC
Alpha Centre
Hillfoots Road
Stirling

Mr G R Waters
MAFF
Nobel House
17 Smith Square
London

Dr T A Watt
Wye College
University of London
Wye
Ashford
Kent
TN25 5AH

Mr R A Weston
Fairways
8 Lichfield Avenue
Hereford
HR1 2RH

Mr A M Whitfield
EAU Woolerton Truscott
Stable Yard
Kent Street
Kendal
Cumbria
LA9 4AT

Prof. R J Wilkins
AFRC IGER
North Wyke Research Station
Okehampton
Devon
EX20 2SB

Mr P Wilson
4 Prospect Place
Grove Lane
Redlynch
Salisbury
Wiltshire, SP5 2NT

Mr K Wind
Wageningen Agricultural
University
Dept. of Agronomy
Haarweg 333
6709 RZ Wageningen
The Netherlands

Dr R Wolton
English Nature
37 North Street
Okehampton
Devon
EX20 1AR

Ms F Woolmer
Little Wittenham Nature
Reserve
Little Wittenham
Abingdon
Oxon, OX14 4RA

Ms S Woolven
English Nature
Institute for Applied Biology
The University of York
York
YO1 5DD

Dr I A Wright
MLURI
Craigiebuckler
Aberdeen
AB9 2QJ

Dr A Younger
Department of Agriculture
King George VI Building
The University
Newcastle upon Tyne
NE1 7RU

Mr D Younie
SAC Aberdeen
581 King Street
Aberdeen
AB9 1UD

Publications in the BGS Occasional Symposium Series

1.★ **The Agronomic Evaluation of Grassland** (Eds) Baker, H.K. & Tayler, R.S. (1963).

2.★ **Beef Production and Marketing** (Ed) Cannell, R.Q. (1966).

3.★ **Fodder Conservation** (Ed) Wilkins, R.J. (1967).

4.★ **Hill-Land Productivity** (Ed) Hunt, I.V. (1968).

5.★ **Grass and Forage Breeding** (Eds) Phillips, L.I. & Hughes, R. (1969).

6.★ **White Clover Research** (Ed) Lowe, J. (1970).

7.   Forage on the Arable Farm (Ed) Kimber, D.S. (1972).

8.★ **Pasture Utilisation by the Grazing Animal** (Eds) Hodgson, J. & Jackson, K. (1974).

9.   **Green Crop Fractionation** (Ed) Wilkins, R.J. (1977).

10. **Changes in Sward Composition and Productivity** (Eds) Charles, A.H. & Haggar, R.J. (1979).

11. **Forage Conservation in the '80s** (Ed) Thomas, C. (1980).

12. **Effective Use of Forage and Animal Resources in the Hills and Uplands** (Ed) Frame, J. (1981).

13.★ **Plant Physiology and Herbage Production** (Ed) Wright, C.E. (1981).

14. **Efficient Grassland Farming** (Ed) Corrall, A.J. (1983).

15. **Money from Grass** (Ed) Corrall, A.J. (1984).

16. **Forage Legumes** (Ed) Thomson, D.J. (1984).

17. **Machinery from Silage** (Eds) Nelson, J.K. & Dinnis, E.R. (1985).

18. **Weeds, Pests and Diseases of Grassland and Herbage Legumes** (Ed) Brockman, J.S. (1985).

19. **Grazing** (Ed) Frame, J. (1986).

20. **Grassland Manuring** (Eds) Raymond, W.F. & Cooper, J.C. (1986).

21. **Efficient Sheep Production from Grass** (Ed) Pollott, G.E. (1987).

22. **Efficient Beef Production from Grass** (Ed) Frame, J. (1988).

23. **Silage for Milk Production** (Ed) Mayne, C.S. (1989).

24. **Milk and Meat from Forage Crops** (Ed) Pollott, G.E. (1990).

25. **Management Issues for the Grassland Farmer in the 1990's** (Ed) Mayne, C.S. (1991).

26. **Grass on the Move - a positive way forward for the grassland farmer** (Ed) Hopkins, A. (1992).

27. **Forward with Grass into Europe** (Eds) Hopkins, A. & YounieD. (1993).

28. **Grassland Management and Nature Conservation** (Eds) Haggar, R.J. & Peel, S. (1993)

*Out of print